Council of Europe's Heritage Discourse

Interdisciplinary Studies on the Council of Europe and Its Conventions

VOLUME 2

The titles published in this series are listed at *brill.com/isce*

Council of Europe's Heritage Discourse

Critical Perspectives on the History, Policy, and Politics of European Heritage

By

Marija Kamber

BRILL | NIJHOFF

LEIDEN | BOSTON

The Library of Congress Cataloging-in-Publication Data is available online at https://catalog.loc.gov

Typeface for the Latin, Greek, and Cyrillic scripts: "Brill". See and download: brill.com/brill-typeface.

ISSN 2950-3612
ISBN 978-90-04-72626-0 (hardback)
ISBN 978-90-04-75625-0 (e-book)
DOI 10.1163/9789004756250

This book is printed on acid-free paper and produced in a sustainable manner.

Contents

Tables

CHAPTER 1

Setting the Stage

The Council of Europe (CoE) is uniquely positioned as a policy-making and standard-setting body for 46 European states. Since its establishment in 1949, the CoE has aimed to promote human rights, the rule of law, and democracy, influencing European policies across a wide range of fields. Over more than seven decades, its responsibilities have extended into culture and heritage, with the organisation's conventions, recommendations, and policies shaping how heritage is understood, preserved, and managed across Europe.

Despite the CoE's long-standing and comprehensive engagement with heritage policy, including five core conventions and numerous policy guidelines and initiatives, its contributions remain underexplored in heritage scholarship. Most studies in this area focus on international frameworks, primarily those developed by UNESCO and ICOMOS, with the critique of their Eurocentric perspectives as a prominent subject of discussion. This prominent place of the 'problem of Eurocentrism' in international heritage scholarship led me to question the nature of the European heritage discourse – a term often used to describe the dominance of certain European perspectives in global heritage practices. What was the role the CoE played in the process of shaping international heritage discourse? Is what is considered 'European heritage discourse' aligned with Smith's definition of Authorised Heritage Discourse (AHD),[1] or is it more accurately reflected in the distinctly European approach advanced by CoE policy texts and initiatives? Are these discourses identical? The recurrent use of 'Eurocentrism' in heritage literature, coupled with a general lack of in-depth analysis of the CoE's role, seems to imply that they are. However, as this book aims to demonstrate, this assumption could not be further from the truth. The CoE's heritage discourse, while rooted in a European context, offers a more nuanced and context-specific perspective that deserves closer examination and certainly justifies the research presented in this volume.

Today, the evolving field of critical heritage studies is framed by the concept of Authorised Heritage Discourse and its critique. Smith, in her book *Uses of Heritage*, defined AHD as the discourse that dominates international and national heritage policies, emphasising the preservation of material and monumental heritage and privileging historical narratives deemed valuable

1 Laurajane Smith, *Uses of Heritage* (Taylor & Francis Group 2006).

 | DOI:10.1163/9789004756250_002

by experts and usually used in forging the national identity. At its core, AHD is based on an idea of heritage that centres around tangible, aesthetically pleasing material objects, sites, and places that current generations 'must' care for, protect, and revere so that they may be passed on to nebulous future generations for their education.[2] Moreover, Smith argues that it is European ideas of conservation, as well as the nature and meaning of monuments that have become internationally naturalised, 'so that these principles become global "common sense"'.[3] Therefore, the historical context of heritage conservation and understanding of 'heritage' that emerged in late nineteenth-century Europe provides an essential background for AHD, labelling it as 'Eurocentric'.

Consequently, the critique of the framework established through policy instruments within the AHD focuses heavily on reducing the Eurocentric character of the global heritage discourse. Rudolff and Buckley, in their proposition for the reform of the UNESCO World Heritage system, identified several interrelated problems where focused reform could deliver a significant 'alternative' and better future for the World Heritage system.[4] The problem of Eurocentrism, according to Rudolff and Buckley, appears to be the critical challenge to be met.[5] While this post-Western perspective among heritage scholars certainly does not imply questioning the need for studies on Europe, it might well continue to perpetuate the interpretation of Eurocentrism that constructs a homogenous picture of pan-European historical and cultural governance (AHD) and leaves current European contributions to the ongoing discussions in the field to the side. In this sense, I argue, it is essential to look closely at the work of the CoE. The organisation is a crucial heritage policy body in Europe, and what the analysis presented in this book will show is that its heritage policies, underpinned by the organisation's broader goals of promoting human rights and democratic participation, were/are far more 'post-Western' than acknowledged. The notion of heritage and its role within the policies promoted by the CoE has drastically evolved in comparison with what is usually understood as 'Eurocentric'.

Examining the CoE's nuanced approach offers an opportunity to rethink the often-cited 'Eurocentrism' of international heritage policies. While certain European ideas of heritage protection and conservation have undeniably influenced global heritage practices, particularly during the early period of

2 Smith (n 1).

3 Ibid 21.

4 Britta Rudolff and Kristal Buckley, 'World Heritage: Alternative Futures' in William Logan, Máiréad Nic Craith and Ullrich Kockel (eds), *A Companion to Heritage Studies* (Wiley-Blackwell 2015).

5 Ibid 522–540.

CHAPTER 1

Setting the Stage

The Council of Europe (CoE) is uniquely positioned as a policy-making and standard-setting body for 46 European states. Since its establishment in 1949, the CoE has aimed to promote human rights, the rule of law, and democracy, influencing European policies across a wide range of fields. Over more than seven decades, its responsibilities have extended into culture and heritage, with the organisation's conventions, recommendations, and policies shaping how heritage is understood, preserved, and managed across Europe.

Despite the CoE's long-standing and comprehensive engagement with heritage policy, including five core conventions and numerous policy guidelines and initiatives, its contributions remain underexplored in heritage scholarship. Most studies in this area focus on international frameworks, primarily those developed by UNESCO and ICOMOS, with the critique of their Eurocentric perspectives as a prominent subject of discussion. This prominent place of the 'problem of Eurocentrism' in international heritage scholarship led me to question the nature of the European heritage discourse – a term often used to describe the dominance of certain European perspectives in global heritage practices. What was the role the CoE played in the process of shaping international heritage discourse? Is what is considered 'European heritage discourse' aligned with Smith's definition of Authorised Heritage Discourse (AHD),[1] or is it more accurately reflected in the distinctly European approach advanced by CoE policy texts and initiatives? Are these discourses identical? The recurrent use of 'Eurocentrism' in heritage literature, coupled with a general lack of in-depth analysis of the CoE's role, seems to imply that they are. However, as this book aims to demonstrate, this assumption could not be further from the truth. The CoE's heritage discourse, while rooted in a European context, offers a more nuanced and context-specific perspective that deserves closer examination and certainly justifies the research presented in this volume.

Today, the evolving field of critical heritage studies is framed by the concept of Authorised Heritage Discourse and its critique. Smith, in her book *Uses of Heritage*, defined AHD as the discourse that dominates international and national heritage policies, emphasising the preservation of material and monumental heritage and privileging historical narratives deemed valuable

1 Laurajane Smith, *Uses of Heritage* (Taylor & Francis Group 2006).

 | DOI:10.1163/9789004756250_002

by experts and usually used in forging the national identity. At its core, AHD is based on an idea of heritage that centres around tangible, aesthetically pleasing material objects, sites, and places that current generations 'must' care for, protect, and revere so that they may be passed on to nebulous future generations for their education.[2] Moreover, Smith argues that it is European ideas of conservation, as well as the nature and meaning of monuments that have become internationally naturalised, 'so that these principles become global "common sense"'.[3] Therefore, the historical context of heritage conservation and understanding of 'heritage' that emerged in late nineteenth-century Europe provides an essential background for AHD, labelling it as 'Eurocentric'.

Consequently, the critique of the framework established through policy instruments within the AHD focuses heavily on reducing the Eurocentric character of the global heritage discourse. Rudolff and Buckley, in their proposition for the reform of the UNESCO World Heritage system, identified several interrelated problems where focused reform could deliver a significant 'alternative' and better future for the World Heritage system.[4] The problem of Eurocentrism, according to Rudolff and Buckley, appears to be the critical challenge to be met.[5] While this post-Western perspective among heritage scholars certainly does not imply questioning the need for studies on Europe, it might well continue to perpetuate the interpretation of Eurocentrism that constructs a homogenous picture of pan-European historical and cultural governance (AHD) and leaves current European contributions to the ongoing discussions in the field to the side. In this sense, I argue, it is essential to look closely at the work of the CoE. The organisation is a crucial heritage policy body in Europe, and what the analysis presented in this book will show is that its heritage policies, underpinned by the organisation's broader goals of promoting human rights and democratic participation, were/are far more 'post-Western' than acknowledged. The notion of heritage and its role within the policies promoted by the CoE has drastically evolved in comparison with what is usually understood as 'Eurocentric'.

Examining the CoE's nuanced approach offers an opportunity to rethink the often-cited 'Eurocentrism' of international heritage policies. While certain European ideas of heritage protection and conservation have undeniably influenced global heritage practices, particularly during the early period of

2 Smith (n 1).

3 Ibid 21.

4 Britta Rudolff and Kristal Buckley, 'World Heritage: Alternative Futures' in William Logan, Máiréad Nic Craith and Ullrich Kockel (eds), *A Companion to Heritage Studies* (Wiley-Blackwell 2015).

5 Ibid 522–540.

framing the international heritage agenda in the 1950s and 1960s, the CoE's evolving regional heritage discourse demonstrates a more pluralistic, adaptive, and socially oriented approach. This book, therefore, aims to provide a historical overview of the CoE's contributions through discourse lenses, tracing how the organisation has pioneered alternative frameworks that encourage the democratisation of heritage management and promote cultural rights, inclusivity, and community participation. In doing so, it challenges a one-dimensional view of Eurocentrism in global heritage discourse and reveals the complexities within Europe's own heritage policies, which at times critique and push against the boundaries of traditional heritage norms.

Moreover, the book aims to add to the growing discussion in heritage studies that argues that there is a need for the recognition of the multiplicity of AHDs. Generalised characteristics of the AHD could still be considered the dominant elements in the international heritage agenda; however, it is crucial to acknowledge the different nuances of AHD among distinctive international and regional institutions rather than gloss over them by recognising only the generalised character of the AHD. Therefore, a defining task for this book is mapping the distinctive Council of Europe's heritage discourse by using the prominent AHD characteristics, defined by Smith, as the reference points against which to compare the CoE discourse's divergences and similarities.

In an effort to provide answers to questions regarding the CoE's place in the wider global heritage governance that inspired this research, the volume builds on two equally important blocs that structure it as a coherent whole:

1. **In-depth historical overview of the CoE heritage activities** – this historical approach is critical for our understanding of the evolution of heritage practice under the auspices of the CoE and its impact on global heritage protection trends. The thorough analysis of the historical and political context permits us to understand how the CoE's heritage conventions and other texts came about, and what combination of timing and relevance enabled their success (or lack thereof). Consequently, it became necessary to dedicate a certain amount of space to historical narrative and the analysis of specific paths taken since the actions and texts of the CoE were shaped mainly not by abstract theory but rather by political and other conditions. Attention is therefore given to analyses of the motives, stakeholders, and political and institutional context (most of the time more pragmatic than theory-based), which influenced the development of specific texts and ideas that, in themselves, demonstrated how the CoE's heritage protection practices were tailored to respond to changing political and social circumstances during the last 70 years.

2. **Discourse-oriented focus on the CoE texts and activities** – the development of a CoE-oriented discussion holds broader relevance in a debate on the AHD's inevitable changes and variations through time and space. In addition to understanding the AHD as a reflection of a European sense of historical monuments, it is valuable to investigate the role that the CoE's heritage activities have played in legitimising the AHD in the formative years of international heritage agenda – but also, more interestingly, in contesting it. The CoE conventions and recommendations led to the unification of European heritage legislation and were a decisive factor in how heritage is valued and protected across the continent. Thus, using the CoE as a specific body for analysis, it is possible to look simultaneously at the legitimisation of the AHD in the international heritage arena, where the CoE played an important part in its early years (until the late 1990s), and, more importantly, at the examples of departure and discrepancy, where one discourse (AHD) gives way to another (the CoE's twenty-first-century discourse).

The present volume, thus, seeks to push the heritage scholarship discussion towards the recognition of the multiplicity of nuances of generalised AHD and to contribute to our understanding of the regional contributions to the ongoing change in the international heritage discourse, policy, and law-making.

As Blake[6] and Lixinski[7] note, the policies and laws in the regional context allow for greater ambition and freedom than on the global scale. They also have a more noticeable impact on the standards and legislation of the Member States, as those countries are more likely to have more apparent shared values as well as shared challenges, which can allow for more innovative approaches to protection and regulation. Vrdoljak suggests that regional approaches hold transformative potential for reshaping our understanding of cultural heritage and its legal protections at the multilateral level, shifting the focus from a traditional emphasis on state and national cultures to an emphasis on human rights and cultural diversity.[8] With its recent heritage conventions and a number of recommendations and declarations, the CoE, together with other regional organisations, most notably the African Union and Organisation of American States (OAS), has significant potential for a major influence over the development of global international law in the field. All three regional bod-

6 Janet Blake, *International Cultural Heritage Law* (Oxford University Press 2015).

7 Lucas Lixinski, 'International Cultural Heritage Regimes, International Law, and the Politics of Expertise' (2013) 20(4) *International Journal of Cultural Property* 407.

8 Ana Filipa Vrdoljak, 'Human Rights and Cultural Heritage in International Law' in Federico Lenzerini and Ana Filipa Vrdoljak (eds), *International Law for Common Goods* (Hart Publishing 2014) 139.

ies have noticeably put their recent focus on the human rights approach to heritage, the relationship between heritage and sustainable development, and a focus on broader participation (democratisation of heritage), moving the regional heritage discourses further from established AHD norms. Building on the understanding of these scholars, my intention with this book is to bring into the spotlight the CoE's chain of texts and projects that framed and still frame a distinctive regional European heritage approach.

1 Theoretical Underpinnings of the Book

As it has been made clear up to now, the aim of the present volume is, while taking stock of the almost 70 years of the CoE's engagement in the field, to pinpoint the ideas and elements in the chain of its legal heritage instruments which challenged the AHD and enabled a more radical shift in the discourse to happen at the beginning of the 2000s. With this aim in mind, this research takes a particular interest in the intersection of the authorised heritage discourse, as characterised by Smith[9] and the CoE's intensive agenda of developing (or, more precisely, harmonising) its heritage discourse with the organisation's wider goals of social inclusion, promotion of human rights, democratic participation, and intercultural dialogue.

Before going into the theoretical aspects underlying the discursive approach to heritage adopted in this volume, it is essential to clarify that the research draws on the notion of public policy instruments as a reflection of values and relations between the governing and the governed.[10] As Pierre Lascoumes and Patrick Le Galès point out:

> Public instruments are not tools with perfect axiological neutrality, equally available: on the contrary, they are bearers of values, fuelled by one interpretation of the social and by precise notions of the mode of regulation envisaged.[11]

In other words, the public policy instrument, such as the CoE heritage conventions, determines the ways in which the actors on different policy levels are

9 Smith (n 1).

10 Pierre Lascoumes and Patrick Le Galès, 'Introduction: Understanding Public Policy through its Instruments – From the Nature of Instruments to the Sociology of Public Policy Instrumentation' (2007) 20(1) *Governance* 1.

11 Ibid 4.

likely to behave; they determine what resources can be used and by whom; they drive forward a particular representation of problems, and they eventually privilege certain actors and interests and exclude others.[12] In this respect, the overview of the chain of conventions and other regulatory instruments adopted by the CoE allows for reflection on the main concepts and relations articulated in the heritage field in Europe.

Going back to the discourse-focus of the book, it is worth noting that the theoretical and analytical foundations – Critical Realism and Critical Discourse Analysis – used by Smith to develop her 'catchphrase' of AHD also inevitably informed the research presented in this book. The clear discourse-oriented approach to heritage used here unavoidably pushes the idea of 'discourse' to the forefront. The notion of discourse is widely referenced in contemporary humanities and social sciences, and researchers from different theoretical backgrounds and fields of study may use it with different meanings. Naturally, those different perspectives have resulted in several approaches to discourse and its analysis, such as Foucauldian research, conversation analysis, and critical discourse analysis, among others. Based on the strong public (CoE) policy focus of this volume, the tradition of discourse analysis that was primarily utilised is critical discourse analysis (CDA).

It is hard to speak about discourse without referring to Foucault. He is undeniably one of the most influential writers on discourse, and it is through his original contribution that the study of discourse became so widely used in different disciplines. For him, discourse is a set of 'practices which systematically form the objects of which they speak'.[13] As Hall clarifies, for Foucault, 'nothing has any meaning outside of discourse'; that is to say, discourse produces the world as we know it.[14]

Building on Foucault's understanding of discourse but also on its critique, Fairclough, whose approach to CDA predominantly informed this research, defines the notion of discourse in two ways. When 'discourse' is used as an abstract noun, it signifies 'language use conceived as social practice'.[15] On the other hand, when 'discourse' is used as a countable noun, it refers to a 'way of signifying experiences from a particular perspective'.[16] Similarly, in Gee's view, a discourse has two fundamental meanings, which he distinguishes by

12 Ibid 1–21.

13 Michel Foucault, *The Archaeology of Knowledge* (Tavistock 1977) 49.

14 Stuart Hall, 'Representation, Meaning and Language' in Stuart Hall (ed), *Representation: Cultural Representations and Signifying Practices* (SAGE Publications 1997) 45.

15 Norman Fairclough, 'Critical Discourse Analysis and the Marketization of Public Discourse: The Universities' (1993) 4(2) *Discourse & Society* 138.

16 Ibid 138.

using the capital letter 'D' and a small letter 'd'. By 'discourse', with the small letter 'd', Gee refers to language-in-use; that is to say, language is seen as an action that is taking place in and is influenced by specific settings.[17] 'Discourse' with a capital 'D', on the other hand, is about 'ways of acting, interacting, feeling, believing, valuing, and using various sorts of objects, symbols, tools, and technologies – to recognise yourself and others as meaningful and meaningful in certain ways'.[18] The focus on the policy texts in this volume inevitably oriented the understanding of 'discourse' towards Fairclough's use of it as an abstract noun, and Gee's definition of 'discourse' with the small letter 'd'.

Most of Foucault's work focuses on the epistemological issues of knowledge construction and practice. For him, to be knowledgeable about something means that we are in the regime of the discourse that constructs that thing. Consequently, our ways of being and acting are then constrained or controlled by that knowledge and discourse; in other words, knowledge and the discourse that produces it exercise power upon us.[19] The power-knowledge relation was vital for Foucault, as he identified knowledge as a particular technique of power. However, as Hall argues, a major critique of Foucault's work on discourse is that he tends to 'absorb too much into the idea of discourse' and tends to neglect the material, economic, and structural factors in the way power and knowledge are deployed.[20] In other words, he was more focused on identifying techniques of power rather than on general political struggles.[21] In addition, Foucault did not offer a clear methodological approach, particularly concerning the links between knowledge and practice and social change.[22] Critical discourse analysis (CDA) has matured out of this critique and developed into a well-established interdisciplinary methodology for analysing dis-

---

17 James Paul Gee, *Social Linguistics and Literacies: Ideology in Discourse* (1st published 1990, Taylor and Francis 2011); See also: James Paul Gee, *An Introduction to Discourse Analysis: Theory and Method* (1st published 1999, 2nd edn, Routledge 2005).

18 Ibid 7.

19 Foucault (n 13); see also: Zhiyong Wu and Shuang Hou, 'Heritage and Discourse' in Emma Waterton and Steve Watson (eds), *The Palgrave Handbook of Contemporary Heritage Research* (Palgrave Macmillan 2015) 37.

20 Stuart Hall, 'Foucault: Power, Knowledge and Discourse' in Margaret Wetherell, Stephanie Taylor, and Simeon J Yates (eds), *Discourse Theory and Practice: A Reader* (SAGE Publications 2001) 72.

21 Joseph Rouse, *Knowledge and Power* (Cornell University Press 1987); Joseph Rouse, 'Power/Knowledge' in Gary Gutting (ed), *The Cambridge Companion to Foucault* (Cambridge University Press 1994) 95.

22 Fairclough (n 15).

course and discursive practice, positioning itself within critical social scientific theory and analysis.[23]

The CDA offers a theoretical and methodological approach to exploring the links between discourse and practice, i.e., how language use contributes to shaping and transforming social, cultural, and historical realities and, in turn, how a social, political, or cultural context influences language choice. However, it is important to stress that CDA has become a substantial and diverse field of research. There have been many attempts to systematise it, namely in work by Fairclough[24] (1992, 1995, 1999, 2001, 2003, 2010), Chouliaraki and Fairclough,[25] Van Dijk,[26] Wodak,[27] Wodak and Meyer,[28] Scollon,[29] Gee,[30] and Van Leeuwen.[31] Even though they differ significantly in technical specifications, their strategy is shared. As Luke points out,

> CDA involves a principled and transparent shunting back and forth between the microanalysis of texts using varied tools of linguistics, semi-

23 Lilie Chouliaraki and Norman Fairclough, *Discourse in Late Modernity: Rethinking Critical Discourse Analysis* (Edinburgh University Press 1999).

24 Norman Fairclough, *Discourse and Social Change* (Polity Press 1992); Norman Fairclough, *Critical Discourse Analysis: The Critical Study of Language* (Pearson Education Limited 1995); Norman Fairclough, 'Linguistic and Intertextual Analysis in Discourse Analysis' in Adam Jaworski and Nikolas Coupland (eds), *The Discourse Reader* (Routledge 1999) 183; Norman Fairclough, 'Critical Discourse Analysis as a Method in Social Scientific Research' in Ruth Wodak and Michael Meyer (eds), *Methods of Critical Discourse Analysis* (SAGE Publications 2001) 121; Norman Fairclough, *Analysing Discourse – Textual Analysis for Social Research* (Routledge 2003); Norman Fairclough, *Critical Discourse Analysis* (2nd edn, Longman 2010).

25 Chouliaraki and Fairclough (n 23).

26 Teun A van Dijk, 'Discourse, Power and Access' in Cecilia R Caldas-Coulthard (ed), *Studies in Critical Discourse Analysis* (Routledge 1993); Teun A van Dijk (ed), *Discourse as Structure and Process – Discourse Studies: A Multidisciplinary Introduction* (Vol 1, SAGE Publications 1997); Teun A van Dijk, 'Multidisciplinary CDA: A Plea for Diversity' in Ruth Wodak and Michael Meyer (eds), *Methods of Critical Discourse Analysis* (SAGE Publications 2001) 95.

27 Ruth Wodak, *Disorders of Discourse* (Longman 1996).

28 Ruth Wodak and Michael Meyer (eds), *Methods of Critical Discourse Studies* (SAGE Publications 2001).

29 Ron Scollon, *Analysing Public Discourse: Discourse Analysis in the Making of Public Policy* (Routledge 2008).

30 Gee (n 17).

31 Theo Van Leeuwen, *Discourse and Practice: New Tools for Critical Discourse Analysis* (Oxford University Press 2008).

> otic, and literary analysis and the macroanalysis of social formations, institutions, and power relations that these texts index and construct.[32]

Consequently, the CDA draws simultaneously from theories and models of linguistic analysis of texts and political and sociocultural theories. While relying on linguistic analysis of texts, it also critically analyses visible practices of text interpretation and use. Moreover, the CDA can be seen as a critical political project. Fairclough clearly states in his 'manifesto for CDA' that he '... begins from the political case for [his] research, aiming to respond to present-day issues and problems'.[33] Underpinned by Critical Realism (CR) and the work of Bhaskar,[34] Fairclough developed a critical research programme that focuses on social wrong (in its semiotic aspect), that identifies obstructions in addressing the social wrong, and offers possible ways around identified obstacles.[35] Thus, as Wodak and Mayer argue, CDA, among other critical theories, wants to produce critical knowledge that enables human beings to emancipate themselves from forms of domination through self-reflection.[36]

It is easy to perceive Smith's critique in such a research agenda, as she tends to reveal ideologies and power structures in heritage management – 'that in its semiotic element, she argues, take a form of an Authorised Heritage Discourse'.[37] Waterton, Smith, and Campbell argue that the usefulness of CDA is that it allows researchers to analyse how a particular discourse acts to constitute and mould the various representations of heritage.[38] Therefore, the useful consequences of this kind of analysis are not only that it prompts a critical discussion of what heritage is, but that it ideally facilitates the development of more open dialogue between a range of stakeholders. This book builds on this understanding of CDA and its utility as a method.

As the concept of AHD represents an important notion to which I will be coming back numerous times in this book, I find it necessary to provide a brief overview of the arrival of this hegemonic discourse in the international heri-

---

32 Allan Luke, 'Beyond Science and Ideology Critique: Developments in Critical Discourse Analysis' (2002) 22 *Annual Review of Applied Linguistics* 103.

33 Fairclough 2003 (n 24).

34 Roy Bhaskar, *Scientific Realism and Human Emancipation* (Verso 1986).

35 Joar Skrede and Herdis Hølleland, 'Uses of Heritage and Beyond: Heritage Studies Viewed through the Lens of Critical Discourse Analysis and Critical Realism' (2018) 18 (1) *Journal of Social Archaeology* 77.

36 Wodak and Mayer (n 28).

37 Skrede and Hølleland (n 35) 81.

38 Emma Waterton, Laurajane Smith and Gary Campbell, 'The Utility of Discourse Analysis to Heritage Studies: The Burra Charter and Social Inclusion' (2006) 12(4) *International Journal of Heritage Studies* 339.

tage policy arena, its main characteristics, and the particular set of consequences it has. This overview not only exposes how the AHD is legitimised and its notions perpetuated throughout the chain of international heritage texts (specifically UNESCO conventions) but also makes us wonder what the role of the CoE in this process was.

Ideology, power, and knowledge are of particular importance in the discourse approach to heritage. Hall asserted that heritage is a discursive construction through which the nation-state creates collective identity, gains political legitimacy, and educates its citizens.[39] Building on this, Smith, in her work *Uses of Heritage*, offered a characterisation of this hegemonic discourse and its set of consequences. The authorised heritage discourse is reliant on the power/knowledge claims of experts, who have a responsibility to 'steward' and 'act for' a universal past.[40] This past comprises 'tangible', 'monumental', and 'aesthetically pleasing' sites, monuments, and buildings. The AHD, therefore, 'privileges monumentality and grand scale, innate artefact/site significance tied to the time depth, scientific/aesthetic expert judgment, social consensus and nation building'.[41]

With its focus on materiality that needs to be 'conserved as found' for future generations and its role in building national identity, the AHD has a particular set of consequences. Smith argues that one of the consequences of the AHD is that it defines who the legitimate spokespersons for the past are. The current generation is best represented by 'experts' whose role is to demonstrate the benefits of heritage to the 'public'. This leaves the 'public' largely disengaged from the active use of heritage and obscures the multi-vocality of many heritage values and meanings of communities today. Moreover, this 'public' in most of Europe is represented by a particular and privileged social group – 'white' upper-middle and upper-class men. According to Smith, 'it is as much a discourse of nationalism and patriotism as it is of certain class experiences and social and aesthetic value'.[42]

While today it is generally accepted in heritage literature that heritage is multi-faceted and ultimately experienced in the present (Cleere;[43] Low-

39 Stuart Hall, 'Whose Heritage? Un-Settling "The Heritage", Re-Imagining the Post-Nation' (1999) 13(49) *Third Text* 3.

40 Emma Waterton, *Rhetoric & 'Reality' – Politics, Policy and the Discourse of Heritage in England* (PhD thesis, University of York 2007).

41 Smith (n 1) 11.

42 Ibid 28.

43 Henry Cleere (ed), *Archaeological Heritage Management in the Modern World* (1st published 1989, Routledge 2000).

enthal;[44] Meskell;[45] Waterton and Watson;[46] Logan, Craith, and Kockel[47]), the AHD is still the predominant discourse in heritage policies and management, nationally and internationally. It is, therefore, necessary to understand its historical formation and the rise to dominance of its aforementioned characteristics if, as is the case in this book, one intends to explore and map out a competing or alternative discourse (the CoE heritage discourse). The AHD developed within a particular timeframe and under a specific set of influences, and its core characteristics are recognised in the range of heritage literature.

1.1 *Heritage and National Identity*

The current concept of heritage, well-reviewed in heritage literature, emerged in Europe within the context of nineteenth-century modernity (Jokilehto;[48] Walsh;[49] Barthel;[50] Pearce[51]). Much of the changes that came with the Industrial Revolution, the associated urbanisation and opening of the globalised world, and the related social changes that took place due to them, draw on antecedents beginning in the Enlightenment. The overturning of the perceived 'irrationality' and 'superstition' of the fifteenth and sixteenth centuries that came with the Enlightenment and its claims about the possibility of objective, scientific truth is the origin of wider societal change in Europe throughout the eighteenth and nineteenth centuries. It was a period of significant progress reflected in numerous discoveries and technological advancements. It was also a period where the idea of the cultural (and racial) superiority of (Western) Europe emerged, which subsequently legitimised and reinforced European colonial and imperial expansions. The colonial expansion also brought a dialogue about race to the foreground, and ethnic and cultural identity became firmly linked with the notions of 'blood', 'homeland',

44 David Lowenthal, 'Fabricating Heritage' (1998) 10(1) *History and Memory* 5.

45 Lynn Meskell, 'The Intersections of Identity and Politics in Archaeology' (2002) 31 *Annual Review of Anthropology* 279.

46 Emma Waterton and Steve Watson (eds), *Culture, Heritage and Representation: Perspectives on Visuality and the Past* (Ashgate Publishing Limited 2010).

47 William Logan, Máiréad Nic Craith and Ullrich Kockel (eds), *A Companion to Heritage Studies* (John Wiley & Sons 2015).

48 Jukka Jokilehto, *History of Architectural Conservation* (Routledge 1999).

49 Keith Walsh, *The Representation of the Past: Museums and Heritage in the Post-modern World* (Routledge 1992).

50 Diane Barthel, *Historic Preservation: Collective Memory and Historical Identity* (Rutgers University Press 1996).

51 Susan Pearce, 'The Construction and Analysis of the Cultural Heritage: Some Thoughts' (1998) 4(1) *International Journal of Heritage Studies* 1.

and 'territory'. Europeans believed in their technical, cultural, and intellectual superiority, and the humanitarian impulse underpinning the Enlightenment was gradually replaced with class tensions, racial prejudice, and intellectual stratification.[52]

The Industrial Revolution, the emergence of modern trade, the rise in open market economies, and the rapid urbanisation of the nineteenth century perturbed a sense of social and geographical security for many people. As Trigger argues, it was an attempt to respond to those tensions that forged the 'unity of nations'.[53] As a result, nation-states emerged, and the development of their social, political, and cultural projects became inseparably linked with the notions of national identity and nationalism (Díaz-Andreu and Champion;[54] Trigger;[55] Lowenthal;[56] Graham, Ashworth, and Tunbridge[57]). Material remains of the past played the utmost importance in the process of nation-building, and it is within this context of developing a narrative of nationalism and national identity that a new, more noticeable concern for heritage emerged.[58] The material (monumental) remains presumably represented a narrative of European progress and superiority. The sense of a new Modern Europe, arising from the nineteenth century, was best expressed in monuments, as they were seen as a 'testimony of the culture and continuity of the entire nation'.[59] As Smith points out, 'material or tangible heritage provides a physical representation of those things from "the past" that speaks to a sense of place, a sense of self, of belonging and community'.[60] Object-oriented heritage was an instrumental element in the process of building national identities. Together with the homogenisation of national languages, national defence, and the unification of national education, monumental heritage played a vital role in providing the national 'consciousness', 'mem-

52 Waterton (n 40).

53 Bruce G Trigger, 'Romanticism, Nationalism, and Archaeology' in Peter L Kohl and Claire Fawcett (eds), *Nationalism, Politics, and the Practice of Archaeology* (Cambridge University Press 1995) 268–9.

54 Margarita Díaz-Andreu and Tim Champion, 'Nationalism and Archaeology in Europe: An Introduction' in Margarita Díaz-Andreu and Tim Champion (eds), *Nationalism and Archaeology in Europe* (Routledge 1996) 1.

55 Trigger (n 53).

56 David Lowenthal, *The Heritage Crusade and the Spoils of History* (Viking 1997).

57 Brian Graham, Greg Ashworth and John E Tunbridge, *A Geography of Heritage: Power, Culture and Economy* (Arnold Publishers 2000).

58 Smith (n 1).

59 Mark Glendinning, 'The Conservation Movement: A Cult of the Modern Age' (2003) 13 *Transactions of the Royal Historical Society* 362.

60 Smith (n 1) 30.

ory', and feeling of 'belonging' for newly defined nation-states (Waterton;[61] Graham, Ashworth, and Tunbridge;[62] Meskell;[63] Harvey[64]). Consequently, the primary form of identity associated with heritage is that of the nation (Smith;[65] Macdonald;[66] Graham, Ashworth, and Tunbridge[67]). Heritage, thus, became a significant, tangible manifestation used to legitimise particular national narratives and, as such, is one of the central elements of AHD.[68] One of the main consequences of the AHD's role in providing a sense of national community is that it inevitably plays a role in ignoring the diversity of other sub-national cultural and social identities.

1.2 *Privileging the Aesthetics and the Elite View of Male History*

The concept of aesthetics is another characteristic of the AHD that needs to be accentuated. It is a concept that has been largely universalised within the fields of heritage and conservation and reappears in a number of current policy and legislative materials. Beyond its background in romanticism (Edensor;[69] Trigger[70]), the aesthetic value within conservation studies is primarily associated with the philosophies of two influential British art and social critics, John Ruskin (1819–1900) and William Morris (1834–1896), even though the influence of French architect Eugène Viollet-le-Duc (1814–1879) and Austrian art-historian Alois Riegl (1858–1905) should not be underestimated.[71] Morris stated in his manifesto proclaiming the interests and objectives of The Society for the Protection of Ancient Buildings (SPAB):

> If...it be asked us to specify what kind of amount of art, style, or other interest in a building makes it worth protecting, we answer, anything which can be looked on as artistic, picturesque, historical, antique, or

61 Waterton (n 40).

62 Graham, Ashworth and Tunbridge (n 57).

63 Lynn Meskell, 'The Intersections of Identity and Politics in Archaeology' (2002) 31 *Annual Review of Anthropology* 279.

64 David Harvey, 'Heritage Pasts and Heritage Presents: Temporality, Meaning and the Scope of Heritage Studies' (2001) 11(4) *International Journal of Heritage Studies* 269.

65 Smith (n 1).

66 Sharon Macdonald, 'Museum, National, Postnational and Transnational Identities' (2003) 1(1) *Museum and Society* 1.

67 Graham, Ashworth, and Tunbridge (n 57).

68 Waterton (n 40).

69 Tim Edensor, *Industrial Ruins: Space, Aesthetics and Materiality* (Berg Publishers 2005).

70 Trigger (n 53).

71 Michael V. Thompson, *Ruins Reused: Changing Attitude to Ruins since Late Eighteenth Century* (Heritage Marketing and Publications Ltd 2006).

> substantial: any work, is short, over which educated, artistic people would think it worthwhile to argue at all.[72]

Morris's statement above exposes not only the privileging of artistic and aesthetic value, but it clearly declares that 'it was only the well-educated who had the necessary cultural literacy to understand grand social and national narratives that were inherent in the fabric of such monuments'.[73] As a result, it was the ruling and upper-middle class's idea of monuments, grand scale, and aesthetic taste that imposed itself as dominant in conservation practice. The privileging of a particular expression of heritage, such as churches, country houses, and other great estates, and the assumption that national relevance derives from this elite architecture presupposes, in Lowenthal's words, that 'the historic fabric belongs to the Great and the Good; heritage is the pastoral care of **gentlemen**'.[74] This idea, which draws directly from Morris, that the sense of identity engendered by heritage is specifically 'middle and upper-class,' still underwrites heritage policies today.[75] Consequently, such elite heritage (because it represents the 'right' aesthetics, the 'right' age, and the 'right' historical interest) is equated with the nation and national heritage.[76]

In addition, this heritage is gendered. Smith argues that the AHD, with a noticeable masculine perspective informed by class-specific values and perceptions, tended to dominate the way in which heritage has been preserved, valued, and interpreted. As a result, this bias contributed to legitimising an elite view of male history – the history of great men and their deeds, which is perpetuated through the selection of sites, monuments, artefacts, and places that come to count as 'heritage'.[77] A number of scholars have addressed this intersection between gender and heritage (Edensor and Kothari;[78] Lowenthal;[79]

72 William Morris, *Manifesto of the Society for the Protection of Ancient Buildings* (Society for the Protection of Ancient Buildings 1877).

73 Smith (n 1) 21.

74 Lowenthal (n 56) (emphasis in original).

75 Anders Karlström, 'Spiritual Materiality: Heritage Preservation in a Buddhist World?' (2005) 5(3) *Journal of Social Archaeology* 338.

76 Waterton (n 40) 34.

77 Silvana Colella, 'Not a Mere Tangential Outbreak: Gender, Feminism and Cultural Heritage' (2018) 18 *Il Capitale Culturale* 251.

78 Tim Edensor and Uma Kothari, 'The Masculinisation of Stirling's Heritage' in Vivienne Kinnaird and Derek R. Hall (eds), *Tourism: A Gender Analysis* (Wiley 1994) 164.

79 David Lowenthal, 'Fabricating Heritage' (1998) 10(1) *History and Memory* 5.

Labadi;[80] Blake[81]), emphasising that women 'have been largely invisible and misrepresented in the archives of history'[82] and that both tangible and intangible heritage has been often selected from a perspective of 'heritage masculinisation'.[83] Moghadam and Senftova,[84] as well as Labadi[85] and Shortliffe,[86] argued that the androcentric interpretation of heritage dominates how heritage is identified and selected at national and international levels. Drawing on Labadi's examination of nomination dossiers for the UNESCO World Heritage List, Shortliffe states that sites being proposed for inclusion 'were most often associated with historical men or successful male entrepreneurs, especially in the case of industrial heritage'.[87] The question of how to change this structural bias is at the centre of the ongoing discussion among scholars addressing the issue (Smith;[88] Colella;[89] Levy[90]). Their critiques highlight two main concerns: the use of falsely genderless language (in conventions, documents, sites, and monuments' interpretations) and the marginalisation of gender issues in heritage discourse, even as the voices of minorities or indigenous peoples are progressively making themselves heard.

1.3 *Sense of Patrimony, the Role of Experts, and Community Participation*

The work of Ruskin and Morris not only emphasised the importance of the aesthetic but their doctrine was also rooted in a sense of the pastoral care of

80 Sophia Labadi, 'Representations of the Nation and Cultural Diversity in Discourses on World Heritage' (2007) 7(2) *Journal of Social Archaeology* 147.

81 Janet Blake, 'Gender and Intangible Heritage: Illustrating the Inter-Disciplinary Character of International Law' in Wera Grahn and Ross J. Wilson (eds), *Gender and Heritage: Performance, Place and Politics* (Routledge 2018) 207.

82 Graham, Ashworth and Tunbridge (n 57) 45.

83 Edensor and Kothari (n 78).

84 Valentine M. Moghadam and Lucie Senftova, 'Measuring Women's Empowerment: Participation and Rights in Civil, Political, Social, Economic, and Cultural Domains' (2005) 57(184) *International Social Science Journal* 389.

85 Sophia Labadi, *UNESCO, Cultural Heritage, and Outstanding Universal Value: Value-Based Analyses of the World Heritage and Intangible Cultural Heritage Conventions* (AltaMira Press 2013).

86 Sarah Shortliffe, 'Gender and (World) Heritage: The Myth of a Gender-Neutral Heritage' in Laurent Bourdeau, Maria Gravari-Barbas and Mike Robinson (eds), *World Heritage, Tourism, and Identity: Inscription and Co-production* (Routledge 2015) 107.

87 Ibid 108.

88 Laurajane Smith, 'Indigenous Archaeologies: Decolonizing Theory and Practice' (2008) 82(315) *Antiquity* 236.

89 Colella (n 77).

90 Janet Levy, 'Gender, Feminism, and Heritage' in Peter Bihel and Christopher Prescott (eds), *Heritage in the Context of Globalization: Europe and the Americas* (Springer 2013) 85.

the material past. In Morris's words, 'They (monuments) are not in any sense our property, to do as we like with. We are only trustees for those that come after us'.[91]

The idea of moral obligation and the idea of patrimony, together with the primacy of eternity of the monuments and 'old' buildings, as proclaimed by Ruskin and Morris, are the essence of the conservation movement. Together with aesthetic and artistic value, these ideas, coupled with historical associations and the monuments' significance in the nation-building process, offered the parameters for patrimony.[92] These parameters have also endured within the AHD and were inscribed in national and international heritage legislation. Central to this sense of patrimony are monuments that, firstly, are symbols of the nation-state and national identity and that need to be 'properly handed on to future citizens';[93] secondly, their value lies within their fabric: intrinsic, unchallengeable, and universal (Labadi;[94] Waterton[95]).

The AHD emerged from nineteenth-century debates (beginning with Ruskin and Morris), and the aforementioned parameters are embedded within it. The AHD defines heritage as material, non-renewable, and fragile.[96] Waterton points out that three major consequences were generated with such an understanding of heritage.[97] Firstly, the idea of inheritance and the moral obligation of the current generations to care for and protect aesthetically pleasing material objects, sites, and places so that they may be passed to 'nebulous future generations' unavoidably disengages the present from the active use of heritage.[98] Consequently, the AHD defines who the legitimate spokespersons for the past are. Based on the heritage's materiality, its architectural importance, and its focus on old age, the 'experts', predominantly archaeologists and conservation architects, therefore dominated the process of heritage management and policy formulation. Secondly, Waterton argues, the AHD continues to sustain an understanding of heritage as something that belongs to human-

91 William Morris, 'Address at the Twelfth Annual Meeting – SPAB' (1889) https://www.marxists.org/archive/morris/works/1889/spab16.htm accessed 7 November 2020.

92 Noha Nasser, 'Planning for Urban Heritage Places: Reconciling Conservation, Tourism, and Sustainable Development' (2003) 17(4) *Journal of Planning Literature* 467.

93 Miles Glendinning, 'The Conservation Movement: A Cult of the Modern Age' (2003) 13 *Transactions of the Royal Historical Society* 359.

94 Labadi (n 85).

95 Waterton (n 40) 35.

96 Laurajane Smith, 'Intangible Heritage: A Challenge to the Authorised Heritage Discourse?' (2015) 40 *Revista D'Etnologia de Catalunya* 135.

97 Waterton (n 40).

98 Smith (n 1) 29.

kind collectively as a 'common heritage'.[99] However, paradoxically, by declaring something a 'public', 'common' or 'universal' heritage, different stakeholders outside of the circle of experts are excluded from any control over or access to it. Consequently, a third implication resulting from the two aforementioned points is the significant alienation of non-experts from the decision-making process and the naturalising of the privileged position of 'experts' within the management process. This means that, as Smith points out, distinctive groups and organisations supporting that discourse are afforded a sense of expertise and authority and a privileged position in the debate about the past and heritage and how both may be used.[100] By favouring intrinsic aesthetic and scientific values and the materiality of heritage, the real cultural, political, and social work that the heritage process does has been disguised. The privileging of the scientific value and assertion of scientific expertise and authority helped to legitimise the public claims of architects and archaeologists as stewards over the past and became authorised and authoritative due to its appeals to universal applicability.

This was the discourse that mostly underpinned the international twentieth-century conventions. The formulation of the AHD is predominantly the result of the extensive collaboration between newly created organisations with the mandate in heritage protection in the 1950s and 1960s, particularly between UNESCO, the CoE, and ICOMOS. Through the texts of those international bodies, the roles of architects, art historians, and archaeologists were strengthened; these professions were deemed the only ones capable of distinguishing the sites, monuments, and buildings worthy of protection and transmission to future generations. It is also important to bear in mind the fact that the most prominent experts at the time (archaeologists and architects)

---

99 Waterton (n 40);
See also: David Lowenthal, 'Fabricating Heritage' (1998) 10(1) *History and Memory* 5;
Lindsay V Prott, 'International Standards for Cultural Heritage' in UNESCO, *World Culture Report* (UNESCO Publishing 1998) 222;
Lynn Meskell, 'The Social Life of Heritage' in Ian Hodder (ed), *Archaeological Theory Today* (2nd edn, Polity Press 2012) 229;
Lynn Meskell, 'UNESCO's World Heritage Convention at 40: Challenging the Economic and Political Order on International Heritage Conservation' (2013) 54(4) *Current Anthropology* 483;
Lynn Meskell, 'States of Conservation: Protection, Politics and Pacting within UNESCO's World Heritage Committee' (2014) 87(1) *Anthropological Quarterly* 217;
Lynn Meskell, *A Future in Ruins: UNESCO, World Heritage and the Dream of Peace* (Oxford University Press 2018).

100 Laurajane Smith, *Archaeological Theory and the Politics of Cultural Heritage* (Taylor & Francis Group 2004).

simultaneously participated in the work of those organisations, trying to find the best platform for the dissemination of their ideas. In this context of enthusiastic exchange, it is central to the argument of this book to show how much of the ideas and discussions developed at the CoE have influenced the debate on the global level and, in fact, the formulation of the AHD at the time.

In addition, the question of community participation in AHD needs to be addressed. The predominant attitude of experts at the international level, not only towards monumentality but also towards the communities as passive observers and passive recipients of knowledge, was legitimised in a series of conventions at the CoE and UNESCO levels. In Smits's view of the AHD, visitors are instructed *about* heritage but are not invited to engage *with* it more actively.[101] However, since the 1990s, heritage management theory and practice have seen an increased use of terms like community involvement, community engagement, participatory approach, heritage community, and public archaeology. It was a sign of a changing discourse that evolved from a monuments-focused approach towards a value-based and, recently, a person-oriented approach.[102] Even though the signs and certain visionary proclamations concerning community participation can be traced to the policy documents of international heritage organisations during the twentieth century, the fundamental paradigm shift took place only in the 1990s. The results of it came in the form of a number of policy documents throughout the 2000s, such as the revised Burra Charter,[103] the Convention for the Safeguarding of the Intangible Cultural Heritage (2003), the Convention on the Protection and Promotion of the Diversity of Cultural Expressions (2005), and the Council of Europe Framework Convention on the Value of Heritage for Society (Faro Convention, 2005). With the underpinning of these documents, international organisations now increasingly give attention to community engagement in their policies and create a legal basis for the promotion of civil society participation in the field of cultural heritage.

This concise portrayal of the roots and characteristics of the AHD was critical, as it offers a foundation upon which one could build a more complex understanding of the AHD and, more importantly, its nuances within the preceding chapters.

---

101 Smith (n 1).

102 Koen Van Balen and Aziliz Vandesande (eds), *Community Involvement in Heritage* (Garant 2015).

103 Australia ICOMOS, *The Burra Charter: The Australia ICOMOS Charter for Places of Cultural Significance* (The International Council on Monuments and Sites, 2013).

2 Data and Methods of Investigation

From an academic point of view, as portrayed earlier in this chapter, this research is nourished by studies on the discursive nature of heritage. Principally, the book builds on Smith's proposal that there is a dominant hegemonic authorised heritage discourse, legitimised through an international and national chain of texts and policies (AHD), as well as on the growing body of literature that analyses its consequences.

The second proposition this research draws upon, and that offers both a theoretical and methodological framework, is Critical Discourse Analysis (CDA). It is a fundamental methodology employed in this volume, and the arguments that this book aims to develop are underpinned by CDA's concern with identifying and understanding how people organise themselves and act through particular discourse.[104] For Fairclough, integral to CDA is not solely an analysis of discourse but also an analysis of that discourse's social and political context and its social effects.[105] The idea that discourses are not just about sustaining and legitimising certain practices and social relations, but may also be engaged with social change, is an important notion to keep in mind. The critical point here is to recognise that any given dominant discourse does not enjoy an undisputed sense of pre-eminence and will be challenged and contested, and thus put at risk, in the course of social struggles.[106]

The CDA offers a theoretical and methodological approach to exploring the links between discourse and practice, i.e., how language use contributes to shaping and transforming social, cultural, and historical realities and, in turn, how a social, political, or cultural context influences language choice. Fairclough, thus, developed a critical research programme that focuses on social wrong (in its semiotic aspect), identifies obstructions in addressing the social wrong and offers possible ways around identified obstacles.[107] It is easy to perceive Smith's critique in such a research agenda, as she tends to reveal ideologies and power structure in heritage management – 'that in its semiotic element, she argues, take a form of an Authorised Heritage Discourse'.[108]

---

104 Norman Fairclough, *Analysing Discourse: Textual Analysis for Social Research* (Routledge 2003).

105 Ibid.

106 Norman Fairclough, 'Critical Discourse Analysis as a Method in Social Scientific Research' in Ruth Wodak and Michael Meyer (eds), *Methods of Critical Discourse Analysis* (SAGE Publications 2001).

107 Skrede and Hølleland (n 35).

108 Ibid 81.

Therefore, Smith's assertion of the AHD as a paradigm of dominant heritage discourse and the framework offered by critical discourse analysis forms a basis for examining the CoE's heritage policy and texts in this book. The CDA, both in terms of theory and method, allows us to analyse and comment upon the AHD characteristics recognisable in the CoE's texts, but at the same time, it also permits us to identify those features of the particular CoE's discourse, which more readily recognised and encouraged the use of heritage in broader agendas for social change.

The critical dataset that permitted a comprehensive analysis of the construction of the CoE's heritage discourse comes from two areas of qualitative research: (1) archival research, and (2) a number of semi-structured interviews undertaken with a range of key former and current CoE staff and external experts working on the CoE's heritage conventions.

The argument in this book is primarily built upon the CoE's archival documents. The data collected through the intensive study of the CoE archives provided thorough information on the evolution of the CoE heritage policies, its origins, its use for wider political goals, and its relationships with other international heritage organisations. Therefore, the arguments developed here are primarily based on a range of published and unpublished CoE policy documents. These include a collection of published policy guidelines, recommendations, resolutions, and strategies freely available online, covering a period between 1949 and 2023. In addition to these published texts, the analysis is based upon extensively employed evidence collected from a number of unpublished sources, such as preparatory work for policy documents, meeting records, consultation discussions and responses, internal letters, experts' reports, thematic reports from the Member Countries, reports from conferences, round tables and seminars organised by the CoE, memos, and policy drafts, gathered from institutional archival sources (the archives of the CoE, Parliamentary Assembly, and Committee of Ministers). While final, adopted texts reflect the agreed stance of the organisation on certain issues, and in that sense, they are the reflection of agreed-upon discourse, the exploration of the preparatory work proved to be much more rewarding for our understanding of the interplay of multiple factors that led to the final text. It was those documents that revealed the background behind every provision in conventions' texts and offered the opportunity to understand them from multiple perspectives. Putting the timeline of all documents gathered (regarding the specific convention) allowed for following the development of the process and how certain issues and challenges were overcome. This process also permitted tracking the reasoning behind why some ideas and concepts were included and why others were excluded from the text, what issues were politically sen-

TABLE 1.1 Approximate number of CoE archival documents consulted

Council of Europe activity	Number of documents consulted
Early years of European cultural cooperation and the European Cultural Convention (1954) – Chapter 4	65
Council of Europe activities for the protection of architectural heritage – Chapters 5 and 6	250
Council of Europe activities for the protection of archaeological heritage – Chapter 7	60
Council of Europe change in heritage policies in new millennia – Part 3	110
Council of Europe cultural cooperation	115
Total	600

sitive, and who (which Member State or members of the Committee) had an issue with moving the discourse forward. These documents also clarified the complex interplay among the Secretariat, external experts, and the political committee who had to endorse the text in the end. The interplay between experts' expectations and their agenda and the political reality of committees could only be exposed through a thorough exploration of preparatory documents. These documents disclosed who was behind a particular idea that moved the discourse in one or another direction, i.e., whether the change in discourse came about as the result of political will or the experts' initiatives.

The exhaustive list of all documents consulted can be found in the Bibliography section. However, for a general understanding of the extent of archival resources referred to in this research, Table 1.1 (Above) offers an approximate number by subject.

To place the CoE in relation to other intergovernmental organisations also required the consultation of the CoE's archive sources as well as the archives of UNESCO, as well as official documents from the European Union (EU), ICOMOS, Europa Nostra, and the International Centre for the Study of the Preservation and Restoration of Cultural Property (ICCROM). To these official documents, the textual material obtained during interviews with former and current employees of the CoE and its external experts needed to be added.

With the CDA as a framework and its explicit emphasis on language analysis, archival and textual material became an obvious source of data. The choices made regarding the textual material to be analysed were relatively straightforward, considering the timeframe focused on the formal drafting of the CoE heritage conventions. Thus, the four most important heritage-related CoE conventions were used as signposts for directing the collection of data: (1) the European Cultural Convention, (2) the Convention for the Protection of the Architectural Heritage of 1985, (3) the Convention for the Protection of the Archaeological Heritage of Europe (revised) 1992, and (4) the Convention on the Value of Cultural Heritage for Society of 2005.

One of the limitations this research faced was the inaccessibility of the information confined within the Cultural Heritage Department meetings. These working documents and discussions are not publicly available and are generally out of the reach of the researcher. To tackle this obstacle, interviews with the staff of the Secretariat and particularly the Heritage Department were the first option to consider. However, in this process, the two-month study visit to the Heritage Department in its offices in Strasbourg (15 September–15 November 2022) turned out to be an invaluable source of information. It added a further level of understanding of the Department's internal working processes and offered the unique opportunity to participate in day-to-day tasks with the Heritage Team. It also allowed for a closer insight into specialised committee meetings, such as the Steering Committee for Culture, Heritage and Landscape (CDCPP), that are, generally speaking, closed to the public. This experience was instrumental for multiple reasons – it allowed for more relaxed and non-time-constrained discussions on the CoE's heritage approach with team members of different hierarchical roles and responsibilities; it demystified rather complex working methods that include multiple players (Secretariat, CDCPP, external experts, the Committee of Ministers, and PACE); and it offered insight into the future CoE heritage agenda. The study visit allowed for employing a multivalent approach that ranged between person-centred interviewing, general conversation, and observation of the procedures, which all provided a deeper understanding of the policy processes.

In addition, 12 interviews were conducted with former and current CoE staff members who were running or still run the CoE's heritage-related policy formulation and related projects. They covered a range of roles within the CoE's standard-setting processes, drawing from high-level CoE officials, project managers, department directors, external experts affiliated with the CoE, and retired CoE officials. These interviews were used to obtain qualitative data used primarily to contextualise the findings from archival work, and as a consequence, were semi-structured and relatively non-directive. For each interview, a guide of ten questions was used, usually prepared separately for every interviewee depending on that person's position in the organisation and the work that they were involved with. These questions were used as a guide, helping to monitor the interview process rather than directing it in its entirety. Nevertheless, the series of questions revolved around key themes, such as AHD characteristics identified, the political and social context that triggered the decisions for conventions to be drafted, or the details on individuals and organisations (NGOs) particularly involved. In this way, each interviewee was encouraged to talk about similar issues in accordance with the topic guide, which subsequently provided the firm material with which to supplement the observations and interpretations arising from CDA. The interviews were recorded and transcribed (except for those done in the informal setting during the study visit, which had more the form of an informal exchange of opinions rather than a structured and planned interview), thus offering an important part of the data analysed and interpreted in this research.

To analyse the qualitative data collected from the interviews, a manual coding approach was employed. The reason for the choice of manual coding instead of using software such as NVivo, for example, lies in the obtained number of interviews. This number is relatively limited because the Heritage Department of the CoE is extremely small in size, having only five to seven members at a time; these people stay in their positions for a relatively long period of time. They usually report directly to one to two persons, which leaves us with an extremely limited number of people directly involved in the CoE heritage actions. Even though the interviews and informal discussions with some of those team members happened more than once, which raises the factual number of interviews to some extent, it was assessed that manual coding was the optimal choice for the analysis of the acquired data. The interviews were transcribed, and the descriptive codes were assigned to specific data segments. A deductive coding was used, whereby a predefined set of codes was developed before the data analysis. This set of codes was based on the research framework, using the AHD characteristics, political and social context, as well as characteristics of the 'new heritage discourse' as descriptors. For instance, the code 'AHD – tangible aspects' was applied to segments where participants discussed the approach to heritage as an exclusively tangible phenomenon. In addition, codes 'AHD – Experts' Values', 'Community Participation', 'Heritage and Social Processes', 'Heritage and Human Rights', and 'European Heritage' were ascribed to the segments of data mentioned by the interviewees, which allowed for distinguishing the characteristics of the discourse that participants found important. Another code, 'Political background', was used to label the segments highlighting the participant's view on the context, political and social, that, in their opinion, underpinned certain decisions and provisions in heritage texts they were familiar with. This process of manual coding allowed for the organisation and categorisation of data, facilitating the identification of recurrent patterns and emerging themes. The manual coding also allowed for codes to be relatively easily revised and refined, ensuring the capturing of the richness of participants' experiences and knowledge. By breaking down the interview data into meaningful units and labelling them with codes, it was possible to gain a comprehensive understanding of the participants' perspectives, which ultimately decrypted a number of uncertainties identified in the archive sources. In addition, in the second phase, the transcripts were examined again in order to highlight illuminative quotations. A number of quotations were chosen to be used in the following chapters.

Ultimately, this two-fold method, combination of linguistic-led policy analysis with the qualitative technique of semi-structured interviewing, allowed for the mapping of a range of values and understandings of heritage in the CoE's policy texts and the ways it is understood and managed (discourses). Building on Smith's characterisation of the dominant authorised heritage discourse as suppressive, non-democratic, and elite-cementing, this research, therefore, supports the opinion that there is a need to empirically demonstrate those characteristics by CDA's linguistic tools rather than to just assert them in policies of different organisations. As such, the goal of this volume is to contribute to scholarship that enters into more engaging discussions of the concept of AHD. The empirical material analysed in this research will confirm the observations made by other authors that there are not only several competing heritage discourses, but that there are 'sub-AHDs' at work within the same organisation,[109] and more generally, several AHDs among the various actors operating within the heritage sector, among them the CoE discourse.[110]

3 Structure of the Book

This introductory chapter clarifies the theoretical and methodological framework that structures and guides the analyses of the data and the conclusions drawn from it in the following parts. The book is divided into nine chapters, organised into two broader parts – Part 1 covers the Council of Europe heritage

---

109 John Pendlebury, 'Conservation Values, the Authorized Heritage Discourse and the Conservation-Planning Assemblage' (2013) 19(7) *International Journal of Heritage Studies* 709.

110 Arthur Parkinson, Mark Scott and Declan Redmond, 'Competing Discourses of Built Heritage: Lay Values in Irish Conservation Planning' (2016) 22(3) *International Journal of Heritage Studies* 261.

discourse in the twentieth century, and Part 2 focuses on the organisation's discourse in the twenty-first century.

Chapter 2 introduces us to the Council of Europe and the organisation's relation and use of culture and cultural heritage for its broader political goals. The chapter is rather distinctive from the rest of the book, as it does not evaluate any 'pure' heritage-related convention. On the contrary, it implies that understanding the broader political context behind the establishment of the CoE and the role that culture was supposed to play in its political development is necessary, as it was in this period that the foundations of the organisation's heritage discourse were instituted.

Chapters 3, 4, and 5 sketch out the twentieth-century CoE discourse by tracing its characteristics, which, at the time, were highly in line with the AHD. Chapters 3 and 4, in particular, look at the CoE's approach towards the protection and conservation of architectural heritage, which resulted in documents such as the European Architectural Charter (1975) and the Convention for the Protection of Architectural Heritage (1985), as well as events such as the European Year of Architectural Heritage (1975). Chapter 5 explores the CoE's approach to archaeological heritage, which began with the drafting of the European Convention for the Protection of the Archaeological Heritage in 1969 and its substantial revision in 1992. With an exclusive interest in material manifestations of heritage (architectural and archaeological), the arguments in those chapters revolve around themes of experts' dominance, the assumed physicality of the past, and popularisation of heritage. While traces of the AHD were recognised, the dataset analysis also allowed for the identification of several innovative features in the CoE's discourse, which resulted from the acknowledgement of the AHD's limitations, social aspects of heritage, and an integrated approach to heritage management being the most significant ones.

Part 2 (Chapters 6, 7, and 8) takes particular interest in the twenty-first-century radical shift in the CoE's attitude towards heritage and its role in society, which came with the drafting of the Council of Europe Convention on the Value of Cultural Heritage for Society – Faro Convention (2005). With a focus on the debate about the relationship between heritage and cultural rights as part of the wider human rights agenda, heritage and sustainable development, democratic participation, and the new notion of 'heritage community', Chapters 6 and 7 examine the context which allowed for this shift in discourse to happen. The potential of the new CoE approach in tackling, through the AHD, naturalised values and understanding of heritage is gaining well-deserved attention. However, the debate on how to address the tenacity of the AHD and how to implement a 'new heritage' paradigm will be the focus of heritage scholars and practitioners for years to come. Chapter 8, therefore, explores those heretofore identified implementation strategies on both national levels and that of the CoE and reflects on the ways forward.

Lastly, the overall aim of the concluding chapter (Chapter 9) is to highlight the particularities of the CoE's discourse and the impact it has had on how heritage is managed in Europe today. To do this, the arguments that emerged from the CoE conventions and activities analysed will be framed by the three sets of questions that framed this research, as they allow for capturing and illustrating the stages through which the CoE's heritage sector has progressed, as well as describing the evolution of the organisation's heritage discourse.

PART 1

The Council of Europe's Heritage Discourse in the 20th Century

CHAPTER 2

Foundations of European Heritage Cooperation

1 Introduction

The immediate post-WWII period saw unprecedented growth in a number of intergovernmental organisations with mandates in a variety of fields. In parallel with creating the United Nations (UN) system as the most critical one on the global scale, dedicated to maintaining international peace and security, developing friendly relations among nations, achieving international cooperation, and harmonising the actions of governments, there was also a similar process happening at the regional level. This book focuses on one of those regional post-WWII organisations – the Council of Europe. The CoE emerged as a reaction to the trauma Europe endured through WWII, with the aim of creating a more peaceful, democratic, and prosperous European society based on human rights, the rule of law, and democracy. The CoE was just one among many newly created organisations covering several fields to shape the regulations and legislations of their Member States. In the context of this research, the place of, and importance given to culture and cultural cooperation in those newly created international bodies are of specific interest. It was during this period that the basis for future European cultural policy and discourse was shaped, and it is necessary to look at these early endeavours and their origins as they formed the foundation for all subsequent developments.

In the European context, the organisations created post-WWII, such as the Council of Europe (CoE), the Brussels Treaty Organisation (subsequently known as the Western Union (WE) and the Western European Union (WEU), which was its formal title from 1955), the Nordic Council, and even the North Atlantic Treaty Organization (NATO), have all included cultural cooperation in their mandates. The cultural dimension has been seen by newly formed European institutions as a sort of unifying factor, suggesting positive feelings about Europe. In the case of the CoE, culture has been seen as 'any subject throwing light upon the way of life, … and by taking an interest in all activities which aim at developing a better reciprocal knowledge of the basic principles of European civilisation'.[1] Consequently, culture (and cultural heritage) has been recur-

1 Parliamentary Assembly, 'Five Years' Work by the Committee of Cultural Experts – Report presented on behalf of the Committee of Cultural Experts by M. Reinink' [1955] AS/CS (6) 41, 1.

 | DOI:10.1163/9789004756250_003

rently used in European organisations' political texts as a means of evoking the common imagery of Europe.

As this chapter will illustrate, the issues covered under the pretext of cultural cooperation at the CoE level have included actions in the fields of education, the visual and performing arts, cultural heritage (at the time, only its tangible aspects), the media (television, film, publishing, the press), exchange of students and teachers, language teaching and translation, and issues around copyright. Science, sport, and youth were also areas of policy considered at various times to be part of cultural cooperation under the CoE. While acknowledging all the aforementioned different aspects of the CoE's cultural work, the choice was made to focus solely on the cultural heritage policies of the organisation in this volume, partly to relate to a single policy field but also to keep the subject matter manageable. While the following chapters will exclusively explore the heritage-related texts and policies of the organisation, this one holds that a look at the organisation's origins, specifically its view on the wider role of culture in society, to be critical. This not only places heritage issues in the context of the CoE's broader aims but also offers insight into the interplay of ideas and influences among different players in the field at the time.

Therefore, this chapter explores the events and texts that led to the development of European cultural cooperation, focusing on the CoE's approach that resulted in one of the most important CoE conventions: the European Cultural Convention (1954). Understanding this foundational text and the ideas behind it is essential, as it serves as the groundwork for all future developments in the European intergovernmental cultural sphere, including cultural heritage issues.

The chapter is divided into three different thematic sections. Firstly, the chapter offers a historical overview of the CoE's origins and the role attributed to the cultural aspects in its creation. An examination of the ideas that led to the creation of the CoE will serve not only to better apprehend the origins of its heritage discourse – as its philosophical base was established at that point in time – but also it will serve to demonstrate an intense interchange of ideas and influences among different European organisations, one that resulted in the chain of texts regulating the field of culture and cultural heritage that inevitably authorised the specific discourse. The second section of the chapter will pay close attention to the first five years of the cultural cooperation organised under the auspices of the CoE. It was during this period that the early foundations of the CoE discourse were inaugurated, and the first discrepancies could be observed between the organisation's human-rights-based understanding of the role of heritage and culture in society and the reality of the hereditary elitist attitude towards culture that dominated the political discourse at the time. The third part of the chapter aims to guide the reader through the 'life cycle' of the 1954 European Cultural Convention. Starting with the events leading to the decision that such an instrument was needed in the context of cooperation between the CoE Member States, coverage will also be provided relative to the drafting process and its provisions before concluding by considering the impact the document has had and still has on the CoE cultural heritage activities.

2 Origins of European Cultural Cooperation

To understand the CoE in general and the organisation's engagement in cultural matters, initial reference must be made to the Congress of Europe of 1948 (The Hague Congress). The Congress was essentially the expression of the determination of Western European countries for more evident European unification, and the establishment of the CoE can be perceived as a direct result of it. Taking into account the overall interest of this volume, the focus here will be on the Cultural Committee of The Hague Congress and the ideas it communicated. The intellectual framework advocated by the Cultural Committee that put culture at the heart of the project of European unity had served as a base for cultural cooperation work of newly created European organisations and, among them, most significantly, on the cultural policy of the CoE.

Even though the 'European idea', as a multiform process, has inspired many projects since the nineteenth century, it was in the aftermath of WWII that the term 'United States of Europe' and the 'Council of Europe' entered the political discourse. Usually, in the literature on the subject,[2] the reference is made to Winston Churchill's speech from 1946 that he gave at the University of Zurich, where he called on Europe to unite in the regional structure that may be called the United States of Europe. Churchill also saw 'the creation of a Council of Europe as the first practical step in this process'.[3]

Several factors contributed to the widespread support for uniting Europe into an international organisation. The first and main issue that a unified Europe could solve was the problem of securing peace; in this context, it was

2 Wendell R Mauter, 'Churchill and the Unification of Europe' (1998) 61(1) *The Historian* 67; Richard Toye, 'Churchill and the "United States of Europe"' in Allen Packwood (ed), *The Cambridge Companion to Winston Churchill* (Cambridge University Press 2023) 362–78.

3 Winston Churchill, *Speech delivered at the University of Zurich, 19 September 1946* (Council of Europe) https://rm.coe.int/16806981f3 accessed 3 March 2018.

important to include post-war Germany in the new world order. It was also evident not only that European powers had lost their universal relevance, with the US and USSR dominating world politics, but also that their national economies would not be able to compete on a global scale, and they could only 'survive' if they acted together. In addition, common control over natural resources (primarily coal) and steel production seemed unavoidable.[4]

The will to address these concerns resulted in the remarkable development of European intergovernmental organisations that occurred just a few years after WWII. Even though different in character, these organisations had some overlapping competencies. Before the Congress of Europe, which promoted the creation of the CoE, the Brussels Treaty Organisation[5] and the Organisation for European Economic Cooperation (OEEC)[6] had already been created in 1948. A short period following the Congress and the creation of the CoE in 1949 saw the establishment of the European Coal and Steel Community (1952), the Nordic Council (1952), the Conference of Ministers of Transport (1953), and the European Organisation for Nuclear Research (1954). The distinctive character of these institutions reveals the complexity of the European unity idea and the multiplicity of solutions to which it gave rise. The Brussels Treaty Organisation and the OEEC had a traditional pattern of intergovernmental cooperation; the Nordic Council was a purely parliamentary body, while the

4 Stefanie Schmahl and Marten Breuer (eds), *The Council of Europe: Its Law and Policies* (Oxford University Press 2017).

5 The Brussels Treaty (17 March 1948) is the Treaty of Economic, Social and Cultural Collaboration and Collective Self-Defence, signed in Brussels by Belgium, France, Luxemburg, the Netherlands, and the United Kingdom. While this treaty stipulates only 'cooperation' between the signatory countries and does not provide for establishing an international organisation, in practice, it led to the creation of the Brussels Treaty Organisation (also known as the Western Union). It was primarily a collective defence alliance but also designed to facilitate cooperation in economic, social, and cultural matters. NATO and the Council of Europe developed out of that framework. In 1954, the Treaty of Brussels was amended as the Modified Brussels Treaty – the Western Union was transformed into the Western European Union, and the Federal Republic of Germany and Italy were admitted. Western European Union ceased to exist only in 2010.

6 The Organisation for European Economic Cooperation (OEEC) came into existence on 16 April 1948. It emerged from the Marshall Plan and the Conference of Sixteen which demanded the establishment of a permanent organisation to work on a joint recovery programme and economic cooperation. It had 16 member states – France, United Kingdom, Austria, Belgium, Denmark, Greece, Iceland, Ireland, Italy, Luxemburg, the Netherlands, Norway, Portugal, Sweden, Switzerland, and Turkey. In 1961, the OEEC was replaced by the Organisation for Economic Co-operation and Development (OECD), a worldwide body (www.oecd.org).

CoE incorporated both systems. The European Coal and Steel Community (which developed into the European Union) was, from the beginning, in quite a special position, as it was not an international but a supra-national organisation, with its members surrendering a certain part of their sovereignty to it.

These organisations developed from numerous visions of European unity. But essentially, two main groups dominated the discussion in the post-war period: (a) the Federalists (mainly French, Italian, and Belgian) called for a radical solution – a federation of the states of Europe under a supranational authority, whereas (b) the Unionists (mostly British) preferred intergovernmental cooperation among sovereign states.[7] Winston Churchill, one of the leading political figures, was often praised for his role in the European unity project. He was aware that, in order for the idea of European unity to be successful, he needed to mobilise a large public and incorporate both sides.[8] By organising the different branches of private *Movements for European Unity* under the International Coordination Committee, he and his particularly pro-European son-in-law, Duncan Sandys, managed to ensure that disagreements would not jeopardise the shared aim of uniting Europe. Three working committees of the International Coordination Committee – Political, Economic, and Cultural – were set up to prepare for the Congress of Europe, where the prospects and outlines of the European unity project were to be discussed.[9]

The Congress of Europe (The Hague Congress) was held in May 1948. This ambitious Congress, with the participation of more than 700 eminent figures from nearly 30 countries and chaired by Winston Churchill, wanted to demonstrate the existence of public opinion in support of European unity.[10] Opinion leaders, political activists, civil society representatives, politicians of all political shades (except communists), trade unionists, lawyers, and professors could all claim to represent almost every important aspect of life and opinions in Europe. However, it is necessary to clarify that The Hague Congress was not an official international conference with the governments' representatives, even though its influence over the official politics of participating countries is unquestionable. The work of the Congress was divided into three committees: the Economic and Social Committee, the Political Committee, and the Cultural Committee.

---

7 Birte Wassenberg, *History of the Council of Europe* (Council of Europe Publishing 2013).

8 Tanja E.J. Kleinsorge (ed), *Council of Europe* (Kluwer Law International BV 2015).

9 Wassenberg (n 7).

10 John Coleman (ed), *The Council of Europe* (Council of Europe Publishing 1999).

Whereas the main discussion of the Congress was in its Political Committee, with its particular concern of finding the balance between the two rival visions of Europe and the future Council of Europe's institutional structure, the conclusions of its Cultural Committee are at the heart of our understanding of the role of culture in the early processes of European integration.[11] The Cultural Committee was chaired by Denis de Rougemont,[12] a Swiss philosopher, journalist, and the leader of the European Union of Federalists (UEF). Rougemont was a driving force behind the 'idealist' wing of European federalism, and according to Deering, it was he who synthesised a version of federalism which brought together different aspects into a 'theology' within which culture was a central element of the federalist agenda.[13] In Rougemont's opinion, without culture as an active agent for change, the project of European unity had no point. Rougemont defended the idea that the objectives and aims of future European institutions could not be achieved without taking culture into account. The remarkable work on the idea of European unity by Rougemont is out of the scope of this volume; however, it could be argued that his ideas provided the intellectual framework not only for the future position of cultural cooperation under the auspices of the CoE but also for the foundation of the organisation itself. Rougemont's ideas are accurately articulated in the Message to Europeans, issued by the Cultural Committee and delivered at the end of the Congress.[14] This message contains the essence of what would soon

---

11 Council of Europe, *Congress of Europe* (Council of Europe Publishing 1999).

12 The Cultural Resolution and the 'Message to Europeans', delivered at the end of The Hague Congress, were written by Denis de Rougemont, a Swiss writer whose name is highly associated with the European Movement and with the cultural dimension of Europe. He was born in Switzerland in 1906. He was a reader in French at the German University of Frankfurt-on-Main in the 1930s and returned to Switzerland in 1936 with a clear awareness of Nazism, which he actively opposed. He spent war years in the United States and returned to Europe in 1947, where he became active in the European Federalist Movement. With the actuality of the nuclear issues at that period, he co-founded CERN (European Centre for Nuclear Research) in Geneva. He also guided the work of the European Cultural Centre (ECC), which he founded in 1950 (CERN developed from the ECC). He was also involved with Robert Schuman in creating the European Cultural Foundation in 1954. At the end of the 1950s, his interest turned towards the dialogue between cultures (L'avenire occidental de l'homme, 1957), the concept which UNESCO would adopt later. He died in Geneva in 1985.

13 Mary Jo Deering, *Denis de Rougemont l'Européen* (Lausanne: Fondation Jean Monnet pour l'Europe 1991).

14 1. We desire a United Europe, throughout whose area the free movement of persons, ideas and goods is restored;
2. We desire a Charter of Human Rights guaranteeing liberty of thought, assembly and expression as well as the right to form a political opposition;

become the organisational foundation of the CoE: human rights, diversity, and the European Assembly.

This being the case, it is clear why the Congress of Europe is seen as one of the most significant events in the history of European integration. It was where the prospect of a radical restructuring of political authority was opened, and the unification of Europe was put irreversibly on the political agenda. And although this Congress played a crucial role in creating the CoE as such, we cannot underestimate the significance it gave to cultural cooperation. Undeniably, the European countries were aware of the importance of cultural diplomacy and cooperation well before the European Congress, but that cooperation was mainly bilateral and oriented towards national interests. The change the Congress introduced was in emphasising the role of cultural cooperation in the European unity project. As a result, the Brussels Treaty Organisation (BTO), the Nordic Council, NATO, and, later on, the European Communities/European Union all included culture as one of their core competencies. At the same time, for the CoE, the preparatory cultural work of the Congress ultimately became the basis of its cultural policy.

Before turning our full attention to the Council of Europe and its work in the fields of culture and heritage, the next section will briefly examine the approaches taken by the Brussels Treaty Organisation, NATO, and the Nordic Council. These organisations and their activities significantly influenced the framework for cultural cooperation that the Council of Europe developed in its early years.

3 Cultural Cooperation in Post-WWII Europe

3.1 *The Brussels Treaty Organisation (BTO)/Western European Union (WEU)*

The Brussels Treaty Organisation (BTO), also known as the Western Union (WU), emerged in March 1948 following the signing of the Treaty of Economic,

---

3. We desire a Court of Justice with adequate sanctions for the implementation of this Charter;
4. We desire a European Assembly where the live forces of all our nations shall be represented;
5. And pledge ourselves in our homes and in public, in our political and religious life, in our professional and trade union circles, to give our fullest support to all persons and governments working for this lofty cause, which offers the last chance of peace and the one promise of a great future for this generation and those that will succeed it (Council of Europe 1999, p. 421).

Social and Cultural Collaboration and Collective Self-Defence by France, Belgium, the Netherlands, Luxembourg, and the United Kingdom. Structurally, the BTO reflected the conventions of a classic intergovernmental body: decision-making rested with a Consultative Council composed of Foreign Ministers, without either a parliamentary assembly, as would be the case with the Council of Europe (CoE), or the national commissions characteristic of UNESCO. While principally a military alliance, the treaty's first three articles concerned economic, social, and cultural cooperation, offering a broader vision of post-war reconstruction and unity.

This brief account of BTO cultural cooperation is included in the volume for two interrelated reasons. First, it was the BTO that played a catalytic role in translating the aspirations of the 1948 Congress of Europe into institutional reality, directly influencing the creation of the CoE. Second, the BTO represents the earliest attempt at a multilateral cultural cooperation framework in post-war Europe among states that, unlike the Nordic countries, lacked an existing linguistic or historical infrastructure for collaboration.[15]

Despite its significance, the cultural activities of the BTO have received limited scholarly attention. This section draws primarily on the work of Haigh,[16] Parry,[17] and archival material from the UK Foreign Office. A former head of the Cultural Relations Department at the Foreign Office and member of both the BTO Cultural Committee (from 1952) and later the CoE's Committee of Cultural Experts, Haigh offers a first-hand, if largely descriptive, account of the BTO's cultural work. His trajectory, culminating in his role as Head of Education and Cultural and Scientific Affairs at the CoE from 1962, also illustrates the personal continuity that characterised European intergovernmental cooperation during this period. Parry, in turn, provides the only sustained academic analysis of BTO cultural policy, though his focus remains primarily on the British position.

Why, then, was cultural cooperation included in what was ostensibly a defence treaty? The motivations of the drafters remain opaque, but Article III of the treaty makes the intention clear:

> The High Contracting Parties will make every effort in common to lead their peoples towards a better understanding of the principles which

---

15 Joy Parry, *Companies of Clouds: The Development of Multilateral Cultural Cooperation in Western European International Organisations* (PhD Thesis, University of Warwick 2000).

16 Anthony Haigh, *Cultural Diplomacy in Europe* (Council of Europe 1974).

17 Parry (n 15).

> form the basis of their common civilisation and to promote cultural exchanges by conventions between themselves and by other means.
>
> Article III

Despite this formal commitment, the early work of the BTO Cultural Committee was marked by uncertainty. As Haigh noted, the Committee's members had only a vague sense of what cultural cooperation ought to achieve. Diverging national views on the meaning and purpose of cultural collaboration further complicated matters.[18] The United Kingdom insisted that multilateral cultural work should rest on a foundation of bilateral conventions – a perspective informed by its disillusionment with the perceived inefficiencies of UNESCO. The Foreign Office was adamant that the BTO should avoid replicating that model.[19] Other members, however, held contrasting views. French officials imagined a forum for debating common cultural issues but were wary of establishing a new institution akin to a European UNESCO. The Dutch openly supported the creation of such an institution, while Belgium and Luxembourg focused on practical proposals for joint cultural activities.

Eventually, a compromise was reached. The four continental states accepted the British preference for bilateral foundations but insisted this should not preclude the development of a joint cultural programme. The Committee of Cultural Experts was thus tasked with drafting such a programme. Although larger projects were not ruled out, the absence of a central budget limited ambitions. The proposals focused on facilitating the circulation of cultural and educational materials and the mobility of cultural workers. One of the most notable initiatives was the introduction of the 'Cultural Identity Card', which offered practical benefits such as free museum access and reduced travel costs. The CoE later adopted the scheme in 1950 and maintained it until the early 1980s.

Other areas of BTO engagement included efforts to regulate the audiovisual sector, foster cooperation in non-fiction film production, and convene conferences of European university rectors. In the field of cultural heritage, the protection of artworks during wartime initially appeared as a priority. A working party addressed the issue in 1950, followed by the 1951 Brussels Treaty Civil Defence Conference. However, the matter was ultimately referred to UNESCO, culminating in the 1954 Hague Convention for the Protection of Cultural Property in the Event of Armed Conflict. According to proceedings of the Assembly of the Western European Union (WEU), this was part of a broader

18 Haigh (n 16).

19 Parry (n 15).

tendency to transfer questions to UNESCO either to prevent duplication or to scale up initiatives developed under the BTO framework.[20]

Throughout the BTO's lifespan, tensions persisted over the aims and methods of cultural cooperation. The UK promoted activities such as training courses for teachers, civil servants, and youth leaders, viewing cultural cooperation as a means of promoting democratic values and Western European solidarity. In contrast, the continental partners emphasised 'high culture' and artistic appreciation, which the British viewed as disconnected from the political objective of fostering a shared European identity. Parry convincingly argues that this ideological divide stemmed from Britain's unique post-war experience – unlike its partners, the UK had not endured occupation, and its limited appreciation for the role of 'high culture' in restoring a shattered European sense of self.[21]

The lack of a coherent vision among member states meant that the BTO Cultural Committee functioned largely through experimentation, often advancing initiatives that provoked the least resistance. Nevertheless, its work provided a valuable testing ground for the cultural programme of the Council of Europe. As noted in a 1955 WEU report, the BTO's cultural efforts were 'to some extent experimental, similar to that done in a laboratory', and promising initiatives were expected to be extended to the CoE.[22]

From the outset, the potential for convergence between the BTO and CoE was evident. Both created Cultural Committees composed of government-appointed experts, tasked with advising their respective governing bodies – the Council of BTO/WEU and the Committee of Ministers of the CoE, on cultural cooperation. Significantly, many committee members served in both organisations (notably R. Seymour, A. Haigh, and M. Reinink), facilitating coordination and avoiding duplication. With several initiatives already transferred to the CoE and the 1954 European Cultural Convention providing a legal framework for wider cooperation, the merger of cultural programmes appeared inevitable.

Following the 1954 amendment of the Brussels Treaty, which created the WEU and added Italy and the Federal Republic of Germany as members, the Cultural Committee continued its work with an emphasis on education. By 1962, it had been fully integrated into the Council of Europe's Council for Cultural Cooperation.

---

20 Assembly of Western European Union, 'Proceedings – Third Session' [1957].

21 Parry (n 15).

22 Council of Western European Union, 'First Annual Report of the Council of Western European Union (1 June–15 October 1955) – Cultural and Social Sections' [1955].

Therefore, while the cultural activities of the BTO/WEU may appear modest and underdeveloped in retrospect, their historical significance lies elsewhere. They marked the first sustained attempt to embed culture within an international framework where cultural engagement served broader political goals, in this case, fostering trust and cohesion within a Western European defence alliance. The legacy of the BTO is thus not measured by its cultural achievements alone, but by the institutional and conceptual groundwork it laid for cultural cooperation under the Council of Europe.

3.2 *The North Atlantic Treaty Organization: NATO*

The North Atlantic Treaty Organization (NATO) provides another instructive example of how cultural cooperation was incorporated into organisations primarily established for defence and military purposes. This section presents a brief examination of NATO's cultural dimension, not to suggest it was central to its mission, but rather to highlight how the idea of incorporating cultural elements became a recurrent feature in post-war international institutions. It appears that the inclusion of cultural cooperation had become an accepted norm in newly established organisations of the post-1945 period. A British official captured this tendency with ironic flair, comparing the widespread insistence on adding cultural programmes to a form of contagious cultural enthusiasm, likened to 'a species of cultural mumps'.[23]

Despite its relevance, the cultural dimension of NATO has rarely been addressed in broader studies of the alliance. During the 1960s, a limited number of authors, including Beloff[24] and Jordan,[25] discussed aspects of cultural cooperation within NATO. Their work has since been revisited by Parry, primarily in the context of British cultural diplomacy.[26] Building upon these sources and drawing on archival documents from NATO and the Council of Europe (CoE), the following discussion focuses on the rationale for the inclusion of cultural cooperation within NATO and the outcomes of such efforts.

The North Atlantic Treaty, signed in 1949, does not refer explicitly to culture. However, Article II provided the legal and political basis for non-military cooperation, including the potential for cultural engagement. The Working Group on Social and Cultural Co-operation was formally established in September 1952, with participation from all NATO member governments. The

---

23 Parry (n 15) 154.

24 Michael Beloff, *New Dimensions in Foreign Policy: A Study in British Administrative Experience 1947–59* (Routledge 1961).

25 Robert S Jordan, *The NATO International Staff/Secretariat 1952–1957* (Oxford University Press 1967) vii.

26 Parry (n 15).

available literature offers only partial explanations for the creation of this group. Among the most frequently cited reasons is the insistence of Canada that the alliance should possess a broader political dimension. According to Beloff and Parry, as well as internal NATO documents from 1953, Canada advocated for the use of NATO's structure to support political consultation and cooperation in non-military areas.[27]

Another important factor may have been the establishment of the NATO Information Service in 1950. Parry has noted that this initiative paralleled a model already developed by the United States Department of State, which had long treated cultural relations as part of its broader public diplomacy efforts.[28] Ninkovich observed that American officials regarded cultural relations primarily as intellectual engagement. During the Cold War, this form of engagement was interpreted as a battleground for competing ideological systems.[29] Within this context, NATO's public information policies followed the American model, with culture positioned as a tool for both internal cohesion and external messaging.

Lord Ismay, NATO's first Secretary-General, offered a compelling justification for cultural cooperation in his book *NATO: The First Five Years, 1949–1954*.[30] He argued that cultural engagement served two essential functions. First, it demonstrated the unity of NATO member states to external audiences, particularly the Soviet Union. Second, it reassured the populations of NATO countries themselves about the value and necessity of the alliance.

This belief that NATO should be presented not only as a military alliance but also as a community of shared values contributed to growing support for cultural initiatives. In 1953, a report on the prospects for NATO cultural cooperation was prepared by Mr. Reinink, who held a senior position in the Netherlands Ministry of Education.[31] Reinink was also a member of the Brussels Treaty Organisation's Cultural Committee and the Council of Europe's Com-

27 Beloff (n 24); Parry (n 15);
NATO, Working Group on Social and Cultural Co-operation, NATO Armed Forces and Cultural Co-operation [1953] AC/31-D/6;
NATO, Working Group on Social and Cultural Co-operation, Draft Recommendations Relating to Cultural Exchange Between the NATO Countries [1953] AC/31-D/7.

28 Parry (n 15).

29 Frank Ninkovich, *The Diplomacy of Ideas: US Foreign Policy and Cultural Relations, 1938–1950* (Cambridge University Press 1981).

30 Hastings Lionel Ismay, *NATO: The First Five Years 1949–1954* (North Atlantic Treaty Organization, Paris 1955).

31 NATO, Committee on Information and Cultural Relations, 'Report to the Secretary General from the Temporary Cultural Consultant on Strengthening Cultural Co-operation Among NATO Countries' [1953] AC/52-D/53.

mittee of Cultural Experts. His proposals grouped possible activities into four areas: education, science, the arts, and cooperation with military forces. He recommended programmes that would facilitate exchanges between Western European countries on one hand and the United States and Canada on the other. Although Reinink's report offered a structured vision for a NATO cultural programme, the practical outcomes remained very limited. According to Beloff, NATO's civilian and cultural activities were constrained by financial limitations. Many of the suggested projects were never implemented due to insufficient resources.[32]

Hopes for a more substantial role in cultural cooperation emerged with the formation of the Committee on Non-Military Cooperation, also known as the Committee of Three, in 1956. This committee issued a report in the same year, proposing several initiatives.[33] These included courses and seminars for educators, fellowships associated with NATO, efforts to build links between NATO and youth organisations, and the funding of cultural projects deemed to be of shared interest.

In light of the growing number of international organisations active in similar fields during the post-war period, NATO and the Council of Europe agreed to exchange documents on matters of mutual concern. They also established joint consultations at the level of their respective Secretariats. The primary goal of these arrangements was to prevent duplication of efforts. However, there was also a secondary objective: to allow the Council of Europe to carry out cultural initiatives that could extend to NATO members who were not themselves members of the Council. The Council of Europe documents from this period indicate that cooperation with NATO, up until 1965, focused primarily on science and the provision of research grants.[34] Nevertheless, and in line with Parry's analysis, there is no evidence that NATO ever developed initiatives specifically related to cultural heritage or what might be called 'pure' cultural engagement.[35] This omission is striking. The protection of cultural property in times of armed conflict had become a central theme within the heritage policies of several post-war organisations. Given the inherently

32 Beloff (n 24).

33 NATO, 'Report of the Committee of Three on Non-Military Cooperation in NATO' [1956] C-M(56)126.

34 Parliamentary Assembly, Cultural Committee, 'Cultural Activities within NATO – Report of the Conference of Members of PACE from the NATO Countries' [1958] AS/Cult(9)30; Parliamentary Assembly, Cultural Committee, 'NATO Cultural Co-operation – Information Note Published by the NATO Secretariat' [1960] AS/Cult(12)29; Parliamentary Assembly, 'Report on NATO Cultural Activities' [1959] Doc 1020.

35 Parry (n 15).

military context of this issue, NATO's absence from such discussions appears to represent a missed opportunity.[36] It might have served as a relevant platform for such concerns, particularly in coordination with civilian cultural institutions.

In conclusion, the case of NATO illustrates the limits and ambiguities of post-war cultural cooperation when it emerged within security-focused institutions. While cultural engagement was acknowledged as valuable by several member states, and while some proposals were formally adopted, the results remained modest. Nonetheless, the debates and documents generated in this context reveal important insights about how Western nations understood the role of culture in international relations during the early Cold War period. NATO may not have become a cultural actor in the fullest sense, but its engagement with cultural questions reflects the broader tendency of post-war organisations to frame unity and legitimacy through shared values and intellectual collaboration.

3.3 *The Nordic Council*

In order to complete the picture of early efforts in European intergovernmental cultural cooperation, it is necessary to consider the collective efforts undertaken by the five Nordic countries (Sweden, Norway, Denmark, Finland, and Iceland). These states developed a consistent practice of cultural collaboration that preceded the Second World War and stands out as one of the few significant examples of multilateral cultural cooperation in Western Europe during the interwar period. Their collaboration was grounded in both official and non-governmental initiatives. On the official level, it involved regular meetings of parliamentary representatives. On the unofficial level, cooperation was promoted through the work of the Norden Associations, voluntary societies committed to fostering unity among the Nordic countries in various sectors, including culture.

The first systematic account of Nordic cultural cooperation in the post-war period was provided by Ingeborg Lyche in a report prepared for the Council of

36 NATO has, over time, assumed a role in the protection of cultural heritage within areas of its intervention. In its publication *The Safety and Security of Cultural Heritage in Zones of War or Instability* (2021), NATO recognises a range of challenges associated with conflict contexts, including cultural genocide, the illicit trade in antiquities, and their connections to terrorism financing. The document further reflects on NATO's potential contribution to cultural heritage protection and underlines the necessity of developing a coherent policy framework in this domain. (Folliero, Antonello, et al. *The safety and security of cultural heritage in zones of war or instability*. IOS Press, 2021.)

Europe (CoE) in 1974.[37] A condensed synthesis of her findings appears in Haigh's study of European cultural diplomacy,[38] while a more recent update can be found in the work of Archer.[39] The broader context of Nordic cooperation (political, social, economic, and cultural) has been widely analysed in the literature.[40] However, the present section concentrates specifically on the cultural aspects of early Nordic cooperation, in order to illustrate how cultural matters were accorded a high degree of importance in the emerging framework of international organisations during the early 1950s.

Two particular features distinguish the Nordic model of cultural cooperation in its formative phase. First, unlike the case of the Brussels Treaty Organisation (BTO), whose cultural cooperation was devised in order to fulfil an explicit treaty obligation, the Nordic initiative preceded formal treaties and was instead followed by formalisation only after the cooperative practices had already taken root.[41] Second, while the BTO's cultural dimension was ultimately absorbed into the Council of Europe following the establishment of the Council for Cultural Cooperation in 1962, the Nordic countries succeeded in maintaining their own cooperative structures while simultaneously participating in broader European frameworks, including the CoE.

Despite many shared characteristics that facilitated cohesion, such as linguistic proximity, comparable political systems, adherence to Lutheran Protestant traditions, and a widespread sense of belonging to a common cultural sphere, the Nordic countries also demonstrated substantial divergences in other areas of policy, particularly in foreign affairs, defence, and economic alignment. Sweden remained militarily neutral and outside NATO; Denmark and Norway were founding members of NATO; and Finland maintained a special position due to its 1948 treaty with the Soviet Union, which influenced its alignment during the Cold War. Notably, Finland was not a member of the Council of Europe until 1989. Against this complex geopolitical background,

37 Ingrid Lyche, *Nordic Cultural Cooperation: Joint Ventures 1946–72* (Universitetsforlaget 1974).

38 Haigh (n 16).

39 Clive Archer, *Organising Europe: The Institutions of Integration* (2nd edn, Edward Arnold 1994).

40 See for example: Johan Strang, 'Introduction: The Nordic Model of Transnational Cooperation?' in Johan Strang (ed), *Nordic Cooperation* (Routledge 2015);
Stanley V Anderson, 'The Nordic Council and the 1962 Helsinki Agreement' (1964) 34 *Nordisk Tidsskrift for International Ret* 278;
Svein Efjestad, 'The Nordic Region' in John Andreas Olsen (ed), *Security in Northern Europe* (Routledge 2019).

41 Haigh (n 16).

culture emerged as the least controversial area for cooperation, offering a neutral and widely accepted foundation for unity.[42]

The Nordic Cultural Commission was established in 1947 without the formal enactment of a treaty. It functioned through regular meetings, typically attended by university professors. During this early phase, the principal concern was the harmonisation of educational systems. However, the Commission lacked both administrative capacity and dedicated financial resources. As a result, its recommendations eventually led to proposals for the creation of a more structured mechanism for ongoing cooperation. This led to the formation of the Nordic Council in 1952, which became the primary inter-parliamentary body for formal cooperation among the Nordic states. The Council was designed as an advisory institution across a wide range of policy areas, including culture, which was one of its five main domains of activity. The Council's Cultural Committee addressed subjects such as higher education and research, lower levels of education, adult learning, youth programmes, as well as artistic domains including music, theatre, cinema, broadcasting, libraries, and museums. It also initiated two cultural awards: one for literature and another for music.

Initially, the Nordic Council did not have a clearly defined relationship with the governments of its member states. However, beginning in 1960, it began to advocate for a formal clarification of its status. These efforts culminated in the adoption of the Nordic Cooperation Treaty, also known as the Helsinki Agreement, in 1962. This treaty gave legal recognition to existing practices, outlined future forms of cooperation, and introduced mechanisms for implementation.[43] The treaty was later revised to strengthen cultural cooperation, resulting in the signing of the Nordic Cultural Agreement in 1971.

In contrast to the integration of the BTO cultural mechanisms into the Council of Europe framework, the Nordic countries succeeded in preserving their distinctive cultural cooperation model through the Nordic Cultural Agreement, while simultaneously engaging with other European and global institutions. Although ideas and policies certainly circulated among these overlapping systems, the working methods developed by the Nordic group remained distinct. According to Stålvant, close coordination of national positions and continuous information sharing were routine practices among the Nordic representatives.[44] These practices allowed the group to form a cohe-

42 Lyche (n 36).

43 Haigh (n 16).

44 Carl-Einar Stålvant, 'The Council of Baltic Sea States' in Andrew Cottey (ed), *Subregional Cooperation in the New Europe: Building Security, Prosperity and Solidarity from the Barents to the Black Sea* (Macmillan 1999).

sive and influential bloc within the Council of Europe and also at UNESCO. Council of Europe records indicate that the Nordic approach was viewed as a model of effective multilateral behaviour, particularly in preparation for UNESCO General Conferences. Despite this, few other Council of Europe member states adopted similar strategies. Most preferred to prioritise their national agendas within the frameworks of the CoE and UNESCO, which made it difficult to replicate the Nordic model of collaboration in those settings.

The early post-war period saw a variety of experiments in cultural cooperation across different intergovernmental frameworks, each reflecting specific geopolitical alignments and regional identities. While the Brussels Treaty Organisation and NATO integrated cultural elements into broader political and defence agendas, the Nordic Council developed a parallel, regionally grounded model based on shared cultural heritage and parliamentary collaboration. These examples illustrate both the strategic and symbolic value attributed to culture in the early architecture of international cooperation. Against this backdrop, the Council of Europe emerged as the first pan-European institution to place cultural cooperation at the centre of its mandate, offering a more systematic and inclusive approach to culture in the service of European unity.

4 The Council of Europe's Cultural Cooperation Framework

The impetus The Hague Congress gave to the creation of the Council of Europe and the role given to culture in this process was crucial for the development of multilateral cultural cooperation in Europe. While the previous section offered the context for the creation of the CoE, the philosophy behind the organisation's creation, and its aims, the following part of the chapter moves on to describe in some detail the first five years of the CoE's effort to establish broader cultural cooperation among its Member States. With the book's focus on the cultural heritage discourse of the CoE in mind, an understanding of the background and provisions of the European Cultural Convention (which was a fundamental result of this formative period of the CoE activity) is of the utmost importance, as these formed the framework for all the subsequent heritage-related CoE texts. In addition, it should be borne in mind that it was in this period that the AHD began to formalise in the international heritage arena, and the role of the CoE in this process was not negligible.

In 1948, as a direct result of the Congress of Europe, negotiations on the creation of the Council of Europe started between the Brussels Treaty powers. As described by Bitsch, these negotiations proved long and demanding since the French and British positions on the future organisation were fundamentally opposed.[45] The French and Belgian proposal was for a European Assembly, while the British delegation was in favour of a European Council of Ministers to meet periodically and discuss matters of common interest, except defence and economic issues.[46] As a final result of the negotiations, the Council of Europe emerged as a particular intergovernmental organisation, differing from similar organisations by the contrast between and unique relation of its two organs, the Committee of Ministers and the Consultative Assembly (Parliamentary Assembly – PACE). The Committee of Ministers comprises the Ministers of Foreign Affairs. At the same time, the PACE is an original creation, with its members elected or appointed by national parliaments but who work in an independent capacity.[47] The PACE, however, has no powers of decision and depends on the Committee of Ministers to give effect to its proposals.[48] The Secretariat of the CoE assists those two bodies.

On 5 May 1949, the Treaty of London (the Statute of the Council of Europe, ETS No. 001), which officially established the CoE was signed by ten states – Belgium, Denmark, France, Ireland, Italy, Luxembourg, the Netherlands, Norway, Sweden, and the United Kingdom. The organisation was given a wide range of competencies, covering action in the social, cultural, scientific, legal, and administrative fields, and the Committee of Ministers and the Consultative Assembly, as the organs of the CoE, were able to set up advisory and technical committees on a specific question. Given its links with the Congress of Europe, cultural matters were integrated into the work of the CoE from its creation. Cultural cooperation was regarded as an important vehicle for enhancing the idea of a united Europe,[49] and the CoE's main objective in

45 Marie-Thérèse Bitsch, *Histoire de la construction européenne de 1945 à nos jours* (Edition Complexe 2004).

46 Arthur H Robertson, *The Council of Europe: Its structure, functions and achievements* (Frederick A Praeger 1961).

47 For the detailed account of the period preceding the signing of the Treaty of London see the work of Marie-Thérèse Bitsch 'La role de la France dans la naissance du Conseil de l'Europe' (1986) and 'Histoire de la construction Européenne' (1996).

48 Council of Europe/Conseil de l'Europe (eds), *European Yearbook / Annuaire Européen*, vol 1 (Brill/Nijhoff 1955);

Understandably, the foundation of the Council of Europe, and especially the role of the Consultative Assembly, did not bring the satisfaction to the promoters of a parliament-led Europe. Even though the contribution of this first European Assembly in creating a supranational forum for discussion should not be underestimated, the idea of the strong European Assembly as a main institutional actor had been defeated at this point.

49 Haller, Bruno, *An Assembly for Europe: The Council of Europe's Parliamentary Assembly 1949–1989* (Council of Europe Publishing 2006).

the cultural field was an intensification of cultural exchange between its Member States and the launching of a plan for cultural cooperation.[50]

At its First Session (10 August–8 September 1949), the Consultative Assembly created six Committees, among them the Committee on Cultural and Scientific Questions,[51] which showed that the Assembly had seen cultural cooperation as one of the keys to rebuilding Europe, healing divisions, and securing peace for the future.[52] For its part, the Committee of Ministers agreed during its Third Session (30 March–1 April 1950) to convene the Committee of Cultural Experts 'to study the cultural recommendations of the Assembly'.[53]

The first official action in the field of culture came in the shape of the Assembly's eight-point plan for cultural cooperation.[54] This document was greatly influenced by the preparatory cultural work of the Congress of Europe,

---

50 Council of Europe, *The First Five Years – 5.V.1949 – 5.V.1954* (Directorate of Information of the Council of Europe 1954).

51 Committees on General Affairs, Economic Questions, Social Questions, **Cultural and Scientific Questions** (M. Casati from Italy was its first Chairmen from 1949–51), Legal and Administrative Questions and Rules of Procedure and Privileges (*Assemblee Europeenne 1949–1969*, 1969).

52 Haller (n 48).

53 European Yearbook 1955 (n 47) 267;

Chronology of the advisory committees of the Committee of Ministers with the mandate in cultural heritage issues:

1950–1961 – Committee of Cultural Experts
1959–2001 – Cultural Fund
1961–2001 – Council for Cultural Co-operation (CDCC)
1970–1976 – Committee on Monuments and Sites
2001–2012 – Steering Committee for Cultural Heritage and Landscape (CDPATEP)
2012 – Steering Committee for Culture, Heritage and Landscape (CDCPP)

54 Parliamentary Assembly, Committee on Culture, Science and Education, 'Report – Methods by which the Council of Europe can develop cultural cooperation between its members' (Doc. 59, 1949);

Guided by the preparatory cultural work of the Congress of Europe, at the beginning of its work in 1949, the Parliamentary Assembly of the CoE already had several proposals ready for consideration, as the Report from Assembly's Committee on Culture, Science and Education shows (Doc. 59). The plan for cultural co-operation, as suggested by the Consultative Assembly, should relate in particular to the following points:

1. 'Comparative study of the teaching programmes in the different countries in that the best features of each may be available to all;
2. The development of the teaching of the leading European languages;
3. The conditions under which Universities degrees and diplomas may be recognised in other countries;
4. The preparation of a series of impartial books dealing with the geography and the history of European countries, which bring out the links between them;
5. The arranging of university courses and lectures on European problems and organisations;

and the focus was principally on educational issues such as the teaching of European languages, recognition of university degrees among Member States, the revision of geography and history books of European countries, and creation of scholarships. An early focus on educational issues aimed to undo the nationalist appropriations and distortions of history.[55] Besides, with the political goal of European unity in mind, the exchange of cultural works (cinema, music, art, and folklore exhibitions) and particularly archaeological treasures 'which constitute one of the fundamental elements of the common heritage of the European peoples' was planned.[56] The Assembly believed that their cultural programme would help bring Europeans closer to each other and show them the cultural aspects they have in common. Securing the framework that would allow for intensifying the exchange of people (especially young people), books, and works of art was crucial in these formative years of the CoE's cultural efforts.

While the 'practical' points and activities of the Assembly's cultural programme established the foundations for European cooperation in the cultural field, it is interesting to cite the principles the Assembly had already agreed upon in 1949. These principles express the underlying philosophy behind the CoE's heritage discourse. As such, they underpin the CoE's heritage texts still today (particularly as explored in Chapter 7, this is evident in the 2005 Faro Convention):

> European culture has its sources in the thought and work of free peoples based on centuries of tradition… It is one in its respect for the human person, for the supremacy of the spirit, for freedom of opinion and the unfettered expression of ideas; in its uncompromising opposition to every form of tyranny; It is at the service of man, and not of any one nation or class; No national or ideological consideration may prevail against it; No power can be allowed to prohibit or impede the individ-

---

6. The creation of as large a number as possible of scholarships and periods of study in universities and higher teaching and research institutes abroad;
7. The methods to be adopted in the interest of European unity to raise the cultural level of the population by adult education, university extension lectures, broadcast and the cinema, exchange of records and films between nations and art and folklore exhibitions;
8. The collective utilisation, to the best advantage, of the works of art, and particularly, archaeological treasures, which constitute one of the fundamental elements of the common heritage of the European peoples' (Doc. 59, 1949).

55 Council of Europe, *50 years of the European Cultural Convention* (2004).

56 PACE Doc. 59, 1949 (n 53).

> ual's search for truth; Culture must not be the privilege of a minority; Every man is entitled to it, just as he is to freedom, and it is the duty of every democracy to ensure access to it for each of its citizens, irrespective of economic and social inequalities.[57]

This clear expression of a human rights–based approach to culture and, in that context, to heritage is, as I argue in this volume, the foundation for a specific CoE heritage discourse that the organisation has developed over the 70 years of its existence. The above-quoted principles noticeably echo the Universal Declaration of Human Rights (1948) and its provision for the right of all persons to freely participate in cultural life (Article 27). The CoE's approach was, therefore, from its inception, primarily attuned to individuals and the role of culture in an individual's quality of life and development. This could be considered a critical element that underlines the CoE's discourse; as the following analysis shows, this element is more or less accentuated during different periods of the CoE's activities.

By taking the propositions suggested by the Assembly as a base, the Committee of Cultural Experts organised its tasks on two parallel fronts: (1) the 'practical front', which brought the Council of Europe Cultural Programme to life, and (2) the 'legal front' which culminated in the European Cultural Convention of 1954.

4.1 *Practical Front*

The actions on the 'practical front' in the period before the European Cultural Convention (1950–1954) were extremely small-scale and focused on working out a programme and preparing the way for its implementation. This quite limited and mostly theoretical work was a direct consequence of the non-existent funds allocated to cultural activities. In striking opposition to its political proclamations on the importance of culture in its formative process, the first budget for cultural programmes was allocated only in 1952. It was finally possible for the Committee of Cultural Experts to apply and develop some of the ideas presented in the Assembly's eight-point plan.[58]

---

57 PACE Doc. 59 [1949] (n 53).

58 Parliamentary Assembly, 'Five Years' Work by the Committee of Cultural Experts – Report presented on behalf of the Committee of Cultural Experts by M. Reinink' [1955] AS/CS (6) 41;

'I wish to drive home this basic idea, for it is too important to be treated summarily, that in its first years of existence, the Committee of Ministers did not feel itself impelled to seek a genuine European cultural policy, nor had it the power to do so. At that time, it felt bound to deal with first things first, and the most urgent task was to do every-

The look at these early projects is valuable in the context of this volume for two reasons – they exemplify the values and understanding of the role of culture and heritage in the CoE's cultural policy at the time, and they serve as an illustration of the role the CoE played in the broader legitimisation of the specific heritage discourse (AHD) that started to take shape at the time. As the examples in the following section show, the actions on the 'practical front' displayed little of the agreed principles that promoted an inclusive vision of heritage, and they fairly continued authorising the practices and attitudes towards heritage and culture that had emerged within the context of the nineteenth-century conservation ethic. With such activities in place, the CoE, during the 1950s, actively participated in legitimising the AHD in the field of international heritage.

The Cultural Identity Card is one of such illustrative projects. It was initiated by the Brussels Treaty Organisation and was taken over by the CoE and remained in its cultural programme until the early 1980s. This card was originally planned to serve as a cultural passport, valid for travel as a standard passport. The initial ambitious proposal was scaled down, and the card allowed its holder free access to museums and collections and reduced accommodation and travel costs. A survey from 1968 showed that around 30,000 Cultural Identity Cards had been issued.[59] Its impact on the number of cultural visits may not be impressive; however, one can agree with Parry when stating that the great merit of the card was that it embodied the first visible benefits of multilateral European cooperation.[60] However, while the initial principles declared by the CoE asked 'of every democracy to ensure access to culture for each of its citizens, irrespective of economic and social inequalities', the projects developed in this early period seemed not to be in line with those political aspirations.[61] The Committee of Cultural Experts, for example, took the decision to have 'the issue of the card deliberately confined to intellectuals: university graduates and students, men of letter or artists'.[62] This decision was noticeably underlined by the upper class's dominance in the field of culture (and

thing possible to strengthen the process of political integration. The first function of the Committee of Cultural Experts was therefore to buttress the general policy of the Council of Europe by means of its own particular programme. Such had been the principle which guided the Committee of Ministers, such was to be the action of the Committee of Cultural Experts' (Reinink 1955, p. 2).

59 Michael Palmer and John Lambert, *European Unity: A Survey of the European Organisation* (Allen & Unwin 1968).

60 Parry (n 15) 145.

61 PACE Doc. 59 [1949] (n 53).

62 AS/CS (6) 41 [1955] (n 57).

heritage conservation), which derived from the nineteenth-century developments whereby the European social and political elite secured the legitimacy of and the dominant place in national cultural policies. The CoE Committee of Cultural Experts itself, composed of politicians and university professors, reflected that privilege and their understanding that the interaction of intellectuals and artists was the necessary first step that would lead to better understanding between European nations. It was this group of educated individuals, the CoE believed, that would, through the educational system of their countries, spread the idea of European unity, culture, and values to the wider public. It was, therefore, through those kinds of initiatives that the AHD gained primacy in international cultural heritage policies.

The example of another project developed by the CoE during this period reproduced the same attitude. The series of Council of Europe Art Exhibitions that started in 1954 and remained a constant part of the CoE's cultural programme disclose several AHD-underlined characteristics (30 exhibitions were held to date).[63] Although the CoE's Art Exhibitions deserve a significant place in the field of art historiography,[64] their importance for this research rests in their exemplification of what the CoE considered/considers to be shared European cultural heritage. Arguably, those exhibitions certainly deserve more attention and analysis than it is possible to give in this volume, but even a rudimentary evaluation of them unveils the elements of the CoE's understanding of Europeanness[65] and what this notion *embraces* and what it *disregards*.

The idea for such a project came from the French delegation, but the official proposal for the event was made by Belgian delegate Julien Kuypers at the

63 https://www.coe.int/en/web/culture-and-heritage/past-exhibitions

64 Some ideas pioneered by the CoE, which since the time of the first exhibition become commonplace, deserve some merit. Firstly, the ideas behind the exhibitions were developed by a committee of experts, whose members were usually directors or curators of major European museums (Lefteris 2019). This extensive collaboration created a network of partnerships among European museums and scholars that did not exist on that scale before. Those exhibitions remain distinctive by their scale, quality, scholarly approach, and significant public appeal. This practice of big-scale collaboration of major museums, galleries and private collectors later became standard in the field of exhibitions. The same stands for the organisation of thematic exhibitions, which later had the CoE examples as a guiding principle (Council of Europe 2004).

65 Known to the author, H. Koike's master thesis titled *How Art Has Been Presented as Common Culture for Europe. The Case Study on the Art Exhibitions of the Council of Europe since 1954* (Strasbourg and Udine, 2018) is the only academic attempt to shed some light on the history of these exhibitions.

Committee's 5th Session in 1952.[66] Exhibitions would 'illustrate some of the more outstanding epochs, transcending national bounds, of European culture: renaissance Europe, baroque Europe, neo-classical Europe, romantic Europe, realistic Europe etc.'.[67] Consequently, the exhibitions would demonstrate 'the universal character of the European spirit and the unity of its artistic heritage down the ages'.[68] These events, as a 'spectacular display of European unity', as Kuypers pointed out, would catch the 'imagination of the general educated public, if not the broad masses of people'.[69]

The meeting of the art specialists was organised in 1953, preparing the first exhibition that they characterised as 'a valuable source of spiritual propaganda' that would help to 'arouse the European conscience without being subjected to criticism from political or nationalist quartiers'.[70] Certain details from the approach to this event are of interest as regards AHD characteristics, specifically their suggestions on public participation and their understanding of 'common European culture and heritage'.

Starting with the proposal for the project, Mr. Kuypers referred to a 'general educated public'. In line with the aforementioned approach with the Cultural Identity Card, this position also reiterates the predominant understanding of culture and the arts in Europe at the time as something that only the 'educated public' could understand – a characteristic deeply enshrined in the AHD. It echoes a deeply class-underpinned understanding of heritage that mostly represents the history of the elite of the nations, and consequently of Europe. In this early period, the CoE, as the subjects of the exhibitions show, adopted this notion whereby European culture and heritage consists exclusively of old, grand, and aesthetically pleasing sites, all too often associated with the aristocracy, the church, and European virtuosities. The addition in the exhibitions' proposal, suggesting that the event might be of interest even to the 'broad masses of people', implies that early CoE cultural policy was firmly established on the principle of assimilation, whereby those 'lacking' the 'appropriate cul-

66 Council of Europe, Committee of Cultural Experts, Proposal Concerning the Organisation of a Series of European Exhibitions – Submitted by the Belgian Delegation [1952] EXP/Cult (52) 27.

67 Ibid.

68 Ibid.

69 Ibid.

70 Council of Europe, Committee of Cultural Experts, 'Memorandum Presented by the Belgian Delegation in the Meeting of Art Specialists' [1953] EXP/Cult/Art (53) 1.

tural capital can be educated, if exposed to appropriate sites, places and artefacts' and instructed by experts and intellectuals.[71]

The first exhibition in the series was inaugurated in Brussels (Palais des Beaux-Arts) in December 1954, three days before the signing of the European Cultural Convention. The subject was sixteenth-century humanism, as 'humanism is surely the foundation of what Europe is and what Europe wishes to share with the rest of mankind'.[72] Following the initial success of the first exhibition, the following series of CoE art exhibitions succeeded in illustrating all the great artistic styles in Europe, from the Bronze Age, through the Middle Ages, the Renaissance, the Classical, and the Romantic periods to the present day. Each exhibition attracted hundreds of thousands of visitors and was considered to be one of the major art events in Europe, usually opened by the head of the host state. What becomes clear from the concepts of its early projects is that the CoE chose the same model to promote European unity as that used for nation-building – a historicising argument. The sense of Europe was to be expressed in these monuments and works of art for the education of the public as a physical representation of European taste, achievements, and social evolution.

Judging solely from the selection of the exhibitions' themes throughout the years, one can easily see the apparent presentation of what the European project of heritage-making decided to include and what to exclude. Europe, in the CoE's exhibitions, has been represented as the cradle of civilisation, with exhibitions covering all important artistic styles, from Mannerism, Classicism, and Baroque to Realism, Rococo, and the Romantic movement. Not only was Europe interpreted through splendid artworks, mostly commissioned by, collected by, and devoted to its aristocracy, but also through its Christian core, elitist, and masculine side. As already touched upon in Chapter 1, the representation of Europe adopted by the European institutions, while glorifying Europe's virtuosity, largely marginalised minorities and women and overlooked its colonial past in their cultural policies. The choice of subjects for the CoE's exhibitions is illustrative of this, as most of the heritage and art connected with those marginalised groups are not defined and presented as parts of the inheritance of Europe. As stated by Smith, the AHD does not constructively engage with discomfort, dissonance, and diversity, and the CoE's

71 Laurajane Smith, *Missing Out on Heritage: Socio-Economic Status and Heritage Participation* (Conference, English Heritage, March 2009).

72 Council of Europe, *50 Years of Council of Europe Art Exhibitions* (Council of Europe Publishing 2004).

early projects are vibrant examples of this.[73] Despite the organisation's pronounced principles promoting that 'Culture must not be the privilege of a minority',[74] its actions echoed numerous exclusions.

With its understanding of Europe as utterly Christian, the influences and presence of other cultures, especially those of its eastern and southern neighbours, were largely undermined. In addition, exhibitions are a clear example of 'heritage masculinisation',[75] whereby women 'have been largely invisible and misrepresented in the archives of history', with only the eleventh exhibition dedicated to a woman, Queen Cristina of Sweden (Graham 2000, p. 45).[76] In this case, as well, the class representation visibly stayed in the realm of the upper class, representing Cristina through the art collection from her 'Rome palazzo' where she was 'surrounded by artists and intellectuals'.[77] Moreover, colonisation in this CoE project was approached from a rather curious perspective. The seventeenth exhibition presented the colonial history of fifteenth-century Portugal as 'great voyages of discovery' which brought to the country 'enormous wealth, growth, and great buildings'.[78] If some conclusions on the CoE's project of European heritage-making could be made from this simple analysis of the Art Exhibitions, it seems that the CoE was building European identity largely through a denial of Europe's transcultural histories, especially its entanglement with the Islamic world and particularly by a disavowal of colonialism.[79] Even though such criticism of the project appears, from a brief survey, to be correct, a thorough analysis of the exhibitions' catalogues, covering the items included and their descriptions, would be needed to support it absolutely.

In addition to the art exhibitions as its most notable action during the early period of the CoE cultural programme, the organisation carried out additional work on (1) the recognition of university degrees and diplomas, (2) revisions of history and geography textbooks, (3) exchanges of students and teachers, and

73 Smith (2009) (n 70).
See also: Vesna Kisić, *Governing Heritage Dissonance: Promises and Realities of Selected Cultural Policies* (European Cultural Foundation 2016).

74 PACE [1949] Doc 59 (n 53).

75 Tim Edensor and Uma Kothari, 'The Masculinisation of Stirling's Heritage' in Vicki Kinnaird and Derek R Hall (eds), *Tourism: A Gender Analysis* (Wiley 1994).

76 Brian Graham, Greg Ashworth and John Tunbridge, *A Geography of Heritage: Power, Culture and Economy* (Arnold Publishers 2000).

77 Council of Europe, *Past Exhibitions* (Europe and Cultural Heritage) https://www.coe.int/en/web/culture-and-heritage/past-exhibitions

78 Ibid.

79 Chiara De Cesari, 'Memory Voids and the New European Heritage: A Proposal for Studying Transnational Memory' (2012) 25 *Journal of Museum Ethnography* 152.

(4) the establishment of a European Cultural Centre. Even though limited in scope and somehow basic, the cultural activities developed in the first five years of the CoE's existence are significant for two reasons – they illustrated the discrepancy between the CoE's theoretical human-rights based approach to culture and heritage in its early documents and the reality of values promoted by its 'practical' projects and secondly, they showed the determination of the Member States to use culture as a means to strengthen their unity.[80] Thus, with European unity in mind, the need for a legal framework for cultural cooperation became obvious.

4.2 *Legal Front*

The outlook of organising the new programme for cultural cooperation in Europe under the auspices of the CoE was faced with rather unambitious initial propositions. Most cultural experts in the CoE Cultural Committee believed the best legal framework for cultural cooperation under the CoE should be a continuation of bilateral relations under already signed bilateral cultural conventions. This proposed development of the system of bilateral cultural conventions reflected the still predominant philosophy in the field of cultural relations in Western Europe at the time. However, not all the Member States had that kind of agreement signed among them, and the role of the CoE, those experts suggested, would be to encourage them to do so. The Assembly's Recommendation 24 (1949) and the Committee of Ministers' Resolution (49) 28 confirmed the intention of the Member States to continue the actions that they had already undertaken in this field under the bilateral agreements. However, the policy on a bilateral basis that was promoted resulted in very sporadic cooperation, and no negotiations were opened among the Member States for the conclusion of new cultural conventions in those early years of the CoE's existence.[81] While the policy of encouraging cooperation on a bilateral basis continued through 1951 with the first comprehensive Cultural Programme of the CoE (known as Seymour's Memorandum), it was also a year when the first critique of this approach appeared.[82] Seymour's Memorandum, even though seen as a starting point of the official thinking about the cultural mission of the CoE, reflects the expertise and practice of the British Council (of which Mr. Seymour was Secretary) in bilateral cultural cooperation:

---

80 AS/CS (6) 41 (n 57).

81 Parliamentary Assembly, Committee on Culture, Science and Education, 'Report – Cooperation in Cultural Matters' (Doc 3, 1950).

82 Council of Europe, Committee of Cultural Experts, 'Cultural Relations and the Council of Europe – Note by Mr Seymour' [1951] CM/WP III (51) 45.

> It seems to me that the main purpose of the Council of Europe, in this context, should be the maximum development of cultural relations between the Member States and that this should take precedence over the initiation of joint projects.[83]

On the other hand, Professor Bodelsen, a Danish member of the Committee of Cultural Experts, was, in his response to Seymour's Memorandum, one of the first voices to oppose this exclusively bilateral-based approach. In his own words,

> I think it stresses the importance of bilateralism a little too much. After all, we have two important multilateral projects (the Convention about the recognition of school-leaving certificates and the Cultural Identity Card), and there seems to be no reason why we should stop at that.[84]

The effect of this criticism could already be noticed at the beginning of 1952, with the Committee of Cultural Experts' Report restating the essential role of bilateral relations to European cultural cooperation but urging the CoE to encourage multilateral agreements whenever possible, especially the possibility of a general cultural agreement between Member States.[85]

This report opened the door for the negotiations of the European Cultural Convention, the subject that would be analysed shortly. At this stage, it is also important to briefly consider the Council of Europe's early interactions with UNESCO, particularly in light of the concerns at the time about potential duplication of efforts and the broader aim of promoting multilateral cultural cooperation among their respective member states.

4.3 *Early Collaboration Between the Council of Europe and UNESCO*

From the outset, the CoE had to navigate its position within a broader landscape of, already mentioned, regional and global international organisations,

83 CM/WP III (51) 45 (n 81) 2.

84 Ibid 1; Dr Carl Bodelen was a professor of English at the University of Copenhagen and the sole Danish delegate to the Committee of Cultural Experts in the early stage of its existence. He particularly deserves credit for signing the CoE's European Convention on the Equivalence of Diplomas leading to Admission to Universities in 1953. Having successfully directed this first convention through the Committee of Cultural Experts to the stage of approval by the Committee of Ministers, he became a strong supporter of multilateral cooperation. He was equally successful in bringing to life the European Convention on the Equivalence of Periods of University Study.

85 Council of Europe, Committee of Cultural Experts, 'Report' [1952] CM/12 (52) 49.

including UNESCO, with its global remit in the cultural field. Given these overlapping mandates, it is necessary to explore how the CoE positioned itself in relation to UNESCO, with which it established early formal ties. This section focuses on the first phase of their interaction, beginning in the early 1950s, to understand the nature and extent of their cooperation.

There are two main reasons for this focus. First, UNESCO was the only international organisation at the time developing multilateral cultural cooperation on a global scale, and it is important to consider whether, and how, this shaped European efforts under the Council of Europe. Second, while the notion of overlapping competencies is often raised, the actual extent of duplication or divergence in practice requires clarification.

Despite the significance of this relationship, existing literature on the dynamics between UNESCO and the Council of Europe remains sparse. Much of what is available originates from institutional narratives that present the cooperation as harmonious and effective. Analytically grounded studies based on archival evidence are rare, therefore the following brief account aims to fill this gap by examining the complex and layered exchanges between the two organisations.

Cooperation between UNESCO and the CoE began informally around 1950, largely driven by the Council's concerns over potential duplication of activities in the cultural field. As early as its first report, the Committee of Cultural Experts urged the Committee of Ministers to seek cooperation with UNESCO in order to avoid overlapping efforts.[86] This led to formal negotiations, and by 1952, the two organisations signed an agreement establishing regular consultation and coordination on matters of common interest. From this point forward, channels of communication remained open. UNESCO sent biannual reports on its activities to PACE, which responded with references to its own work and potential areas for cooperation. UNESCO observers were routinely present at CoE-organised events, and joint Secretariat meetings were held annually. PACE also encouraged member states to include in their national UNESCO delegations the individuals involved in the CoE's cultural work, in an effort to build stronger personal ties between the two organisations.[87]

Although this exchange of information was consistent, it is difficult to assess the extent of mutual influence. A case in point is 1954, when both organ-

86 Council of Europe, Committee of Cultural Experts, 'Report of the Committee of Cultural Experts to the Committee of Ministers' [1950] CM (50) 34.

87 Council of Europe, Committee of Cultural Experts, 'Report of the Council of Europe/UNESCO Inter-Secretariat Meeting to Cultural and Scientific Questions of Mutual Interest' [1955] EXP/Cult/CE-UNESCO (55) 1.

isations adopted major conventions in the heritage field: UNESCO adopted The *Hague Convention on the Protection of Cultural Property in the Event of Armed Conflict*, while the CoE introduced the European Cultural Convention. UNESCO's initiative was acknowledged early on by the PACE, which in 1951 recommended that member states support it (Recommendation 19). However, internal CoE records suggest that The Hague Convention was not pursued further within the organisation until 1958, when the PACE recommended its ratification to member states (Recommendation 162). What is particularly notable, however, is that both organisations introduced in these conventions the idea that cultural heritage extends beyond national ownership. The CoE referred to a shared 'cultural heritage of Europe', while UNESCO promoted the idea of the 'cultural heritage of all mankind'. While the origins of this conceptual framing cannot be exclusively attributed to either institution, it is likely that the influence of European intellectuals active within both UNESCO and the CoE contributed to the development of this shared language.[88]

In practice, both organisations operated according to different structures and working methods. UNESCO, despite its international standing, faced operational difficulties in the 1950s, including internal tensions between Eastern and Western member states and ongoing US pressure to reform its bureaucracy. The UK even considered withdrawing from UNESCO in 1957.[89] These factors led several Western European countries, notably France and the UK, to look toward the Council of Europe as a more stable and focused platform for regional cultural cooperation. As UNESCO's Director-General René Maheu admitted in 1972, its programme contained no initiatives specifically dedi-

88 The first instance of more concrete collaboration came with UNESCO's Major Project on the Mutual Appreciation of Eastern and Western Cultural Values (1957–1966). Adopted in 1956, the project aimed to foster better understanding between Western and Asian societies, following the rapid decolonisation and growing membership of non-Western states in UNESCO. The PACE responded in 1957 with Recommendation 128, urging the Committee of Ministers to align the Council with the project. Proposed measures included sending European art exhibitions to the East and organising educational programmes on European values. However, the Committee of Ministers remained cautious, instructing the Committee of Cultural Experts to monitor developments and to consider the Council's involvement at a later stage (AS/Cult(9)50). Eventually, the CoE made some of its cultural materials, such as exhibition catalogues, films, books, and educational resources, available to UNESCO. It also offered publications such as *Notre Europe* and the annotated bibliography *European Cultural Values* for dissemination in Eastern countries. While these contributions demonstrated goodwill, the cooperation was modest. The CoE's participation was largely limited to sharing resources developed for its own internal programmes. Plans for more visible collaboration, such as the creation of a gallery of European art in Asia, initially proposed for New Delhi, never materialised.

89 Richard Hoggart, *An Idea and Its Servants: UNESCO from Within* (Chatto & Windus 1978).

cated to Europe, despite European countries contributing nearly half of the organisation's budget.[90] Against this backdrop, the CoE was seen by its members as a more appropriate forum for pursuing cultural initiatives linked to the broader goal of European integration.

In this context, the Council's concern over overlapping mandates appears overstated, at least during this early period. Archival sources show little evidence of UNESCO shaping the Council of Europe's cultural agenda in any substantive way, nor do they indicate direct interventions. UNESCO's broader significance for Europe, at least until the late 1980s, lay primarily in its unique position as one of the few spaces where both Western and Eastern European states could engage on equal footing.

5 European Cultural Convention: Draft and Implementation

The European Cultural Convention (ECC) is regarded today as one of the fundamental CoE Conventions. Its eventual success, however, was far from assured. In the early 1950s, the majority of the CoE Member States prioritised bilateral cultural relations over multilateral ones, with some questioning the necessity of multilateral conventions as such.[91] However, with cultural cooperation as an important complement to the political action of uniting Europe, the need for a legal framework to underpin cultural policy became increasingly evident. Simultaneously, other international organisations, such as UNESCO and regional groups like the Brussels Treaty and Nordic countries, were advancing multilateral cultural cooperation. To remain relevant and provide its Member States with a foundational text for collective cultural action, the CoE initiated work on the ECC.

The first phase of the CoE cultural cooperation programme is often denoted as the phase of reconciliation, reflecting the broader post-war European context. As noted by Grosjean, the primary goal was to foster awareness of a shared

---

90 UNESCO, 'Address by Mr René Maheu, Director-General of UNESCO at the Opening Meeting of the Intergovernmental Conference on Cultural Policies in Europe' [1972] DG/72/12;

See also: Parliamentary Assembly, Cultural and Scientific Committee, 'Summary of the Debate in the Consultative Assembly on the Speech Made by Mr Maheu, Director General of UNESCO on 30th September 1966' [1966] AS/Cult (18) 51.

91 Council of Europe, Committee of Cultural Experts, 'Draft Report of the Seventh Session (1st–3rd December 1953)' [1953] EXP/Cult (53) 48.

European civilisation while countering the resurgence of extreme nationalism.[92] Consequently, the CoE decided to work on a text that would, at the same time, assert both Europe's fundamental unity and its cultural diversity through a policy of common action designed to safeguard and encourage the development of European culture.[93]

After the first Committee of Cultural Experts' tentative draft from 1952, the United Kingdom government took the initiative and submitted its proposal for the Convention at the beginning of 1953.[94] The structure of the UK draft noticeably echoed the UK's idea of multilateral cultural cooperation as an extension of the bilateral form.[95] This bilateral methodology was allied with the expectations of other members for multilateral cooperation and stated in the provision of the Preamble that 'it is desirable not only to conclude bilateral cultural conventions' but also to develop collective actions.[96] Even though the text turned out to be one of the most successful multilateral European conventions, the statement in the Preamble reminds us of the initial scepticism towards multilateralism Member States displayed at that point in time.

Its provisions outlined specific commitments for signatory states, including:

- Safeguarding and promoting their national contributions to Europe's common cultural heritage (Article 1).
- Encouraging the study of other nations' languages, history, and civilisation (Article 2).
- Engaging in concerted cultural actions under the CoE framework (Article 3).
- Facilitating the exchange of cultural objects and individuals (Article 4).
- Treating European cultural assets within their control as integral parts of Europe's shared heritage (Article 5).

Moreover, Article 9 allowed non-CoE Member States to accede to the Convention, showcasing its inclusive and open-ended approach.

Even though, as Haigh put it, this Convention 'has the merit of great simplicity of thought and expression', it could be argued that this is the exact reason

---

92 Etienne Grosjean, *Forty Years of Cultural Co-operation at the Council of Europe, 1954–94* (Council of Europe Publishing 1997).

93 Council of Europe, European Cultural Convention (adopted 19 December 1954, entered into force 5 May 1955) ETS No 018.

94 Council of Europe, Committee of Cultural Experts, 'Draft European Cultural Convention – Submitted by the United Kingdom Delegation' [1953] EXP/Cult B (53) 2.

95 This approach reflected the working method of the British Council, which had obtained its expertise exclusively in the field of bilateral cultural relations.

96 European Cultural Convention [1954] (n 92).

for its accomplishments.[97] Today the ECC has been ratified by all 46 CoE Member States as well as by the Holy See, Russia, Belarus, and Kazakhstan, and it served as the perfect medium and the first step for many countries in their accession process to the CoE.

5.1 *Key Innovations*

Two critical, innovative notions in the text are 'responsible' for the Convention's success. The first is the concept of the 'common cultural heritage of Europe' in Articles 1 and 5, and the second is the Convention's openness to accession for non-member states of the CoE in Article 9.

1. The 'Common Cultural Heritage of Europe'

The Committee of Cultural Experts introduced, in its amended version of the initial UK draft, the first 'radical element', as seen by Parry, of the Convention: the 'common cultural heritage of Europe'.[98] The proposed Article 1 stated:

> Each Contracting Party shall take all appropriate measures to develop and safeguard its national contribution to the common cultural heritage of Europe (EXP/Cult (53) 1).[99]

Here, a 'common cultural heritage' is acknowledged as a key concept of the ECC.[100] There are two important points in this short construction. Firstly, it was the first time that a post-WWII international organisation had used the term 'cultural heritage' in its official text. Differing from UNESCO's concept of 'cultural property' as understood in The Hague Convention of 1954, the CoE, in this early text, widened the notion of heritage and declared heritage to be not just an object to be preserved, but also one to be developed.[101] What this could mean is that the CoE understood that cultural heritage has an active role in society and that it is not only important to protect it for future generations,

97 Anthony Haigh, *Cultural Mission of the Council of Europe* (Council of Europe, Strasbourg 1970) 131; Anthony Haigh was a British diplomat with a strong personal commitment towards development of cultural cooperation and was one of the drafters of the ECC.

98 Parry (n 15).

99 This article didn't change much in the final text. The final version of Article 1 reads: 'Each Contracting Party shall take appropriate measures to safeguard and to encourage the development of its national contribution to the common cultural heritage of Europe.'

100 Grosjean (n 91).

101 Werner von Truetzschler, 'The Evolution of "Cultural Heritage" in International Law' (paper presented at the 15th ICOMOS General Assembly and International Symposium: Monuments and Sites in Their Setting – Conserving Cultural Heritage in Changing Townscapes and Landscapes, Xi'an, China, 17–21 October 2005).

but also to use it and interact with it today. Nevertheless, judging from the Grosjean statement, it seems that the interpretation of Articles 1 and 5 leaned more towards instituting an inseparable pair of responsibilities that heritage professionals are called upon (to preserve cultural heritage and to promote and enhance it), rather than towards more effective participation of the general public in heritage issues.[102] It is in this way that the AHD mapped out the authority of expertise, legitimising the experts as the only ones capable of defining and protecting cultural heritage. The ECC, therefore, represents one of the earliest texts in a chain of international conventions institutionalising certain aspects of the AHD in European heritage policies and legislation.

Secondly, the reference to a 'common cultural heritage' in ECC is considered central, as it highlights, in Grosjean's words:

> ...at a crucial and extremely early stage of European construction, the idea of fundamental solidarity between states regarding a system of values which each of them acknowledges is not its own but which, on the contrary, makes each State individually responsible for its share of an 'indivisible' heritage.[103]

The inclusion of the phrase 'common heritage' in the text of the ECC was a political statement supporting the aims of the CoE to ensure European unity and to make its citizens aware of their common culture. The content of that common heritage was, at this stage, left undefined, and indeed, this content was the subject of a series of discussions in Rome (1953) and Strasbourg (1956), as well as during the preparatory work for the European Art Exhibitions of the early 1950s. The CoE considered it to be its duty to ensure that the message of unity among Europeans and the existence of their common heritage receive wider publicity and recognition, but also to strengthen this unity by cultural means. In this respect, the ECC, with the recognition of the existence of a common cultural heritage, is a crucial document offering a legal framework for further work in the field.[104] Nevertheless, it needs to be emphasised that the duty to protect and manage that 'share' of 'common European heritage', as Grosjean refers to it, still rests on the nation-states.[105]

---

102 Grosjean (n 91).

103 Ibid 112.

104 It should be emphasised that there are no instances in which the CoE can call to account its Member States for any alleged lack of safeguarding this common heritage. In that context, the CoE does not have any authorisation, under the European Cultural Convention, to oversee Member States' national standards or to impose such standards.

105 Grosjean (n 91).

Looking from a contemporary perspective, with an awareness of the results the ECC has had during the nearly 70 years of its existence, it may be appealing to praise this text for its innovative features, particularly in relation to cultural heritage. It could be said that the ECC was an extremely forward-looking text for its time. It refers to both tangible ('objects of European cultural value' in Article 5) and intangible ('languages, history and civilisation' in Preamble and Article 2) dimensions of the cultural heritage of the different European nations. To this, the third, political, dimension of this cultural heritage can also be added, expressed in the first sentence of the Convention referring to 'the ideals and principles which are the common heritage' of the CoE Members. By covering these three main dimensions of cultural heritage, the drafters, almost certainly involuntarily, created a document flexible enough to embrace all different interpretations of the concept of the cultural heritage of today.[106] However, by looking at the archive documents and the position that was given to the protection of cultural heritage under the CoE in the 1950s showed in them, it is evident that originally, the Convention's obligation to safeguard that common cultural heritage was not seen as a European issue but as a national one. As a result, the CoE started developing its actions in a 'purely' heritage-related field only in the 1960s, as those issues in the immediate post-ECC period continued to be regarded as the exclusive responsibility of the nation-state. As the following chapters will illustrate, while the ECC offered a legal framework for cultural cooperation, the CoE administratively developed its heritage activities outside of the Committee of Cultural Cooperation, including them under this committee only in the 1990s.

2. Inclusivity and Accession by Non-member States

A Dutch member of the drafting committee of the ECC, Mr. Reinink, introduced the second innovative feature of the ECC.[107] He proposed to the Secretary-General of the CoE that the Convention should be extended to the Euro-

106 Irish Delegation, in its Memorandum on the Draft, saw this article referring to 'common cultural heritage' unnecessary:

'The duty to develop and safeguard its national cultural heritage is a duty that a state owes to itself rather than to other member states and is therefore inappropriate in this context' (Amendment 2 to EXP/Cult (53) 1) Nevertheless, at the sixth session of the Committee of Cultural Experts (Strasbourg, 11 –13 May 1953) after the Netherlands Delegation expressed concern at the proposed deletion of Article 1 by the Irish Delegation, the latter stated that it is willing to keep this article in text (EXP/Cult (53) 15).

107 The same Mr Reinink, who was already mentioned in this chapter as the Secretary-General in the Netherlands Ministry of the Education, the expert in NATO's cultural committee, the member of the BTO Cultural Committee as well as a member of the drafting sub-committee of ECC.

pean Member States of UNESCO even if they were not members of the CoE.[108] This proposal was accepted and incorporated into the amended initial UK draft:

> The Committee of Ministers of the Council of Europe may invite any State which is not a Member of the Council to accede to this Convention. Any State so invited may accede by deposing its instrument of accession with the Secretary-General of the Council of Europe which shall take effect on the date of its receipt.[109]

This original feature of the ECC allowed non-member states to participate in the CoE's cultural activities on the same footing as members. With this provision, the Council extended a hand to states held back from joining it by geopolitical factors and associated them with a vast range of cultural activities, covering heritage, education, and the free circulation of values and ideas.[110] It can be argued that the major impact of the Convention was this open-handed approach, as clearly can be seen from the process of its ratification.

Three ratifications were required for the text to enter into force – the first ratification came from Ireland, followed by France and the UK in 1955. By January 1989, seven states had ratified the Convention despite not being mem-

---

108 Jean Petaux, *Democracy and Human Rights for Europe – The Council of Europe's Contribution* (Council of Europe Publishing 2009).

109 Council of Europe, Committee of Cultural Experts, 'Draft European Cultural Convention – Amendments Proposed by the Secretariat-General' [1953] Amendment to EXP/Cult (53) 1;
Council of Europe, Committee of Cultural Experts, 'Draft European Cultural Convention – Amended Version of the Draft Submitted by the UK Delegation' [1953] EXP/Cult/B (53) 2 Revised;
Council of Europe, Committee of Cultural Experts, 'Memorandum of the Irish Delegation on the Draft European Cultural Convention' [1953] Amendment 2 to EXP/Cult (53) 1;
Council of Europe, Committee of Cultural Experts, 'Draft European Cultural Convention – Drafting Amendments Proposed by the United Kingdom Delegation' [1953] Amendment 3 to EXP/Cult (53) 1.

110 Bruno Haller, *An Assembly for Europe – The Council of Europe's Parliamentary Assembly 1949–1989* (Strasbourg: Council of Europe Publishing 2006); Yet, it must be noted that all Member States did not immediately accept this provision. For example, in drafting amendments to the proposed text, United Kingdom Delegation has not included this provision (Amendment 3 to EXP/Cult (53) 1). Nevertheless, it stayed in the new draft proposed by the drafting sub-committee at the end of the sixth Session (EXP/Cult (53) 17).

bers of the CoE at the time: Spain, the Holy See, Switzerland, Finland, Portugal, San Marino, and the Socialist Federal Republic of Yugoslavia (SFRY). All these countries, except the Holy See, acceded to the CoE later at different times. Spain ratified the text as early as 4 July 1957, at the height of the Francoist dictatorship, and it took another 20 years before Spain joined the organisation. Finland, for its part, ratified the Convention on 23 January 1970 and joined the CoE in 1989, 19 years later. Switzerland ratified the ECC on 13 July 1962, less than a year before joining the CoE. Under Salazar's dictatorship (1932–1968), which denied and rejected any form of cultural development as 'socially polluting', Portugal did not ratify the Convention until 16 February 1976, a few months before joining the CoE. San Marino ratified the text three years before becoming a member of the organisation (1986). SFRY ratified the Convention on 7 October 1987, before the other states of Central and Eastern Europe, which followed from 1990 onwards. However, Yugoslavia withdrew when the country dissolved in 1992, and the states born of the breakup of SFRY ratified the Convention and joined the CoE individually in the late 1990s. The other states of Central and Eastern Europe also used the ECC as a stepping stone towards CoE membership. This was the case for 28 out of the 49 signatory states of this Convention.[111] This open-handed approach highlighted the ECC's role as both a legal framework for cooperation and a diplomatic tool for European integration, as it is clearly expressed in the Summary of the ECC by the Treaty Office:

> The purpose of this Convention is to develop mutual understanding among the peoples of Europe and reciprocal appreciation of their cultural diversity, to safeguard European culture, to promote national contributions to Europe's common cultural heritage respecting the same fundamental values and to encourage in particular the study of the language, history, and civilisation of the Parties to the Convention. The Convention contributes to concerted action by encouraging activities of European interest.

5.2 *Legacy and Contemporary Relevance*

Over nearly seven decades, the ECC has had a profound impact on cultural heritage and cooperation in Europe. Its innovative features – recognition of both tangible and intangible heritage, inclusivity, and adaptability – have

111 Petaux (n 107); since CoE currently encompasses almost the entire European continent, the openness of the ECC was used also from 2002 as a framework for the intercultural dialogue with the south Mediterranean countries.

allowed it to remain relevant across changing political and cultural landscapes.

The ECC's flexible definition of heritage, encompassing arts, languages, and historical narratives, has also supported its evolution. While its early focus remained at the national level, CoE heritage activities expanded in scope, particularly from the 1960s onwards, eventually incorporating broader themes of cultural diversity, youth engagement, and conflict resolution.

The ECC has been celebrated for its universal values, which align with fundamental human rights and democratic ideals. At the Wroclaw conference in 2004, which celebrated the fiftieth anniversary of the ECC, the Convention was praised for its universalism, its role in combating totalitarianism, and its relevance in conflict resolution and peacekeeping.[112] As Robert Palmer noted, 'Culture is no longer just about art. Culture is a profound security issue.'[113] In line with the statements on the role of culture in relation to conflict in the early 2000s that reflected political reality in Europe at the time, currently, after 70 years of the ECC in place, the CoE went back the whole circle, and highlighted again, as in the 1950s that without culture there is no democracy. In the current political environment where a decline of democracies around Europe can be observed and where the notion of culture, together with heritage, identity, and tradition, has been hijacked by the populist nationalists, the call for renewal of initial ECC ideas is urgent as it was in post-war Europe in the 1950s. The investment in culture and heritage is seen today as an investment into the resilience of Europe's democracies. And the ECC, in the CoE's opinion, again has a critical role to play in this process.

6 Conclusion of the Chapter

The insight into the background of the first CoE cultural convention (European Cultural Convention), as well as the motives and ideas behind the cre-

112 The 'universal nature' of the ECC was stated in clear terms by Professor Jerzy Wiatr, who was a general rapporteur at the Wroclaw Conference:

> The common European heritage consists of such elements of European culture which are consistent with the fundamental values of human rights and individual freedom. The authors of the Convention rightly believed that these values are universal. They give European culture a distinctly humanistic and democratic character and prove the rationale for human solidarity... While the European Cultural Convention deals with European heritage, there is nothing in it that could be considered exclusive. The core values of European culture constitute a message which is not exclusively directed to the European nations. It has a universal meaning (Petaux [2009] 193).

113 Petaux (n 107) 194.

ation of the organisation as such, as presented in this chapter, serves as a necessary foundation for better understanding the philosophy and approaches that underpinned the CoE's future heritage endeavours. Among the core ideas underlining the organisation's cultural and heritage policies over the years of its existence, the building of European unity and accentuating a European common ground by using culture and heritage is certainly one that needs to be emphasised. The following chapters will inevitably refer to the diverse levels of 'use' and 'definitions' of the concept of 'common heritage of Europe' that the organisation felt was needed during different periods, depending on its political aims. However, understanding the origins of the ECC and the political reality behind it in the formative years of the CoE helps us to understand the main parameters of the heritage discourse the organisation would develop in the following years.

Another fundamental element that underlines all subsequent CoE heritage texts and activities is the human rights dimension of culture and heritage. The CoE's human rights-based approach was, from its early days, primarily focused on individuals and the role of culture in the individual's quality of life and development. This could be considered as a critical element that underlines the CoE's discourse that was, as the following analysis shows, more or less accentuated throughout different periods of the CoE's activities.

The importance of drafting the European Cultural Convention (ECC) in this early formative period of the European unity project, resides in the fact that it enabled multilateral European cultural cooperation, which had been nearly non-existent up to that point. The ECC turned out to be an overarching text for numerous conventions and recommendations in the fields of culture, education, and sport. On the CoE's website,[114] the Convention is referred to as one of the most relevant documents concerning cultural heritage, and it is considered as such by some commentators.[115] The text is important, as it illustrates the early CoE's position on culture and its political role. It also served as a starting point for any future culture-related work, including the organisation's heritage protection activities. The following chapters in the volume focus on the 'purely' cultural-heritage-related conventions developing from the ECC framework, starting with the actions related to architectural heritage and its protection in Chapters 2 and 3, and continuing with the issues of protection of archaeological heritage in Chapter 4.

---

114 https://www.coe.int/en/web/herein-system/council-of-europe

115 For example: Oriane Calligaro, *Negotiating Europe: EU Promotion of Europeanness since the 1950s* (London: Palgrave Macmillan 2013); Parry (n 15); Petaux (n 107).

CHAPTER 3

Shaping Europe's Architectural Heritage Policies

1 Introduction

The 1960s and 1970s marked a critical juncture in the evolution of international conservation doctrine and policy. During this period, the predominantly European ideas about conservation and the meaning and nature of heritage were 'universalised' through a growing number of intergovernmental texts. What Smith has characterised as the authorised heritage discourse (AHD) was, therefore, chiefly shaped and internationally authorised during this period.[1] Amid rapid urbanisation, industrialisation, and post-war reconstruction, the accelerated pace of change posed unique challenges to the preservation of cultural heritage. Within this dynamic context, the Council of Europe emerged as a significant yet under-researched actor, developing a distinctive approach to heritage conservation that set it apart from other major international organisations such as UNESCO, ICOMOS, and ICCROM. This chapter, therefore, explores the CoE's contributions to conservation doctrine during this pivotal period, with a particular focus on its efforts to address the protection of historical cities.

This chapter aims to situate the CoE's work within the broader landscape of international conservation efforts while drawing attention to its unique regional perspective. As a European organisation, the CoE was deeply attuned to the complexities of the continent's historic urban fabric and its diverse architectural heritage. This sensitivity informed its focus on historic centres and the integration of heritage protection into urban planning, areas that became central to its conservation agenda. By examining the CoE's key initiatives during this period – most notably the symposia on architectural heritage held between 1965 and 1968 and the European Architectural Heritage Year (EAHY) of 1975 – this chapter highlights how the organisation shaped conservation policy and doctrine both within Europe and beyond.

The CoE's contributions were driven by a recognition of gaps in the existing conservation frameworks. The Venice Charter of 1964, while considered a canonical text that underlines and provides a philosophical basis for the conservation and preservation movement of the twentieth century, primarily emphasised the restoration of individual monuments and neglected broader

1 Laurajane Smith, *Uses of Heritage* (Taylor & Francis Group 2006).

 | DOI:10.1163/9789004756250_004

considerations of urban and architectural ensembles. The CoE sought to address this limitation by advancing a more holistic approach to heritage conservation. This involved not only preserving the physical integrity of historic centres but also safeguarding their social and cultural dimensions, acknowledging the living nature of these spaces. Guided by the mindset, boldly expressed by Piero Gazzola, that 'the whole of Europe is a "historic centre"' that needs urgent protection, the CoE committed itself to the urgent reorganisation of the preservation of architectural heritage in historic centres, specifically by defining the role of heritage protection in town planning.[2] Such efforts culminated in the production of influential texts, including the Amsterdam Declaration and the European Charter of Architectural Heritage, which articulated principles that are foundations of the CoE's twentieth-century heritage discourse.

In examining the CoE's role, this chapter responds to a critical gap in heritage scholarship. Much of the existing literature on international conservation efforts has centred on the contributions of UNESCO, ICOMOS, and other global organisations, often overlooking the CoE's equally significant influence.[3] By foregrounding the CoE's initiatives and their impact, this chapter seeks to

2 Council of Europe, Committee of Ministers, 'Memorandum presented by Mr Pietro Gazzola on Preservation and Development of Groups and Areas of Buildings of Historical or Artistic Interest' [1965] CCC/CDS/CT (65) 8, 1.

3 See for example:

Miles Glendinning, 'The Conservation Movement: A Cult of the Modern Age' (2003) 13 *Transactions of the Royal Historical Society* 359;

Miles Glendinning, *Modern Architect: The Life and Times of Robert Matthew* (RIBA Publishing 2008); Miles Glendinning, *The Conservation Movement: A History of Architectural Preservation – Antiquity to Modernity* (Routledge 2013);

Dennis Rodwell, *Conservation and Sustainability in Historic Cities* (Blackwell Publishing 2007);

Dennis Rodwell, 'Urban Conservation in the 1960s and 1970s: A European Overview' (2010) 21(1) *Architectural Heritage* 1;

Matthew Hardy (ed), *The Venice Charter Revisited: Modernism, Conservation and Tradition in the 21st Century* (Cambridge Scholars Publishing 2009);

Pietro Gazzola, *The Past in the Future* (DAPCO 1969);

John H Stubbs, *Time Honored: A Global View of Architectural Conservation* (Wiley & Sons 2009);

Robert Pickard (ed), *Management of Historic Centres* (Spon Press 2001);

Robert Pickard, 'A Comparative Review of Policy for the Protection of the Architectural Heritage of Europe' (2002) 8(4) *International Journal of Heritage Studies* 349;

Robert Pickard, *European Cultural Heritage* (vol 2, Council of Europe Publishing 2002);

Robert Pickard, 'Management Strategies for Historic Towns in Europe' in Sophia Labadi and William Logan (eds), *Urban Heritage, Development and Sustainability* (Routledge 2015) 151.

enrich the historiography of conservation discourse and offer a more nuanced understanding of the interplay between regional and global influences in shaping modern conservation practice.

The analysis presented in this chapter is largely informed by a combination of archival research and textual analysis of archival texts. Archival documents provide detailed insights into the CoE's activities, decisions, and outputs, offering a valuable record of the organisation's contributions. Secondary literature on the history of conservation and the theoretical underpinnings of the Authorised Heritage Discourse (AHD) further situates the CoE's work within the broader intellectual and policy landscape of the time.

The CoE's initiatives during the 1960s and 1970s exemplify the interconnectedness of heritage discourse during this period. Far from operating in isolation, the CoE engaged in a dynamic exchange of ideas with other international bodies, building on existing frameworks while addressing their limitations. For instance, the Venice Charter provided an important foundation for the CoE's conservation philosophy, but the organisation also identified critical areas where the Charter fell short, particularly in its treatment of historic centres.[4] In addressing these gaps, the CoE not only developed a distinctive heritage discourse but also influenced the broader trajectory of international heritage policy.

2 Architectural Heritage: Council of Europe's First Steps

The post-war period was marked by a growing recognition of the urgent need to protect architectural and cultural heritage in the face of modernisation and industrialisation. International cooperation in the field of conservation was

4 See for example: Smith (n 1);
Raymond Lemaire, *Prémices de la Charte de Venise* (1964);
Cevat Erder, *The Venice Charter Under Review* (1977);
Jukka Jokilehto, *Comments on the Venice Charter with Illustrations* (1995);
Jukka Jokilehto, 'The Context of the Venice Charter (1964)' (1998) 2 *Conservation and Management of Archaeological Sites* 229;
Claudine Houbart, 'Deconsecrating a Doctrinal Monument: Raymond M. Lemaire (1921–1997) and the Revisions of the Venice Charter' (2014) 4(2) *Change Over Time* 218;
Claudine Houbart, 'Towards an "Integrated Conservation": The Contribution of R.M. Lemaire and Piero Gazzola during the First Decade of ICOMOS (1965–1975)' (2016) 1(3) *Heritage for Future* 117;
Randolph Starn, 'Authenticity and Historic Preservation: Towards an Authentic History' (2002) 15(1) *History of the Human Sciences* 1.

seen as the only effective way to guarantee the future of the world's heritage, and the contributions of different international bodies in the area need to be looked at as an outcome of the exceptional interchange of ideas and influences among experts and professionals participating in their work at the time.[5] The most important initiatives of UNESCO, the CoE, and ICOMOS at the time demonstrate how guidelines for this new conservation doctrine were gradually worked out throughout the 1960s, how the values and assumptions they propagated were given an international presence, as well as how 'the sense and self-referential authority of conservation and management philosophy and practice' were achieved.[6] The normative activities carried out by those institutions helped to legitimise and maintain the canons of art and architecture, and the notion of intrinsic value related to the fabric or history of a particular site persisted.[7]

In this context, on a global international scale the first initiative to be mentioned is Resolution 4.62 of the UNESCO General Conference of 1958, which authorised the Director-General to assist the Member States in improving and developing technical and legal measures for the protection and preservation of cultural property, in particular, by 'launching an international campaign for the preservation of historic monuments', which was followed by its 1968 Recommendation concerning the Preservation of Cultural Property Endangered by Public or Private Works. In addition, the International Centre for the Study of the Preservation and Restoration of Cultural Property – ICCROM was established in 1958 and worked extensively to circulate information on restoration and preservation issues to specialists worldwide.

---

5 The cooperation, or more strictly, the exchange between UNESCO and the Council of Europe began already in 1950, mostly as the result of the organisations' anxiety (in this respect the concern was more evident on the side of the Council of Europe) over overlapping competencies and duplication of the actions. The Agreement between two organisations entered into force in 1952, opening the possibility of coordination of their activities and regular consultations on matters of common interest (Agreement between the Council of Europe and the UNESCO). The information channels between the two organisations were wide open during this period. UNESCO was sending the reports on its activities which could be of the Council's interest to the Consultative Assembly after its General Conferences (every two years). Reciprocally, the Consultative Assembly would in its reply made particular reference on Council of Europe's activities in the cultural field and would examine to what extent two organisations can collaborate on specific questions.

6 Smith (n 1) 94.

7 Sophia Labadi, *UNESCO, Cultural Heritage, and Outstanding Universal Value: Value-Based Analyses of the World Heritage and Intangible Cultural Heritage Conventions* (AltaMira Press 2013).

In its turn, the CoE PACE Committee on Culture and Education in 1962 presented a motion for a recommendation on the subject.[8] This significant early step to address the preservation and development of Europe's architectural heritage culminated in PACE Recommendation 365 in 1963. These efforts were informed by the PACE Report known as the Weiss Report, which provided a comprehensive framework for understanding and tackling the threats facing historic buildings and sites across Europe.[9] The report emphasised the urgency of these efforts, as rapid post-war modernisation posed significant risks to the continent's cultural landmarks.

Weiss highlighted the profound cultural and symbolic value of architectural heritage, portraying it as a testament to Europe's shared history, diversity, and identity. The report stressed that in an era of standardisation, historic buildings and sites served as anchors of cultural individuality and continuity. Their preservation was framed as not only a cultural imperative but also a societal necessity in creating environments that balanced modern development with human dignity and cultural richness. The Weiss Report proposed a systematic protection campaign, combining national and international efforts under a shared European framework. It suggested a range of measures, including the preparation of inventories, the establishment of a European institution for preservation, and enhanced cooperation among member states.[10] A pivotal recommendation was the creation of a pilot project for the restoration of a historical quarter in Venice, recognising its importance as a symbol of European culture. This project, supported by the *Italia Nostra* association and

---

8 Article 24 of the Statute permits the Assembly to establish Committees to consider and report on any matter that falls within its competencies. One of the first Committees established was the Cultural Committee. Over the years, this Committee changed its name and broadened the field of its competencies as follows:
- 1949–1950 – the Committee on Cultural Questions
- 1950–1957 – the Committee on Cultural and Scientific Questions
- 1957–2002 – the Committee on Culture and Education
  It had, from 1968, the Sub-Committee on Historical and Artistic Monuments and Sites; from 1975 – The sub-committee on Monuments and Sites; from 1977 – The sub-committee on the Architectural and Artistic Heritage of Europe; and from 1998 – The sub-committee on the Cultural Heritage.
- 2002–2012 – the Committee on Culture, Science and Education (the Sub-Committee on the Cultural Heritage)
- 2012 – present – Committee on Culture, Science, Education and Media (The Sub-Committee on Culture, Diversity and Heritage)

9 Parliamentary Assembly, 'Report on the Preservation and Development of Ancient Buildings and Historical and Artistic Sites (presented by Mr Weiss)' [1963] Doc 1570.

10 Ibid.

the Italian government, exemplified the collaborative and demonstrative approach advocated by the Council of Europe.

To operationalise these ideas, the Parliamentary Assembly advocated convening a European conference on heritage preservation. This conference would serve as a platform to raise public awareness about the gravity of the situation, develop a joint programme of action, and explore the feasibility of establishing a permanent European body for heritage conservation. The report also proposed the creation of a comprehensive list of historic sites of European significance, reflecting a commitment to identifying and protecting the most emblematic elements of the continent's heritage (an early idea of the World Heritage List!).

These proposals laid the groundwork for Recommendation 365, which was instrumental in elevating the preservation of architectural heritage to a priority issue within the Council of Europe.[11] By calling for a unified European approach, the Recommendation underscored the necessity of integrating conservation into broader regional and urban planning frameworks. It also highlighted the role of municipalities and local authorities, as well as the importance of involving non-governmental organisations in the heritage discourse.[12] This initial phase of the Council of Europe's involvement in architectural heritage protection marked a pivotal moment in shaping a distinctly European approach to conservation. Through a combination of visionary proposals and practical measures, it set the stage for more detailed discussions and initiatives in subsequent years, including the series of symposia that would further refine and implement these ideas.

The symposia (1965–1968) that would be discussed shortly need to be looked at in conjunction with the acknowledged necessity by the professionals in the field to reassess the 1931 Athens Charter and to organise the Second International Congress of Architects and Technicians of Historic Monuments in 1964. The outcomes of this congress – the Venice Charter and the creation of ICOMOS played, as the following analysis shows, a pivotal part in the way how the CoE framed its heritage policy.

---

11 In this document PACE recommended to the Committee of Ministers to (1) call a European Conference, within the framework of the CoE, on the preservation and development of ancient buildings and historic and artistic sites, (2) within the framework of its cultural cooperation, organise series of meetings on the subject and (3) consider the possibility of setting up a European body for the preservation of European heritage or to arrange some other permanent machinery for cooperation in the cultural heritage field.

12 Supported by the PACE, the private organisations for preserving and developing ancient buildings and sites created the pan-European Federation of non-governmental heritage organisations in 1963 – *Europa Nostra*.

2.1 *Venice Charter: Influence on the Council of Europe Heritage Discourse*

The post-war reconstruction of Europe brought to the forefront the urgent need to preserve its architectural heritage. Initial efforts predominantly focused on restoring monuments that were legally protected and eligible for state financial aid. These monuments were often celebrated as cultural symbols, representing continuity and resilience in the wake of destruction. However, the broader urban settings of these monuments, comprising more modest structures that formed the unique character of historic cities, were often overlooked. Modern developments frequently replaced these unprotected buildings, eroding the coherence and authenticity of many urban landscapes. The selective nature of these restoration efforts led to widespread concern among architects, urban planners, and policymakers, who grappled with how to reconcile historic city centres with the demands of modernity without destroying their essence.

This dilemma was not unique to individual nations but resonated across Europe. A 1968 report from England on historic towns captured this tension, emphasising the need to 'reconcile our old towns with the twentieth century without actually knocking them down'.[13] Similar sentiments echoed within the Council of Europe, particularly in the Parliamentary Assembly's 1962 report, which warned of the dangers posed by a 'cult of gigantic' developments and 'dehumanised' environments that 'begged for advocacy in favour of groups of older buildings that should not be regarded as a "museum" or a "foreign body", but rather [as] a context for a way of life' and 'symbol of the dignity and civic spirit of their community'.[14] The report called for an approach where 'the new civilisation will draw its vitality and strength from the richness and diversity of its tradition'.[15] These early reflections set the stage for the CoE's evolving discourse on heritage preservation, which moved beyond the isolated preservation of individual monuments to consider broader urban ensembles and historic cityscapes.

In this context, the 1964 Venice Charter represented a milestone in the development of international conservation doctrine. The charter introduced a broader understanding of heritage, acknowledging the importance of not only monuments but also their settings. Article 1 of the Venice Charter recognised 'modest works of the past which have acquired cultural significance' as

---

13 Dennis Rodwell, 'Urban Conservation in the 1960s and 1970s: A European Overview' (2010) 21(1) *Architectural Heritage* 2.

14 PACE, Doc. 1570 (n 9) 9.

15 PACE, Doc. 1570 (n 9) 8.

deserving of preservation. This marked a departure from earlier approaches that focused exclusively on iconic monuments, signalling an awareness of the interconnectedness between individual structures and their broader contexts. The charter's provisions, particularly Articles 6, 7, and 14, emphasised the need to protect the settings of monuments to safeguard their integrity.

Despite these advancements, the Venice Charter revealed significant limitations, particularly regarding the conservation of urban ensembles. While it gestured toward the importance of historic settings, its practical application was heavily weighted toward the preservation of individual monuments. Article 14, for instance, advocated for the care of monument sites to 'safeguard their integrity', but its language reflected a static preservation ethos. This focus failed to address the complexities of urban conservation, where the vitality of historic areas depended on their integration into contemporary life. This limitation was recognised even by its principal authors, Piero Gazzola and Raymond M. Lemaire, who sought alternative avenues to address these deficiencies.[16]

Gazzola and Lemaire were central figures in both the drafting of the Venice Charter and the subsequent evolution of heritage policies within the CoE. They played a crucial role in defining the international discourse not only as the signatories of the Venice Charter but also as the President and Secretary-General of the newly created ICOMOS (from 1965 to 1975), but also as the members of the CoE Technical Advisory Body[17] (1965) that was framing the CoE's heritage approach.

Piero Gazzola, to whom a number of scholars[18] ascribe authorship of the Venice Charter (together with Roberto Pane), was, as seen by Lemaire, the

16 Claudine Houbart, 'Towards an "Integrated Conservation": The Contribution of R.M. Lemaire and Piero Gazzola during the First Decade of ICOMOS (1965–1975)' (2016) 1(3) *Heritage for Future* 117.

17 It was not only Lemaire who helped to introduce or close the CoE's debates or wrote the recommendations and conclusions of the CoE's discussions. Among ten members of the CoE's Committee of Technical Advisers, which was responsible for organising five CoE symposia and for defining the subjects for the discussion at those meetings, in addition to Lemaire, three more signatories of the Venice charter were taking part – Piero Gazzola, Gertrud Tripp and François Sorlin (CCC/CDS/CT (65) 5). At the same time, Roberto Pane, Paul Philippot, Harold Plenderleith and Jean Sonnier appeared as the keynote speakers in those symposia.

18 See, among other sources:

Luigi Guerriero, "Piero Gazzola and Roberto Pane's contribution to the draft of Venice Charter," in *The Venice Charter Revisited: Modernism, Conservation and Tradition in the 21st Century*, ed. Matthew Hardy (Cambridge Scholars Publishing, 2008);

Miles Glendinning, *The Conservation Movement: A History of Architectural Preservation, Antiquity to Modernity* (Routledge, 2013), 405.

'true founder of ICOMOS'.[19] Prior to the establishment of ICOMOS, Gazzola participated in the early preparation work of the conference at The Hague, where the UNESCO 1954 Hague Convention was adopted. He was also one of the four *ex officio* members of the UNESCO (1958) appointed Provisional Council of ICCROM responsible for developing that newly created organisation's programme of activities. Gazzola also worked at UNESCO as a Programme Specialist and participated in many of UNESCO's initiatives. His example demonstrates how international discourse and the whole international conservation initiative were coordinated by an extremely limited number of prominent experts who influenced national- and intergovernmental-level decisions and authorised their ideas through a series of charters and conventions (AHD). As well argued by Smith, the expertise that underlines and underwrites the charters and conventions is extremely significant in the authorisation of those documents.[20] Through the enactment and use of charters and conventions, the authority of expertise and 'subsequently the principles they espouse, become so naturalised as to be understood as "common sense" or "good sense"'.[21] Gazzola's words serve as an example:

> We need only recall the creation of the International Council of Monuments and Sites – ICOMOS- the institution which constitutes the ***court of highest appeal in the area of the restoration*** of monuments, and of the conservation of ancient historical centres, of the landscape and in general of the places of artistic and historical importance. That *organisation must supervise* the creation of specialised personnel, its recruitment and advancement...But above all, it is to be recognised that the most important positive result by far of this assembly has been the formulation of the international code for restoration: not simply a cultural episode but a text of historical importance. *In fact, it constitutes an obligation* ***which no one will be able to ignore,*** *the spirit of which all the experts will have to keep if they do not want to be considered cultural outlaws*. The concerns thus codified constitute for everyone today an

According to Paul Philippot, 'the two driving forces of the Venice Charter were Gazzola and Lemaire' – from Gian Giuseppe Simeone and Yves Robert, *La Carta di Venezia. Intervista a Paul Philippot,* TeMa 1 (1999): 8.

19 Raymond Lemaire, 'Report of the President of ICOMOS, 1965–1975 – A Tribute to Piero Gazzola' (1981) https://www.icomos.org/public/publications/JS5_11.pdf accessed 20 June 2018.

20 Smith (n 1).

21 Ibid 89.

> *unassailable document* the validity of which will be affirmed more and more as time passes.[22]

Raymond Lemaire, whose expertise was grounded in his work on projects such as the Great Beguinage of Leuven, brought a critical perspective to the limitations of the Venice Charter. His practical experience highlighted the challenges of applying monument-centric principles to urban conservation, leading him to advocate for more dynamic preservation strategies. The in-depth study of Lemaire's contribution to international preservation doctrine by Claudine Houbart, especially his role in drafting the Venice Charter in 1964, is a valuable contribution to our understanding of the realities behind that particular text.[23] Even more important is Houbart's analysis of Lemaire's prompt understanding, based on his practical work, of the 'inadequacy' of the Venice Charter in the context of the conservation of groups of buildings. The important reflections on the active maintenance of monuments, groups, and areas of buildings of historical or artistic interest within the context of regional planning during the already mentioned CoE symposia convinced the experts, and particularly Lemaire and Gazzola, that the Venice Charter needed to be reviewed. Lemaire, in his contribution to the CoE Bath Symposium (C) in 1966, for example, praised the CoE's approach of 'active preservation of monuments and groups of buildings' as 'the only kind which can guarantee their future in the world today'.[24] As expressed in Lemaire's notes, the concern he and Gazzola had about the limitations of the Venice Charter was related to 'this aspect [which] is scarcely initiated in the charter's text', as well as to 'the experience of the last ten years [which] brought out that a pure and simple application of principles devoted to monuments as such is not always possible, nor always desirable for the ensembles'.[25] Therefore, the symposia discussions, which were primarily focused on historic cities' 'reanimation' and the integration of historic sites and monuments into new city developments, revealed the important limits that this 'unassailable' doctrinal document

22 Gazzola as cited in: Michael Petzet, *Principles of Preservation: An Introduction to the International Charters for Conservation and Restoration 40 Years after the Venice Charter* (2004) https://www.icomos.org/venicecharter2004/petzet.pdf accessed 16 June 2018; [emphasis added].

23 Houbart (n 16).

24 Council of Europe, Committee of Ministers, 'Symposium C – Principles and Practice of Active Preservation and Rehabilitation of Groups and Areas of Buildings of Historical or Artistic Interest, Bath 1966' [1967] COE.H.2.4/67 PR, 53.

25 Claudine Houbart, 'Deconsecrating a Doctrinal Monument: Raymond M. Lemaire (1921–1997) and the Revisions of the Venice Charter' (2014) 4(2) *Change Over Time* 229.

had.[26] Houbart's study points particularly to how, after Lemaire and Gazzola failed in their attempts to revise the 'imperfect' Venice Charter within ICOMOS, Lemaire found in the CoE a much more open milieu to address the limitations he had identified in the Venice Charter.[27] This observation is particularly significant in the context of our understanding of which direction the CoE's heritage policies would go.

The CoE's engagement with the Venice Charter and its evolution in response to its limitations, therefore, marked a critical phase in the development of European heritage policies. The CoE recognised the importance of the charter as a foundational document but sought to address its shortcomings through a series of initiatives that emphasised the preservation of urban ensembles and historic cities. Central to these efforts were the symposia organised by the CoE between 1965 and 1968, which provided a platform for experts and policymakers to explore innovative approaches to heritage conservation.

2.2 *The Council of Europe's Five Symposia*

The Council of Europe's five symposia on the preservation and rehabilitation of historic buildings and urban areas held, between 1965 and 1968, were significant events in shaping the CoE's twentieth-century heritage discourse. Initiated in response to rising concerns about the rapid transformation of European cities and their surrounding landscapes, these symposia marked the CoE's commitment to fostering international collaboration and adopting innovative strategies for safeguarding architectural and urban heritage. The impetus for these symposia can be traced back to Recommendation 365, adopted by the CoE's Consultative Assembly in May 1963. The recommendation emphasised the urgent need for coordinated action to preserve Europe's historic sites and buildings, which were increasingly threatened by urbanisa-

26 Council of Europe, 'Memorandum presented by Mr Pietro Gazzola on Preservation and Development of Groups and Areas of Buildings of Historical or Artistic Interest' CCC/CDS/CT (65) 8 (n 2).

27 The subjects of the conferences organised by ICOMOS during its first years of existence also reveal that, in an attempt to adjust the needs detected in practice with the principles of the Charter, ICOMOS considered preserving historic cities to be one of its main priorities:
- Resolutions on the Regeneration of Historic Urban Sites, Levoca, 20–26 June 1966;
- First conference on the conservation, restoration and revival of areas and groups of buildings of historic interest. Caceres, Spain, 15–19 March 1967;
- Second conference on the Conservation, Restoration and Revival of Areas and Groups of Buildings of Historic Interest; Tunisia, 9–16 April 1968;
- *Kolloquium: Der verkehr in den Historischen Stadtzentren, Graz 5–10 Oktober 1969.*

tion, neglect, and a lack of systematic protective frameworks. By invoking the principles of the European Cultural Convention, the recommendation called for a series of expert meetings to develop and exchange effective methodologies for preservation.

In response, the CoE Council for Cultural Cooperation (CCC) structured a programme of five symposia, each addressing a specific facet of heritage preservation. These symposia were designed not only to examine existing practices but also to generate forward-thinking solutions that integrated cultural heritage into broader socio-economic and urban planning policies.

To ensure that the symposia would be scientifically and practically grounded, the CCC established a Committee of Technical Advisors, composed of distinguished heritage professionals and cultural policymakers. This committee oversaw the preparation and implementation of the symposia, ensuring coherence between their thematic focuses and the overarching objectives of the CoE's heritage initiatives. With close reference to the limitations of the Venice Charter in mind, the list of the members of the committee comes as no surprise. Piero Gazzola and Raymond Lemaire were unsurprisingly there, as well as other signatories of the Venice Charter, such as Gertrude Tripp and François Sorlin. In addition, well-known figures who shaped the CoE's cultural agenda from its creation, such as Hendrik Jan Reinink (Chairman), as well as the Rapporteur of the Cultural and Scientific Committee of the PACE Ludwig Weiss were also included together with others national experts helping them to address the specificities of every singular symposium.[28]

2.2.1 Symposium A

The first meeting (Symposium A) was held in Barcelona from 17 to 19 May 1965 and was devoted to 'Criteria and methods for a protective inventory for the preservation and rehabilitation of groups and areas of buildings of historic and artistic interest' as its subject. Its goal was to establish a standardised framework for documenting heritage sites, which would serve as a prerequisite for their effective protection and integration into modern urban planning. The discussions at Symposium A centred on several critical themes:

- *The Need for a Standardised Inventory System* – Participants underscored the importance of developing a unified inventory system that could be used across Europe. The absence of a common framework had resulted in fragmented efforts, with varying methodologies and criteria across

28 Council of Europe, Committee of Ministers, 'Note on the Action Taken by the Council of Europe in the Field of the Preservation and Rehabilitation of Groups and Areas of Buildings of Historical or Artistic Interest' [1968] CCC/ACV (68) 62.

countries. The symposium proposed a 'Protective Inventory' that would include standardised typological, chronological, and geographical classifications.

- *Balancing Scientific and Administrative Needs* – The inventory was envisioned as having both scientific and administrative components. The scientific aspect would cater to researchers and academics, while the administrative component would provide actionable data for policymakers and heritage practitioners.
- *The Protective Inventory Index Card System* – A key recommendation was the adoption of a model index card system to document heritage assets. This system would capture essential information, such as location, typology, and legal status, enabling a streamlined approach to heritage management. Recognising the diversity of European heritage, participants emphasised that the inventory system should be flexible enough to accommodate national specificities while maintaining a cohesive structure at the European level.

The recommendation adopted at the end of this symposium, known as the 'Palma Recommendation', was adopted by the Committee of Ministers of the CoE in Resolution (66)19 – *Criteria and Methods of Cataloguing Ancient Buildings and Historical or Artistic Sites*. This recommendation laid the groundwork for subsequent symposia by emphasising the urgency of creating a comprehensive inventory and linking heritage conservation to socio-economic development.

2.2.2 Symposium B

In October 1965, Vienna hosted a symposium that tackled a pressing and forward-looking question: how to find new uses for culturally significant buildings that no longer served their original purpose while respecting their natural and aesthetic surroundings. This topic reflected an evolving understanding of heritage conservation, recognising that the survival of many historic structures depended on their ability to adapt to modern needs without losing their cultural value.[29]

Presiding over the meeting was Gertrude Tripp, who, in her role as Rapporteur, highlighted the dual challenges of physical preservation and functional reintegration. Tripp framed the architectural heritage of urban settings as

29 Council of Europe, Committee of Ministers, 'Confrontation B – Problèmes posés par la réanimation des monuments dans leur cadre esthétique ou naturel, offrant un intérêt culturel, qui ne remplissent plus les fonctions pour lesquelles ils ont été conçus' [1965] CCC/CDS/B (65) 27.

being under siege by what she described as the 'civilising' forces of modern development – forces that demanded the radical destruction of cultural heritage to make way for progress. She critiqued the modernist approach, which often viewed the conservation of monuments as a sign of 'weakness of spirit and false piety'.[30]

The symposium convened once again well-known names in the field (Gazzola, Lemaire, Weiss, Reinink, Sorlin),[31] who examined how disused or abandoned monuments, often at risk of neglect or demolition, might be revitalised through adaptive reuse, ensuring their relevance in contemporary society. Responses to a pre-symposium questionnaire circulated among Member States revealed a shared concern: across national contexts, heritage buildings were increasingly imperilled, yet their survival depended on identifying new functions aligned with modern socio-economic realities. Adaptive reuse, it was argued, was not merely a practical solution but also a means of reinvigorating the cultural and historical identity of communities.

Central to the discussions was the tension between adapting heritage buildings for new uses and preserving their architectural and historical integrity. Delegates examined case studies demonstrating how thoughtful planning and innovative design could allow historic structures to coexist harmoniously with their modern surroundings, highlighting the National Trust initiatives in the UK as a good example. These cases underscored the importance of sensitivity to original designs and cultural contexts, ensuring that transformations respected the intrinsic values of the buildings.

The symposium also shed light on the legislative and financial frameworks needed to support these adaptive reuse efforts. Participants noted significant disparities in the legal protections afforded to heritage buildings across Europe, particularly those that had fallen out of use. In some cases, inadequate legal safeguards left these structures vulnerable to redevelopment or neglect. The symposium called for comprehensive policy frameworks to protect and promote the reuse of heritage buildings. Financial mechanisms, such as grants,

---

30 CCC/CDS/B (65) 27 (n 29) 10.

31 Speakers at the Symposium B: Prof. C.A. BEERLI (Switzerland)
Mr. P. GAZZOLA (Italy)
Dr. LEISCHING (Austria)
Mr. R. LEMAIRE (Belgium)
Mr. F. MORENO BARBERA (Spain)
Mr. Henri DE MUN (France)
Min. Rat. C. PUTZ (Austria)
Mr. F. SORLIN (France)
Dr. K. STIGLBAUER (Austria)
Mr. Bruce WATKIN (United Kingdom) Dr. J. ZYKAN (Austria)

tax incentives, and public-private partnerships, were identified as crucial tools for enabling property owners and developers to undertake conservation projects.

Beyond the technical and legal aspects, the symposium emphasised the social and economic potential of repurposed heritage buildings. Delegates highlighted how adaptive reuse could revitalise communities by creating spaces for cultural, educational, or economic activities. This approach reflected an emerging perspective within the Council of Europe's heritage discourse: that heritage is not a static artefact requiring mere protection but an active resource capable of driving societal and economic development. In many ways, this marked a CoE heritage discourse's departure from the more preservation-focused AHD, situating heritage within a broader framework of utility and dynamism.

The culmination of the discussions was the adoption of the 'Vienna Recommendation', later endorsed by the Committee of Ministers of the Council of Europe in Resolution (66) 20 concerning new uses of monuments. By positioning adaptive reuse at the heart of conservation strategies, the symposium advanced a vision of historic buildings as living components of modern life, capable of contributing to contemporary societal needs while preserving their cultural essence.

The principles established in Vienna not only addressed immediate preservation challenges but also became foundational to the Council of Europe's broader commitment to integrated conservation. By advocating for a balance between heritage protection and functional reinvention, the symposium laid the groundwork for policies that continue to influence heritage management across Europe, reaffirming the cultural and economic relevance of historic sites in an ever-changing world.

2.2.3 Symposium C

The Bath Symposium of 1966 (3–7 October) convened experts to address the Principles and Practice of Active Preservation and Rehabilitation of groups and areas of buildings of historical and artistic interest.[32] In line with the previous symposia, the Bath meeting went further and supported the idea of a holistic approach to preservation. Participants advocated for embedding heritage protection within comprehensive urban development plans. This included rethinking traffic systems to prioritise pedestrian accessibility and

32 Council of Europe, Committee of Ministers, 'Symposium C – Principles and Practice of Active Preservation and Rehabilitation of Groups and Areas of Buildings of Historical or Artistic Interest, Bath 1966' [1967] COE.H.2.4/67 PR.

ensuring that urban expansions respected the historic scale and character of older neighbourhoods. Such measures were seen as essential not only for conserving architectural integrity but also for maintaining the social and cultural vibrancy of these areas.

It was at this meeting where the speakers, most notably the authors of the Venice Charter, R. Pane, P. Gazzola, and R. Lemaire took the opportunity to address already detected limitations of the document and to advocate for the integration of the protection of historic buildings into an overall plan covering the whole town. Therefore the Bath Symposium centred on advancing the concept of **integrated conservation**, emphasising the preservation and rehabilitation of groups and areas of historic and artistic value as a holistic endeavour. From this point on the concept of integrated preservation, which would be discussed further in the following chapters, became the key frame for the CoE's heritage policy.

The symposium was based on the ideas presented by Gazzola in his intervention that it was time to move from a single historical monument to the idea of historic, artistic areas.[33] Therefore, their preservation needs to be regarded in the broader context of urban and regional environments. Participants argued that historic areas derive their significance from the interplay of architecture, public spaces, and social functions, making it imperative to protect their cultural and physical coherence. Even though historical and artistic values still dominated the discussion, the significant shift happened in recognising the economic and social values of historic areas as crucial in their survival.

By linking heritage conservation to broader urban and regional plans, the symposium solidified integrated conservation as a guiding principle for cultural and spatial planning. The conclusions of the symposium were pronounced in the 'Bath Recommendation' that was later adopted by the Committee of Ministers of the CoE in Resolution (68)11 – *On the Principles and Practice of the Active Preservation and Rehabilitation of Groups and Areas of Buildings of Historical or Artistic Interest.*

2.2.4 Symposium D

The Hague Symposium of 1967 (22–27 May) brought together experts to explore the *Active Maintenance of Monuments, Groups, and Areas of Buildings of Historical or Artistic Interest within the Context of Regional Planning.*[34] This

33 Symposium C (n 32) 35.

34 Council of Europe, Committee of Ministers, 'Symposium D – Active Maintenance of Monuments, Groups and Areas of Buildings of Historical or Artistic Interest Within the Context of Regional Planning, The Hague 1967' [1967] COE.H.2.4/AC.

meeting marked a critical moment in advancing the integration of cultural heritage preservation into broader urban and regional planning frameworks. Building on earlier discussions, particularly the Bath Symposium of 1966, The Hague meeting reinforced the need for a cohesive approach that bridged the divide between monument protection and urban development, emphasising their mutual dependence for sustainable outcomes.

A key focus of the symposium was the recognition that traditional approaches, which often limited preservation to the restoration of isolated structures, were insufficient in addressing the complexities of contemporary urban expansion and societal needs. F.E. Kuyken, the General Rapporteur, argued compellingly for a shift toward adaptive reuse, ensuring that historic buildings and areas could accomplish new functions in modern contexts while preserving their historical significance.[35] This perspective was a natural evolution of ideas championed by Piero Gazzola, who had advocated for an expanded definition of cultural heritage, one that encompassed not only monumental structures but also their surroundings, vernacular architecture, and the social dynamics they sustain. The Hague Symposium thus reiterated the importance of protecting the cultural and physical coherence of historic environments, emphasising their broader urban and regional significance.

Economic considerations emerged as a prominent theme throughout the discussions. Participants, including Mr. Alomar, underscored the economic potential of heritage sites, particularly their role in fostering cultural tourism and stimulating local economies. The symposium advocated for innovative financial mechanisms, such as integrating preservation costs into urban development budgets and creating incentives for private investment. These strategies were seen as essential not only for ensuring adequate funding for conservation efforts but also for demonstrating the economic value of heritage to both policymakers and the general public.

Public engagement was another critical dimension of the symposium. As Kuyken and others noted, the level of public involvement varied significantly across planning systems.[36] Centralised systems often fostered passive compliance, whereas local systems provided greater opportunities for community participation. Speakers stressed the importance of empowering local populations to act as stewards of their heritage, arguing that well-informed, actively engaged communities were vital for the success and longevity of preservation initiatives.

---

35 Ibid.

36 Symposium D (n 34) 15.

The Hague Symposium ultimately reaffirmed and expanded upon the principles of integrated conservation, establishing it as a central tenet of the Council of Europe's heritage policy. By aligning conservation with urban and regional planning, the symposium framed heritage not as an obstacle to modernisation but as a dynamic asset. It underscored the necessity of interdisciplinary collaboration, participatory processes, and financial innovation in ensuring that Europe's cultural heritage remained a living and vital part of its future.

2.2.5 Symposium E

The fifth symposium, Symposium E, convened in Avignon in 1968 and focused on advancing the implementation of policies for preserving and revitalising historic areas and ensembles of artistic and cultural significance.[37] It reaffirmed the principles established in earlier meetings while introducing a forward-looking perspective: monuments and heritage experts were no longer to be seen as impediments to progress but as essential participants in regional planning and economic development. This shift underscored a vision of cultural heritage as a dynamic force within contemporary urban and economic life.

The Avignon meeting distinguished itself by embracing inclusivity. In the collaborative spirit of the European Cultural Convention, representatives from Eastern European countries, including Czechoslovakia, Yugoslavia, Poland, and the USSR, joined the discussions, alongside Portugal. This was a significant gesture during a time of ideological divides, and their contributions enriched the dialogue with diverse approaches to heritage preservation. Renowned figures like F. Sorlin, P. Gazzola, and R. Lemaire, who authored the Consolidated Report, lent their expertise to this closing gathering.

The concluding meeting in Avignon marked the final stage of what can be regarded as a technical phase of the CoE's actions in the field. Here, the CoE laid the basis for the essential principles of its new policy for the preservation and conservation of architectural heritage, 'this policy being based on the cultural, social and economic reality of a heritage which must be considered no longer as a burden but as a basic element in the life of each country'.[38] Gazzola summarised the principles guiding this vision as follows: (1) the con-

37 Council of Europe, Committee of Ministers, 'Symposium E – Policy for the Preservation and Rehabilitation, Avignon 1968' [1968] COE.H.2.3/68 PO.

38 Parliamentary Assembly, Committee on Culture and Education, 'Draft Report on the European Conference of Ministers Responsible for the Preservation and Rehabilitation of the Cultural Heritage of Monuments and Sites (Rapporteur Mr A Premoli' [1970] AS/Cult (21) 29.

cept of active rehabilitation, that is fundamental to the aim of preserving historical urban centres; (2) the principle of harmony between a monument and its setting; (3) the principle of social order and active rehabilitation – restoring to monuments and groups of buildings a function within the framework of present-day life and its requirements from an individual and social point of view. These principles were reiterated in the 'Avignon Recommendation', which once again highlighted the urgency of the meeting at the Ministers' level in order to define and implement those principles in a common European policy in the field.[39]

The newly defined heritage policy promoted during the CoE's symposia further accentuated the need to revise the Venice Charter. The process of reviewing the text, led by Lemaire and Gazzola, lasted through the 1970s and proved to be an unattainable ambition.[40] This long attempt illustrated the (to some extent surprising) unwillingness of the experts to challenge this, as Houbart called it, 'doctrinal monument'.[41] As Lemaire declared in 1995,[42] 'The success of the Charter hinders critique of its content ... It is believed irreplaceable because there is a well-founded fear that a new document might not achieve the same consensus.'[43]

The significance of the initiative for the revision of the Venice Charter, in the context of this research, rests in the fact that Lemaire, when faced with ICOMOS's reluctance to address the weaknesses of the Venice document regarding urban heritage, found the CoE to be a more accommodating environment for developing new principles for urban conservation. In 1971 he became deeply involved in the CoE's Committee on Monuments and Sites. As shown in the following section, this membership would allow him to greatly influence the CoE's heritage discourse by defining the general principles of the new CoE overall doctrine on preserving European architectural heritage: integrated conservation.

---

39 Symposium E (n 37).

40 See: Houbart (n 25) ; Alexander G Chalturin, 'The Fifth General Assembly of ICOMOS – 1978' (1995) 5 *Scientific Journal: Thirty Years of ICOMOS* 38; Jacques Dalibard, 'The Next 20 Years' (1989) 21(1) *APT Bulletin* 4.

41 Houbart (n 25).

42 Raymond Lemaire, *Faut-il Revoir la Charte de Venise?* (1995) 57.

43 Original text: Le succès de la Charte bloque la critique de son contenu...On le croit, donc, irremplaçable parce que, non sans raison, on craint de ne plus trouver le même accord général autour d'un document neuf.

2.3 *The Committee on Monuments and Sites*

After the sequence of five symposia had laid the groundwork for investigating the technical aspects of urban conservation, the time came to address the subject in the political context. It was also time to answer another request from the 1963 PACE Recommendation 365, which called for the European Conference on the Preservation and Development of Ancient Buildings and Historic and Artistic Sites to be organised within the framework of the CoE. The First Conference of European Ministers responsible for the Preservation and Rehabilitation of Cultural Heritage of Monuments and Sites was held in Brussels (25–27 November) in 1969, addressing the integration of monuments and sites into contemporary society as a 'major political problem'.[44] In the opinion of the European Ministers, this integration depended solely on the determination of governments, supported by the consensus of public opinion.[45]

The European Ministers acknowledged the results of the preliminary work done by the CoE and, based on it, put forward several recommendations for governments to consider in the form of two Resolutions.[46] Resolution number 2, among others, invited the CoE (1) to set up a specialised committee of government experts that would be responsible for drafting the legal text (convention/recommendation/resolution/charter), the future Committee on Monuments and Sites, and (2) to designate a year devoted to the preservation and rehabilitation of the cultural heritage of monuments and sites, a European Architectural Heritage Year (EAHY). Such a year would aim to raise awareness among the citizens of Europe of their common heritage and the urgent necessity for its preservation and integration into society.

Even though some Member States were not entirely convinced that there was a need for a special Committee on Monuments and Sites and considered that the actions envisaged could be dealt with within the existing CDCC, the majority voted in favour of such a committee. The Committee of Ministers established the Committee on Monuments and Sites in 1970 with a mandate

---

44 Council of Europe, Conference of Ministers Chiefly Responsible for the Preservation and Rehabilitation of Groups and Areas of Buildings of Historic or Artistic Interest, 'Report – Bases for Common European Action to Protect the Architectural Heritage of the Past' [1969] B (69) 71, 2.

45 Ibid

46 These included (1) the compilation of an inventory, defining the sites and monuments to be protected, (2) adaptation of laws and regulations in order to meet the requirements of active preservation and the integration of the monuments and sites within contemporary society, (3) integration of monuments and sites within the framework of a general policy for the town and country planning, (4) allocation of greater resources for financing the work of preservation and rehabilitation, as well as (5) training and awareness-raising measures.

of five years.[47] There are a few names among participants at the Committee's First Session (29 November–3 December 1971) worth emphasising: Italians Piero Gazzola, Cesare Brandi, and Roberto Pane; French Jean Sonnier, François Sorlin, and Michel Parent; Belgians Raymond Lemaire, Paul Philippot, and René Pechère; Austrians Gertrude Tripp and Walter Frodl; British Bernard Fielden and Sherban Cantacuzino; Dutch W.F. Schut; Turkish Cevat Erder.[48] The inclusion of experts in the preservation and rehabilitation of architectural heritage and experts in regional planning in the same committee was intended to generate a constructive dialogue resulting in actions that would integrate conservation into regional, economic, cultural, and social development. The Committee's programme focused on integrated conservation's normative, operational, and publicity aspects.

2.3.1 Committee on Monuments and Sites: Normative Aspect

One should bear in mind that the objective of the CoE, in comparison with ICOMOS and other professional organisations, was not to define or redefine a doctrine or techniques of conservation and preservation, but rather to provoke the evolution of heritage-related legislation and heritage policies in its Member States in line with social developments and changes. Nevertheless, the effectiveness of the planned new policy on the preservation of European built heritage, which would be based on integrating conservation into spatial planning policies, evidently required the definition of general principles that would serve as a basis for future legal texts.[49]

The task of defining the general principles was given to experts from ICOMOS. More specifically, the task was assigned to R. Lemaire, and he took advantage of the opportunity to address/revise the limitations of the Venice Charter concerning urban conservation. His intervention in the form of the general principles enabled the CoE to cultivate its distinctive heritage discourse. However, while Lemaire's General Principles (and, consequently, the CoE's twentieth-century heritage discourse that developed based on them)

---

47 Council of Europe, Committee of Ministers, 'Conclusions of the 191st Meeting of the Ministers' Deputies' [1970] CM/Del/Dec (70) 191.

48 Council of Europe, Committee on Monuments and Sites, '1st Session – Report' [1971] DELA/MS (71) 18.

49 According to the document from the first meeting of the Committee on Monuments and Sites, the common view was that 'the time is not yet ripe for the drafting on the Convention' but also the drafting of the Charter could not be regarded as a 'legal instrument' (DELA/MS(71)2). The drafting of the recommendation seemed like an optimal solution at that moment with the possible addition of a 'white paper' which, in addition to the recommendation, would contain analyses of the implementations of the general principles.

represented a certain evolution of conservation doctrine, generally speaking, they remained deeply rooted in the already established European value system of mid-twentieth-century conservation policies (AHD). This comes as no surprise if we take into account that the Committee on Monuments and Sites had instructed ICOMOS (that is, Lemaire) that, while drafting the General Principles, he should take into account the earlier work of the CoE and other intergovernmental institutions dealing with the matter, particularly: (1) the CoE PACE's Recommendation 612 on a draft outline law for the active protection of immovable cultural property in Europe (1970) and the conclusions of the five symposia; (2) the (at the time just drafted) UNESCO's World Heritage Convention (1972) and the Recommendation concerning the Protection, at National Level, of the Cultural and Natural Heritage (1972); (3) the ICOMOS's work based on the Venice Charter of 1964; and (4) work of Europa Nostra.

In defining architectural heritage, Lemaire repeated the revolutionary development enshrined in the Venice Charter, and further accentuated in outcomes of CoE symposia, the notion that the concept of architectural heritage was no longer confined to isolated architectural monuments but extended to cover a group of buildings, a district, or even an entire town, including 'lesser works that have acquired a cultural significance with the passing of time' (Venice Charter, Article 1). The direct effect this modification of the concept of architectural heritage had on the CoE was the apprehension of the inadequacy of existing legislation and administrative practice in its Member States. Therefore, including this new definition was the crucial element in defining the general principles that would serve as a basis for new CoE heritage policy, which would further inspire changes in the legislation of the CoE Member States. Based on this comprehensive understanding of architectural heritage, Lemaire defined the following general principles:

- The architectural heritage belongs to mankind;
- Responsibility for conservation of the architectural heritage lies first of all with the public;
- The public authorities, as trustees of public property, have a major responsibility for the conservation of the architectural heritage;
- Conservation must embrace the whole of the architectural heritage;
- The architectural heritage must be functionally integrated into the environment;
- The architectural heritage being an essential element of the environment, it is primarily at the level of regional and town planning, which shapes the environment, that measures for its conservation through institutionalised cooperation between those responsible for planning and for the heritage must be taken;

- The methods of conservation and revival of historic monuments and groups of buildings must be based on scientifically valid principles.[50]

These principles noticeably framed the conclusions of the CoE's preparatory work during symposia into a clear vision of the CoE's heritage discourse of the twentieth century. As already stated above while these principles stayed rooted in the well-established AHD value system, certain (and in the opinion of the author, momentous) divergences need to be highlighted.

To start with the recognisable AHD features Lemaire embedded into his principles, an existential assumption about the inherent value of monuments seems to be the most obvious one. As he stated in his report, 'it has come to be accepted that [the architectural heritage] is an invaluable source of history and that it is endowed with artistic merits that are often unequalled'.[51] Based on its historical and artistic values, architectural heritage is perceived to have universal values that belong to the whole of mankind (Principle 1). Therefore, the tendency of the AHD to favour the European elite's notions of heritage values was reaffirmed in Lemaire's principles, and as such in the CoE's twentieth-century heritage discourse. Another notable AHD features, that of the role of the nation-state/public authorities as the trustee of national cultural heritage (Principle 3) as well as the authority of expertise (Principle 7), were also reasserted and consequently authorised in the CoE's heritage texts.

Nevertheless, in line with the aim of the book to map the specific CoE heritage discourse the noticeable shifts from the AHD are more curious to look at. One example of this shift is seen in Lemaire's second principle, which states that 'responsibility for the conservation of the architectural heritage lies first of all with the public'. Even though he recognised in his third principle the role of the state and public authorities in conservation and preservation, he argued that 'in a democratic State action by the authority depends essentially on the will of its citizens'.[52] The second principle reflected, at the time, considerable concern about how social and economic changes experienced in the post-war period affected people's environment. The public fear of losing architectural heritage emerged as a part of the wider debate about environmental, political, and social issues, where care for heritage provided a point of focus through which the present and its relationship to the past can

50 Council of Europe, Committee on Monuments and Sites, 'Council of Europe Action for the Preservation and Rehabilitation of the Cultural Heritage of Monuments and Sites' [1971] DELA/MS (71) 1.

51 Council of Europe, Committee on Monuments and Sites, 'Towards a Comprehensive Policy of Conservation of the Architectural Heritage: General Principles – Professor R Lemaire' [1973] DELA/MS/CD (73) 1, 6.

52 DELA/MS/CD (73) 1 (n 51) 12.

be understood and negotiated.[53] The recognition by the CoE of the social value of heritage and the importance of public participation in its conservation represented a substantial modification from the up-to-then prevailing situation, in which historical heritage was utterly divorced from social life. As Lemaire pointed out,

> This awareness of the past is not, of course, equally shared by all and the physical need for it is far from being uniform. There can be no doubt, however, that, for a growing number of persons, this need [to preserve architectural heritage] is a real one and *determines the development of their personality*.[54]

With those observations in mind, the CoE understood that the effort to make people aware of their heritage and their rights and duties regarding its protection should be the basis of any future CoE policy aimed at conservation. This is not to say that the CoE did not sustain much of its debate about heritage around specific technical issues of heritage management and conservation practice. Rather, it enlarged certain elements within its discourse that distinguished and pursued agendas for social change. Another citation from Lemaire's report exemplifies this focus on the social aspect of heritage, which would be essential for the CoE AHD:

> The heritage as a whole fulfils a vital function for the twentieth-century citizen, going beyond his desire for culture or his scientific curiosity which, in themselves alone, justify and have in the past justified a policy of preservation; more than ever before, *conservation of that heritage is a major political fact fundamentally conducive to his way of life and his full development*.[55]

The CoE implied that the conservation of historic cities could not be approached solely as a problem of material conservation and protection. It was essential to consider the complexity and interdependence of numerous characteristics of historic towns, such as their architectural homogeneity, harmony, sense of place, and functionality for its citizens. The functional integration of the architectural heritage of historic cities in the environment (Principle 5), its harmonious coexistence with modern urban developments and its

---

53 Smith (n 1).

54 DELA/MS/CD (73) 1 (n 51) 8, [emphasis added].

55 DELA/MS/CD (73) 1 (n 51) 15, (emphasis added).

practical utilisation as the guarantee of a more balanced life for cities' citizens, formed the core of the CoE heritage conservation doctrine. The emphasis on the social value of heritage (built heritage) certainly reflects the organisation's preoccupation with the number of social issues in its Member States that the CoE was reflecting on. It undoubtedly echoed the organisation's priority of protecting human rights and its concern with the protection of individuals.

This CoE's pioneering recognition of the social aspects of heritage seems to be completely ignored in the growing literature that discusses and reflects on values in heritage debates and practices. As shown in Labadi,[56] social value does not figure in Riegl's[57] or Lipe's[58] typology and is usually presented as the originality of the Australian Burra Charter.[59] This impression that it was only with the Burra Charter that the social value of heritage was introduced has been repeated constantly in heritage studies literature and became, one could argue, 'the fact' connected with the Burra Charter. Nevertheless, as the overview of the CoE's activities presented here shows, the CoE recognised the social value of heritage as early as the late 1960s and developed its heritage discourse around it.

The same goes for economic value, which was included in Lipe's typology 'only' in 1984. Lemaire's report for the CoE from 1973 clearly stated,

> Apart from its high cultural and social value and its value in providing indispensable balance to the environment built by man and the community, the architectural heritage also has an unquestionable economic value that justifies its conservation.[60]

Contrary to the present-day direct association of tourism and the economic value of heritage, the CoE interestingly emphasised the importance of conservation of built heritage as a substantial element of housing for 'one half of the

56 Sophia Labadi, 'Representations of the Nation and Cultural Diversity in Discourses on World Heritage' (2007) 7(2) *Journal of Social Archaeology* 147.

57 Alois Riegl, 'The Modern Cult of Monuments: Its Essence and Its Development' in Nicholas Stanley-Price, Mansfield Kirby Talley Jr., and Alessandra Melucco Vaccaro (eds), *Historical and Philosophical Issues in the Conservation of Cultural Heritage* (Getty Conservation Institute 1996) 69.

58 William Lipe, 'Value and Meaning in Cultural Resources' in Henry Cleere (ed), *Approaches to the Archaeological Heritage: A Comparative Study of World Cultural Resource Management Systems* (CUP 1984) 1.

59 Australia ICOMOS, 'The Burra Charter: The Australia ICOMOS Charter for Places of Cultural Significance' (1979, revised 1981, 1988, 1999).

60 DELA/MS/CD (73) 1 (n 51) 9.

European population'.[61] The maintenance and conservation of historic urban centres, in the strictly material sense of the word, has been seen as a matter of good national resource management and, it can be argued, echoed the idea of sustainable development even though the concept of sustainable development was described only decades later by the 1987 Brundtland Commission Report. It is not to say that the economic value of heritage deriving from tourism wasn't recognised and underlined as an additional argument in favour of preserving the historic centres; nonetheless, this aspect of the economic value of heritage wasn't accentuated. This was to be expected, as this attitude mirrored the somewhat anti-commercial and anti-tourism ethos propagated by ICOMOS at its 1969 General Assembly in Oxford, and by Lemaire personally, who was continually warning against the over-exploitation of tourism and the threat to historic cities posed by tourism (even before the time of mass tourism as we know it today). This philosophy, as described shortly, would be prominent within the 1975 EAHY.

Therefore, by taking a more holistic approach to architectural heritage by recognising its cultural and historical but also social and economic values, Lemaire aimed to encourage CoE policymakers to shift their focus from the protection of single monuments towards policies that would look at the conservation of heritage as an essential part of wider spatial planning processes. The following part of the chapter will look closely at how these principles of integrated conservation were further promoted (EAHY), authorised and legitimised once they became built into the European Charter of the Architectural Heritage (1975) and, more importantly, into the CoE Convention for the Protection of the Architectural Heritage of Europe (1985) and as such became the basis of the CoE twentieth -century heritage discourse and European heritage legislation.

2.3.2 Committee on Monuments and Sites: Publicity Aspect

Once the General Principles[62] of integrated conservation were defined, the Committee of Monuments and Sites was committed to raising the public's interest in the problems faced by architectural heritage and to promoting its new conservation policy through the European Charter of the Architectural

---

61 DELA/MS/CD (73) 1 (n 51) 9.

62 However, not all the proposed ICOMOS/Lemaire's principles were accepted by the Committee on Monuments and Sites. Certain doubt was expressed by the Member States' politicians, stating that 'it seemed difficult not to say impossible for it to be made into a document that would attract universal support', however, 'it would have to remain in the form which its author had given it, and as such it would be a valuable contribution to the Committee's work' (DELA/MS (73) 15, p. 15).

Heritage. The publicity aspect of the work by the Committee on Monuments and Sites, that is, the public relations work with the purpose of developing public support for the new political decisions, was quite different from the legal and administrative actions directed at policymakers. It took the form of the European Architectural Heritage Year (EAHY), which was organised under the slogan 'A FUTURE FOR OUR PAST', and which aimed to 'make Europeans alive to the dangers threatening their heritage and the urgent need for measures of protection and of integrating this precious heritage in the society of today and tomorrow'.[63] The CoE's Committee of Ministers decided in January 1971 to declare 1975 the European Architectural Heritage Year. A conference in Zurich in 1973 launched the campaign, culminating two years later with the congress in Amsterdam where the European Charter of the Architectural Heritage (1975) was adopted.

The CoE's idea of organising the campaign and mobilising a range of actors in heritage protection can be considered a somewhat forward-looking approach when compared to, for example, ICOMOS' focus on promoting the Venice Charter exclusively to national authorities and professionals in the field. This was primarily because the CoE recognised that mobilising the public and spreading awareness of the importance of heritage among the public was a prerequisite for any successful heritage policy. And secondly, the CoE acknowledged early on that regional and local authorities, rather than national ones, have a central role to play in the process of heritage protection.[64]

The model of public engagement for the EAHY was found in the UK's Civic Trust, the charitable organisation founded in 1957 by Duncan Sandys. Indeed, not only was Sandys' model of public engagement applied as the 'best practice', but he personally became a guiding 'spirit' of the EAHY, marking the event with his political and social network. Before going back again to the roles of ICOMOS and Lemaire in drafting the European Charter of the Architectural Heritage and the Amsterdam Declaration as the final products of the EAHY, and the Charter's contribution to further enhancing the CoE heritage discourse, the next section of this chapter will look more closely into Sandys' success in turning the EAHY into a milestone of the CoE's heritage-related activities. More precisely, the next section will highlight certain AHD features,

63 Council of Europe, Committee on Monuments and Sites, 'Council of Europe Action for the Preservation and Rehabilitation of the Cultural Heritage of Monuments and Sites' [1971] DELA/MS (71) 1, 3.

64 This CoE's identification of the significance of local and regional authorities is manifested with the establishment of the Conference of Local Authorities of Europe in 1957. Already in 1963, the Conference expressed its interest in the protection of monuments and historic cities as a part of local development.

such as the role of the nation-state, of experts, the upper-class, and the establishment that the EAHY perpetuated, as well as innovative aspects of the event.

Duncan Sandys was the chairman of the Organising Committee of the EAHY and the author of a series of reports and recommendations on the programme's details.[65] The structure of the Organising Committee shows the remarkable interplay of ideas and influences of different players in the field, but also their unquestioned support for the event; representatives of the participating CoE Member States were on the board, along with representatives of other CoE bodies such as PACE and the European Conference of Local Authorities as well as representatives of other intergovernmental organisations such as the European Community, UNESCO, ICOMOS, Europa Nostra, and the European Travel Commission. With such membership, Sandys' role in linking various institutions and their interests was decisive for the EAHY to succeed.

Initially, as a well-known British pro-European politician, he played a significant role with his father-in-law Winston Churchill in the project of uniting Europe, starting from the Congress of Europe in 1948. Chapter 2 showed in some detail how much importance that Congress placed on cultural issues, and Duncan Sandys was one of the leading politicians advocating for it.[66] Consequently, following the creation of the CoE that was initiated at the Congress of Europe, he became deeply involved in the cultural work of the newly created organisation. At the time of the preparations for the EAHY, being the chairman of the Organising Committee was just one of the positions he held. Sandys was also a member of PACE's Cultural Committee, a long-serving member of the Committee on Monuments and Sites, and the president of Europa Nostra from 1969 to 1984.[67] In this regard, the EAHY is also a great illustration of where the influence of personal, political, and transnational networks on a specific project could be observed.[68]

---

65 See, for example, PACE Recommendation 532 (1972) and Recommendation 681 (1972) on the protection of Europe's architectural heritage; PACE [1972] Doc. 3183 – Report on the protection of Europe's architectural heritage; CoE, PACE [1974] Doc. 3522 – Report on the conservation of Europe's architectural heritage; PACE Recommendation 750 [1975] on the conservation of Europe's architectural heritage.

66 Council of Europe, *Congress of Europe* (Council of Europe Publishing 1999).

67 He was succeeded at the position of president by Hans de Koster, who had previously presided over the Parliamentary Assembly.

68 Kiran Klaus Patel and Oriane Calligaro, 'The True "EURESCO"? The Council of Europe, Transnational Networking and the Emergence of European Community Cultural Policies, 1970–90' (2017) 24(3) *European Review of History* 399.

2.3.3 Public Engagement vs. Elitism as Part of AHD

When the CoE referred to the role of the public in the context of the EAHY, an immediate connection was made with Europa Nostra, the pan-European federation of non-governmental heritage organisations. Its importance in the context of the EAHY lies in the fact that Europa Nostra's participation was considered to be a crucial element of the EAHY's public engagement. However, even though the potential of the citizens' initiatives was recognised as critical by the CoE, this prospect was essentially obscured by the reality of Europa Nostra's strong political, elitist, and expert influence, with the end result that it supported a series of effectively top-down projects as part of the EAHY.[69] Europa Nostra's activities and ideas of heritage derived primarily from the experiences of the ruling and upper-middle class. Its members were predominantly elitist private organisations originating in the upper class's involvement in the early preservation and conservation movement. Its political network also accentuates the elitist aura of the organisation. It is important here to underline that Europa Nostra originated in the CoE. The PACE's Cultural and Scientific Committee, in which Sandys had a prominent role, called for a meeting of representatives of private organisations for the preservation and development of ancient buildings and sites. This initiative led to the creation of Europa Nostra in 1963.[70] Since its creation, it was closely connected with the work of the CoE and has had a consultative status within the organisation. Through several reports and recommendations, Sandys assured its central role in realising not only the EAHY but also a number of other CoE heritage projects.[71] As a leading German CoE cultural politician stated in Patel and Calligaro, 'Sandys accomplished that great job of turning *Europa Nostra* into a heavyweight; an index fossil for our work at the Council of Europe.'[72]

Thus, it is not surprising that with all the influence of the strongly expert-dominated establishment bodies like ICOMOS, Europa Nostra's upper-class connotations, and political establishment support, the EAHY was seen as a decidedly elitist event.[73] The EAHY, even though it referred to the social values

69 Michael Falser and Wilfried Lipp (eds), *A Future for Our Past: The 40th Anniversary of European Architectural Heritage Year (1975–2015)* (Hendrik Bäßler Verlag 2015).

70 Parliamentary Assembly, Committee on Culture and Education, 'Information Document on 6th General Assembly of Europa Nostra' [1969] AS/Cult (21) 13.

71 For example, by securing the CoE funding for the EAHY film project done by *Europa Nostra.*

72 Patel and Calligaro (n 68) 405.

73 Miles Glendinning, 'The European Architectural Heritage Year and UNESCO World Heritage: The Hare and the Tortoise?' in Michael Falser and Wilfried Lipp (eds), *A Future for Our Past: The 40th Anniversary of European Architectural Heritage Year (1975–2015)* (Hendrik Bäßler Verlag 2015).

of heritage and the importance of public engagement, mostly strengthened the degree to which the establishment and upper class's experiences and understanding of the importance of material culture became embedded in the CoE twentieth-century heritage discourse.[74]

This elitist manifestation was reproduced further in the EAHY National Committees in the participating countries. One, possibly the most palpable, example of this could be seen in the United Kingdom's Council for EAHY. This Council's President was HRH the Duke of Edinburgh, and it included four Secretaries of State as Vice-Presidents; among its 114 members were the Archbishop of Canterbury, the Archbishop of Westminster, and the Chief Rabbi. The Countess of Dartford chaired the Executive Committee of fourteen members, including Lord Duncan Sandys, the Duke of Grafton, and Viscount Muirshiel.[75] On the other hand, the example of the Dutch organising committee, with members who were predominantly amateurs (lovers of heritage), could be regarded as a more genuine public engagement effort. However, in terms of class, those members belonged foremost to the 'civilised establishment', and even though the rehabilitation of the Jordaan district in Amsterdam – originally built for the working class – was selected as one of the EAHY pilot projects, it was hard to subdue the impression of cultural elitism.[76]

2.3.3.1 *Role of Local and Regional Authorities vs. Nationalism as a Part of* AHD

In line with the EAHY's priority of public engagement, the recognition of the role of local and regional authorities in heritage conservation and protection was an additional element that the event promoted heavily. Nevertheless, the role of the nation-state – yet another feature of the AHD embedded in the EAHY – was favoured through the establishment of national organising committees. While the CoE coordinated the activities at the European level, most of the actions, given the CoE's limited budget, had to be planned and organised at the national, regional, or local levels.[77] Therefore, Sandys prioritised setting up influential National Committees (under the highest patronage) to

74 Smith (n 1).

75 John Delafons, *Politics and Preservation: A Policy History of the Built Heritage, 1882–1996* (E & FN Spon 1997).

76 Marieke Kuipers, 'Dutch Conversions in Conservation: The European Architectural Heritage Year and its Aftermath in the Netherlands' in Michael Falser and Wilfried Lipp (eds), *A Future for Our Past: The 40th Anniversary of European Architectural Heritage Year (1975–2015)* (Hendrik Bäßler Verlag 2015) 239.

77 Council of Europe, Committee on Monuments and Sites, 'EAHY 1975 – Table of Activities Undertaken by the National Committees' [1975] DELA/MS/Inf (75) 4.

manage the campaign in member countries. Those national committees acted as umbrella organisations for various local events. Since the EAHY initiative was centred around raising awareness of the threats to and the importance of architectural heritage, a significant part of the national committees' work encompassed the dissemination of information. Printed material, numerous radio and television reportages, film (produced by Europa Nostra), news, interviews and discussions on national televisions, and commemorative stamps and coins were some of the means that national committees used in celebrating the EAHY.[78]

In addition to promotional activities, Sandys was aware that mere declarations of good intent and statements of broad principle would not be enough. The attempt to influence public opinion had to be made with concrete examples that would demonstrate the soundness of the philosophy underlying the new policy and the effectiveness of the methods used for its implementation. Each participating country was asked to nominate a site(s) representing exemplary restoration. Among the 51 selected projects proposed were Colmar and Rouen in France, Salzburg in Austria, Bruges in Belgium, Bologna, Taranto, and Verona in Italy, and Amsterdam and Middelburg in the Netherlands.[79] Even though there were certain attempts at local voluntary participation, these projects were unsurprisingly dominated by (national) experts. The result of the establishment-dominated organisational formula of the EAHY national initiatives was that only conventional and well-established national projects were featured in the pilot studies, and an exceptional opportunity for a more bottom-up approach was missed.[80] The lessons of these pilot projects were evaluated and synthesised in the European Charter at the EAHY closing event, the Congress in Amsterdam, discussed in the following section.

2.3.3.2 *The Political Aspect of the EAHY*

Furthermore, mention must be made of the political influence of the EAHY. In line with the earlier CoE practice introduced with the European Cultural Convention (1954), Sandys, who saw heritage as a pan-European phenomenon that could be used for the development of cooperation among otherwise ideologically divided countries, supported the idea of opening the EAHY for participation to European societies beyond the CoE membership.[81] The EAHY,

78 A detailed table of activities undertaken by the national committees during the EAHY can be found in the document DELA/MS/Inf (75) 4 (n 77).

79 DELA/MS/Inf (75) 4 (n 77).

80 Glendinning (n 73).

81 Duncan Sandys, 'European Architectural Heritage Year' (1975) 23 *Annuaire Européen/European Yearbook* 124.

with its seemingly non-ideological character, was also acceptable for non-democratic European states; Spain, Portugal, Czechoslovakia, Yugoslavia, Poland, Hungary, Romania, and the Soviet Union all participated in the campaign.

Furthermore, the event was used for building stronger relations around heritage matters with the European Community (EC). Sandys' success in getting the endorsement for the event from the EC also marks one of the first actions carried out by the EC on European heritage issues. Besides Sandys, other British politicians played a significant part in this process. While completely inactive in the heritage field during the formative stage of the EAHY, the EC stepped in only in 1974 with the Report for the European Parliament's Committee on Cultural Affairs and Youth, authored by conservative British MP Lady Elles. The Elles Report suggested creating an inventory of Europe's artistic treasures, proposed a fund that would provide financial support for the most urgent restoration work, and called for support for the EAHY, among other things.[82] According to Patel and Calligaro, some specific links could also be behind this 'sudden support' for the EAHY.[83] Elles's report drew heavily on the initiative submitted by the Liberal and Allies group in the EP in 1973.[84] This initiative, considered to be the starting point for the discussion on heritage at the EP, was authored by Italian MP Augusto Premoli, a Chairman of the EP Sub-Committee on Historical and Artistic Monuments and Sites. Even though Elles was a member of the conservative party, and in this capacity, a colleague of Duncan Sandys in the House of Lords, that did not impede her collaboration with liberal Premoli on the subject. Premoli, however, had only joined the EP in 1972 after spending some years in PACE, where he worked on cultural issues with Sandys. The fact that he was also a member of the CDCC and that, in 1970, he had been the rapporteur recommending the EAHY in PACE explains his actions at the EC level.[85] Ultimately, he played a key role in starting the debate within the CoE,

---

82 European Parliament, 'Report Drawn Up on Behalf of the Committee on Cultural Affairs and Youth on the Motion for a Resolution Submitted by Mr Premoli on Behalf of the Liberal and Allies Group on Measures to Protect the European Cultural Heritage' [1974] (Rapporteur Lady Elles, Document 54/74).

83 Patel and Calligaro (n 68).

84 European Parliament, Motion for a Resolution Submitted by Mr Hougardy on Behalf of the Liberal and Allies Group on Measures to Protect the European Cultural Heritage [1973] Document 73/73.

85 Parliamentary Assembly, Committee on Culture and Education, 'Draft Report on the European Conference of Ministers Responsible for the Preservation and Rehabilitation of the Cultural Heritage of Monuments and Sites (Rapporteur Mr A Premoli' [1970] AS/Cult (21) 29.

and he came to play the same role in the EC a few years later.[86] Elles's report was discussed at the EP Session of May 1974, where the EAHY was endorsed and the EP adopted the Resolution supporting the event.[87] The EC Commission followed up in December 1974 with its Recommendation, urging the EC Member States to sign or ratify the UNESCO World Heritage Convention and also to 'actively support the actions taken in execution of the initiatives of the CoE in connection with the European Architectural Heritage Year, 1975' (Commission Recommendation).[88] With these details and individuals in mind, it can be argued that inter-organisational cooperation among CoE and the EC on specific projects, like the EAHY, was not the initiative of the organisations *per se* but rather the enterprise of a few individual actors who managed to influence not only national but also European policies. Nonetheless, the EC support for the EAHY marks the beginning of a long period of cooperation between two European organisations, in which, most of the time, the CoE worked as the laboratory of ideas that the EC/EU later embraced.

2.3.3.3 *European Charter of the Architectural Heritage*

The EAHY campaign culminated in the Amsterdam Congress, which brought together the most prominent players from all parts of Europe working on preserving architectural heritage. As the final act, the Congress adopted two documents: the *European Charter of the Architectural Heritage* and the *Declaration of Amsterdam*, which are still considered landmarks in scientific thinking and the CoE's policy orientations in heritage matters.[89] The Declaration of Amsterdam addressed its detailed recommendations and conclusions based on the discussions at the Congress. It was presented to the CoE, the EC, and the governments of all the countries represented in Amsterdam, as well as to the principal NGOs in the field, local authorities, industry, architectural and cultural associations, and other interested stakeholders. On the other hand, the European Charter of the Architectural Heritage, adopted by the Committee of Ministers of the CoE and proclaimed at the Congress, was dedicated to the wider public and specifically designed to impact public opinion regarding the new European preservation policy.

---

86 Patel and Calligaro (n 68).

87 Debates of the EP, May 1974, No 176.

88 European Commission, 'Recommendation to Member States Concerning the Protection of the Architectural and Natural Heritage' [1974] 75/65/EEC.

89 Council of Europe, 'European Charter of the Architectural Heritage' (1975); Council of Europe, Congress on the European Architectural Heritage, 'Amsterdam Declaration' (1975).

The Charter, which was tailored to the specific circumstances of Europe, aimed to define (and authorise and legitimise) the principles of the new common European policy for the protection of architectural heritage. Just as the 1979 Burra Charter was arguably drafted for the specific Australian context as a response to the unchangeable Venice Charter, the European Charter did the same for the European context, demonstrating that even though the Venice Charter was and is considered to be an essentially Eurocentric document, it did not offer a sufficient framework for regional (European) specific problems.

In its ten principles, the European Charter defined the nature of European architectural heritage and the threats to it and offered the integrated conservation approach as the solution.[90] Lemaire's General Principles were essentially reasserted and legitimised in the Charter, addressing the shortcomings of the Venice Charter. Sensitive restoration techniques, the correct choice of appropriate functions for architectural heritage, the effective use of laws and regulations, the appropriate administrative support, and adequate technical and financial support represented the main components of this new approach.[91] And while most of the technical aspects repeated the principles declared in the Venice Charter and other notions already discussed at different levels, in the European Charter, the CoE introduced the heretofore rather neglected social aspect of heritage.

In including the social aspect of heritage (such as its role in attaining a balanced and complete life for individuals (Principle 2) or its importance for achieving a harmonious social balance that includes a more satisfactory social mix (Principle 4)), the European Charter departs substantially from the AHD,

---

90 Principles of the European Charter:
1. The European architectural heritage consists not only of our most important monuments: it also includes the groups of lesser buildings in our old towns and characteristic villages in their natural or manmade setting;
2. The past as embodied in the architectural heritage provides the sort of environment indispensable to a balanced and complete life;
3. The architectural heritage is a capital of irreplaceable spiritual, cultural, social and economic value;
4. The structure of historic centres and sites is conducive to a harmonious social balance;
5. The architectural heritage has an important part to play in education;
6. This heritage is in danger;
7. Integrated conservation averts these dangers;
8. Integrated conservation depends on legal, administrative, financial and technical support;
9. Integrated conservation cannot succeed without the cooperation of all;
10. The European architectural heritage is the common property of our continent.

91 European Charter of the Architectural Heritage [1975] (n 89).

acknowledging the 'work that heritage does as a social and cultural practice'.[92] According to Interviewee 3, the inclusion of social aspects in the document was largely the work of the CoE Secretariat, who insisted on and managed to insert this provision in the final text of the Charter.[93] More specifically, according to Interviewee 3, it was a personal endeavour of Nicolaus Sombart, a German cultural sociologist, historian, and writer working at the CoE Division on Regional Planning, Monuments and Sites.[94] His ideas on the social importance of heritage aligned with Lemaire's and Gazzola's attitudes. They were, in addition, influenced by the work of the pioneers of modern preservation and conservation, such as Max Dvořák and Alois Riegl, but mostly by the early twentieth-century work of Gustavo Giovannoni.[95]

In this sense, one can identify the intellectual roots of the European Charter and the whole EAHY project in Giovannoni's model of urban conservation. His model, which at the time contrasted with the prevailing trend of one-dimensional urban development suggested by CIAM (the International Congress of Modern Architecture), focused on connecting the historic city and modern developments as well as the functional utilisation of historic areas. Giovannoni argued that as a precondition for his model to succeed, historical areas needed to be considered an integral part of urban and regional planning that embraced both social and functional aspects. He emphasised the significance of the everyday 'lesser' important urban heritage and the need for socially committed conservation embedded in the planning and education system.[96]

Giovannoni's model of urban conservation presented the most important counterbalance to the radically anti-historic doctrine of CIAM. His influence on Gazzola, who was one of his students,[97] and consequently on Lemaire and ICOMOS, who played a crucial role in defining the philosophy behind the EAHY, ensured that a somewhat anti-modern and anti-commercial ethos

92 Smith (n 1) 11; Principle 7 argue among others: 'Their deterioration must be undertaken in a spirit of social justice and should not cause the departure of the poorer inhabitants.'

93 Interview 3 with Former Employee of Council of Europe's Cultural Policy Division (3 February 2020).

94 Interview 3 (n 93); Nicolaus Sombart was the son of Werner Sombart, who was one of the leading European social scientists at the beginning of the twentieth century.

95 Michael Falser and Wilfried Lipp (n.69).

96 Glendinning (n 73).

97 A generation of architects was trained as experts in monument restoration at the height of Giovannoni's prestige as a scholar and theorist; among them were Piero Gazzola, Alfredo Barbacci, Guglielmo De Angelis d'Ossat, Roberto Pane, to name just a few of those who later influenced the development of European (and international) urban conservation doctrine (Zucconi 2014).

would be prominent within the EAHY.[98] The European Charter (Principle 3) reflects this ethos clearly when stating that 'the destruction of any part of [heritage] leaves us poorer since *nothing new that we create*, however fine, will make good the loss'.[99] The charter argues further that people, faced with a rapidly changing civilisation, have 'an instinctive feeling for the value of this heritage'.[100] In addition to seeing the EAHY as what Glendinning calls a celebration of victory in Western Europe over the 'fallen colossus of modern architecture',[101] ICOMOS used the campaign to propagate its anti-tourism agenda further. The idea of a threat to heritage posed by tourism was already present at the ICOMOS General Assembly in 1969 (Oxford). It was further emphasised during the EAHY when ICOMOS convened a symposium on the challenges facing small historic towns in Rothenburg ob der Tauber.[102] Its proceedings, chaired by Lemaire, warned against the over-exploitation of tourism, and this notion was firmly incorporated in the philosophy of EAHY and the European Charter, mostly through Lemaire's authority.

The inclusion of the social aspect of heritage, and its role for the individual's balanced life, along with the definition of the integrated conservation concept in the European Charter are unquestionably the most important achievements of the EAHY campaign. They form the basis for the CoE's twentieth-century heritage discourse. However, the mention of another important element that diversifies the European Charter from the Venice Charter needs to be acknowledged – the role of training for specialised architects, technicians, and craftsmen (Principle 8). The question of training of the specialists required for the successful implementation of the integrated conservation concept was already incorporated in the preparatory work of the EAHY.[103] Its inclusion in the European Charter as one of the essential elements on which integrated conservation depends was highly supported by ICCROM, for which the training of specialists became a priority.[104] The training element of integrated conservation, as described in greater detail in the next chapter, would also represent a signifi-

98 Guido Zucconi, 'Gustavo Giovannoni: A Theory and a Practice of Urban Conservation' (2014) 4(1) *Change Over Time* 76.

99 European Charter of the Architectural Heritage [1975] (n 89) Principle 3.

100 Ibid, Principle 2.

101 Glendinning (n 73) 93.

102 Ibid.

103 Cevat Erder, *The Venice Charter Under Review* (1977).

104 Jukka Jokilehto and Mehr-Ali Soheil, 'Development of ICCROM's Architectural Conservation Training in Reference to Council of Europe Initiatives' in Michael Falser and Wilfried Lipp (eds), *A Future for Our Past: The 40th Anniversary of European Architectural Heritage Year (1975–2015)* (Hendrik Bäßler Verlag 2015) 104.

cant part of the CoE's activities in the architectural heritage domain for decades to come.

3 Conclusion of the Chapter

The formative years of international conservation policies saw intense cooperation and the exchange of opinions and ideas among international organisations with a mandate in heritage protection. Therefore, it is clear that the CoE's interest and involvement in the subject cannot be looked at in isolation. As explored in the chapter, ICOMOS and its Venice Charter in particular, or rather the reaction to it, had a critical impact on the discourse the CoE decided to develop. The CoE understood that the conservation of historic cities could not be approached solely as the problem of material conservation and protection. It was essential to consider the complexity and interdependence of numerous characteristics of historic towns, such as their architectural homogeneity, harmony, sense of place, and functionality for its citizens. The defining of the CoE's General Principles of Integrated Conservation approach in the early 1970s, whereby the CoE's discourse was clearly outlined, marked a critical point in scientific thinking and the CoE's policy orientations in heritage matters.

In this context, two essential CoE contributions of the time, the EAHY and its final product, the European Charter, can also be seen as key moments in the evolution of integrated conservation approaches as the base for the CoE's twentieth-century heritage discourse. As described in this chapter, the campaign was part of a much longer process. The concept of integrated conservation, which had been developing over years of preparatory work at the CoE level, has finally 'become the major requirement of any cultural heritage policy' in Europe.[105] In this context, the EAHY succeeded in serving both purposes: it sparked a renewed interest in architectural heritage among the public and promoted its active defence. The campaign undoubtedly stimulated governments to pass new laws and encouraged local authorities to show increased attentiveness to the protection of their heritage.

The end of the campaign, at the CoE level, marked only the beginning of an important chapter in the organisation's involvement in heritage matters, and

---

105 Jean-Louis Luxen, 'Les fondateurs de l'ICOMOS et la Campagne européenne de 1975' in Michael Falser and Wilfried Lipp (eds), *A Future for Our Past: The 40th Anniversary of European Architectural Heritage Year (1975–2015)* (Hendrik Bäßler Verlag 2015) 89; Original text: 'devenue l'exigence majeure de toute politique du patrimoine culturel'.

it firmly established the basis for a distinctive CoE twentieth-century heritage discourse. The chapter that follows moves on to consider the *Convention for the Protection of the Architectural Heritage* (Granada Convention, 1985), which set up a legally binding procedure (rather than a charter) for signatory parties to establish statutory measures of integrated urban conservation.

CHAPTER 4

Convention for the Protection of the Architectural Heritage of Europe

1 Introduction

As discussed in the previous chapter, the CoE started developing its distinctive approach to the protection of architectural heritage at the same time as other international organisations with a mandate in the field (UNESCO, ICOMOS). The CoE's involvement in the matter, in particular, came as a response to widespread threats to the urban heritage of European historic cities. It became obvious to the CoE that the predominant policy of piecemeal conservation of monuments that neglected the protection of monuments' surroundings was no longer sustainable and needed to be revised. The CoE's heritage discourse, shaped as a response to acknowledged limitations in heritage policies across Europe, developed gradually over several years.

The principles on which the new CoE policy for conservation of architectural heritage was based, defined, and promoted in several documents that were to become the foundation for the CoE's future actions in the field: the European Charter of the Architectural Heritage, the Amsterdam Declaration, and Resolution (76) 28 concerning the adaptation of laws and regulations to the requirements of integrated conservation of architectural heritage. The two most important principles underlying the new European conservation policy framed by the CoE were (1) the transition from the piecemeal conservation of monuments to a comprehensive conservation of the architectural heritage and (2) the transition from conservation in the sense of restoration to integrated conservation, promoting the inclusion of heritage in urban planning. These principles were widely promoted during the European Architectural Heritage Year (1975). According to the CoE's report, integrated conservation schemes were 'enthusiastically received by local communities and authorities'.[1] However, the new CoE conservation policy also implied major reforms

1 Parliamentary Assembly, 'Communication from the Committee of Ministers Transmitting to the Assembly the Report of the Steering Committee for Regional Planning and the Architectural Heritage on the Situation of the Architectural Heritage in Europe' [1979] Doc 4300.

 | DOI:10.1163/9789004756250_005

in legal, financial, scientific, and technical means of action that Member States needed to address.

In this chapter, the focus will be on the CoE's efforts to maintain political and public interest in heritage conservation issues in the period after the EAHY in 1975 and to help its Member States in their efforts to implement a newly defined conservation policy. The first part explores the impact of the CoE's initial integrated-conservation-based actions. More precisely, a section will offer a review of the impact those activities had on the state of architectural heritage in Europe and the reasons why the CoE felt the drafting of the Convention for the Protection of the Architectural Heritage in 1985 (Granada Convention) was desirable.

The second part of the chapter will look closely at the text of the Granada Convention, especially its role in authorising and legitimising the concept of 'integrated conservation' as an essential part of the CoE's heritage discourse. As it will be argued through the rest of this volume, even though integrated conservation was officialised in a rather 'conservative' 1985 Convention, it continued to be a critical part of the CoE's heritage discourse and was reflected in all subsequent CoE heritage conventions and projects (even after the CoE's profound heritage discourse shift in the new millennium that came with the Faro Convention).

The development of other projects, like the Council of Europe Technical Cooperation and Consultancy Programme (TCCP), European Heritage Days (EHD), or Cultural Routes of the Council of Europe, which originated within the framework of the Granada Convention, can serve as an illustration of this statement. As the short overview of TCCP will show, the CoE developed, to a certain extent even inadvertently, a concept that proved to be adjustable enough to accommodate and adapt to all consecutive advances in heritage protection theory and practice, as well as all consequent CoE's political priorities.

This chapter, which is informed primarily by archival resources and information gathered through interviews, aims to explore the context and motivations behind one of the most successful CoE heritage texts, the 1985 Convention for the Protection of the Architectural Heritage. As will be argued, it was with this convention that the CoE framed its heritage discourse more clearly and established, with the introduction of the concept of integrated conservation, an enduring model for its heritage policies.

2 Towards the Architectural Heritage Convention

The EAHY of 1975 certainly had a significant influence in establishing the protection of heritage as one of the CoE's competencies, and it was important for the organisation to use the success of that event for its future actions. The concept of integrated conservation was successfully introduced through the EAHY and has been enshrined in the European Charter of the Architectural Heritage and the Declaration of Amsterdam. Those texts marked an important landmark in European thinking about the conservation of architectural heritage as well as comprising a critical step in how the CoE moved its heritage discourse away from the AHD. The need to 'integrate' conservation in town planning, to preserve groups of historic buildings and their environment, and to see heritage as a part of economic and social life was thereafter generally recognised as the specificity of the CoE discourse and, as such, was welcomed by the CoE Member States (Explanatory Report to the Convention for the Protection of the Architectural Heritage of Europe). However, the Member States further asked the CoE to develop a more comprehensive basis for adapting laws and regulations to meet the requirements of integrated conservation.

The result came in the form of the Resolution Concerning the Adaptation of Laws and Regulations to the Requirements of Integrated Conservation of the Architectural Heritage.[2] This Resolution marked the beginning of enhanced intergovernmental cooperation in heritage protection among the CoE Member States, and together with the European Charter and Amsterdam Declaration, marked the beginning of a uniform European heritage protection standard-setting. Resolution (76) 28 specifies that:

> By the 'integrated conservation' of the cultural heritage of monuments and sites is meant the whole **range of measures** aimed at ensuring the perpetuation of that heritage, its maintenance as part of an appropriate environment, whether man-made or natural, its utilisation and its adaptation to the needs of society.[3]

These measures should aim to ensure the physical preservation of monuments and groups of buildings but also should make sure that monuments and his-

2 Council of Europe, Committee of Ministers, '*Resolution (76) 28 – Concerning the Adaptation of Laws and Regulations to the Requirements of Integrated Conservation of the Architectural Heritage*' [1976].

3 Resolution (76) 28 (n 2) 2, (emphasis added).

torical buildings are integrated into the physical environment of present-day society. The revitalisation and rehabilitation of monuments and old buildings by assigning them a social purpose and adapting them to the needs of modern life were among the main objectives promoted by the Resolution. These Resolution's objectives, as seen by Pickard,[4] are still relevant today because their approach ultimately echoes sustainable development principles.[5] In addition, these objectives, by introducing the protection of vernacular heritage ('particularly those intended for habitation'),[6] clearly differentiated the CoE heritage discourse from the AHD and its focus on 'aesthetically pleasing material objects, sites, places and/or landscapes', that have intrinsic and immutable cultural values.[7] This is a point the discussion will return to shortly.

The predominant opinion in the immediate post-EAHY period (1976–1980) among the CoE Member States was that it was too early for a convention on the subject and that the principles of the new discourse outlined in the 1975 Charter and Resolution (76) 28 would be sufficient for the desirable changes in heritage conservation in Europe to take place. Nonetheless, the CoE tried further to influence Member States' actions and to sustain their interest in the issues of integrated conservation with additional recommendations.[8] Firstly, it was recognised that new skills would be indispensable for a new policy to be successfully implemented. The need for specialised, multidisciplinary training of architects, town planners, civil engineers, and landscape designers was underlined in the Committee of Ministers' Recommendation No. R (80) 16. Even though the authority of expertise is clearly emphasised in the Recommendation, it can be argued that, here again, the CoE's text extends debate and practice outside of the framework established by the AHD. It advocated for the training to begin in primary and secondary schools which 'should above all encourage a sense of observation, the perception of space, a critical spirit, creativity, awareness of social interdependence, a pride in past values

4 Robert Pickard, 'Management Strategies for Historic Towns in Europe' in Sophia Labadi and William Logan (eds), *Urban Heritage, Development and Sustainability* (Routledge 2015) 151.

5 Even though the concept of sustainable development as is known today was not defined in 1976.

6 Resolution (76) 28 (n 2) 2.

7 Laurajane Smith, *Uses of Heritage* (Routledge 2006) 29.

8 PACE Recommendation 880 (1979) on Conservation of the European architectural heritage; Committee of Ministers' Recommendation No. R (80) 16 on the specialised training of architects, town planners, civil engineers and landscape designers; Recommendation No. R (81) 13 on the action in aid of certain declining craft trades in the context of craft activity.

and respect for the environment'.[9] This approach, the CoE envisaged, would lead to an appreciation of architectural heritage and an eagerness for its protection across a broad sector of society and would incite public participation in decision-making.

Moreover, as stated by PACE Rapporteur Mr. Schwencke, 'Conservation needs craftsmen'.[10] In that regard, the CoE steadily promoted the importance of the transmission of old crafts and skills. For example, Recommendation No. R (81) 13 aimed at preventing the decline of traditional crafts that 'have helped to shape the artistic and cultural heritage of Europe'.[11] Another noteworthy project was the establishment of the European Centre for Training Craftsmen in the Conservation of the Architectural Heritage in Venice (1977). The aim was to provide specialised training in conservation to as many European craftsmen as possible and, at the same time, to play a part in saving Venice's architectural treasures. It was also important for the CoE to demonstrate, through the example of Venice, the worth of the concept and policy of integrated conservation, where the aim was not merely to save the great monuments, but to preserve a living city in 'which the past may find a future'.[12]

However, notwithstanding all the aforementioned initiatives, there was a general dissatisfaction among members of the PACE and the CoE Secretariat with the somehow unambitious and limited CoE Medium-Term Plan (1976–1980) for actions in heritage matters. In its report, the PACE expressed discontent with the work done on maintaining public interest in the architectural heritage created by the campaign of 1975.[13] It stated that despite repeated assurances from the representatives of the Committee of Ministers, very little had been done, and the resources (funds and staff) had not been available for the Secretariat to handle or produce suitable information material.[14]

---

9 Council of Europe, Committee of Ministers, '*Recommendation No R (80) 16 of the Committee of Ministers to Member States on the Specialised Training of Architects, Town Planners, Civil Engineers and Landscape Designers*' [1980] 2.

10 Parliamentary Assembly, 'Report on the European Foundation Pro Venetia Viva and the European Centre for the Training of Craftsmen in the Conservation of the Architectural Heritage' [1978] Doc 4190, 9.

11 Council of Europe, Committee of Ministers, 'Recommendation No R (81) 13 on the Action in Aid of Certain Declining Craft Trades in the Context of Craft Activity' [1981] 1.

12 PACE Doc, 4190 (n 10) 9.

13 The activities of making citizens aware of their architectural heritage resulted in CoE's bulletin 'Future for our past', with the first issue only in 1980.

14 Parliamentary Assembly, Committee on Culture and Education, Sub-Committee on the Architectural and Artistic Heritage of Europe, 'Draft Minutes of the Meeting (14 September 1978)' [1978] AS/Cult/AA (30) PV 2.

Further insight into the state of the architectural heritage in Europe was offered in the two reports on the issue requested by the PACE in 1979 and 1982.[15] On the positive side, the report from 1982 confirmed the general picture of steady improvement in legislation dealing with both conservation and planning in all Member States. However, this improvement was not as rapid as the situation requested everywhere, and more problematically, it seems that in many cases, even though the legal provisions were in place, they were not enforced.

While most of the countries reported positive patterns emerging after 1975 and saw them as encouragement, the report primarily testified to a multiplicity of 'main' problems.[16] The first underlined 'main' problem in heritage conservation in Europe was an insufficiency of resources, mainly financial; however, the lack extended to include a workforce with specific knowledge and a paucity of appropriate materials for heritage conservation to be successfully performed. At the time, Europe was faced with a deep recession, and consequently, funds allocated to heritage were greatly restricted. Throughout its recommendations, the CoE encouraged the Member States to search for new funding models, including fiscal incentives and private or public-private partnerships, among others.

Another dominant problem detected was the unsuccessful integration of conservation within urban planning. Most of the countries reported a lack of clear division of responsibilities and powers, as well as a lack of cooperation between authorities responsible for conservation and those responsible for planning and development control. As the Italian government put it in their contribution to the report, 'despite all the successful experiments in coordination in integrated conservation, we are still far from a general integration of planning measures and real planning controls'.[17] Statements like this one, and the general conclusion of the 1982 Report, that even though the concept of 'integrated conservation' was praised by governments, it was not implemented enough in practice, signalled to the CoE that its (non-binding) 1975 Charter and

15 PACE Doc. 4300 (n 1);
Parliamentary Assembly, 'Report on the Conservation of the European Architectural Heritage (Rapporteur Lord Duncan Sandys)' [1979] Doc 4396;
Council of Europe, Steering Committee for Urban Policies and the Architectural Heritage (CDUP), 'Report on the Situation of the Architectural Heritage in Europe' [1981] CDUP (81) 16;
Council of Europe, Steering Committee for Urban Policies and the Architectural Heritage (CDUP), 'Rapport sur la Situation du Patrimoine Architectural en Europe, par Mr H L Warburton' [1982] CDUP (82) 59.

16 CDUP (82) 59 (n 15).

17 CDUP (82) 59 (n 15).

subsequent recommendations would not suffice for the new conservation policy to become an accepted European norm. An argument in favour of the Convention that would present an obligation, rather than an incentive, for more radical adjustment of legal, administrative, and financial resources was obvious. In this context, it could be argued that, with this certain reluctance towards the new CoE conservation policy revealed in the 1982 Report, governments and professionals in the field showed uneasiness towards even the slightest challenge/change to the dominant AHD. The CoE's 'integrated conservation' concept, while unquestionably (and in line with the AHD), gave attention primarily to 'things', also recognised that the management of heritage has a significant consequence beyond the preservation of historic fabric.[18] The CoE's concept of 'integrated conservation', one could argue, marks an important step in the CoE's departure from the AHD. This divergence from the AHD became more and more pronounced, as will be shown in subsequent CoE heritage texts. However, it is important to keep in mind that this volume does not only offer a critique of the AHD through the lens of the CoE policies and texts that challenge it, but also a case in point of the multiplicity of AHDs that could be mapped.

The above-mentioned reports were undoubtedly the motivation for another CoE body, the Conference of Local and Regional Authorities of Europe, to call for the convention on the protection of heritage in its Resolution 127 (1982) on the 4th European Symposium of Historic Towns.[19] This resolution also requested the CoE's Committee of Ministers to organise the second European Conference of Ministers Responsible for Architectural Heritage where further measures and policies would be promoted.

As a response to the aforementioned Report and Resolution 127 from 1982, studies on the possibility and desirability of preparing a European Convention for the Protection of the Architectural Heritage were prepared by the Secretariat (1982) and by the European University Centre in Nancy.[20] The studies primarily took the legal implications and obstacles (at the national and international levels) of the introduction of the new convention on the heritage issues into consideration, rather than analysing substantial aspects of the text.

18 Smith (n 7).

19 Council of Europe, Conference of Local and Regional Authorities of Europe, 'Resolution 127 (1982) on the 4th European Symposium of Historic Towns' [1982].

20 Council of Europe, Steering Committee for Urban Policies and the Architectural Heritage (CDUP), 'Study on the Legal Feasibility and Desirability of a European Convention on the Protection of the Architectural Heritage – by the European University Centre Nancy' [1983] CDUP (83) 4.

In the context of national legislation, the binding nature of a convention that imposes obligations on the Member States essentially required sufficient uniformity of national legal systems. A comparative analysis of the various laws and regulations showed that the principles of architectural heritage protection were common to all Member States and that, despite certain variations, the legislation was similar in content.[21] Thus, the convention as a means of proclaiming the European standard of protection for the architectural heritage which all the Member States accept to observe has been seen as highly appropriate.[22]

The introduction of new international texts inevitably raised the question of possible overlaps or even incompatibility with other existing instruments. In this context, the UNESCO World Heritage Convention has been particularly taken into consideration. The conclusion was that the two conventions would become complementary, with the World Heritage Convention referring to that heritage with outstanding universal value and (thus concerned only with a very limited number of monuments and sites) and the European convention attempting to provide overall protection for monuments and sites and their surroundings through a European integrated conservation model which it would define.

At the European level, the interest of the European Community (EC) in heritage issues started to gain momentum in the 1980s, and, in this context, the EC expressed its intention for operational actions in the field.[23] However, the EC was primarily referring to the financial aspect, while the new CoE convention would be quite different in scope. Therefore, concerning other international instruments, the conclusion was that there was no foreseeable incompatibility between the proposed CoE convention and other international instruments on heritage conservation issues.[24] The final opinion in favour of the convention that came from the studies was undoubtedly not a surprise; it would more likely appear to be a justification for an already made political decision. The prevailing opinion was that the lack of a European convention created a legal vacuum, and, in that sense, the convention would

---

21 Ibid.

22 Council of Europe, Steering Committee for Urban Policies and the Architectural Heritage (CDUP), 'Comparative Analysis of Legislation in the Field of Conservation of Monuments and Sites – Report of the Meeting' [1983] CDUP (83) 89;

Austria, Denmark, and the United Kingdom had reservations about the practical value and desirability of drawing up a convention in the architectural heritage field but were nevertheless prepared to cooperate in the drawing up of a draft text.

23 CDUP (83) 4 (n 20).

24 Ibid.

be an ideal instrument to consolidate past achievements by introducing compulsory minimal requirements for heritage protection in Europe.

While the reasons in favour of the convention are certainly valid and, indeed, the only ones visible in the archival documents, the comments made by a former CoE Secretariat member suggest that the simple 'required' dynamic to produce conventions on a certain subject every few years could also be one of the reasons why the decision to draft the convention was made. As that staff member implied, the numerous committees needed to justify their existence to the Committee of Ministers, and the 'production' of conventions played a vital role in it.[25]

3 1985 Granada Convention: Draft and Implementation

Once a decision on the desirability of the Convention had been made, the swiftness of producing the final draft was remarkable. The CoE Steering Committee for Urban Policies and the Architectural Heritage (CDUP) set up a committee of select experts to prepare a draft in 1983.[26] The basis for discussion was a preliminary draft prepared by the Secretariat, which drew heavily on the previous CoE recommendations and resolutions on heritage protection.[27] It took only three meetings for the drafting committee to adopt the final text which, as witnessed by the member of the Secretariat at the time, was one of the shortest procedures for adopting a draft convention in the CoE's history.[28]

---

25 Interview 3 with Former Employee of Council of Europe's Cultural Policy Division (3 February 2020).

26 Council of Europe, Steering Committee for Urban Policies and the Architectural Heritage (CDUP), 'Report of the 5th Meeting of the Plenary Committee' [1985] CM (85) 61/ CDUP (85) 20;

The states represented on the Select Committee of Experts responsible for preparing the draft were: Austria, Belgium, Denmark, France, Germany, Greece, Ireland, Italy, Portugal, Spain, Switzerland, and the United Kingdom.

27 Council of Europe, Steering Committee for Urban Policies and the Architectural Heritage (CDUP), 'European Convention for the Conservation of the Architectural Heritage – Preliminary draft revised by the Secretariat following the meeting of the group of experts' [1984] CDUP (84) 1.

28 Council of Europe, Steering Committee for Urban Policies and the Architectural Heritage (CDUP), 'Commentaires des Membres du Comité Restreint d'Experts sur le Projet révisé No 1 du Secrétariat' [1984] CDUP (84) 46;

Council of Europe, Steering Committee for Urban Policies and the Architectural Heritage (CDUP), 'Selected Committee of Experts Responsible for Drafting a European Convention for the Protection of the Architectural Heritage, 2nd Revised Draft of the Convention' [1984] CDUP (84) 73;

There are a few reasons for such a 'procedural' success. The first and most obvious reason could be that the text represents a stock-taking of more than 15 years of joint work and development of the already well-known and commonly accepted notions in the conservation of architectural heritage. The other reason could be more technical, but equally important: that the quality of the preliminary Secretariat's draft satisfied both the legal and heritage-related requirements.[29]

The Convention for the Protection of Architectural Heritage (Granada Convention, ETS No. 121) was opened for signature at the Second European Conference of Ministers Responsible for Architectural Heritage, held in Granada in 1985.[30] It entered into force in 1987 after three necessary ratifications, and to date (June 2025), it has been ratified by 41 CoE Member States (Albania, Austria, Iceland, Monaco, and San Marino did not ratify it), as well as by the Russian Federation. The Convention is considered by many to be one of the key texts on the protection of architectural heritage in Europe.[31] The first European Conference on architectural heritage issues held in Brussels (1969) was, as we saw in the previous chapter, a starting point for the CoE's work in the heritage protection field. With the Second Conference in Granada, the CoE intended to reactivate public interest and political debate in support of heritage protection (that, the organisation felt, had been lost in the post-EAHY period), as well as to propose concrete steps for future CoE intergovernmental cooperation. The Granada Convention was therefore seen not only as a political and legal confirmation of the previous work of the CoE-established European cooperation, but also as a text which provides a strong foundation for more harmonised European heritage protection legislation. The text of the Convention was structured to reflect this twofold purpose: (1) to promote and reinforce policies for protecting and enhancing the heritage in the Member States and (2) to foster practical cooperation between states and regions of Europe.[32]

Council of Europe, Steering Committee for Urban Policies and the Architectural Heritage (CDUP), 'Selected Committee of Experts Responsible for Drafting a European Convention for the Protection of the Architectural Heritage, Working Paper for the Meeting 27–29 November 1984' [1984] CDUP (84) 92.

29 Interview with Interviewee 1 (former employee of the Council of Europe's Directorate of Culture and Cultural and Natural Heritage, 1 April 2020).

30 Council of Europe, *Convention for the Protection of the Architectural Heritage* (European Treaty Series No 121, Granada, 3 October 1985) ('Granada Convention').

31 Robert Pickard, *European Cultural Heritage* (vol 2, Council of Europe Publishing 2002).

32 The first part of the Convention covers the provisions for the minimum protection needed and the conservation policies to be implemented. This part is covering sections like (1) Definition of the architectural heritage, (2) Identification of the properties to be

The importance of the text rests in the fact that not only did it give additional impetus to a newly developed CoE integrated conservation policy, but it also asked the contracting parties to implement legally binding *statutory measures* to protect architectural heritage by using the concept of integrated conservation. In addition, it could be argued, the Granada Convention was the first CoE's binding instrument that stipulated a distinctive organisation's heritage discourse. This discourse, as the following section will show, did not depart drastically from the AHD at that time. However, the CoE's discourse did challenge the AHD sufficiently via several emerging ideas (developed throughout the years and reiterated in the Convention's text), that it is possible to look at it disjointedly. Therefore, the purpose of this section of the chapter is twofold. Firstly, to look at the developments introduced by the CoE that noticeably demonstrate and in line with Pendlebury's[33] criticism, that the AHD has changed/is changing and becoming more flexible since its initial characterisation by Smith.[34] And secondly, the analysis offered here will not only offer a critique of the dominant understanding of heritage through the challenges that the CoE's texts presented it with, but will also offer a case in point within which to observe the tenacity of the AHD.

More precisely, and as it will be argued throughout this book, the CoE's actions in the heritage field, starting with the Granada Convention, should be looked at through the notion of 'hybridity', which essentially moves the examination away from a binary model of the AHD and its critical response and opens discursive terrain beyond the oppositional. This 'hybridity' that offers what Bhabba terms as 'third place' decidedly resonates with the case of the CoE's heritage approach.[35] It permits the CoE to take into account voices of alternative discourses in line with its wider focus on human rights, social inclusion, and democracy, but without departing radically from the core values of the AHD. This hybridity with different concepts will become more

---

protected, (3) Statutory protection procedures, (4) Ancillary measures, (5) Enforcement, (6) Conservation policies, (7) Participation and associations, and (8) Information and training.

The purpose of the second part of the Convention's text (Article 17–21) is to lay down the principles of European coordination of conservation policies covering consultations between countries, exchange of experience and specialists.

33 John Pendlebury, 'Conservation Values, the Authorised Heritage Discourse and the Conservation-Planning Assemblage' (2013) 19(7) International Journal of Heritage Studies 709.

34 Smith (n 7).

35 Bhabba (1990) as cited in: Gillian Rose, 'The Cultural Politics of Place: Local Representation and Oppositional Discourse in Two Films' (1994) 19(1) Transactions of the Institute of British Geographers 46.

and more obvious in the CoE's later heritage text, but its first indications can be observed within the Granada Convention. The notion of 'hybridity' within the Granada Convention allowed the CoE, as a European organisation (and, at the time covered in this chapter, a fundamentally Western European organisation) to maintain the fundamental European ideas about conservation and the nature and meaning of heritage that were predominant in the international discussion (the central components of the AHD). Still, this hybridity of the AHD and a number of other discourses existent in the CoE policies, allowed the CoE to be at the origin, in many instances, of the (more or less) pronounced departure from the AHD and to delineate its specific discourse. The text of the Granada Convention offers us noteworthy evidence to support this argument.

Generally, commentators place an emphasis on the rather 'conservative' and 'technical' appearance of the Granada Convention.[36] Yet, one can argue that this assessment can easily undermine the work the Convention has done in challenging the AHD. The fact that the Convention instituted and legitimised sufficiently comprehensive principles for heritage protection (integrated conservation), which ultimately allowed further theoretical and practical developments in the heritage field to be successfully incorporated into the following CoE's texts and activities, should not be overlooked. It also represents one of the earliest international policy documents that promote wider participation in heritage planning as much as it seeks a wider understanding of what architectural heritage covers and what significance it has relative to social and communal values. A closer look at those elements (the broader notion of architectural heritage, the social aspects of heritage, and the concept of integrated conservation) will demonstrate the importance of the Convention in laying down the European conservation standards and discourse which proved to be much more flexible and inclusive than is frequently portrayed in academic discussions.

3.1 *Enlargement of the Concept of Architectural Heritage*

'Architectural heritage', according to Article 1 of the Granada Convention, comprises monuments, groups of buildings, and sites. It is evident that these classifications follow the definition contained in the UNESCO Convention for

36 Pickard (n 31);
Robert Pickard, 'A Comparative Review of Policy for the Protection of the Architectural Heritage of Europe' (2002) 8(4) International Journal of Heritage Studies 349;
Interview with Interviewee 1 (n 29);
Interview with Interviewee 4 (former Head of Division of Culture and Cultural Heritage, 10 October 2022).

the Protection of the World Cultural and Natural Heritage (1972); however, a closer look at Article 1 exposes an evident shift in the CoE's discourse.[37] As Smith notes in her comment on the World Heritage Convention, the categories of monuments and groups of buildings represent the 'grand and unproblematic aspects of authorised heritage'.[38] However, while the World Heritage Convention suggests that these things have a universal value that lies in 'history, art or science', the CoE, in its definition, reflected the trend towards the enlargement of the concept of heritage by adding the 'social and technical interest' of architectural heritage. This addition resulted in extending the scope of the Granada Convention to works of vernacular architecture, as well as civil engineering works, private houses, industrial heritage in its various forms, and certain contemporary architectural works, among others.[39] Hence, in the Granada Convention, the CoE normalised more everyday examples of heritage, including those with arguably no sense of aesthetic grandeur.[40] In close correlation with this expansion of what is considered heritage, it is also important to mention that the Convention promoted the approach that age should not be a consideration for protecting items of architectural heritage.[41] This is undoubtedly the first important element of departure from the AHD in this Convention.

One can observe this shift in the focus and scope of conservation of architectural heritage in numerous studies. The reality of a wider approach to what is considered architectural heritage has been documented across numerous analyses of European/national heritage policies and management practices.[42] As a matter of example, here the reference is made to Ludwig's and Pendle-

---

37 The CoE clarifies that it is referring exclusively to the architectural heritage in its Convention rather than the heritage in general, as the UNESCO convention suggests. The Explanatory Report points out that 'the Convention is concerned with buildings and sites' (p. 5). It also extended its scope to fixtures and fittings, which may apply to the part of a protected building, as well as to the movable objects which have a particular historical association with a protected building.

38 Smith (n 7) 96.

39 Council of Europe, *Explanatory Report to the Convention for the Protection of the Architectural Heritage of Europe* (European Treaty Series No 121, 1985).

40 Françoise Choay, *The Invention of the Historic Monument* (Cambridge University Press 2001).

41 Recommendation No. R (91) 13 of the Committee of Ministers on the protection of the twentieth-century architectural heritage states that this period is 'an integral part of Europe's historical heritage and that the preservation and enhancement of its most significant elements serve the same aims and principles as those of the conservation of the architectural heritage as a whole', 1.

42 Emma Waterton, *Rhetoric and 'Reality': Politics, Policy and the Discourse of Heritage in England*(PhD thesis, University of York 2007);

bury's work focusing on the English conservation planning system. Their research took place in the 2000s, when arguably the broader approach to heritage had already been widely accepted. However, the authors largely overlooked the impact the CoE could have had on this shift in focus. The significance of Ludwig's and Pendlebury's research undoubtedly lies in the fact that they have clearly illustrated how the AHD, in the context of English conservation planning, noticeably displays some degree of flexibility. Ludwig specified in her research that all her sources implied that the AHD in local conservation planning in England had evolved from a discourse that prioritised grandeur and elitist heritage over one which normalises more everyday examples, as suggested by the Granada Convention.[43] On the other hand, Pendlebury discussed this development through the series of what he calls 'sub-AHDs'.[44] Such sub-AHDs, Pendlebury explains, deploy 'a challengingly flexible interpretation of what constitutes acceptable and desirable conservation practice, often far removed from the traditional emphasis on the authenticity of material fabric'.[45] Even though an explicit reference to the CoE's work is missing in those studies, one can argue that the flexibility of the discourse detected by Ludwig and Pendlebury undoubtedly reflected the wider debate on heritage issues under the auspice of the CoE and, notably, the UK's ratification of the Granada Convention in 1987. The earlier, rare reference to the CoE made by Pendlebury in his work from 2009 could undoubtedly support this assumption.[46] He recognised that documents such as the CoE's Amsterdam Declaration (1975) (together with the UNESCO Nairobi Statement (1976) and the ICOMOS Washington Charter (1987); but not, interestingly, the Granada Convention) extended the discussion in the heritage field into areas beyond the traditional conservation issues to include the wider social relevance of conservation as an activity. Pendlebury further noted 'with the benefit of hindsight' that the CoE 1975 EAHY formed an important cusp in this process, when 'the tide had truly turned', suggesting thus that the move forward in the heritage discourse in England was, to a certain degree, initiated by the CoE's activ-

---

Carol Ludwig, 'From Bricks and Mortar to Social Heritage: Planning Space for Diversities in the AHD' (2016) 22(10) International Journal of Heritage Studies 811; Pendlebury (n 33).

43 Carol Ludwig, 'From Bricks and Mortar to Social Heritage: Planning Space for Diversities in the AHD' (2016) 22(10) International Journal of Heritage Studies 811.

44 Pendlebury (n 33).

45 Ibid 722.

46 John Pendlebury, *Conservation in the Age of Consensus* (Routledge 2009).

ities.[47] Yet, the impact the CoE's heritage approach had in the national contexts went largely unnoticed by academia.

The CoE further reiterated the broadening in scope of categories and types of architectural assets that should be protected in several recommendations of the PACE and Committee of Ministers following the Granada Convention. Industrial heritage, for example, was covered by two recommendations in 1987 and 1990: Recommendation No. R (87) 24 on European Industrial Towns, which considers the issues arising from the economic decline in older industrial areas and the need for their regeneration, and Recommendation No. R (90) 20 on the Protection and Conservation of the Industrial, Technical, and Civil Engineering Heritage in Europe.[48] Rural built heritage was a subject of Recommendation No. R (89) 6 on the Protection and Enhancement of the Rural Architectural Heritage, and PACE recommended the Protection of Disused Hospitals and Military Buildings in its Recommendation 1485 (2000). With all these additional texts in mind, the initial broadening of the types and categories of architectural heritage worth protecting seems to be one of the major Granada Convention's accepted and implemented provisions that have set a minimum standard for European conservation policy.

While the definition of architectural heritage discussed above reshaped an important aspect of the AHD, the protection procedures and measures identified in Articles 2–9 cling firmly to traditional core values that privilege a social 'elite' and the requisite responsibilities of experts. The provisions of those articles ask the Parties to the Convention to introduce legislation protecting architectural heritage, which covers the creation and maintenance of the inventories of the architectural heritage to be protected, setting up an administrative system for the implementation and supervision of policies, and providing the financial support for maintaining and restoring the architectural heritage. The wording of those articles, particularly Article 5, which draws directly from the Venice Charter, illustrates this clearly. In this aspect, the Granada Convention stays confidently in line with the plethora of other UNESCO and ICOMOS charters, conventions, recommendations, and guidelines that aim to protect, conserve, safeguard, and manage different aspects of heritage. The intertextuality of the chain of texts that can be observed here demonstrates how the AHD has been legitimised across the heritage field at the time.[49] This intertextuality, Smith argues, '*is* the AHD', and it undoubtedly

47 Ibid 63.

48 Pickard (n 31).

49 Lilie Chouliaraki and Norman Fairclough, *Discourse in Late Modernity: Rethinking Critical Discourse Analysis* (Edinburgh University Press 1999), 118–119;

positions the Granada Convention among other intergovernmental texts that collectively reinforce the authority of the AHD.[50] The Convention's framing in relation to other texts, more explicitly the Venice Charter implies a choice, and thereby 'highlights a sense of what is being excluded and insulated against, and what is being worked into the interaction'.[51] However, the persistence of the AHD given in Articles 2–9 does not undermine two other important innovative elements of the Granada Convention: its reference to the social value of heritage and its legitimisation of the concept of integrated conservation. And while the intertextuality of the Granada Convention with external texts reasserted the principles of the AHD, its relation to other CoE texts, such as the CoE's Statute or the European Charter of the Architectural Heritage, permitted the Convention to depart from the AHD to a certain extent. The content of the Convention marked the first sign of hybridisation of the AHD in the CoE's texts with foundational aims of the organisation, such as the protection of human rights and fundamental freedoms, as well as fostering of the economic, social, and cultural development of its Member States.

3.2 *The Social Relevance of Heritage Conservation*

The second essential element where the Granada Convention departs from the AHD is its reference to the social aspects of architectural heritage and the social weight of conservation as an activity. The expression of the social aspect in the Granada Convention is the result of more than a decade of the CoE's reflection on the value of heritage. A brief reference to those texts is necessary for our understanding of some of the Convention's provisions in this respect.

Social value is a complex concept that has been variously used today to refer to some or all of the following: community identity, attachment to place, symbolic value, spiritual association, and social capital.[52] Aspects of, what today we call social value, were alluded to in nineteenth-century conservation debates, but early to mid-twentieth-century international charters overwhelmingly privileged historic, scientific, and aesthetic values. As noted by François Sorlin

---

Norman Fairclough, 'Linguistic and Intertextual Analysis in Discourse Analysis' in Adam Jaworski and Nikolas Coupland (eds), *The Discourse Reader* (Routledge 1999) 183; Norman Fairclough, 'Critical Discourse Analysis as a Method in Social Scientific Research' in Ruth Wodak and Michael Meyer (eds), *Methods of Critical Discourse Analysis* (SAGE 2001) 233.

50 Smith (n 7) 94.

51 Waterton (n 42) 75.

52 Siân Jones, 'Wrestling with the Social Value of Heritage: Problems, Dilemmas and Opportunities' (2017) 4(1) Journal of Community Archaeology and Heritage 21.

in his report prepared for the CoE in 1971, 'consequently, a situation arose in Europe which led to the historical heritage being divorced from social life throughout the 19th century and the early years of the 20th'.[53]

As this report suggests, together with additional documents discussed shortly, a re-emerging of the social and emotional aspects of heritage in the discussions on conservation matters in the 1970s was largely initiated by the CoE. While many recognise the Burra Charter as a key document in bringing social value into the focus of heritage conservation and management, the plethora of the earlier CoE's texts suggests, nevertheless, that it was indeed the CoE that recognised the social aspect of heritage almost a decade before the first version of the Burra Charter.

As early as 1969, European ministers responsible for the preservation and rehabilitation of cultural heritage stated in their resolution at the Brussels Conference that 'the realisation of the social value of this heritage confers on it a new dimension which necessitates its preservation and its active integration into the setting of men's life'.[54] The CoE further, in the document that outlines general principles for its future heritage policy in 1973 together with the enlarged concept of architectural heritage, fostered the idea that architectural heritage is also 'intricately bound up with the environment of daily life, constantly serves the numerous activities of the people who occupy it'.[55]

The following section from the same document extremely resonates with Smith's argument (almost 30 years later) that heritage is a cultural process that 'engages with acts of remembering that work to create ways to understand and engage with the present':[56]

> It is a mistake to believe, as has often been claimed, that this need for the past is fundamentally the expression of antagonism between yesterday and tomorrow. To ponder on the significance of the past is not to deny the importance and irreversibility of the present. It is not to seek escape from the problems of the past but **rather a fundamental act of**

53 Council of Europe, Committee on Monuments and Sites, 'Towards a New European Polity for the Preservation and Rehabilitation of Groups of Buildings and Sites of Historical Value – Extracts from the Consolidated Report on the Possibilities Resulting from the CCC's Work 1964–69' [1971] DELA/MS (71) 5.

54 Council of Europe, First Conference of European Ministers Responsible for the Preservation and Rehabilitation of the Cultural Heritage of Monuments and Sites, 'Resolutions of the Conference' (Brussels, 25–27 November 1969).

55 Council of Europe, Committee on Monuments and Sites, 'Towards a Comprehensive Policy of Conservation of the Architectural Heritage: General Principles – Professor R Lemaire' [1973] DELA/MS/CD (73) 1, 5.

56 Smith (n 7) 44.

> **our civilisation to analyse and grasp the significance and value of the past ages and their legacy**...[the men's awareness of the heritage] is not necessarily the same as it had been in the past, but constitutes a will **to recreate it in the context of the present and endows it with a kind of unquestionable present value.**[57]

It is apparent from these statements that the CoE started to look at heritage and its protection and conservation as a *process* and more importantly as a *capital* needed for the cultural, social, and economic development of society. That approach, arguably, significantly challenged the AHD's notion of heritage as something finite, fragile, and non-renewable that needs to be conserved as found for future generations. The relevance of the past to contemporary life has been emphasised further in the European Charter of the Architectural Heritage of 1975, which stated that 'architectural heritage is a capital of irreplaceable spiritual, cultural, social and economic value' (Article 3) that 'is conducive to a harmonious social balance' (Article 4). The Charter's reference to the importance of the 'atmosphere' of the place (Article 1) and its 'instinctive feeling' (Article 2) is framed by the language resonant in the later Burra Charter that basis the conservation process on cultural significance 'that provides a deep and inspirational sense of connection to community and landscape and to lived experiences'.

In most of the CoE's aforementioned texts, there is also evidence of a more instrumental concern with social value. The aspect of maintaining the social fabric and social balance in historic urban centres turned out to be the CoE's main issue of concern. The 1976 Resolution 28 clearly stated that:

> ...maintaining the social fabric and improving the living conditions of all levels of the population, particularly the less affluent ones, should be one of the main concerns of anyone responsible for drawing up a programme for the integrated conservation of a group of urban or rural buildings.[58]

This focus on the potential problem of gentrification and property speculation that the conservation and rehabilitation of historic architectural complexes could bring about surely signifies the concern of political authorities over how to prevent the general departure of the poorer section of the population and foster a social balance in rehabilitated areas. Conversely, this discussion

---

57 DELA/MS/CD (73) 1 (n 55) 8 (emphasis added).

58 Resolution (76) 28 (n 2) 7.

on the social weight carried by conservation activities also signalled the CoE's deeper understanding of the notion that it is the people and community at and around historical architectural heritage that make that heritage valued.

The provisions of the Granada Convention reiterated the messages of those previous texts. Article 15, for example, asks the contracting parties to promote policies that would demonstrate 'the unity of the cultural heritage and the links that exist between architecture, the arts, popular traditions and ways of life at European, national and regional levels alike'.[59] Even though one could argue that social value was not in the foreground of the Granada Convention, the text reaffirmed the CoE's recognition of the social aspect of heritage, which would later become central to a number of its succeeding charters and conventions, notably the European Landscape Convention (2000) and the Council of Europe Framework Convention on the Value of Cultural Heritage for Society (2005). The social effect of conservation was undoubtedly echoed throughout Granada and especially through its connotation within the concept of integrated conservation, which is the third element of Granada's departure from the AHD that this chapter aims to explore.

3.3 *Integrated Conservation*

The concept of 'integrated conservation' as discussed in the previous chapter was, according to Pickard, 'one of the most important developments in policy for the European architectural heritage'.[60] Its origins in the 1960s were directly connected with the identified need to associate heritage protection with territorial planning. The concept was firmly established and promoted by earlier CoE (non-binding) texts such as the European Charter of the Architectural Heritage, the Amsterdam Declaration and Resolution (76) 28. Restating the main principles promoted by those earlier documents, the Granada Convention is of great importance in the fact that it requires the Member States to adopt and incorporate integrated conservation policies into their legislation.[61] Article 10 of the Convention devotes five paragraphs to the principles of integrated conservation that serve as the basis for adopting and adapting national laws and regulations. More importantly, as will be explored in the following paragraphs, the model of integrated conservation not only evolved from individually considered elements and the legal concepts and actions for the protection of heritage into a more encompassing approach, but it also offered a

59 Granada Convention, Article 15.

60 Pickard (n 31) 33.

61 Patrick J O'Keefe and Lyndel V Prott, *Cultural Heritage Conventions and Other Instruments: A Compendium with Commentaries* (Institute of Art and Law 2011).

model demonstrably flexible enough to accommodate broader social, economic, and political developments.

The hybridity potential of the concept of integrated conservation, whereby the AHD came into relation with other external concepts such as territorial planning, social inclusion, or environmental concerns, ensured its permanence in the CoE's policies to date. One of the notions that echoed perfectly with the principles of integrated conservation, and that will be highlighted here, is the concept of sustainable development. Sustainable development is generally defined, in the words of the World Commission on Economic Development (the Brundtland Report), as 'development that meets the needs of the present without compromising the ability of future generations to meet their own needs'.[62] The concept is often looked at through a balance between its pillars – economic, social, and environmental.[63] In 2015 UN's Transforming Our World: the 2030 Agenda for Sustainable Development these pillars were redefined as the '5 Ps': people, planet, prosperity, peace, and partnership. While more in-depth reference to the CoE's heritage work within the framework of sustainable development will be made in the following chapters covering the post-1992 Earth Summit period, here a section looks closely at different understandings of the ideas of sustainable development implicit in the Granada Convention, especially through the concept of integrated conservation.

At the time of Granada's drafting, the global discussion on the concept of sustainable development was still undeveloped, and explicit reference to it is obviously missing. However, the essential themes of the Granada Convention and the previous related CoE texts concerning integrated conservation are highly connected to the theme of sustainable development. The Granada Convention explicitly refers to the term 'development' in its Preamble, and the understanding of (sustainable) development seems to be implicit throughout the convention. While the Preamble evokes the Convention's underlying purpose and expresses a European philosophy of conservation (a demonstration of the AHD's tenacity!), at the same time, it aims to both (1) 'bequeath to Europeans a system of cultural reference and to improve their environment, and (2) foster balanced economic and social development in states and localities'.[64]

Borrowing from Labadi's analysis of the World Heritage Convention and sustainable development and her three different understandings of develop-

62 World Commission on Environment and Development, *Our Common Future* (Oxford University Press 1987) Paragraph 27.

63 As adopted at the Earth Summit in Rio de Janeiro in 1992.

64 Explanatory Report (n 39) 4.

ment which seem to be implicit in the 1972 UNESCO Convention, a parallel can be made with respect to the Granada Convention and integrated conservation as its essential segment.[65] Labadi identified a relationship between heritage conservation and development as a reference to '(1) heritage conservation in opposition to development, (2) heritage conservation as sustainability and (3) heritage conservation as community development'.[66] Whereas it is worth accentuating the interplay of (sustainable) development and heritage conservation in the concept of integrated conservation in its own right, putting the CoE's approach in comparison to Labadi's analysis of the World Heritage Convention offers, in addition, an interesting comparison of the two Conventions and the discourses of the two organisations at the time.

The threats to cultural heritage caused by rapid urbanisation and technical progress in the post-World War II context were at the origin of the initial CoE involvement in heritage protection matters. An anti-development sentiment was indeed excessively present in the early CoE documents.[67] Yet, contrary to the World Heritage Convention's standing in opposition to the modern forces of development,[68] in the outlining of the integrated conservation concept the CoE embraced social progress and urban development and saw heritage conservation as 'an essential town and country planning objective'.[69] This relationship between heritage conservation and (sustainable) development has been worked out through more than a decade of preparatory activities leading to the 1985 Granada Convention. The aforementioned Resolution (76) 28 and its integrated conservation objectives are worth underlining here as an example of the CoE's approach: the measures of heritage conservation should have as their objective the integration of monuments, groups of buildings, and sites into the physical environment of present-day society through programmes designed to revitalise that heritage by assigning to it a social purpose

65 Sophia Labadi, 'UNESCO, Heritage and Sustainable Development: International Discourses and Local Impacts' in Peter Gould and Karen A Pyburn (eds), *Promise and Peril: Archaeology Engaging with Economic Development* (Springer 2017) 45–60.

66 Ibid 47.

67 Council of Europe, Committee on Monuments and Sites, '*European Charter for the Preservation and Rehabilitation of the Architectural Heritage – Preliminary Draft*' [1974] DELA/MS (73) 27;

Council of Europe, Committee on Monuments and Sites, '*Draft European Charter of the Architectural Heritage – Adopted at the 4th Session of the Committee on Monuments and Sites*' [1975] DELA/MS (75) 32 (CM (75) 171).

68 Labadi (n 65).

69 Granada Convention, Article 10.

and adapting it to the needs of modern life while still carefully preserving features of cultural interest and keeping with the character of their setting.[70]

The second reference made by Labadi, to what she calls 'heritage as sustainability/sustainable development' refers to the World Heritage Convention's recognition that heritage should be identified, protected, and transmitted to future generations (Article 4).[71] The idea of protecting finite resources for future generations is also explicitly restated in the Granada Convention's Preamble:

> ...the importance of handing down to **future generations** a system of cultural reference, improving the urban and rural environment and thereby fostering **the economic, social, and cultural development** of States and regions.

This notion, according to Labadi, was echoed in the Brundtland Report a decade later, which she argues positions the World Heritage Convention as a 'precursor of the Brundtland Report's implication that governments need to develop novel approaches to growth that take into account and protect non-renewable resources'.[72] However, while the World Heritage approach echoed the notion of 'conserve as found' in preserving a limited number of heritage sites in their finite, unchangeable state, the Granada Convention goes further in recognising that in order to preserve architectural heritage, it has to be used 'in the light of the needs of contemporary life' (Article 11). It could be argued here that the adaptation of old buildings for new uses and the reuse of already existing built capital/resources lies perfectly within the spirit of sustainable development, reaffirming the CoE's conviction that architectural heritage is a cultural but also an economic and social capital which use and reuse for the benefit of society is not negligible.

Whereas it is undeniable that the World Heritage Convention's aim to preserve, protect, and transmit outstanding heritage to future generations resonates with the philosophy behind the concept of sustainable development, the Convention's problem lies in the fact that its approach, underlined by the AHD, disengages the present (or at least certain social actors in the present) from the active use of that heritage. If we go back to Smith's argument that according to the AHD, heritage is 'inevitably saved "for future generations" a rhetoric that undermines the ability of the present...to alter or change the meaning and

70 Resolution (76) 28 (n 2).
71 Labadi (n 65) 48.
72 Labadi (n 65) 48.

value of heritage sites or places',[73] it is clear that the original Convention was not much concerned with a range of matters implied by sustainable development, particularly the role of communities as necessary stakeholders for achieving the sustainable conservation and management of the listed properties. On the other hand, the role of architectural heritage in contemporary life and its active use by communities is central to the Granada Convention and the integrated conservation approach promoted by the CoE. It is an important difference between the discourses of the two organisations (at the time) to keep in mind.

It was indeed this role of community and its development that Labadi identified as the third element of sustainable development that was implied in the World Heritage Convention.[74] The implicit link between heritage and community development was made in the World Heritage Convention's Article 5. However, this linkage has become explicit only in 2002 with the Budapest Declaration (UNESCO 2002) and developed further with the Operational Guidelines in 2011. The CoE has followed the same path of developing further a European methodology for heritage management with a focus on community development in a framework of sustainable development once the concept entered the mainstream of public policies globally.[75] However, contrary to the World Heritage Convention, the CoE had a much more solid base in this respect. The philosophy behind the CoE approach was denoted in the principles of integrated conservation, which were defined in the early 1970s:

> Integrated conservation of the cultural heritage of monuments and sites is one of the basic constituents of regional and country planning. This new broader concept of conservation should serve as a **basis for a more human approach** to regional and town planning policy.
>
> **The integrated conservation of a country's cultural heritage of monuments and sites concerns its citizens first and foremost.** A balance

---

73 Smith (n 7) 29.

74 Labadi (n 65).

75 Fourth European Conference of Ministers responsible for the Cultural Heritage: Resolution No. 2 (Helsinki 30–31 May 1996);
- Guidance on the development of legislation and administration systems in the field of cultural heritage, Technical Cooperation and Consultancy Programme (2000);
- Guiding Principles for Sustainable Spatial Development of the European Continent, adopted at the 12th – Session of the European Conference of Ministers responsible for Regional Planning (Hanover, 2000);
- European Landscape Convention (Florence, 2000).

> should be maintained between man and his traditional environment, and the assets inherited from the past and on which the quality of the environment largely depends should not be debased.[76]

The Granada Convention, consequently, reiterated those elements. Jones and Silva's[77] definition of community development that includes collective actions, problem-solving, and community building, such as the ability for individuals to participate freely in the life of their community and to build and express their own cultural identity, resonates throughout the Convention. Article 15 asks the Contracting Parties to promote policies aiming 'at demonstrating the unity of the cultural heritage and the links that exist between architectural heritage, the arts, popular traditions and ways of life'. It also acknowledges the value of conserving architectural heritage as an element of cultural identity, but also as a source of inspiration and creativity for present and future generations. Article 14 is even more explicit in the reference to community development. It asks Contracting Parties to:

> …establish in the various stages of the decision-making process, appropriate machinery for the supply of information, consultation, and cooperation between the State, the regional and local authorities, cultural institutions and associations, **and the public.**

The prominence of fostering the development of NGOs working in the field (Article 14) is another important aspect of community development implied in the Convention. This feature was another reiterated element from the CoE's earlier texts and activities (e.g., the creation of Europa Nostra), exposing the organisation's recognition of the role community development has in an overarching concept of sustainable development.

This section, which highlighted three understandings of conservation of heritage and development, had a twofold purpose; it recognises certain forward-looking aspects of the Granada Convention in comparison to the World Heritage Convention, and its sustainable development spirit, but more essentially, it demonstrates the potential flexibility of its central element: integrated conservation. The capacity of integrated conservation and its role within the framework of sustainable development has been further developed through a number of CoE mechanisms. Firstly, this took place in Resolution No. 2 of the Fourth European Conference of Ministers Responsible for the Cultural Heri-

76 Pickard (n 31) 92 (emphasis added).
77 Referenced in Labadi (n 65) 48.

tage (Helsinki, 1996), which was asked to rethink a European methodology for heritage management within the framework of sustainable development, and later through the Technical Cooperation and Consultancy Programme (TCCP). The short overview of the TCCP that follows will additionally illustrate the flexibility that the integrated conservation approach demonstrated in accommodating various social, political, and economic changes that took place from its creation in 1973 up to the present (2024).

4 Technical Cooperation and Consultancy Programme (TCCP)

The Council of Europe's Technical Cooperation and Consultancy Programme (TCCP) was developed from the initial Technical Assistance and has been a principal tool of the CoE's intervention in the field of heritage for more than 45 years. Since the mid-1970s, the TCCP has been advising national, regional, and local authorities and heritage professionals on a wide range of issues relating to the conservation, rehabilitation, and management of cultural heritage. The 'Rules for Technical Assistance relating to the Integrated Conservation of the Cultural Heritage of Monuments and Sites' were agreed upon as early as 1973, and the programme was given a significant stimulus by the European Architectural Heritage Year (1975). As indicated in the title of the Programme's Rules, the integrated approach is at its origin, and it was this approach that allowed the TCCP to develop an impressive capacity to respond flexibly and innovatively to changing socio-economic and political circumstances, situating heritage at the heart of solutions to social questions.[78]

This section of the chapter is largely informed by John Bold's and Robert Pickard's comprehensive analysis of the programme.[79] They laid out the main steps taken by the TCCP over the decades and offered, through them, an overview not only of the evolution of the concept of integrated conservation approach but also of the CoE's AHD.

78 John Bold and Robert Pickard (eds), *An Integrated Approach to Cultural Heritage: The Council of Europe's Technical Co-operation and Consultancy Programme* (Council of Europe Publishing 2018).

79 See for example: John Bold, 'The Technical Co-operation Programme: Context and Evolution' in John Bold and Matthew Cherry (eds), *The Politics of Heritage Regeneration in South-East Europe*(Council of Europe Publishing 2016) 17;

Robert Pickard (ed), *Management of Historic Centres* (Spon Press 2001);

Robert Pickard, 'Area-Based Protection Mechanisms for Heritage Conservation: A European Comparison' (2002) 8(2) *Journal of Architectural Conservation* 69.

In its first phase (1975–1991), characterised as the phase of expansion, the TCCP was based on the early notion of integrated conservation that promoted the idea that conservation should be one of the first considerations in all urban and regional planning.[80] The EAHY, which was predicated on the notion of heritage at risk, promoted the integrated conservation approach as a promising response, and the role of the TCCP was to endorse this concept in practice, offering comprehensive responses to requests coming from Member States for advice on specific heritage problems. Consequently, it was made clear from the beginning of the programme that technical assistance was to be directed exclusively towards integrated conservation projects, i.e., those that tackled all the challenges coming with the requirement of striking a balance between conservation and enhancement of old districts and improvement of the local economy and quality of life. Throughout decades, more than 100 projects have been carried out, and more than 40 of them were focused on the conservation and rehabilitation of historic town centres (for example, Valencia, Segovia, Funchal, Cracow, Telc). This programme, which was prompted by individual national needs and which was, in its first phase, principally informed by the European Charter of the Architectural Heritage (1975) and the Granada Convention (1985) played a significant role in situating the CoE at the heart of setting standards for heritage management in Europe. Importantly, the CoE repeatedly highlighted that its approach was not a 'top-down' one, but rather one of creative dialogue between its appointed experts and local professionals and authorities. According to Bold and Pickard, 'the recipients of the advice have taken part in a dialogue based on their needs, rather than being told what to do'.[81] The implementation of agreed-upon and achievable solutions to local problems was then the responsibility of the host country.

The turbulent political changes in Central and Eastern Europe from 1989 onwards asked for the adaptation and extension of the TCCP to the new Member States of the CoE. The new rules drawn up in 1992 marked the beginning of a new phase – diversification.[82] This phase significantly extended the scope of applications for assistance and introduces the concept of sustainable development into the TCCP remit and with it, adjustments of the initial model of integrated conservation. This broadening of the scope put an emphasis on new concepts, such as sustainable development and the role of heritage in it, but it also demonstrated the procedural continuity of the TCCP. It is this continuity, allied with the readiness to respond to ever-evolving situations, that

80 Bold and Pickard (n 78).

81 Bold and Pickard (n 78) 16.

82 Ibid.

assured the longevity of the programme. Notwithstanding significant progress made until the 1990s, it was evident during this phase that many of the issues identified during the European Architectural Heritage Year (1975) have been shown to be recurrent. The old problems, like how to balance sustainable growth with the retention of historic sites and town centres; how to encourage tourism without compromising the qualities which draw tourists in the first place; how to enlist the support of the local population (sustainable regeneration should not be a top-down strategy); how to ensure public/private collaboration or how to finance restoration and rehabilitation, re-emerged in new situations.[83] The TCCP projects developed during this phase tried to respond to those problems, especially by dealing with the specific issues related to sustainable development at monuments and sites and in historic towns and wider territories, and with institutional management.

The late 1990s marked an even more pronounced shift in the TCCP approach – from viewing heritage as an object to positioning it as an agent and catalyst for social improvements. The activities developed in this phase were characterised by an increase in the scope and scale of the interventions, an increase in the duration of the projects, and an increase in the involvement of local people and a wide range of stakeholders.[84] The integrated approach to heritage protection that the TCCP promoted evolved further and extended to societal issues, recognising heritage as a fundamental agent in the management of societal and environmental changes. In line with the CoE's aims, the emphasis of the TCCP has been placed on the need to foster mutual understanding and respect between communities and individuals. By setting the integrated conservation of heritage within the context of broad cultural and social development in its projects, the TCCP started the process that ultimately led to the Faro Convention that 'legitimised' this fundamental shift in the CoE AHD. The Regional Programme on Cultural and Natural Heritage in South-East Europe, the Kyiv Initiative and the COMUS – Community-Led Urban Strategies in Historic Towns of the Caucasus are examples of the programmes the CoE developed during this period.

This fundamental shift, which happened in the CoE's heritage policy at the beginning of the new millennium, and that promoted heritage as a unique resource contributing to the creation of a more peaceful, just, and cohesive society, will be the subject of upcoming chapters. Nevertheless, it was important to make reference to this shift here, as it perfectly illustrates the flexibility that the integrated conservation approach has shown through time – from the

83 Bold and Pickard (n 78).

84 Ibid.

early notion that conservation should be one of the first considerations in all urban and regional planning, to relating heritage to the concept of sustainable development and ultimately recognising the cultural heritage as a recourse that contributes to the creation of more peaceful just and cohesive society. The TCCP's work throughout the decades exemplified this flexibility and demonstrated in practice all those major shifts in the CoE's heritage policy and discourse.

5 Conclusion of the Chapter

The Convention for the Protection of the Architectural Heritage (1985) has served a twofold purpose in the CoE's heritage policy: it legitimised, in the legally binding instrument, the approach to heritage conservation the organisation promoted since the 1960s, and at the same time it anticipated the progress of heritage theory and practice and offered a model (integrated conservation) for accommodating it. Some commentators, even among the CoE staff interviewed, argued that the draft of the Convention remained trapped in the past, re-establishing once again the ideas promoted by the CoE for its first 20 years of heritage-related activities, resulting in a predominantly 'technical' convention. And undeniably, the 'technical' issues the Convention refers to in its Articles 2–9 kept it aligned with the majority of the rest of the international charters and conventions of the time, and as such part of the texts legitimising the AHD. On the other hand, it could be argued that the signing of the more 'conservative' Convention marked the end of a crucial stage in the CoE's heritage work and created a sufficiently secure foundation for the more ambitious texts on heritage protection of the future. It seems that this apparently 'conservative' text was exactly what the CoE's Member States needed at the time, making much of what the Convention required a standard for the protection of the architectural heritage across Europe. The high number of 42 ratifications is a clear sign of the text's success. The 2015 CDCPP Report on the state of implementation of the CoE heritage conventions offered additional proof of how important the Convention's principles have been in the State Parties' legislation. Out of 29 observed Member States, 26 ratified the Convention and declared that its provisions are implemented through national heritage legislation.[85]

---

85 Council of Europe, Steering Committee for Culture, Heritage and Landscape (CDCPP), 'Review of the Council of Europe Conventions under the Responsibility of the CDCPP – Classification by State' [2015] CDCPP (2015) 3 Addendum I Bil Rev.

And while the Convention's 'technical' and 'conservative' characteristics were welcomed by public administration on the national levels, such a categorisation of the text significantly undermined its innovative elements when it came to most of the academic commentary. And yet, its reference to the social value of heritage is an extremely important development that needs to be acknowledged and constitutes one of the major divergences from the AHD in the CoE's discourse.[86] Its enlargement of what constitutes architectural heritage, with the inclusion of vernacular, industrial, and technical heritage, is another significant challenge to the AHD's existence in the Convention. In addition, the principles of sustainable development echoed through its model of integrated conservation is another element that reflected the CoE's understanding of the widened notion of heritage and its role in a cultural and social environment, its economic impact, and its importance in the development of the society. The CoE's understanding of the flexibility of the integrated conservation model in accommodating all these different aspects and roles of heritage protection, and moving it from its focus on particular monuments, played a crucial role in all further CoE heritage policy developments. The next chapters dealing with the CoE's approach to archaeological heritage will further demonstrate the extended use of the integrated approach, proving once again its effectiveness for the CoE's heritage discourse.

86 In its Explanatory Report the explicit reference to the World Conference on Cultural Policies held in Mexico City in 1982 and its broader approach to heritage has been made – 'heritage includes both tangible and intangible works through which the creativity of that people finds expression: languages, rites, beliefs, historic places and monuments, literature, works of art, archives and libraries' (Cultural Heritage, Point 23).

CHAPTER 5

The Council of Europe: Protection of Archaeological Heritage

1 Introduction

As reviewed in the previous chapters, particularly Chapters 3 and 4, the CoE's work in the domain of cultural heritage saw its peak during the 1970s and 1980s, which was a response to major construction projects being carried out all over Europe and the threats they posed to architectural and archaeological heritage. As presented in Chapter 4, the Granada Convention of 1985 consolidated the CoE's important achievements regarding the inclusion of architectural heritage in the town planning and development policies of Member States. 'Integrated conservation' became the predominant doctrine in all of the CoE's heritage activities at the time. However, curiously, the relationship between archaeological heritage and development stayed inadequately addressed by the CoE during this period.

The early 1969 European Convention on the Protection of the Archaeological Heritage (London Convention) primarily focused on archaeological excavation and extracting information from those excavations. It did not satisfactorily address the major problem of clandestine excavation and the illicit trade of archaeological finds, which was the main motive for this convention in the first place, nor did it anticipate or tackle the threats from large-scale development projects, even though they were very much present at the time of its drafting. Against this background, the need for a revised text reflecting changing approaches to the management of archaeological heritage and the changing nature of threats to it since 1969 was evident.

This chapter looks at the context and events at the CoE level that steered the organisation's understanding of the inadequacy of its 1969 Convention and the need for its revision in 1992. The first part of the chapter considers the key changes and aspirations that occurred from 1969 to 1992 and stimulated the revision process of the 1969 London Convention. The second part looks at the fundamental features of the revised European Convention on the Protection of the Archaeological Heritage (known as the Valletta or Malta Convention): the drafting process, the text's characteristics, and its impact and implementation. While the Convention's enormous impact on the management of European archaeological heritage will be acknowledged, as informed by extensive writ-

 DOI:10.1163/9789004756250_006

ing and analysis of many authors,[1] its weight for this book mostly rests in the fact that its drafting process presents a perfect example of how the authorised heritage discourse was shaped and embedded within documents and processes of heritage, management, and conservation. More specifically, it illustrates how archaeology and archaeologists found in the CoE the perfect forum to attain larger political recognition and relevance for their profession in European heritage policymaking, and consequently to legitimise the authority of their expertise and, together with architectural heritage conservators, render the past an exclusive subject of their judgments. Thus, the Valletta Convention has a significant place in the chain of international texts that institutionalised the AHD. Even though, as will be discussed further, the CoE's actions in the heritage field were motivated by the organisation's wider aims of creating a more democratic European society, with community participation in heritage and culture playing a pivotal role, the Valletta Convention, it will be argued (despite certain departures from the AHD), remains a largely technical document that helped the European field of archaeology to institute its position in political arena as well as in the spatial planning and decision-making processes.

The Valletta Convention was adopted on 16 January 1992 and came into force on 25 May 1995 (CoE, Treaty Series No. 143).[2] As of January 2025, 46 states had ratified the Convention, with Iceland and Montenegro being the only two CoE Member States not party to it.

1 See: Willem JH Willems and Monique H van den Dries (eds), *Quality Management in Archaeology* (Oxbow Books 2007);
Patrick J O'Keefe, 'The European Convention on the Protection of the Archaeological Heritage' (1993) 67(255) Antiquity 406;
Gustav Trotzig, 'The New European Convention on the Protection of the Archaeological Heritage' (1993) 67 Antiquity 414;
Alexander Olivier, 'The Valletta Convention: Twenty Years After – A Convenient Time' in Victoria M van der Haas and Peter AC Schut (eds), *The Valletta Convention: Twenty Years After – Benefits, Problems, Challenges* (EAC Occasional Paper No 9, Europae Archaeologia Consilium 2014) 11;
Monique H van den Dries and Willem JH Willems, 'Quality Assurance in Archaeology, the Dutch Perspective' in Willem JH Willems and Monique H van den Dries (eds), *Quality Management in Archaeology* (Oxbow Books 2007) 50.

2 European Convention on the Protection of the Archaeological Heritage (Valletta, 16 January 1992) ETS No 143 ('Valletta Convention').

2 Towards the Archaeological Heritage Convention

The CoE's heritage-related activities gained significant momentum in the 1980s and the beginning of the 1990s, covering the issues of protection of architectural heritage, archaeological heritage, underwater heritage, and offences relating to cultural heritage. The result was the drafting of four conventions on those issues during this period – the 1985 Granada (architecture) and 1992 Valletta (archaeology) Conventions are today considered core CoE texts in the heritage protection field; the Draft Convention on the Protection of the Underwater Cultural Heritage[3] (1984) remained in draft form, while the European Convention on Offences Relating to Cultural Property (1985) was adopted but remained unratified and it was revised in 2017 (Nicosia Convention).[4]

There are a few reasons for this noteworthy focus on heritage matters at the CoE. Firstly, a growing awareness among heritage professionals that archaeological and architectural heritage was rapidly disappearing as a result of booming development and large-scale works across Europe required an urgent response. This situation required new approaches, and the CoE offered an appropriate setting for international discussion by putting the issue on the political agenda. The spread of new ideas on managing and protecting heritage was greatly accelerated in Europe by CoE initiatives, resulting in a more harmonised heritage legal framework in the CoE Member States. As viewed by Interviewee 3, the new focus on more technical aspects and the standard-setting part of the CoE's activities in the 1980s and 1990s was possible because of a political atmosphere that shifted from the initial goals of helping Europeans to know each other better through culture and heritage activities and to build a more democratic society, as presented in the 1954 European Cultural Convention, towards the more technical part of heritage management once the organisation assumed that its core values of democracy, rule of law, and human rights were firmly embedded in its Member States.[5]

In addition to the response to the changing situation and ever-growing threats to heritage, the CoE had to react to the reality of growing European

3 Adopted in March 1984 by the Ad hoc Committee of Experts on the Underwater Cultural Heritage (CAHAQ).

4 Convention had been signed by six countries: Cyprus, Greece, Italy, Liechtenstein, Portugal and Turkey.

5 Interview with Interviewee 3, former employee of the Council of Europe's Cultural Policy Division, 3 February 2020.

Communities' (EC) interest and action in the field of heritage protection.[6] Namely, during the 1980s, the competition between the CoE and the EC in the cultural field became a reality, and a general feeling in the CoE was that the EC was challenging the CoE's primacy, and that the organisation could increasingly lose ground. The CoE was aware that it could not compete with the growing political, financial, and administrative resources of the EC, and it tried to fight this challenge by strengthening its cooperation with the EC, true to the motto 'if you can't beat them, join them'.[7] The increase in actions and number of texts produced during this period by the CoE might reflect the need of the organisation to extend its competencies to as many areas as possible before the EC took the lead.

Before moving to the activities in the archaeological field and the adoption of the 1992 Valletta Convention as a central part of this chapter, it is worth making a brief overview of the other heritage issues discussed during the 1980s, as all of them illustrate the range and intensity of the organisation's involvement in shaping European heritage doctrine. In addition, all these initiatives brought on board a new layer of the CoE's understanding of what is considered to be heritage and how it was supposed to be protected. As the main question leading the actions in the heritage field during this period was 'How do we protect heritage?', the CoE tried to bring as many different types of heritage as possible under its protection. The subject of the preservation of architectural heritage was dealt with within the context of the Granada Convention of 1985 (Chapters 3 and 4). In addition to protecting architectural and archaeological heritage, the CoE addressed the issues of protecting underwater cultural heritage and offences related to cultural property.

2.1 *The CoE and the Protection of Underwater Heritage*

It is well established among commentators in the field that the CoE played a pioneering role in the protection of underwater heritage.[8] In close relation to its revision of the CoE's approach to the archaeological heritage, the PACE

---

6 Kiran Klaus Patel and Oriane Calligaro, 'The True "EURESCO"? The Council of Europe, Transnational Networking and the Emergence of European Community Cultural Policies, 1970–90' (2017) 24(3) European Review of History 399.

7 Ibid 408.

8 Janet Blake, 'The Protection of the Underwater Cultural Heritage' (1996) 45(4) International and Comparative Law Quarterly 819;

Patrick J O'Keefe, 'Fourth Meeting of Governmental Experts to Consider the Draft Convention on the Protection of Underwater Cultural Heritage' (2002) 11(1) International Journal of Cultural Property 168;

Sarah Dromgoole, '2001 UNESCO Convention on the Protection of the Underwater Cultural Heritage' (2003) 18(1) International Journal of Marine and Coastal Law 59;

Committee on Culture and Education published its report, The Underwater Cultural Heritage (widely referred to as the 'Roper Report') in 1978, in which a thorough examination was made of the legal protection of underwater cultural heritage, the nature of underwater archaeology as a discipline, and existing legislation in the CoE's Member States.[9] According to Mr Roper, the need for the PACE report on the matter was first recognised during the debate at the UN Conference on the Law of the Sea in 1977. The growing sense of frustration with the slow progress of the UN Conference in the preparation of an international treaty on the law of the sea and the recognition of the undervalued status of archaeology, in general, in the context of discussions relating to economic, ecological, and spatial planning considerations, was enough incentive for the CoE to take action on the European level 'which might eventually form the basis of wider international agreement'.[10] The report set out the minimal legal requirements for effective protection of underwater cultural heritage. It introduced many useful proposals that resonate in the field even today. The Roper Report was one of the first detailed studies concerning underwater cultural heritage, and it proved to be hugely influential.[11] As noted by Blake, what is striking about the Roper Report's innovative points such as introduction of the 'cultural protection zone' or application of the 'nationality principle' is their similarity to many of the central provisions of the later 1994 draft Convention for the Protection of the Underwater Cultural Heritage prepared by the International Law Association (ILA) that in turn served as the basis for the 2001 UNESCO Convention on the Protection of the Underwater Cultural Heritage.[12] Those central proposals framed in the report were reiterated in the PACE Recommendation 848 on underwater cultural heritage (1978), together with the request for the European Convention on the protection of underwater cultural heritage. The decision to draft the Convention was made in 1979 at the Committee of Ministers, 331st meeting at Deputies Level, and the Ad Hoc Com-

Sarah Dromgoole, *Underwater Cultural Heritage and International Law* (Cambridge University Press 2013);

Anastasia Strati, 'The Notion of the Underwater Cultural Heritage' in Anastasia Strati, *The Protection of the Underwater Cultural Heritage: An Emerging Objective of the Contemporary Law of the Sea*(Brill Nijhoff 1995) 7.

9 Parliamentary Assembly, 'Report on the Underwater Cultural Heritage (Rapporteur Mr Roper)' [1978] Doc 4200.

10 Ibid 5.

11 The only earlier study relating to law and the underwater cultural heritage, referred to in the literature, was published by Crane Miller in 1973 (Crane Miller, International law and Maritime archaeology; there is also a more general study of underwater cultural heritage published by UNESCO in 1972, Underwater Archaeology: A Nascent Discipline).

12 Blake (n 8).

mittee (CAHAQ) started its work in 1980. The CAHAQ held six plenary meetings between 1980 and 1985, which resulted in the draft Convention.

The historical overview of the development of the international texts related to the protection of underwater cultural heritage is a remarkable example of the influences UNESCO and the CoE have had on each other's work. As the slow progress of the 1977 UN Conference on the Law of the Sea led to the CoE's Roper Report (1978), the problematic provisions (Articles 149 and 303) of the later 1982 UN Law of the Sea Convention asked to be addressed in the 1985 draft European Convention on the Protection of the Underwater Cultural Heritage. This example not only allows us to understand the texts' motivation but also demonstrates the intertextuality of those texts that collectively reinforce the authority of the dominant international heritage discourse.

Most commentators consider the CoE's draft Convention to be a significant text for the development of international legal texts in the field, containing many beneficial provisions. However, according to Willems, an important reason for its failure to be adopted was the composition of the CAHAQ; the representatives' main motive was not to protect underwater archaeological heritage but was focused rather on protecting territorial waters.[13] In particular, the Turkish government objected to the adoption of the Convention over the proposed jurisdictional scope and the resulting potential problems of delimitation between Greece and Turkey in the eastern Aegean.[14] Out of the sixteen Member States represented at the final meeting of CAHAQ, it seems that only Turkey objected to the final text of the Convention and its adoption.[15]

It is argued by Blake that the context within which the later 1994 ILA draft Convention (and subsequent 2001 UNESCO Convention) was drafted was a direct result of two developments at the CoE level.[16] The first factor was the disappointing failure of the draft of the European Convention to be adopted in 1985, with all the valuable proposals it suggested. And another significant factor that influenced the ILA draft was the adoption of the 1992 Valletta Convention. The Convention and its characteristics will be explored in more detail shortly, but here it is important to briefly note the Convention's consideration of underwater heritage. The CoE used the revision of the European Conven-

13 Willem JH Willems, 'The Work of Making Malta: The Council of Europe's Archaeology and Planning Committee 1988–1996' (2007) 10(1) European Journal of Archaeology 57.

14 Council of Europe, Committee of Ministers, Ad Hoc Committee of Experts on the Underwater Cultural Heritage (CAHAQ), 'Final Activity Report' [1985] CAHAQ (85) 5, 33.

15 Austria, Cyprus, Denmark, France, Federal Republic of Germany, Greece, Ireland, Italy, the Netherlands, Norway, Portugal, Spain, Sweden Switzerland, the UK and Turkey.

16 Blake (n 8).

tion for the Protection of the Archaeological Heritage in 1992 to reconsider once again the question of protecting underwater cultural heritage and to include the materials and sites located underwater under its scope. This is significant in two major ways. Primarily, it introduced the principle of the State's duty to protect underwater heritage. Secondly, the Valletta Convention addressed the developments in methodological approaches toward the study and protection of archaeological material. Thus, the extension of its scope to underwater archaeological heritage meant that the new philosophy of protection promoted by the Convention would also be applied to that heritage.[17]

As the 1985 European Convention on the Protection of the Underwater Cultural Heritage stayed in draft form and has not been adopted, additional consideration of its provisions will not be further examined in this volume.[18] The importance of this succinct overview served here to emphasise the recurrent argument in this volume that the CoE initiated many important heritage-related initiatives in the international sphere, being most of the time the organisation that first recognised emerging problems and was ready to offer solutions. Its texts were also among the first ones to legitimise and authorise new forms of heritage, thus deviating from certain characteristics of the AHD.

2.2 *Convention on Offences Relating to Cultural Property*

The offences relating to cultural property were another important subject of interest for the CoE during the 1980s. The problem of illicit trafficking and clandestine excavations of archaeological treasures was already discussed on the CoE level in the 1960s and served as the main motive for drafting the 1969 European Convention on the Protection of the Archaeological Heritage. The 1969 Convention left the issue inadequately addressed with the hope from the Member States that the 1970 UNESCO Convention on the Means of Prohibiting and Preventing the Illicit Import, Export and Transfer of Ownership of Cultural Property would offer a satisfactory solution. Nevertheless, as evident from a question posed by Lord Duncan Sandys to the CoE Committee of Ministers in 1977, none of the CoE Member States at the time ratified the UNESCO Convention.[19] The question to the Committee was 'whether they will enquire from the governments of the member states concerned the reasons why they

17 Ibid.

18 See extensive analysis by Dromgoole 2013 (n 8).

19 UNESCO, List of the State Parties to the Convention on the Means of Prohibiting and Preventing the Illicit Import, Export and Transfer of Ownership of Cultural Property (1970).

have so far not felt able to ratify this convention'.[20] This discontent with the slow ratification of UNESCO's text and the awareness of the Convention's weaknesses led to a new CoE initiative – the drafting of the European Convention on Offences relating to Cultural Property.[21]

In general, the fact that no obligations under criminal law were imposed on the Contracting Parties and that the Convention only offered the encouragement to adopt measures for the cultural properties' protection were seen as the 1970 UNESCO Convention's weakest points. In 1977, the CoE's Committee on Crime Problems (CDPC) decided to address these inadequacies in international cooperation regarding the punishment of offences against cultural heritage and to raise awareness of the inadequate legal rules on this subject. A Selected Committee of Experts on International Cooperation in the Field of Offences Relating to Works of Art (PCROA) started its work on the draft in 1978, initially aiming to present the Convention at the Conference of European Ministers of Justice in Athens in 1982. However, the final draft was opened for signature only in 1985 (Delphi, 1985). With this draft, the CoE aimed to look at the problem primarily through the lens of criminal law and to offer principally a criminal law convention to combat the illicit trafficking of cultural property. Commonly known as the Delphi Convention, the text intended to establish a legal standard for the international protection of cultural property by introducing definitions of the different offences against cultural property[22] as well as a list of the wide range of items that can be described as cultural property; in general, those regarded as being of great importance from an artistic, historical, archaeological, scientific, or other cultural interest.[23] However, as argued by Ulph and Vigneron, there are several reasons that explain why the Delphi

20 Parliamentary Assembly, Written Question No 194 by Lord Duncan-Sandys on the UNESCO Convention of 1970 for the Protection of Art Treasures against Theft [1977] Doc 3972.

21 Report by Mr Schutter, The Harmonisation of Criminal Law and International Criminal Co-operation as Instruments of Protection (13th Colloquy on European Law, Delphi, 1983) [1983] CJ-DE/13 (83) 6.

22 The list of offences includes:
- Thefts of cultural property
- Appropriating cultural property with violence or menace
- Handling cultural property obtained as the result of an offence against the property other than theft
- Destruction or damage of the cultural property of another person
- Actual or attempted exportation of cultural property exportation of which is prohibited by the law of a Party

(ETS 119 – Convention on Offences relating to Cultural Property, Appendix III).

23 Robert Pickard, *European Cultural Heritage* (vol 2, Council of Europe Publishing 2002).

Convention remained unratified.[24] Firstly, its formulations were vague, and the criminal offences it listed uncertain in scope. Secondly, rather than offering a text that would homogenise European criminal law, the implementation of the Convention was à la carte. Lastly, the Convention did not contain a unique definition of cultural property and instead gave States the freedom to add further offences to the list it defined (Appendix III), which risked limiting inter-State cooperation.[25] From the point of view of criminal law, commentators argue, the fact that the Delphi Convention remained a dead letter (since it was signed only by six States, none of which went on to ratify it) must be considered a 'lost opportunity'.[26]

Its specific attention to the criminal law dimension that particularly focused on the direct protection of the cultural assets, their restitution, and the repression of crime in this sector was seen as a significant effort toward harmonisation of some rules of criminal law in the CoE Member States. However, in the context of this book, its criminal law dimension makes it less relevant regarding the formulation of a distinct CoE heritage discourse. By the nature of its focus on cultural property, the materiality of the cultural heritage the Convention covers is self-evident. Its consideration of 'cultural property' as any category of movable or immovable property 'presenting an artistic, historical, archaeological, scientific interest' (Article 2)[27] is rather in line with the AHD's understanding of cultural heritage. A slight deviation from this predominant understanding could be traced in the phrase 'or other cultural interest' in the same article (Article 2). This expression, it could be argued, leaves the possibility for different communities to declare an item that is not necessarily considered of great importance by experts to be 'cultural property' and as such subject to this Convention. However, the view that this Convention primarily touches on criminal law resulted in the decision to not include the extensive discussion on it, or the matter of offences relating to cultural heritage, in the scope of this volume (nor the new more successful, and in force, 2017, Council

---

24 Janet Ulph and Sophie Vigneron, 'The Significance of the Convention on Offences Relating to Cultural Property 2017' in Deborah M Fabiani, Kate M Burmon and Saskia Hufnagel (eds), *Cultural Property Crime and the Law: Legal Approaches to Protection, Repatriation, and Countering Illicit Trade* (Routledge 2024).

25 Ibid.

26 Stefano Manacorda, 'Criminal Law Protection of Cultural Heritage: An International Perspective' in Stefano Manacorda and Duncan Chappell (eds), *Crime in the Art and Antiquities World* (Springer 2011) 37.

27 Article 2 (3) reads: Any Contracting State may, at any time, declare that for the purposes of this Convention it also considers as cultural property any category of movable or immovable property, presenting an artistic, historical, archaeological, scientific or other cultural interest, that it not included in Appendix II.

of Europe Convention on Offences relating to Cultural Property (Nicosia Convention).[28] It was important, however, to touch upon this subject in this section as it illustrates the wide CoE concern with the issues in the heritage field at the time.

The failed initiatives for the ratification of the European Convention on the Protection of the Underwater Cultural Heritage and the Delphi Convention were surely an additional motivation for the process of revision of the 1969 Convention on the Protection of the Archaeological Heritage of Europe to be successful. The following sections of this chapter will look at the archaeology-specific developments in the post-1969 period that led to the Valletta Convention and its implementation around Europe.

2.3 *Florence and Nice Colloquies*

In this section, the emphasis is on the significant changes that have occurred in the field of archaeology since the formulation of the 1969 London Convention, which pushed the CoE towards the drafting of the Valletta Convention. This fairly descriptive historical overview of the developments of the archaeological heritage activities in the intergovernmental sphere in the next section is needed as it reflects on the inter-organisational dynamics and sets the scene for the ideas developed and promoted in the Valletta Convention.

The intense transition of archaeology from a purely scientific and academic field (as treated in the 1969 London Convention) to a field that became actively involved in spatial planning that also asked for the development of more comprehensive management of archaeological heritage that happened during the 1970s and 1980s, was deeply reflected in the CoE's approach to the subject. Following the passage of the Archaeological and Historic Preservation Act in the USA in the early 1970s, the necessity to protect threatened archaeological heritage spread internationally and, importantly, into the consciousness of international bodies. For this protection to be successful, there had to be strong doctrinal and legislative texts that would form a needed framework within which archaeological heritage would be managed. In those formative years of what is today known as 'archaeological heritage management' or, broadly, 'heritage management', archaeologists had to find their place at the table of influential international bodies.

---

28 Currently (June 2025), the 2017 Nicosia Convention has been ratified by seven countries: Albania, Cyprus, Greece, Hungary, Italy, Latvia and Mexico (Mexico is not a Member of the CoE, but the Convention is open for ratification also for a non-Member States) and signed by additional seven countries: Armenia, Montenegro, Portugal, the Russian Federation, San Marino, Slovenia and Ukraine. It entered into force in April 2022.

On the international level, the doctrinal setting was provided in 1984 by the International Committee on Archaeological Heritage Management of the ICOMOS (ICAHM). The successful campaign launched in 1981 by archaeologists to make their views heard in ICOMOS, which was hitherto predominantly the sphere of influence of architects and architectural historians, led to the creation of ICAHM. ICAHM's primary task was to draft an international charter comparable to the hugely successful Venice Charter of 1964 that would provide the philosophical basis for preserving and managing archaeological heritage. The Charter for the Protection and Management of Archaeological Heritage was ratified by the General Assembly of ICOMOS in 1990. The Charter, which by the necessity of its universal application is general in its language, nonetheless articulated the broad principles of archaeological heritage management. However, according to Cleere, it received very little publicity after it was approved.[29] Its principles, such as protection policies integrated with general planning, the need for clear and adequate legislation, the need for an inventory of the country's archaeological heritage, the study of that heritage, its maintenance and conservation, its presentation to the public, and its relationship with economic development, were already fairly established in the predominantly European archaeological community and, as the following examination of archival sources shows, had already been discussed in detail on the CoE level and legitimised in its texts.

On the European level, as already touched upon in the previous chapter, the exceptional economic growth and development in most of the CoE Member States in the 1960s and 1970s meant, as Gauthier put it, 'glory for the economy and disaster for archaeology'.[30] One could have hoped that the CoE would have considered the situation on the ground during these decades and addressed these concerns in the 1969 Convention. Regrettably, this was not the case. From today's perspective, the absence of an adequate response to those hazards is even more surprising if we know that the organisation addressed the issues and the same threats to the architectural heritage during this period. Arguably, however, the treatment of archaeology, as in the 1969 London Convention, reflects the discipline's struggle to accept its role in wider social processes. The emergence of archaeological heritage management (AHM) as an important area of archaeological practice in the 1960s and 1970s still meant that many

29 Henry Cleere, 'The Charter for the Protection and Management of the Archaeological Heritage' (1993) 67(255) Antiquity 402.

30 Martine Gauthier, 'The Origins and Aims of the Valletta Convention: Its Implementation in France' in Victoria M van der Haas and Peter AC Schut (eds), *The Valletta Convention: Twenty Years After – Benefits, Problems, Challenges* (EAC Occasional Paper No 9, Europae Archaeologia Consilium 2014) 31.

archaeologists did not, and in terms of their philosophies of science, could not, consider AHM to be 'real' science or 'real' archaeology.[31] It could be argued that it is mostly due to this struggle among archaeologists to find the theoretical framework for the AHM at the time that they missed the opportunity to address already-emerging threats to archaeological heritage in Europe in the 1969 Convention. In other words, it was not the misperception or unwillingness of the CoE to address the issue. Rather, the adopted texts reflected the preoccupations of the discipline's experts and their lobbying for those concerns they found relevant at the time. So, the London Convention was drafted with the motive to fight illicit excavations and counterfeits on the antiquity market and had as a priority the protection of archaeological excavations.

The welcomed change of direction in the CoE's rapport towards archaeology and the threats to archaeological heritage was taken in the early 1980s. It certainly reflected the consolidation of AHM and archaeologists' understanding of it on the international level, as witnessed by the archaeologists' campaign to establish the ICAHM that started in 1981. The CoE has certainly been another organisation archaeologists looked at as a relevant international body that needed to be influenced by their new approach to protecting and managing archaeological heritage. The first sign of the CoE's adjustment to the new developments in archaeology and to the need to react to the already critical situation regarding the threats to archaeological heritage took shape in creating the group of experts (1982) whose purpose was to make proposals on the protection and preservation of archaeological heritage within the framework of urban planning.[32] The work of this expert group led to the organisation of the Florence Colloquy on Archaeology and Planning in 1984, which brought together around a hundred participants from eighteen CoE Member States.

The four-day meeting was a chance for archaeologists to pronounce their priorities and preoccupations. Those priorities can be summarised as follows:

1. Effective protection of important sites, with the collaboration of planners;
2. Prevention of the destruction of archaeological evidence (including paleo-environmental elements) before it has been adequately studied;
3. Ensuring that, where excavation is necessary, it is carried out in proper conditions, for example, by anticipating archaeological investigation in development procedures;

31 Laurajane Smith, *Archaeological Theory and the Politics of Cultural Heritage* (Routledge 2004) 41.

32 Council of Europe, 'Archaeology and Planning – Report of the Florence Colloquy' [1984] PUBDGIV008.

4. Consideration of physical conservation of archaeological material, whether in situ, in the museum, or not at all, subsequent to excavation and evaluation, alongside other considerations of the environment and land use;
5. Consolidation of the discipline of archaeology in all its aspects and improvement of archaeological techniques (prospection, excavation, and conservation) considering the development of planning techniques.[33]

By looking at those priorities, an obvious parallel could be drawn with the actions and the priorities of the conservators and architectural historians in the 1960s and 1970s, as reviewed in Chapters 3 and 4. The archaeologists essentially asked the CoE to implement the integrated conservation approach to the field of archaeology and to formulate recommendations on the subject to the Member States. Their more specific proposals were made in the complementary note of the Florence meeting where the participants defined, without using the term explicitly, ideal preventive archaeology.[34] All the objectives to be reached were pronounced under eight themes,[35] which, one may notice, were largely reiterated in the ICOMOS Charter for the Protection and Management of the Archaeological Heritage in 1990. Still, as the event was dominated by archaeologists, a desired dialogue with spatial planners and developers needed to be included and the need for a more inclusive debate and further colloquy was suggested by the CoE.

And indeed, there was a strong political determination at the CoE level to ensure that these proposals did not remain a list of good intentions. In 1985, the creation of a Committee of Experts on Archaeology and Rural and Urban Planning was initiated, composed mainly of archaeologists from ten CoE Member States. The group decided to concentrate on the comparative study of archaeology and large public works and to organise the second colloquy based on the results of the study. The colloquy Archaeology and Major Public Works was held in Nice in November 1987. After the Florence meeting with its fairly abstract discussion, some groups of problems needed further consider-

33 Report of the Florence Colloquy (n 32) 97.

34 Gauthier (n 30).

35 (1) undertaking of the systematic national archaeological survey and inventory, (2) integration of archaeological considerations in planning procedures, (3) legislation – all planning legislation should cover the protection of the cultural heritage, (4) financial aspects – adequate resources for archaeological work must be assured, (5) increasing public awareness – a more open dialogue should be developed between the experts, the authorities, elected representatives, developers and public, (6) training, (7) exchange of information between member states, and (8) research.

ation on a more practical level. The first problem the participants brought up was the need for more dialogue and understanding between archaeologists, planners, and decision-makers. The organisers of the meeting in Nice made sure that this time representatives of all considered professions were invited, and town planners, architects, engineers, jurists, administrators, and archaeologists 'discovered each other at last'.[36]

The initial Florence meeting also highlighted the importance of legal aspects in protecting archaeological heritage. The results of the comparative study of legal solutions across Europe, carried out by the CoE group of experts, showed extreme diversity. All different types of legal systems were identified, between the example of Norway, where all remains earlier than 1537 were protected, to the case of Belgium, which in 1987 did not have legislation or administration relating specifically to archaeology.[37] Considering this diversity of legal solutions, the need for a more harmonised European approach was welcomed among participants in Nice, and the frame for future CoE Recommendation R (89)5 was set up.[38]

The Nice Colloquy was the occasion for taking stock of new working methods that emerged across Europe related to cooperation between archaeologists and developers. New solutions were developed in three fields: technical and scientific, legal, and financial. The solutions and methods advocated in the conclusion of the meeting were largely considered and implemented in the text of Recommendation R (89)5, which was the first step toward a more binding European treaty.

Recommendation R (89)5 Concerning the Protection and Enhancement of the Archaeological Heritage in the Context of Town and Country Planning Operations was adopted by the Committee of Ministers of the CoE in April 1989 (425th meeting of the Ministers' Deputies). All the desires expressed in Nice by experts were accounted for, reflecting the evolution of archaeological research after 1969. The text's recommendations included, among others: (1) the establishment of national inventories and maps that planners can use, (2) creating or reinforcing scientific and administrative structures capable of handling development projects involving archaeological data, (3) increasing

---

36 Gauthier (n 30).

37 Council of Europe, 'Archaeology and Major Public Works – Report of the Nice Colloquy' [1989] PUBDGIV018.

38 Council of Europe, Committee of Ministers, 'Recommendation No R (89) 5 of the Committee of Ministers to Member States Concerning the Protection and Enhancement of the Archaeological Heritage in the Context of Town and Country Planning Operations' [1989].

the financial and human resources dedicated to preventive archaeology, and (4) raising awareness of the importance of archaeology for the community.

This instrument, in principle, gave archaeology a legitimate place in Europe, recommending to the CoE Member States that they should have regulations in place making it mandatory for archaeological services to be consulted before any work that might damage archaeological heritage commences. On the other hand, archaeologists were respectively invited to enlarge their audience by 'explaining the importance for the community of the archaeological heritage as a major element of the European cultural identity'.[39] A more detailed review of this provision, which was also incorporated in the Valletta Convention, will be given in the following section of the chapter. In summary, the text of the Recommendation underlined ideal preventive archaeology. However, given that it is meant to be just a recommendation and, as such, non-binding for the Member States, its provisions were easily accepted. Unsurprisingly, as noted by Egloff and Comer, the ICAHM Charter was inspired by this CoE work, having the same European heritage specialists involved in drafting those texts and influencing the efforts of these organisations (for example, Gustaf Trotzig, who was a founder of ICAHM, was an influential member of the CoE working group that organised the Florence and Nice colloquies, as well as the Chairman of the CoE Committee of Experts on Archaeology and Planning that drafted the Valletta Convention).[40] The example of the interconnection of these CoE and ICOMOS texts demonstrates how texts, individually and collectively, create a consensus that gains international presence and, according to Smith, 'the sense of self-referential authority of conservation and management philosophy and practice is achieved'.[41] It is precisely in this way that the authority of the AHD was reinforced, or to quote Smith once again, 'their intertextuality *is* the AHD'.[42]

Additionally, for many, including the Committee of Experts preparing Recommendation R (89)5, it was clear that for more cohesive European action in the field of archaeology, the Recommendation was not enough and the drafting of the new convention or the revision of the 1969 London Convention was

---

39 Recommendation R (89) 5 (n 38).

40 Bruno Egloff and Douglas Comer, 'Conserving the Archaeological Soul of Places: Drafting Guidelines for the ICAHM Charter' in *16th ICOMOS General Assembly and International Symposium: Finding the Spirit of Place – Between the Tangible and the Intangible* (Quebec, 29 September–4 October 2008).

41 Laurajane Smith, *Uses of Heritage* (Routledge 2006) 94.

42 Ibid 94.

essential.[43] The Committee of Experts decided on the latter option for two reasons: (1) a revision of the text would not prevent adding to it or restructuring it profoundly, and, more importantly, (2) this would avoid the very demanding procedure that a new text would have to go through, without any guarantee that it would be adopted at all.[44]

The next section will look in detail at the revision process of the Convention and its final draft, which aimed to reflect the new risks and threats to archaeological heritage but also the exceptional scientific and methodological developments in the field as well as the previously identified objectives and aspirations of the archaeological community.

3 European Convention for the Protection of the Archaeological Heritage: Draft

With the preparatory work done, and with clear objectives stipulated in Recommendation R (89)5, the revision of the Convention was a rather swift endeavour – it took only five meetings (in the period from June 1990 to June 1991) for the Selected Committee of Experts on Archaeology and Planning (PH-R-MA)[45] to complete the draft. It did, however, require the experts to leave the ideal that had motivated their work since 1984 for the necessary realism that would permit the Convention's successful adoption.[46] In other words, the archaeologists who dominated the work of the PH-R-MA easily agreed on the text's main scientific and technical objectives. Still, they also had to readjust their expectations considering the legal domain of the text's provisions, the necessary diplomatic balance, the economic aspects, the tax systems, and the issues related to land ownership in the Member States, among other issues.

Keeping in mind all the steps that this kind of political text needs to go through and, most importantly, the required approval of political authorities,

43 Council of Europe, Steering Committee for Integrated Conservation of the Historic Heritage (CDPH), 'Select Committee of Experts on Archaeology and Planning (PH-R-MA) – Meeting Report' [1988] CDPH (88) 66.

44 Gauthier (n 30).

45 Since June 1990, the *Select Committee of Experts on Archaeology and Planning* has been operating within the Cultural Heritage Committee (CC-PAT) programme. The CC-PAT replaced the Steering Committee for Integrated Conservation of the Historic Heritage in June 1990 and became the specialised committee attached to the Council for Cultural Co-operation – CDCC. (CC-PAT (91) 41).

46 Gauthier (n 30).

the fact that such a document could be prepared predominantly by archaeologists rather than politicians or jurists in a political organisation has been welcomed and praised by European archaeologists. The composition of the drafting committee ensured that the professional voice of the archaeologists would be heard, or rather, would be predominant, and it allowed them to legitimise their position as the only ones capable of determining the meaning and values of archaeological sites through the international heritage text. It is a rather clear example of the AHD's authorisation of experts' positions and values. On the other hand, the dominant role given to the archaeologists in drafting the Valletta Convention has been met with certain reservations by some interviewed former and current CoE staff who worked on the text. While not negating the need for a text to formalise the role of archaeology and archaeologists in the wider planning processes in Europe as urged by archaeologists, the critique heard was that the text is lacking any political dimension, as could be expected from the political organisation. In the words of Interviewee 3 '…the text looks like the text produced by ICOMOS rather than the CoE. It does not reflect the organisation's values or political goals'.[47] The general impression of the Secretariat was that the archaeologists took the opportunity to address all the pending professional issues while completely ignoring the wider context and organisation's values and aims in the drafting process.[48]

Following the successful organisation of the Nice Colloquy, the French delegation took responsibility for drafting the first version of the new Convention.[49] This 'martyr text' served as a base for discussion and was further modified according to the participants' amendments. The text was based on the original 1969 London Convention and the main articles of the 1989 Recommendation. The discussion reflected the main professionals' preoccupation at the time of drafting and the key changes that occurred to archaeology's scientific and technical context since the London Convention. The revised Convention directly responded to the significant impacts of those changes.[50] It is important to specify that the following section will look at the drafting process and characteristics of specific articles of the Convention, while the

47 Interview with Interviewee 3, former employee of the Council of Europe's Cultural Policy Division, (3 February 2020).

48 Interview with Interviewee 1, former employee of the Council of Europe's Directorate of Culture and Cultural and Natural Heritage (1 April 2020).

49 Council of Europe, Steering Committee for Integrated Conservation of the Historic Heritage (CDPH), Select Committee of Experts on Archaeology and Planning, 'Document de Travail soumis par la Délégation Française pour la Réunion des 12–13 juin 1989' [1989] CDPH (89) 28.

50 Willem (n 13).

impact and implementation of those provisions will be discussed in a separate section shortly.

The changing definition of archaeological heritage was the first issue discussed. In any legal instrument seeking to protect cultural heritage, it is of prime importance to define what is to be protected, and the scope of the revised Convention was of great concern among members of the drafting committee. While the London Convention put the emphasis on the objects found during excavations (Article 1 of the London Convention 1969), the revised Convention attempted to set up a more inclusive definition. Article 1 of the Valletta Convention defines archaeological heritage as follows:

> 2. To this end shall be considered to be elements of the archaeological heritage all remains and objects and any other traces of mankind from past epochs:
> i) the preservation and study of which help to retrace the history of mankind and its relation with the natural environment;
> ii) for which excavations or discoveries and other methods of research into mankind and the related environment are the main sources of information; and
> which are located in any area within the jurisdiction of the Parties.
> The archaeological heritage shall include structures, constructions, groups of buildings, developed sites, moveable objects, monuments of other kinds as well as their context, whether situated on land or underwater.

As stated in the Explanatory Report to the Convention, the phrase 'element of the archaeological heritage' was used to emphasise that the importance is not just on the objects, but rather on any evidence, of whatever nature, that can throw light on the past of humanity is important. If that evidence meets the criteria set in paragraph 2, then it is an element of the archaeological heritage.[51]

Article 1.3 was considered by some northern countries to be too broad because it could be interpreted to include 'built heritage', which at the time was largely separated from 'archaeological heritage'. As witnessed by the Secretariat member participating in the experts' meetings, the southern countries were unwilling to limit the definition of archaeological heritage with all their extant historical buildings from Antiquity in mind.[52] On the other hand, the

51 Council of Europe, *Explanatory Report to the European Convention on the Protection of the Archaeological Heritage* (Revised) [1992] (European Treaty Series No 143).

52 Interview with Interviewee 1 (n 48).

northern countries argued that built and archaeological heritage are separated in at least three ways: (1) from an academic viewpoint, the subjects are studied in totally different university departments (archaeology department vs. art history/architecture); (2) in legal terms, with disparities in the legal position between real estate and land; and (3) from the organisational perspective, whereby the two types of heritage are handled by separate government departments in most of the countries.[53] The arguments by northern European countries resonate with Smith's idea that the AHD tends to reduce the concept of heritage to 'manageable' and to emphasise the importance of its identifiable material boundaries. What this discussion additionally shows is how even the tangible/material aspects of the AHD were developed gradually; the European archaeologists took a considerable amount of time to establish themselves and archaeological heritage management in international heritage bodies on an equal footing with the experts in the protection of architectural heritage. The same could be observed regarding underwater heritage; including underwater archaeological remains in the definition was considered an important victory for experts drafting the text.[54]

Another important aspect of Article 1 is the provision stating the aim of the revised Convention, which is to 'protect the archaeological heritage as a source of the *European collective memory* and as an instrument for historical and scientific study' (Article 1.1). This is a rare political statement in the text reflecting the broader aim of the organisation and is one of the important (AHD) elements of the Valletta Convention, clearly articulating the growing awareness that archaeological heritage has scientific importance in informing our understanding of the development of humankind in Europe and that it is an important source of Europe's collective memory. During the last 150 years, the political role of archaeology has tended to swing between local, national, and international perspectives. The CoE's orientation towards the European dimension of archaeological heritage has been seen by commentators[55] as an attempt to break away from the then-predominant national dimension of archaeology

53 Willems (n 13).

54 Willem JH Willems, 'Malta and Its Consequences: A Mixed Blessing' in Victoria M van der Haas and Peter AC Schut (eds), *The Valletta Convention: Twenty Years After – Benefits, Problems, Challenges*(EAC Occasional Paper No 9, Europae Archaeologia Consilium 2014) 151.

55 Kristian Kristiansen, 'Archaeological Communities and Languages' in Robin Skeates, Carol McDavid and John Carman (eds), *The Oxford Handbook of Public Archaeology* (Oxford University Press 2012) 461.

Patrick J O'Keefe, 'The European Convention on the Protection of the Archaeological Heritage' (1993) 67(255) Antiquity 406.

and its renewed focus on historical origins and local histories within it (despite claims of cultural diversity as a preferred framework in some countries). In the 1990s, European societies confronted increasing uncertainty about their regional, national, or supra-national identities. The former Soviet and Yugoslav countries needed to create new national identities, while Western European countries witnessed increasing migration that prompted discussion about cultural differences between 'others' and 'occidental'.[56] All these changes were reflected in the revival of national heritage throughout Europe. At the same time, the accession of new member countries to the CoE and the political will to further develop the EU, both politically and culturally, saw a growing number of examples of using history and heritage in the promotion of Europeanism. The Valletta initiative, among others, was a clear response to the changing political conditions after the fall of the Iron Curtain in 1991. It was a reaction to a new revival of nationalism and national heritage throughout Europe and a first attempt to create a European framework for archaeological research and heritage.[57] The processes of European unification and continually growing political cooperation in the 1990s had a significant influence on archaeology and the community of archaeologists in Europe, and the Valletta Convention was one of the main results coming from the understanding of the new 'political' role of archaeology at the European level.[58] However, the model and role of using heritage in identity building, be it a national one or European, was the same – one based on the difference between 'us/Europeans' and 'others', which as seen by Smith[59] and De Cesari[60] among others, inevitably means that other forms of identity would be obscured or devalued. The well-known mechanism of the AHD was used by the CoE in the same manner as by the nation-states, even if the CoE saw this Europeanness as one promoting diversity and inclusion and opposing nationalism. At this stage, however, the CoE remained unclear about what precisely the notion of 'European' entails. As noted by Willems, for the archaeological community at least, Article 1 of the Valletta Convention

56 Alexander Gramsch, 'Theory in Central European Archaeology: Dead or Alive?' in John Bintliff and Mark Pearce (eds), *The Death of Archaeological Theory?* (Oxbow Books 2011) 48.

57 Kristiansen (n 55).

58 Willem JH Willems, *The Future of European Archaeology* (Oxbow Books 1999);

This increased awareness of and interest in European aspects in archaeology promoted by Valletta and other CoE initiatives developed under the *European Plan for Archaeology* (1992–1997) following the adoption of the Convention resulted also in the creation of the European Association of Archaeologists (EAA) in 1994.

59 Smith (n 41).

60 Chiara De Cesari, 'Memory Voids and the New European Heritage: A Proposal for Studying Transnational Memory' (2012) 25 Journal of Museum Ethnography 152.

remained relatively neutral when referring to archaeological heritage as a '*source* of European collective memory' – archaeologists preferred to focus on the idea of archaeological heritage as a source of information rather than on the 'political' role of that heritage in the unification of Europe.[61] Nevertheless, this short provision in Article 1 was probably the only provision reflecting the CoE's political goal of uniting Europe in this Convention, leaving the rest of the text to deal with technical aspects of archaeological heritage protection.

The mounting threats to archaeological heritage discussed previously in this chapter (major public works, development projects, etc.), which led to the revision of the 1969 Convention, asked for new measures for protection. Article 2 requires the State Parties to institute a 'legal system for the protection of the archaeological heritage'. The comparative study on existing legal systems in the CoE Member States from 1987 showed that most of the countries had legislation that to some extent implemented protective measures.[62] However, for most signatory countries to the revised Convention, it required a certain upgrade of their protection system. This particular point will be discussed further in this chapter's section devoted to the Valletta Convention's implementation. What the Valletta Convention emphasised in this respect is the importance of having detailed inventories of archaeological heritage alongside legal measures and systems to regulate the designation of protected areas, creation of archaeological reserves, and mandatory reporting of finds.

The scientific approach to the work on archaeological heritage is the subject of Article 3. The emphasis was on the use of non-destructive methods of investigation whenever possible and on procedures to ensure that what is excavated is properly preserved, conserved, and managed. Here, the Valletta Convention stays in line with the ICOMOS Charter for the Protection and Management of the Archaeological Heritage (1990), which also promoted the same methodology and reaffirmed already established scientific standards. The requirement from the States to 'ensure that excavations and other potentially destructive techniques are carried out *only* by qualified, specially authorised persons' (Article 3. ii) was raising some questions about the role of volunteers. The prevailing interpretation is that this does not exclude members of the general public from excavation. It rather emphasises that they must be under the control of a qualified person responsible for the excavation. This explanation provided in the Explanatory Report to the Convention allowed a continuation of the prac-

61 Willems (n 54).

62 Council of Europe, Steering Committee for Integrated Conservation of the Historic Heritage (CDPH), 'Archaeology and Major Public Works – The Law and its Application: Comparative Study of the Situation in Several European Countries' [1987] CDPH/Nice (87) 1.

tice in a number of countries of using volunteers for assistance in excavations, but it firmly established the authority of experts and the privilege of their values over those of the non-experts. The role of the general public and its participation in archaeology was thus treated as a 'problem' that needed to be regulated and limited.

This 'problem' was even more accentuated with the issue of metal detectors. The CoE worked on the issue as early as 1981, with PACE's Recommendation 921 on Metal Detectors and Archaeology. However, the problem needed to be addressed again – this time in the revised Convention. The archaeological community, nevertheless, has criticised the CoE's attempt as insufficient. As condemned by O'Keefe, the provision in Article 3.3 can be 'only described as a very weak provision for dealing with the very real problem posed by indiscriminate and unscientific use of metal detectors'.[63] Even though the majority in the drafting committee insisted on a provision that would ban the unlicensed use of metal detectors, the political reality, in this case, having the UK not signing the Convention in case of strong wording on this issue, resulted in a rather watered-down paragraph,[64] hidden in Article 3.3 that reads:

> [Each Party undertakes] to subject to specific prior authorisation, whenever foreseen by the domestic law of the State, the use of metal detectors and any other detection equipment or process for archaeological investigation.

The provision still says what the standard should be, but that does not explicitly oblige State Parties to do anything.[65]

While Articles 2 and 3 are concerned with setting up legal and administrative procedures to enhance the management of archaeological sites, Article 4 imposes measures for the physical protection of archaeological heritage. States are expected to provide protection for archaeological reserves[66] and to privilege the conservation and maintenance of the archaeological site

63 O'Keefe (n 55) 410.

64 Willems (n 13).

65 Ibid.

66 Archaeological reserves are areas of land subject to certain restrictions in order to preserve the archaeological heritage contained within the borders. The UNESCO Recommendation concerning the Preservation of Cultural Property endangered by Public or Private Works (19 November 1968) provides that (Article 24.a): 'Archaeological reserves should be zoned or scheduled and, if necessary, immovable property purchased, to permit thorough excavation or the preservation of the ruins found at the site.' Article 2 of the revised Convention is aimed at preserving the heritage in order that it will be available for later generations. It should be read in conjunction with Article 4, sub-

in situ. This provision again goes in line with the doctrine promoted by ICOMOS in its Charter (Article 6), making preservation in situ a dominant ideology in heritage management after Valletta.

What is considered by most commentators on the text to be the main elements of this Convention are the issues discussed in Articles 5, 6, and 9 that regulate how archaeology should become part of the planning process; that it should be financed through the budget of development schemes; and that its results should be communicated to the public. Still, as witnessed by Willems, these elements were almost beyond discussion (apart from Article 6) during the drafting process.[67] Since they were already established by Recommendation (1989) 5, founding agreement on them was rather unproblematic, and they were integrated into the Valletta Convention in line with the already established CoE views.

According to the member of the Secretariat working on the text, the main goal of the Valletta Convention was to formally set out the integrated conservation of archaeological heritage in the national legislation of CoE Member States.[68] The same approach earlier promoted by the CoE in the Grenada Convention on architectural heritage was now expanded to cover archaeological heritage. The Convention required State parties to ensure that archaeologists and town and spatial planners cooperate throughout the entire planning process. The Convention repeatedly emphasised the importance of consultation between archaeologists and town and spatial planners, especially in two cases; firstly, when the modification of development plans likely to have adverse effects on archaeological heritage is necessary and secondly, if modification is not possible, the sufficient time for site excavation should be made available.[69] It could be rightly said that as a result of this Article, archaeology in contemporary Europe is firmly integrated into spatial planning, and archaeologists are now appropriately included in the relevant decision-making processes.

Another important issue was funding, considered under Article 6. With the Valletta Convention, the archaeological work resulting from development was placed on a much firmer, more structured funding basis than before. Influenced by the environmental movement, the policy of 'the polluter pays all'

---

paragraph *i*. The creation of reserves does not mean that the land cannot be used at all. Normally, it means that operations which disturb the soil cannot be allowed or must first be cleared by the relevant authorities. Any excavation must be subjected to severe scrutiny in the light of scientific objectives (Explanatory Report, Article 2).

67 Willems (n 13).

68 Interview with Interviewee 1, former employee of the Council of Europe's Directorate of Culture and Cultural and Natural Heritage, (1 April 2020).

69 O'Keefe (n 55).

(i.e., whoever destroys an archaeological site should pay for the excavation costs) was discussed at great length and was put forward in the early drafts of the Convention.[70] However, according to Trotzig, because it was considered to be too provocative for certain countries, the proposed provision was modified in the final version that, to the regret of the French delegation, could be interpreted as not explicitly obliging private developers to cover archaeological operation costs.[71] Unfortunately, the discussion on this last-minute change in the text is missing from the archive documents (to the author's knowledge). What is visible is that Article 6 changed from its initial version, which stated that each Party undertakes:

> To increase the material resources for rescue archaeology by taking appropriate measures to ensure that the cost of archaeological operations necessitated by major public or private development schemes is *met in full* from the budget relating to such schemes.[72]

To its final version, which was adopted by the Committee of Ministers (461st meeting, September 1991), that reads:

> Each Party undertakes to increase the material resources for rescue archaeology by taking suitable measures to ensure that provision is made in major public or private development schemes for covering, from the public sector or private sector resources, *as appropriate*, the total costs of any necessary related archaeological operations.
>
> Article 4.2.i

Still, the principle of financial support for archaeological interventions by public or private developers became a common feature in many states, resulting in a significant increase in funding for archaeology. As justly noted by O'Keefe, the importance of the international legal obligation that comes with

70 Council of Europe, Steering Committee for Integrated Conservation of the Historic Heritage (CDPH), 'Select Committee of Experts on Archaeology and Planning (PH-R-MA) – Revision of the European Convention on the Protection of the Archaeological Heritage (2nd Meeting, Report)' [1990] CDPH (90) 22.

71 Trotzig (n 1). See also: Council of Europe, Cultural Heritage Committee, Draft Revised European Convention on the Protection of the Archaeological Heritage – Final Activity Report and Draft Revised Convention [1991] CM (91) 122; CC-PAT (91) 41.

72 Council of Europe, Cultural Heritage Committee, 'Select Committee of Experts on Archaeology and Planning – Final Activity Report' [1991] CC-PAT (91) 31.

the ratification of the Convention can be of significant value to heritage professionals, particularly in times of recession.[73]

The crucial public awareness problem is indicated in Article 9, asking the State Parties to carry out '*educational* actions to rouse and develop awareness in public opinion of the value of the archaeological heritage for understanding the past and of the threats to this heritage' (Article 9). Besides, Article 9 suggests that an essential aspect of those educational activities lies in public access to its heritage. With the Valletta Convention, the public benefit of archaeology came into focus, and the willingness of archaeologists to open up to the general public and start to involve that public as a stakeholder in their work has been tested. In his evaluation of the consequences the Valletta Convention has had on European archaeology, Willems argued that the most obvious difference that the treaty brought was the increase in the level of public awareness and interest in archaeological heritage.[74] Arguably, we can look at this 'increase in the level of public awareness' from different perspectives.

Firstly, archaeologists in the drafting committee made sure that the public engagement with their work stays passive – 'while it may be the subject of popular "gaze", that gaze is a passive one in which the audience will uncritically consume the message of heritage constructed by heritage experts'.[75] The significant work that the AHD does in portraying the public/visitors as passive consumers of the knowledge produced by experts is enshrined in Article 9. Archaeological heritage, therefore, is not seen as an active process or experience but rather as something that the public needs to be allowed access to and instructed about. More excavations and more sites necessarily meant more visitors and an increase in the level of public awareness of archaeology, yet the 'glass case' display mentality identified for museum exhibitions by Merriman was equally present in the presentation and interpretation of archaeological sites.[76]

Secondly, from the archaeological discussions on the impact of the Valletta, it seems that even this limited level of public presence around their work has been seen by experts as a 'sort of cancer'.[77] As the discussion on the imple-

---

73 O'Keefe (n 55).

74 Willems (n 54).

75 Smith (n 41) 31.

76 Nick Merriman, *Beyond the Glass Case* (Leicester University Press 1991).

77 Pascal Depaepe, 'Preventive Archaeology, Scientific Research and Public Outreach: Some Non-politically Correct Thoughts' in Predrag Novaković and others (eds), *Recent Developments in Preventive Archaeology in Europe: Proceedings of the 22nd EAA Meeting in Vilnius, 2016* (Ljubljana University Press 2016) 39.

mentation of the Convention in the following section will show, this provision raised a considerable debate among archaeologists on the main reasons for excavating; i.e., do we primarily excavate for public outreach or for the scientific community? It might be argued that once archaeologists managed to legitimise their position and their values and expertise as the only valid approach to archaeological heritage, they saw the requirement for public outreach not as something the community expects/deserves from their work and has the right to engage with, but rather as a useful concept to obtain more funds to be able to study the sites. This attitude was boldly stated by Depaepe in some of his 'non-politically correct thoughts':

> Indeed, the aim of archaeologists at the beginning of preventive archaeology was to make the public (and the politicians) aware of the problem of the destruction of archaeological sites. Their hidden agenda was to obtain the funds to be able to study the sites....Archaeologists desperately try to convince developers and politicians of the importance of archaeology by offering derivatives such as public outreach...So all agree that the pre-eminence given to public outreach was important during the birth of preventive archaeology but can now be considered a sort of cancer...the time has come to think about our real reasons for excavating.[78]

What can be established from this attitude is that the inclusion of the provision on the role of the public in Article 9 does not have anything to do with meaningful and active engagement of communities with archaeological heritage but everything to do with archaeologists using the public outreach as a means to obtain more funds and power in spatial planning decision-making processes.

Even though its primary purpose is the standardised regulation of archaeological activities, the Convention, upon repeated demands from Greece, Turkey, Italy, and Cyprus, had to address, at least to some extent, the issue of illicit traffic in archaeological heritage. And while the 'export' countries were keen on getting very strong paragraphs on this issue in the Convention, they were strongly opposed by the UK, Switzerland, and the Netherlands, all important centres of international trade in art and antiquities. Article 10 of the Valletta Convention makes provisions to restrict the illegal circulation of artefacts, but with a very soft approach that (1) promotes cooperation between states asking them to inform each other when a suspect object appears on the market and (2)

78 Depaepe (n 77) 39.

promotes the education of public on values of archaeology as the best way of guarding that heritage against illicit trading and excavations.[79] Also, the Convention emphasised the importance of developing policies for museums (and similar institutions) under State control asking the State Parties to ensure that they do not obtain elements of the archaeological heritage with an illegal or unclear background. This practice was already incorporated in most museums' governing statutes and promoted by ICOM's 1986 Code of Professional Ethics. It was hoped that with the adoption of the Valletta Convention, the States will reinforce that practice.[80] Although a stronger position on the issue would be welcomed by many Member States, the attempt by the CoE to essentially deal with this divisive issue in Revision would be inappropriate at the time, especially having in mind the attempts of other organisations to address the problem substantively.[81]

Lastly, the revised text addressed one of the main problems of the 1969 Convention – the absence of a provision for monitoring the application of the Convention. In Article 13 of the Valletta Convention, a provision was made for a committee to monitor its implementation, report to the Committee of Ministers on the position of archaeological protection policies in States Parties, and make proposals for the facilitation of the revised text's application. What could be observed through the monitoring process in the aftermath of its adoption is that there was a clear difference in the implementation of the text by different states. However, what the Valletta Convention changed is that there was for the first time a broadly consistent yet pluralistic framework that sets the core standards for the practice and management of archaeology in Europe.

The Valletta Convention was opened for signatures at the Third European Conference of Ministers responsible for Cultural Heritage (Valletta, 16–17 January 1992). The 25 CoE Member States participated in the Conference, wel-

79 Olivier (n 1).

80 Council of Europe, *Explanatory Report to the European Convention on the Protection of the Archaeological Heritage* (Revised) [1992] (European Treaty Series No 143).

81 Council of Europe, Steering Committee for Integrated Conservation of the Historic Heritage (CDPH), 'Select Committee of Experts on Archaeology and Planning (PH-R-MA) – Revision of the European Convention on the Protection of the Archaeological Heritage (3rd Meeting – Report)' [1990] CC-PAT (90) 17.

At the time of the revision, the European Community was considering a Directive that would regulate certain aspects of trade in arts and antiquity within the Community, the International Institute for the Unification of Private Law (UNIDROIT) have had its draft of Convention on Stolen or Illegally Exported Cultural Objects ready which was intended to complement UNESCO's 1970 Convention on the subject and the CoE itself had adopted the 1985 Convention on Offences relating to Cultural Property.

coming Eastern European countries, such as Hungary and Poland, who joined the organisation in 1990 and 1991 (there were also representatives from Bulgaria and Russia signing the Convention, even though those countries were not yet CoE Members). In total, the Convention saw 20 signatures in Valletta, which signified the beginning of a very profound impact on the practice of archaeology and archaeological heritage management in Europe.

The Conference also meant a two-part radical shift in the CoE's cultural activities and actions.[82] Firstly, as the changed name of the Conference suggests (from the adjective 'architectural heritage' used in Granada in 1985 to 'cultural heritage' used in Valletta), the CoE took a much broader view of what tangible heritage encompasses. The organisation moved from great historic monuments and archaeological sites to the more up-to-date concept of heritage which includes also rural, underwater, technical, and industrial heritage, the architecture of the nineteenth and twentieth centuries, landscape, etc. The adoption of the Valletta Convention marked the end of the predominantly 'technical' approach to heritage preservation and the turn of the CoE's attention to heritage's political, economic, and social role.

Secondly, the new European reality, with many Eastern Bloc countries joining the CoE, meant that the organisation's priority would lie in communicating to the new members the values and approaches promoted by existing CoE Conventions and Recommendations, and certainly not only in the heritage domain. Surely, considering all the dramatic changes happening in Europe at the time, such as, in 1992, the still-ongoing conflict in the former Yugoslavia as well as the rapid accession of the new Member States, issues such as cultural heritage were not a high priority for the organisation. However, the ministers participating in the Valletta Conference invited the CoE's Council for Cultural Cooperation (CDCC) in its Resolutions of the Conference to 'carry out, even before the entry into force of the Convention, a "European Plan for Archaeology" managed by its Cultural Heritage Committee (CC-PAT)'.[83] It is important to emphasise the decision of the ministers to focus on pan-European cooperation, asking the CC-PAT to organise its activities to meet the urgent

82 The major reform of the structures of Cultural Cooperation at the CoE was reflecting the trends laid down in the 1989 Declaration on the future role of the Council of Europe – the promotion of pluralistic democracy and human rights, the development of the European identity and the seeking of the solutions to the major problems of contemporary society. This Declaration was a response to the dynamism of the European society at the time and the role of the CoE in that society, i.e. more and more powerful European Union, changes that had occurred in Central and Eastern Europe (CM (89) PV1).

83 Council of Europe, 'Third European Conference of Ministers Responsible for the Cultural Heritage -Resolutions 1–4' (1992).

needs of 'Greater Europe'.[84] The focus on the eastern and south-eastern parts of the continent would be a reality in the CoE heritage programmes for years to come (for example, programmes like Legislative Support Task Force, Regional Programme on Cultural and Natural Heritage in South-East Europe, Kyiv Initiative, the Regional Programme for Black Sea and South Caucasus, among others). However, the implementation of the Valletta Convention created the theoretical and philosophical framework for all those subsequent CoE activities.

4 European Convention for the Protection of the Archaeological Heritage: Implementation

> The Valletta treaty has been such an integrated part that the younger generation of archaeologists can hardly imagine what the pre-Valletta era was like.[85]

As the quote above illustrates, there is a consensus among European archaeologists on the dramatic significance of the Valletta Convention on the practice of archaeology and archaeological heritage management in Europe. The influence the Convention has had on the changes in the field of archaeological heritage management in the last 30 years has been widely discussed among archaeologists.[86] The Convention, which had been ratified by 46 states (June

84 Resolution No. 3 on the priorities of a pan-European cultural heritage project (n 83).

85 Peter Schut, 'Foreword' in Victoria M van der Haas and Peter AC Schut (eds), *The Valletta Convention: Twenty Years After – Benefits, Problems, Challenges* (EAC Occasional Paper No 9, Europae Archaeologia Consilium 2014) 9.

86 Willems (n 13) (n 54); Olivier (n 1);
Monique van den Dries, 'The Good, the Bad and the Ugly? Evaluating Three Models of Implementing the Valletta Convention' (2011) 43(4) World Archaeology 594;
Victoria M van der Haas and Peter AC Schut (eds), *The Valletta Convention: Twenty Years After – Benefits, Problems, Challenges* (EAC Occasional Paper No 9, Europae Archaeologia Consilium 2014);
Kristian Kristiansen, 'Do We Need the "Archaeology of Europe"?' (2008) 15(1) Archaeological Dialogues 5;
Monique van den Dries, Sjoerd van der Linde and Amy Strecker (eds), *Crossing Borders and Connecting People in Archaeological Heritage Management* (Sidestone Press 2015);
Alexander Olivier and Patrick Van Lindt, 'Valletta Convention Perspectives: An EAC Survey' in Victoria M van der Haas and Peter AC Schut (eds), *The Valletta Convention: Twenty Years After – Benefits, Problems, Challenges* (EAC Occasional Paper No 9, Europae Archaeologia Consilium 2014) 165.

2025), established the core standards for the practice and management of archaeology in Europe. The Valletta Convention firmly integrated archaeology into spatial planning and decision-making processes, moving it from being only an academic discipline to having a place in the world of politics and economics.[87] Its implementation also led to a significant increase in the volume of archaeological work, and consequently to an increase in our knowledge and understanding of the past.

However, it would be misleading to just look at this instrument in those general terms. As is the case with all of the CoE's Conventions, ratification by states is voluntary and its implementation may vary from country to country, depending upon the legislation already in place, but also depending on the degree to which the effects of treaties are taken seriously at the national level.[88] The high number of ratifications today could lead us to the wrong conclusion on swift and cohesive acceptance of the provisions of the Convention. On the contrary, the process has taken almost 25 years, with Italy, Austria, and San Marino ratifying the Convention only in 2015, and Luxembourg only in 2017.

As already mentioned previously, the CoE did not systematically follow the implementation of its earlier heritage-related conventions, and even though provision for the monitoring committee of the Valletta Convention's implementation was made in Article 13, it was rather the heritage sector itself which, through its professional associations (European Association of Archaeologists (EAA) and European Archaeological Council (EAC)), did the monitoring work.[89] In that respect, the survey undertaken by the EAC in 2012–2013 for

87 Willems (n 54).

88 Willem JH Willems, 'Archaeology and Heritage Management in Europe: Trends and Developments' (1998) 1(3) European Journal of Archaeology 293.

89 The launching of the *European Archaeological Council* (EAC) in 1999 showed how well needed and welcomed the Valletta Convention was among European archaeology professionals and scholars. The Valletta Convention is extensively present (and celebrated) in the EAC publications which have served as one of the main sources for this Chapter. Considering the Convention as a 'watershed in the development of European archaeology' (Willems 2007) could explain this interest by EAC members in the text; but a look at the history of the organisation gives us an additional explanation to it. The EAC was founded in 1999 and as explained on its website it is 'a network of heads of national services responsible under the law for the management of the archaeological heritage in the Council of Europe member states' (EAC website). However, its predecessor was the Committee of Experts on Archaeology and Planning who was responsible for drafting the Valletta Convention. The Committee continued promoting the text after the Convention was ratified and it held regular meetings at the annual conferences of the European Association of Archaeologist (EAA). In 1999, it was decided that a group would continue its work as an international NGO. The inaugural meeting of the EAC

its Heritage Management Symposium[90] is of a great significance, allowing us to better understand how the Convention was implemented in different states.[91] Even though this survey provides a very basic benchmark, it is worth indicating some of its main results.

According to the survey by Olivier and Van Lindt (2014), which covered 34 responses[92] from the states that are party to the Convention, 15 states (44%) have adopted new measures specifically formulated to implement the main provisions of the Convention into their legislation. The other 19 states (56%) considered their existing heritage legislation to be sufficiently aligned with provisions of the Convention. Around half of the states reported accounting problems/difficulties with the implementation of the Convention, while 15 states apparently did not encountered any problems.[93]

The overall figure for the successful implementation of articles of the Valletta Convention is quite high; 23 states reported positive results. However, when questions focused on the specific articles of the Convention, the results were slightly less optimistic.[94] In general, respondents stated encountering problems during the implementation of Articles 2–6 (dealing with legal and physical protection, integrated conservation, and the financing of activities). In practice, this reflects the challenges of implementing different forms of *in situ* preservation, preventive archaeology, and the developer-pays-all principle.[95] On the other hand, according to the responses, the implementation of articles 7–12 (dealing with issues such as dissemination of knowledge, exchange of skills, public awareness, and public outreach activities) did not present any significant problems.

---

was held in 1999 at the Council of Europe headquarter in Strasbourg and from that point, the EAC held the status of an NGO observant member to the CoE heritage committees.

90 Victoria M van der Haas and Peter AC Schut (eds), *The Valletta Convention: Twenty Years After – Benefits, Problems, Challenges* (EAC Occasional Paper No 9, Europae Archaeologia Consilium 2014).

91 Olivier and Van Lindt (n 86);

The results of the survey that are published and accessible (EAC Occasional Paper No.9, 2014) were not regarded as the final version of this analysis; however, the anticipated final results, to the knowledge of the author, have never been published.

92 Survey covered 34 responses including a number of multiple responses from federal states or states where the legal responsibility for heritage management is the responsibility of the level below that of the nation (Belgium, Germany, UK).

93 Olivier and Van Lindt (n 86).

94 Ibid.

95 Sjoerd van der Linde and Monique van den Dries, 'Creative Archaeology' in Monique van den Dries, Sjoerd van der Linde and Amy Strecker (eds), *Crossing Borders and Connecting People in Archaeological Heritage Management* (Sidestone Press 2015) 51.

If we look at these results in conjunction with the responses to the question of how effective the implementation of different articles has been, a similar division in articles could be observed. Whereas respondents identified that the implementation of articles 2–6 had generated quite significant achievements, the majority of respondents recognised little significant achievements regarding Articles 7–12.

The contradiction of two answers (on the one hand, not having any problems in implementing Articles 7–12 and, on the other, a generally low level of achievements identified), as argued by authors of the study, could indicate a lower priority generally being accorded to the implementation of these articles than was given to Articles 2–6. Besides, when put in relation to the results of the Discovering the Archaeologists of Europe 2012–2014 Project (2014) concerning the degree to which public engagement activities are embedded in the archaeology profession in Europe, Van der Linde and Van den Dries concluded that the message is essentially that:

> We have not encountered any problems in the Malta articles dealing with the implementation of public outreach, dissemination and exchange of knowledge simply because we have not bothered all too much with them in the first place.[96]

The surveys confirmed once again the same attitude the archaeologists maintained while drafting the Valletta and over the course of its implementation: they saw public outreach as a requirement they needed to offer in exchange for getting more public/private funding for their research. Their attitude is in line with the portrayal of the AHD and its power to obscure the real work that heritage does, undermining the role of non-experts and their engagement with heritage. This discourse has been legitimised in the Valletta Convention and consequently in legal texts and heritage discourses of the States that are Parties to it. An additional illustration of the ways how the AHD mapped out the authority of expertise in the Valletta Convention and subsequently in the legal texts of the States (Parties) can be seen in the example of the Dutch Monument Act from 2007. As noted by Van den Dries and Van der Linde (2012), most of the organisational issues promoted by Valletta have been dealt with and have juridical power through this revised Dutch Monument Act.[97] However,

96 Van der Linde and Van den Dries (n 95).

97 Monique van den Dries and Sjoerd van der Linde, 'Twenty Years After Malta: Archaeological Heritage as a Source of Collective Memory and Scientific Study Anno 2012' (2012) 43/44 *Analecta Praehistorica Leidensia* 9.

the only exception is the promotion of public awareness (Article 9 of Valletta), where no formal or legal provisions have been made to achieve this goal. Nevertheless, the archaeologists recently recognised the need to explore the opportunities that the implementation of Articles 7–12 might produce and to focus more on the social value that their work creates, supplementing the provisions of the Valletta Convention with the public value of heritage promoted in the Faro Convention.[98]

As the survey showed, the focus of most states was on the implementation of Articles 2–6, and it is important to acknowledge that, although the Valletta Convention stipulates the basic principles of preventive archaeology, its implementation varied dramatically among European countries. Willems and Van den Dries distinguished two predominant models of implementation: (1) the 'socialist' approach where the state considers archaeology a public task and exclusively governmental organisations were responsible for archaeological work (France and the Scandinavian countries, for example), and (2) the 'capitalist' or 'market' approach, which allowed a commercial archaeological sector to develop and where the developer chooses the excavator, partly according to heritage administration guidelines, partly by the cheapest bid (the United Kingdom).[99] The reality is that most countries choose some of the variations of those two models, for example, introducing the 'market' model but integrating governmental responsibility towards quality assurance to various degrees, in the Netherlands, for instance.[100] The pros and cons of each model were extensively discussed among European archaeologists;[101] however, as argued by Van den Dries, different approaches can be perceived as neither good nor bad.[102] Depending on the priorities and goals, as well as its possibilities, each state develops a system that suits it the best.

---

98 Monique van den Dries, 'From Malta to Faro, How Far Have We Come? Some Facts and Figures on Public Engagement in the Archaeological Heritage Sector in Europe' in Peter Schut, Diane Scharff and Lotte C van de Wit (eds), *Setting the Agenda: Giving New Meaning to the European Archaeological Heritage* (EAC Occasional Paper No 10, Europae Archaeologia Consilium 2015) 45.

99 Willem JH Willems and Monique H van den Dries (eds), *Quality Management in Archaeology* (Oxbow Books 2007).

100 Van den Dries (n 86).

101 Willems and van den Dries (n 99); Kristensen (n 86); Jean-Paul Demoule, 'Rescue Archaeology: The French Way' (2002) 2 Public Archaeology 170;
Jean-Paul Demoule, 'Answer to Roger Thomas' (2002) 2 Public Archaeology 239;
Roger Thomas, 'Comment: Rescue Archaeology: The French Way, by Jean-Paul Demoule' (2002) 2 Public Archaeology 236.

102 Van den Dries (n 86).

The conclusion of Olivier and Van Lindt's survey is that the overwhelming majority of respondents (31 states), affirmed that even after 20 years, the Valletta Convention continued to be relevant to heritage management in Europe.[103] The results of this survey supported the view that the Convention changed how archaeological heritage is managed across Europe, and it affirmed the positive influence it has had in safeguarding and conserving Europe's heritage.

Nevertheless, since no convention is an ideal text, today it is also possible to identify the negative consequences of Valletta's implementation. In his analysis, Willems referred to those consequences as 'the good, the bad and the ugly'.[104] On the positive side, Willems highlighted three important consequences. The most obvious difference, according to him, was an increase in the level of public awareness and interest. This is surely connected with the other consequence, which is a substantial increase in archaeological research and the new knowledge created, but primarily with the willingness of the practitioners to open to the public and to include that public as a stakeholder in their work, to a certain (arguably, quite limited) degree. This change in the attitude of archaeologists certainly happened due to the fact that the steeply increased cost of undertaking archaeological works and the spending of public funds could only be legitimised by demonstrating the benefits of archaeology to the public.[105]

Another positive aspect emphasised by Willems is the fact that archaeological research and practice have become much better integrated with spatial planning, but also with other related social sciences.[106] Consequently, a major advance has been seen in both the internal integration of cultural historic disciplines (archaeology, historic geography, architectural history) and their external integration with other relevant disciplines from the social sciences.

The whole process of drafting and implementing the Convention was the chief inspiration for getting European archaeology organised, with EAA and EAC as the direct 'product' of the Convention. According to Willems, this can be regarded as the third positive consequence of Valletta.[107]

While today participatory forms of heritage management and public archaeology are gaining importance, Willems remarked that one of the negative, yet probably unintended, consequences of Valletta's implementation was the

103 Olivier and Van Lindt (n 86).

104 Willems (n 54).

105 Ibid.

106 Ibid.

107 Willems (n 54).

diminished role of hobby archaeologists in archaeological practice.[108] With increased regulation, professionalisation, and associated commercial interests in place, an inevitable decrease in the opportunities to include those stakeholders occurred.

The bureaucratisation of archaeology is perceived by Willems as one of the highly undesirable (ugly) consequences of Valletta.[109] As archaeology was already a largely academic discipline in the 1980s, the specialised bureaucracies dealing with archaeological heritage management were run predominantly by people with academic training and attitudes. With the implementation of Valletta, archaeology was introduced into the development and special planning field and thus became a part of the much larger systems, usually state services and ministries of culture or tourism, which have broader and sometimes very different core purposes. Most of the time, the senior staff of these organisations have no academic qualifications in the field of archaeology, and attaining new knowledge from archaeological research is not their priority. In this way, archaeology became a part of the system that often stands in the way of good research instead of encouraging it.

In the countries which accepted the 'market' model, the commercialisation of the sector, according to Willems, is another element with significant negative consequences.[110] It became evident that most of the archaeological work that has been done predominantly includes evaluation work, which is much more in demand by the established bureaucratic system and is much less risky as a business. Only a small percentage of all archaeological work involves excavations, which, in addition, are usually of short duration. This results in fewer and fewer good-quality excavations, and therefore in less and less knowledge about the past, and fewer and fewer stories to tell to attract public interest in archaeology.

The knowledge production capacity and the quality of the reports, especially in the market-driven model, seem to be the crucial preoccupation of the archaeologists.[111] Willems argued that the substantial increase in archaeological work resulted in the rise of unsatisfactory and irrelevant work, with widespread plagiarism of reports which are done only for legal reasons.[112] He classified this as an ugly consequence of the Valletta Convention.

108 Ibid.
109 Ibid.
110 Ibid.
111 Van den Dries (n 86); Kristiansen (n 86).
112 Willems (n 54).

5 Conclusion of the Chapter

The valuable investigations into the benefits, challenges, and problems of the implementation of the Valletta Convention presented in this chapter demonstrate the importance of the text as perceived by the archaeologists (in academia and practice) and suggest that the text succeeded in becoming a stable platform for further developments in the field. Unsurprisingly, since the drafting of the Valletta Convention more than 30 years ago, enormous changes in the field of archaeology and archaeological heritage have taken place, and there is continuous discussion among European professionals in the field concerning whether the provisions of the Valletta Convention are suitable enough to respond to contemporary circumstances. There is a certain number of authors who support the idea of a new convention, which will address the new challenges and changes in the field of archaeology and heritage management.[113] However, it is uncertain that the CoE will go in that direction; the CoE's latest Faro Convention already offers a new approach to embedding archaeology and other aspects of cultural heritage in society. Thus, it would be more realistic to expect a renewed interpretation of Valletta's provisions in line with the aspirations of the Faro Convention. Once the technical provisions of Valletta became the minimum standard in how we deal with archaeology across Europe, will archaeologists again use the 'card' of the public outreach and community participation in order to regain their power in knowledge creation and return the focus to scientific aspects of archaeology as a source of our understanding of the past?

The following chapter will focus on the decisive turn of interest at the CoE in this respect – moving from standard-setting in the field of the protection of European heritage to the important aspects of heritage as they relate to human rights, sustainable development, and democracy. The next Part of the book offers a closer look at how this change has happened and reflects on its significance in relation to AHD.

---

113 Bengt Johansen and Mats Mogren, 'Valetta and Beyond – Ideas and Practice in Sweden' in Victoria M van der Haas and Peter AC Schut (eds), *The Valletta Convention: Twenty Years After – Benefits, Problems, Challenges* (EAC Occasional Paper No 9, Europae Archaeologia Consilium 2014) 143.

PART 2

The Council of Europe's Heritage Discourse in the 21st Century

CHAPTER 6

New Millennium: A Turn in the CoE Heritage Policies

1 Introduction

At the end of the 1990s, ideas and practices of cultural heritage were in transition from a traditional view, where material things were privileged based on intrinsic and scientific-led values (the AHD), to a new, more participatory, and inclusive approach focusing on public values, public benefits, and the role of community in understanding, identifying, caring for, transforming, and creating their heritage. The CoE and other international institutions dealing with heritage followed this development in their policies. The shift from regulation (top-down approach) to participation and from exclusion to inclusion is clearly seen through the evolution of the 'family' of the CoE's heritage conventions discussed in this volume.

As the previous chapters demonstrated, the Council of Europe has been at the forefront of many important evolutions in European cultural heritage law-making and has inspired many actions on the global level as well. Even though the period until the mid-1990s has been characterised by many[1] as the period when the organisation was predominantly focused on technical aspects of cultural heritage protection, with the Grenada and Valletta Conventions and activities based on them, it could be argued that many ideas and notions developed during this period demonstrated a high degree of foresight (such as the previously discussed concept of integrated conservation).

The Council of Europe's approach has traditionally been based on a more holistic approach to heritage derived from the organisation's central mandates to protect and promote human rights. The CoE's heritage policies were also underpinned by its political goals of building a common European identity. Engagement with the idea of European identity was essential for creating regional (European) commonalities that would foster more robust European integration and regional cooperation,[2] and heritage in all its forms, as a 'bearer

1 Interview with Interviewee 3, former employee of the Council of Europe's Cultural Policy Division (3 February 2020).

2 Lucas Lixinski, 'International Cultural Heritage Regimes, International Law, and the Politics of Expertise' (2013) 20(4) International Journal of Cultural Property 407.

 | DOI:10.1163/9789004756250_007

of [that] identity', played and still plays a significant role.[3] The main heritage treaties from the first phase of the CoE's heritage work (Part 1) are regarded as fundamental standard-setting instruments in heritage protection and conservation in Europe, and as such, as 'technical' and exclusively oriented to tangible aspects of heritage (AHD-underpinned). However, they proved to be much more responsive to the value of heritage to society than generally acknowledged. This value, or the role and importance of heritage to society, is a topic of the following part of this book. The Granada and Valletta Conventions, among other of the CoE's recommendations and projects adopted throughout the first phase of the CoE's heritage actions, undeniably created a reliable structure capable of accommodating the radical shift in how heritage is seen and managed that came with the new millennia.

Although aware of the social aspects of heritage, the first-phase Conventions showed rather reduced social and political relevance with regard to demands and expectations coming from heritage scholars and communities that became much more articulated at the end of the 1990s and more obviously at the beginning of the twenty-first century. The CoE was aware that a bold reaction to the new developments in the heritage field was necessary if the organisation wanted to effectively address the role of heritage in the changing Europe.[4] The need for rethinking its approach was even more evident when bearing in mind the evolution of the UNESCO conventions and ICOMOS charters at the time (e.g., the ICOMOS Nara Document on Authenticity (1994), the ICOMOS Stockholm Declaration (1998), and the 2003 and 2005 UNESCO Conventions). The new policy texts, regionally and globally, as well as the academic discussion in the heritage field, reflected the shift in focus from intrinsic values and material heritage (the AHD) to social values and intangible heritage, and the CoE's engagement with the topic, as the following discussion demonstrates, proved to be one of the more audacious examples. The main result of the CoE's process of rethinking the role and value of heritage in

3 Council of Europe, Steering Committee for Cultural Heritage (CDPAT), A Council of Europe Initiative: Heritage from Elsewhere, Heritage of Others [2004] CDPAT (2004) 30 final, 2.

4 Council of Europe, Steering Committee for Cultural Heritage (CDPAT), 'Cultural Heritage, a Vector of Democratic Development – Report of the Cross-sectoral Seminar, Strasbourg, 20–21 June 2002' [2002] CDPAT (2002) 28;

Council of Europe, Steering Committee for Cultural Heritage (CDPAT), 'Exchange of Views on the Future Aims of Council of Europe Co-operation in the Field of Cultural Heritage in the Light of European Union Enlargement' [2003] CDPAT (2003) 37;

Council of Europe, Steering Committee for Cultural Heritage (CDPAT), 'Select Committee of Experts on the Preparation of a Framework Convention on Cultural Heritage – Record of the 1st Meeting' [2003] CDPAT (2003) 43.

society was the Convention on the Value of Cultural Heritage for Society (Faro Convention, 2005).[5]

The CoE's new convention on cultural heritage, which will be discussed in detail in this part of the book, drastically moves away from the AHD and its main characteristics that were more or less enshrined in previous CoE heritage conventions. The 2005 Faro Convention invites us to rethink our position on heritage in a more open, inclusive, flexible, and collaborative way. While the Granada and Valletta Conventions concentrated on 'how' cultural heritage should be conserved and protected, the Faro Convention focuses on 'why' it should be accorded value.[6] The ideas, principles, and ambitions promoted in the Faro Convention have also been reflected in several other regional[7] and global[8] policies and initiatives. However, the Faro Convention has provided these ideas with a structured approach and renewed energy, making it potentially the most impactful in terms of its reach.[9]

There are two critical points on which the Faro Convention is based. The first is to place people at the heart of cultural heritage discussions through a clear connection to the realm of human rights. The second point highlights the advantages of utilising cultural heritage as a resource, thereby ensuring its central role in a new vision of sustainable development.[10] To unpack this ambitious and challenging text, it is evident that one must consider not only heritage issues and the standards for its protection (both global and European) but also the broader perspective in which heritage, as part of culture in general, plays a role in addressing numerous global challenges, particularly within the context of development.

5 Council of Europe, *Council of Europe Framework Convention on the Value of Cultural Heritage for Society* (CETS No 199, 2005).

6 Council of Europe (CETS No 199, 2005).

7 *The Charter of the Association of Southeast Asian Nations*, adopted by ASEAN in Singapore on 20 November 2007;
The Charter for African Cultural Renaissance of 2006; Adopted by the African Union at Khartoum on 24 January 2006;
Organization of American States, *Declaration of Mar del Plata* (2005).

8 UNESCO, *Convention for the Safeguarding of the Intangible Cultural Heritage* (adopted 17 October 2003, entered into force 20 April 2006) 2368 UNTS 3;
UNESCO, *Convention on the Protection and Promotion of the Diversity of Cultural Expressions* (adopted 20 October 2005, entered into force 18 March 2007) 2440 UNTS 311.

9 Janet Blake, 'Development of UNESCO's 2003 Convention – Creating a New Heritage Protection Paradigm?' in Michelle L Stefano and Peter Davis (eds), *The Routledge Companion to Intangible Cultural Heritage* (Routledge 2016) 11.

10 Explanatory Report, CETS 199 (n 6).

To begin with, this chapter aims to offer an in-depth analysis of the organisation's approaches and actions that created the environment in which an innovative text like the Faro Convention could be developed. Therefore, the chapter will first look at the political and social changes in Europe in the 1990s and the early 2000s and the role of the CoE in those processes. In particular, it will explore how the CoE framed its cultural and heritage activities to be meaningful and beneficial for the fundamental values of European unification, development, and social progress. Understanding this background is essential, as it lays out the institutional context for preparing the Faro Convention and, with it, repositions the CoE's heritage discourse away from the AHD.

2 The Background of the Faro Convention: Political and Social Context

The Faro Convention was convened as a result of the broader global and specific European context, and it contributed to a paradigm shift that arose not only in the field of cultural heritage but also in other fields such as human rights, development, environmental protection, and intellectual property protection.[11] Understanding this context is fundamental for understanding why the Convention's text took the form it did. This section highlights prominent lines of, firstly, evolutions of international cultural policy and law that reflected the growing recognition of the role of heritage in society, and secondly, the specific European challenges and 'problems' the CoE Member States sought to address through the CoE's heritage mechanisms.

In terms of policy and law-making at the international level, the long-awaited 'issue' of recognising the variety of manifestations of intangible cultural heritage (ICH) and its values for communities that the international community aimed to address through UNESCO conventions in the late 1990s has had a trickle-down effect on national approaches towards heritage and its protection around the world. The 2003 Convention for the Safeguarding of the Intangible Cultural Heritage is considered the critical text that has created a

---

11 Noel Fojut, 'The Philosophical, Political and Pragmatic Roots of the Convention' in Council of Europe, *Heritage and Beyond* (Council of Europe Publishing 2009) 13;
Graham Fairclough, 'New Heritage Frontiers' in Council of Europe, *Heritage and Beyond* (Council of Europe Publishing 2009) 29;
Claudia Ledig, 'The Faro Convention and the Information Society' in Council of Europe, *Heritage and Beyond* (Council of Europe Publishing 2009) 159.

'new paradigm' in heritage protection at the UNESCO level.[12] In the wide range of heritage literature dealing with the 2003 Convention, it is noted that the text moved away from the 'up until that moment' heritage protection paradigm that prioritised monumental 'European' cultural forms over local and Indigenous ones and that it did so from a position that favoured the experts' interests over those of cultural bearers, essentially one that had all the characteristics of the AHD.[13] Withstanding the criticism that the text received, which argues that even though the 2003 UNESCO Convention legitimised the intangible cultural heritage in global heritage policies, it used the AHD to frame much of the way the intangible cultural heritage was to be understood and safeguarded, the contribution of the Convention in moving the field forward is not negligible.[14] The Faro Convention, on the other hand, 'responded' to this criticism and radically moved the conversation and heritage discourse away from the AHD and the tangible/intangible and cultural/natural binaries that sustains the AHD.[15] The Convention's starting point comes from the idea that the text needs to 'reflect the aspirations and expectations of "grass-roots" citizens in public decisions and investment concerning cultural heritage, in fields that were **previously reserved for an elite**'.[16]

In the context of the Faro Convention, the developments in the field of (sustainable) development have a specific importance. The concept of sustainable development, defined in 1987 as 'development that meets the needs of the present without compromising the ability of future generations to meet their own needs' (Brundtland Report 1987), was further elaborated in the 1992 Rio Declaration (UNCED). The Rio Declaration refined the concept promoted by the Brundtland Report. Among other points, it promoted the value of local and Indigenous cultures and recognised the value of their heritage and traditional knowledge as a resource for its overall development. As Blake points out, the adoption of the Rio Declaration was the most far-reaching moment at the time, as it gave sustainable development an international endorsement.[17]

12 Blake (n 9) 11.

13 Ibid.

14 Lucas Lixinski, 'Selecting Heritage: The Interplay of Art, Politics and Identity' (2011) 22(1) European Journal of International Law 81;
Laurajane Smith and Natsuko Akagawa, 'Introduction' in Laurajane Smith and Natsuko Akagawa (eds), *Intangible Heritage* (Routledge 2009) 1;
Laurajane Smith, 'Intangible Heritage: A Challenge to the Authorised Heritage Discourse?' (2015) 40 *Revista d'Etnologia de Catalunya* 133.

15 Laurajane Smith, *Uses of Heritage* (Routledge 2006).

16 Council of Europe, Steering Committee for Cultural Heritage (CDPAT), '*Work on Cultural Heritage Conventions – 1st Meeting*' [2002] CDPAT (2002) 40 (emphasis added).

17 Blake (n 9).

It also positioned a sociocultural 'pillar' alongside the central economic and environmental ones. This new UN understanding of development reflected important and novel thinking in development theory. The understanding of development moved away from a dominant model wherein culture was often seen as a constraint to development and 'traditional' and indigenous cultures of the less-developed countries were especially poorly viewed by organisations such as the World Bank, International Monetary Fund, and the World Trade Organisation.[18] The challenges to this model that predominantly came from the countries of Africa and Latin America shifted the focus on local cultures and traditional ways of life, which were given a greater value.

Building on the paradigm shift pronounced in the Rio Declaration, organisations with a mandate in culture, such as UNESCO and the World Bank on the global scale and the CoE, the African Union, and the OAS on the regional level, turned their focus to the role that culture can/could play in the wider development framework. The CoE has been actively involved with development issues in its wide-ranging policy areas. The organisation's understanding of the concept of development can be best seen from, among other documents, its report *Sustainable Development at the Council of Europe: proposal for its strategic development*, where it is stated that:

> As an organisation committed to human rights, democracy and the rule of law, the Council of Europe has promoted since the 1960s the adoption of policies carrying **sustainable development values**, in the field of environment in its social sector and in culture, aiming at building cohesive societies, fighting inequality, promoting better living standards and reducing the vulnerability of populations. **Human rights and sustainable development are inextricably linked.** Development is unsustainable when the rule of law and equity are absent. Similarly, human rights cannot thrive without social justice and sustainable development.[19]

Statements like this showed the CoE's commitment to participate actively in international efforts and, most importantly, to use its human-based approach to sustainable development as a framework for its policies in different fields, heritage included. Even though the CoE's standing on development could not be heard in Rio (as witnessed by the member of the CoE Delegation, it 'is hard

18 Mary Douglas, 'Traditional Culture: Let's Hear No More About It' in Vijayendra Rao and Michael Walton (eds), *Culture and Public Action* (Stanford University Press 2004) 85–109.

19 Council of Europe, 'Directorate General IV – Education, Culture and Heritage, Youth and Sport, Sustainable Development at the Council of Europe: Proposal for Its Strategic Development' [2005] GR-C (2005) 13 (emphasis added).

to comprehend why the Council of Europe Secretary General was unable to obtain permission to speak'),[20] the organisation successfully transmitted the above-cited statement in the Political Message to the World Summit on Sustainable Development in Johannesburg in 2002.[21]

As a result of the evolution of the understanding of the role of culture and heritage for development in the 1980s and 1990s, the most crucial heritage conventions from the beginning of the new millennia (UNESCO 2003[22] and 2005 Conventions[23] and the CoE 2005 Faro Convention) made this relationship explicit in their texts. In the case of the CoE, sustainable development was fundamentally a key theme enabling the process of rethinking heritage and heritage discourse as promoted by the Faro Convention.

In addition to the aforementioned advancements in discourses in different subjects, it is necessary to look closely at the European-specific social and political context at the time, which, to a greater extent, shaped the CoE's responses in the field of heritage and led to the decision to draft the Faro Convention.

---

20 Council of Europe, 'Conference of Local and Regional Authorities of Europe, Committee on the Natural and Built Environment – Report on the Rio Earth Summit and Its Implications (presented by Mr H Lässing' CPL/ENV (27) 12) 4.

21 The CoE continues its involvement, and since 2015, it has actively contributed to the UN 2030 Agenda and its 17 *SDGs*. As stated by Max Gilbert (Directorate of External Relations of the Council of Europe) at the session organised by the United Nations Human Rights Council in 2019:

> The Council of Europe contributed from the outset to the process leading to the adoption of Agenda 2030, and we have been clear about our determination to embed it in our work. By definition, our philosophy is that most, if not all, of the Council of Europe's activities contribute to the implementation of the Sustainable Development Goals (SDGS), in particular those related to human rights, as well as empowerment, inclusion and equality. As such, it has not been necessary for the organisation to set up new objectives, instruments or activities, but rather to align existing activities with the relevant *SDGs* (**Human Rights and the 2030 Agenda: Decade of Action and Delivery on the *SDGs*, Geneva, 3 December 2019; *Session 2: Reflections and conversation on human rights and the "Decade of Action and Delivery of the 2030 Sustainable Development Agenda". Building on the pledge of the 2019 High-Level Political Forum Declaration; "Leave No One Behind": How can promoting and protecting human rights accelerate the realisation of the* SDGs**).

22 "Considering the importance of the intangible cultural heritage as a mainspring of cultural diversity and a guarantee of sustainable development…" (UNESCO 2003 Convention for the Safeguarding of the Intangible Cultural Heritage, Preamble).

23 For example in its Preamble: "Being aware that cultural diversity creates a rich and varied world, which increases the range of choices and nurtures human capacities and values, and therefore is a mainspring for sustainable development for communities, peoples and nations" (Convention on Protection and Promotion of the Diversity of Cultural Expressions).

As stated by several interviewees,[24] the adoption of the Valletta Convention in 1992 marked the end of the CoE's focus on the technical side of heritage protection, and the organisation entered a period of profound changes, not only in the heritage-related area but in general. The Vienna Declaration of 1993, which was the result of the first summit of Heads of State and Governments of all CoE Member States, confirmed the CoE's policy of openness and enlargement following the fall of the Berlin Wall and the development of new democracies in Central and Eastern Europe[25] (Vienna Declaration 1993). It confirmed the Member States' reliance on the CoE as the guardian of democratic security founded on human rights, democracy, and the rule of law. Consequently, as the CoE's interviewed official noted:

> The CoE finally returned to the use of heritage for its political goals, as one would expect from the political organisation, rather than dealing with technicalities of conservation. We could say that the CoE went a full circle in its heritage policies – from the values of culture and heritage in building European integration, cultural cooperation and European identity, as aimed with the 1954 European Cultural Convention, through the focus on more technical aspects of the architectural and archaeological heritage conservation and protection when the political goals of the organisation were primarily neglected (with Granada and Valletta Conventions), back to the role of heritage in addressing different social and political challenges in European societies with the Faro Convention.[26]

Few social and political European-specific events have to be considered when discussing the roots of the Faro Convention and the CoE's reorientation in heritage policies, not only because they shaped Europe as we know it today, but in the context of this volume, they played an essential role in how cultural heritage is perceived and currently managed on a European level. Firstly, the specific effects of globalisation have become increasingly apparent. As Thér-

---

24 Interview with Interviewee 1, former Employee of the Council of Europe's Directorate of Culture and Cultural and Natural Heritage (1 April 2020); Interview with Interviewee 6, current employee at the Council of Europe Directorate for Democracy (Strasbourg, 2 November 2022).

25 The CoE membership changed from 23 Member States in 1989. to 32 in 1993. It reached 47 members in 2007 and returned to the current 46 members in 2022 when Russia was expelled following its Ukraine invasion.

26 Interview with Interviewee 2, current employee at the Council of Europe Directorate of Democracy (Strasbourg, 4 December 2020).

ond noted, one could observe the widening gap between cultural heritage's social, symbolic, and collective value and its economic dimension that focuses on heritage as a labour-intensive, job-creating factor in local development.[27] The explosion of mass tourism during this period and the role of heritage in tourism and its commodification are prominent examples. Another aspect of globalisation that needs to be mentioned is rapid digitisation and its effects, not only in terms of dissemination of knowledge about heritage globally and the extreme benefits when it comes to access to heritage by the vast public, but also the challenges created when it comes to intellectual property, for example. Furthermore, a significant social change that had to be reflected in the new approach to heritage involves trends in migration. The emergence of more and more multicultural societies, particularly in the major urban centres, clearly asked for other angles of approach to the heritage concept.

In addition to those societal changes, two important European political events can also be considered, to some extent, as a 'seed' for the critical turn in the CoE's conceptualisation of cultural heritage and its role in European society that culminated with the adoption of the Faro Convention.

The first significant development is the conclusion of the Treaty on European Union (Maastricht Treaty) in 1992, which established the EU and marked a new stage in the process of European integration.[28] This Treaty was driven by the European Parliament's aspiration to give more powers to the European Community in the fields of the environment, economic and social cohesion, social matters, development policy, education, transport, and culture. It was with this Treaty, as Calligaro states, that the EU cultural action obtained a legal basis.[29] Article 128 of the Treaty reads:

> 1. The Community shall contribute to the flowering of the cultures of the Member States while respecting their national and regional diversity and at the same time bringing the common cultural heritage to the fore'.[30]

With the established legal basis for its cultural heritage activities, the EU started, from this point on, to challenge the CoE's primacy in the field at the

27 Daniel Thérond, 'The Council of Europe Conventions in the Field of Cultural Heritage and Landscape: Trends and Prospects' in Mitja Guštin and Terje Nypan (eds), *Cultural Heritage and Legal Aspects in Europe* (Institute for Mediterranean Heritage 2010) 20.

28 During the 1990s, the EU had 15 members.

29 Oriane Calligaro, *Negotiating Europe: EU Promotion of Europeanness since the 1950s* (Palgrave Macmillan 2013).

30 Treaty on European Union [1992] OJ C191/1.

European level. Nonetheless, the CoE had, and still has, an initiating role in new developments when it comes to the heritage field. Most of the time, it serves as a laboratory of new ideas for its heritage initiatives and, to a significant extent, for the EU schemes.[31] Important reasons for the EU's increased relevance in the heritage arena in comparison to the CoE include: (1) it has considerably superior financial means, (2) the EU regulations are more stringent, and (3) it links cultural policy and the market-integration project, for which the CoE has no equivalent.[32] Therefore, it can be argued that at this specific time (during the 1990s), when the EU finally established its competencies in the heritage field, the CoE understood that it could only remain relevant by being more innovative and ambitious in its actions.[33] This opened the door for cutting-edge texts such as the Faro Convention and the radical shift in its heritage discourse.

The war in the former Yugoslavia was the second critical event that influenced the CoE's shift in heritage policies. The destruction of cultural heritage and its use for ethnic cleansing, which had not been seen in Europe since the Second World War, demanded a European reaction. The CoE was one of the first (in 1992) international organisations to send fact-finding missions to collect information on the destruction of heritage in Croatia and Bosnia and Herzegovina.[34] These reports characterised the destruction as 'the cultural catastrophe in the heart of Europe'.[35] They were later used as a source of evidence in the number of cases for war crimes at the International Criminal Tribunal for the former Yugoslavia – ICTY.[36] The heritage destruction in the

31 Oriane Calligaro, 'Which Culture(s) for Europe? The Contrasting Conceptions of the Council of Europe and the European Union from 1949 to the Present Day' (2017) 7(13) Cambio 67.

32 Kiran K Patel and Oriane Calligaro, 'The True "EURESCO"? The Council of Europe, Transnational Networking and the Emergence of European Community Cultural Policies, 1970–90' (2017) 24(3) *European Review of History* 399.

33 Council of Europe, Steering Committee for Cultural Heritage (CDPAT), 'Exchange of Views on the Future Aims of Council of Europe Co-operation in the Field of Cultural Heritage in the Light of European Union Enlargement' [2003] CDPAT (2003) 37.

34 Parliamentary Assembly, Committee on Culture and Education, Sub-Committee on the Architectural and Artistic Heritage, 'Destruction by War of the Cultural Heritage in Croatia and Bosnia-Herzegovina – Information Report (rapporteur Jacques Baumel)' [1993] AS/Cult/AA (44) 16.

35 Parliamentary Assembly, Committee on Culture and Education, 'Information Report on the Destruction by War of the Cultural Heritage in Croatia and Bosnia-Herzegovina' [1993] Doc 6756.

36 András J Riedlmayer, *Destruction of Cultural Heritage in Bosnia-Herzegovina, 1992–1996: A Post-War Survey of Selected Municipalities* (Expert report commissioned by the International Criminal Tribunal for the Former Yugoslavia, 2002).

former Yugoslavia demonstrated the insufficiency of existing heritage international legislation and asked for a revised approach to heritage protection. It also shed new light on the connection between heritage, identity, human rights, dissonance of heritage, and conflicts. As stated by the CoE in its publication *Analysis and Reform of Cultural Heritage Policies in South East Europe* (2008):

> […] After the war in Bosnia and Herzegovina […].
>
> Heritage evaluation became a more complex process, in which the non-material – the symbolic and ontological – value of the heritage carried more weight than the material. The very definition of heritage, as well as its significance changed – its function in maintaining social patterns and the distinctive features of society became as important as its cultural and economic value.
>
> p. 28

These were all grounds for renewing the debate about the value of heritage for society. The initial reaction at the CoE level was an initiative from the ministers responsible for cultural heritage asking for a number of protocols to be added to the Granada and Valletta Conventions. Those protocols would outline procedures for preserving and enhancing built and archaeological heritage 'that reflects the cultural diversity which has emerged over history within a given territory, irrespective of the present-day political context of that territory'.[37] However, it became apparent that adding protocols to existing conventions would not be sufficient in addressing changes and challenges in heritage management in the twenty-first century. A more profound shift in the approach was required.

3 The Background of the Faro Convention: The Council of Europe's Actions

The 4th European Conference of Ministers Responsible for the Cultural Heritage (Helsinki, 30–31 May 1996) presents a starting point for a profound modification in the CoE's heritage policies, one that accentuated the fact that heritage values can help support the idea of democracy as promoted by the CoE.

---

37 Council of Europe, Committee of Ministers, '4th European Conference of Ministers Responsible for the Cultural Heritage (Helsinki) – Report by the Secretary General' [1996] CMD037494/CM (96) 97, 3.

This more political view of heritage was 'welcomed',[38] and the organisation's new approach in considering the contribution of the cultural heritage sector to the CoE's current perspectives and priorities could be seen from the central theme of the conference – 'The Cultural Heritage: An Economic and Social Challenge'. The Conference adopted the Declaration on the Political Dimension of Cultural Heritage Conservation in Europe, the Resolution on the Cultural Heritage as a Factor in Building Europe and the Resolution on the Cultural Heritage as a Factor of Sustainable Development. As a result of these political affirmations, the work of the CoE Cultural Heritage Committee from 1996 centred around subjects that would play a principal role in the Faro Convention: (1) heritage and identity, (2) heritage and society, (3) heritage, information, and training, and (4) methodology for heritage management in a framework of sustainable development.[39]

This significant ideological shift in the perception of heritage itself, but also the perception of the relationship between the environment and the cultural heritage in CoE policy, as declared at the Helsinki Conference, was further marked by the adoption of the European Landscape Convention in 2000[40] (Florence Convention). To date (June 2025), the Florence Convention has been ratified by 40 Member States and represents an integral part of the CoE's political, cultural, and legal framework concerning common European heritage, environment, town planning, sustainable development, and local self-government. Even though the Florence Convention is not considered to be one of the CoE's core conventions on heritage, its recognition of the landscape as one of the essential components of European natural and cultural heritage was welcomed as an initial attempt to legally address the full scope of elements that encompass landscape as heritage (Last 2006).[41] The Euro-

38 Interview with Interviewee 7, former Director General of Education, Culture and Heritage, Youth and Sport at the Council of Europe (5 June 2020).

39 CM (96) 97 (n 37).

40 *European Landscape Convention*, 20 October 2000, ETS No. 176.

41 Kathryn Last, 'Heritage and Identity: The Challenge of Landscapes to the Nature/Culture Dichotomy' in *Landscape as Heritage: Negotiating European Cultural Identity*, EUI Working Papers RSCAS 2006/5, 9–16;

Florence Convention is not seen as one of the exclusive heritage-themed CoE conventions, and as it can be seen from the academic considerations of the subject, it attracted interest mainly from the academics in landscape architecture, spatial planning and management, landscape ecological issues, landscape planning tools and instruments, agricultural policies (Eiter and Pottoff 2007; Olwig and Mitchell 2007; Jones, Howard, Olweg, Primdahl and Herlin 2007; Herlin 2004; Roe 2013; Déjeant-Pons 2006; Olwig 2007; Jones and Stenseke eds. 2011; Scott 2011; De Montis 2014; Jørgensen, Clemetsen, Thorén and Richardson eds. 2016; Bloemers, Kars, Valk and Mijnen eds. 2010; Antrop 2005).

pean Landscape Convention moved away from the nature/culture separation approach of the UNESCO Convention for the Protection of World Cultural and Natural Heritage, initiating the more refined notion of heritage that would be further fully developed in the Faro Convention.

As already noted, underpinned by the effects of globalisation, 'cultural diversity' became the mainstream concept debated on different levels, resulting in the CoE Declaration on Cultural Diversity in 2000 and UNESCO's Universal Declaration on Cultural Diversity in 2001 as well as two fundamental UNESCO Conventions: The Convention for the Safeguarding of the Intangible Cultural Heritage (2003) and The Convention on the Protection and Promotion of the Diversity of Cultural Expressions (2005). In evolving its own approach to heritage, the CoE had to make sure to avoid duplicating UNESCO's efforts. As a response to the developments mentioned above in the heritage field and the changing social and political European context, the Fifth European Conference of Ministers Responsible for Cultural Heritage (Portorož, 2001) called on the CoE to draft a reference text that would incorporate, among other matters, the 'extended concept of heritage [which is going] to encompass the cultural environment and address the need to sustain its cultural values (including material, non-material and spiritual), as perceived by people'.[42] With the call for the new reference text coming from ministers of the Member States and the pressure to avoid overlapping with other international legal texts, the CoE had to look further from a heritage value that connects the tangible and intangible heritage and to search for an inventive and aspiring approach to heritage in the twenty-first century. As a result of this process, the Faro Convention, for many commentators and the CoE Member States' administration, emerged as somewhat over-ambitious text. Nevertheless, it could be argued that it was the only choice the CoE had at the time. All the other options would have resulted in duplicating already existing international texts. In this respect, the CoE should be given credit for creating and adopting the Convention that would destabilise AHD-underpinned policies and practices and open new spaces for dialogue and action at all levels of society regarding the value of heritage.[43]

---

42 Council of Europe, 'Resolution No 2 on the Council of Europe's Future Activities in the Cultural Heritage Field, 2002–2005' (Portorož, 2001).

43 At the three Summits of the Council of Europe Heads of State and Government (Vienna 1993, Strasbourg 1997 and Warsaw 2005), full compliance with the undertakings given for the purpose of securing democracy, respect for human rights and the rule of law throughout Europe was solemnly reasserted as member states' principal obligation, which was inherent in their membership of the Council. Following the Third Summit, the Council of Europe's current priorities now include the protection and promotion of

Major guidelines for the future text emerged from the seminar *Cultural Heritage, a Resource for Democratic Development* organised in Strasbourg in 2002, bringing together around thirty experts from various backgrounds (heritage conservation, cultural development, human rights, social affairs, education). Those guidelines can be summarised as follows:

- The text should focus on rights to heritage (heritage rights) – access to heritage, civil society's participation and public involvement;
- The text should emphasise the function and use of cultural assets in a peaceful and democratic society and clarify the concept of the 'common heritage';
- The new definition of heritage should put forward a universal and cross-disciplinary perception of cultural heritage, leaving behind the definitions traditionally adopted (tangible-intangible distinction, movable and immovable heritage, architectural or archaeological forms, etc.);
- Heritage should be presented as a development resource, a source of wealth for society and citizens; and
- The text should also introduce society's collective responsibility in preserving and handling heritage, new governance methods and procedures for public involvement.[44]

It is apparent from the discussion and the guidelines developed that participants hoped the new convention would aim for cultural heritage and its conservation to play a more active role in social processes. A change in perspective, or rather a transition away from the AHD, was required if the Convention wanted to successfully deliver on the goals it set out. As stated in the Final Activity Report of the Steering Committee for Cultural Heritage (CDPAT), the new convention effectively needed to promote changes in viewpoint at the national and European level from (1) an 'object-centred' view of cultural heritage to a 'people-centred' view, (2) from 'how' to preserve to 'why' to preserve heritage, (3) towards a more explicit recognition of the cultural heritage dimension of human rights, and (4) towards an acknowledgement of physical

---

cultural diversity and intercultural dialogue as factors that contribute to the building of a more humane and inclusive Europe. The Council of Europe's role is to offer member states useful tools for the development of their policies and societies. The Warsaw Declaration refers to Europeans' shared values and **heritage as the foundations of their identity and unity. Cultural heritage must, therefore, form an integral part of the organisation's main lines of action and priority programmes.**

44 Council of Europe, Steering Committee for Cultural Heritage (CDPAT), 'Cultural Heritage, a Vector of Democratic Development – Report of the Cross-Sectoral Seminar, Strasbourg, 20–21 June 2002' [2002] CDPAT (2002) 28.

and intellectual use and misuse of heritage in the course of the conflict, as well as its role as a source of conflict.[45]

Building on the aforementioned guidelines and goals, the selected Committee of Experts responsible for preparing the Convention's draft worked on the text for two years (2003 and 2004). The often-heard critique and the fear coming from the Member States that the Convention wanted to cover too much seemed valid, especially once we look at the preliminary outline of the instrument's content.[46] Namely, the text aimed to cover subjects from the broader definition of heritage and right to heritage, to heritage and human security, heritage and conflict prevention, and sustainable development and globalisation, as well as collective responsibility for cultural heritage and participation, among others (CDPAT (2002) 40).[47] Three groups of experts (the group on 'Principles and definitions', the group on 'Sustainable development and cultural diversity', and the group on 'Monitoring the convention') were entrusted to articulate those wide-ranging aspirations in a convention that would radically challenge traditional ways of looking at heritage and our relation to it (the AHD), but which would, at the same time, be possible to implement.

4 Conclusion of the Chapter

The Faro Convention, as the text that frames the CoE's twenty-first-century heritage policy, emerged as a result of number of global and Europe-specific social, political, and cultural changes. The paradigm shift that arose at the time took place not only in the field of cultural heritage but also in other fields

45 Council of Europe, Steering Committee for Cultural Heritage (CDPAT), 'Final Activity Report – Preparation of a Framework Convention on Cultural Heritage in a Changing Europe' [2005] CM (2005) 17 Addendum.

46 Interview with Interviewee 9, current employee at the Directorate of Democracy, Council of Europe (October 2022).

47 Council of Europe, Steering Committee for Cultural Heritage (CDPAT), 'Work on Cultural Heritage Conventions – 1st Meeting' [2002] CDPAT (2002) 40;

The first outline of the Convention's content includes Article 1: The Cultural Heritage, Article 2: Common European Heritage, Article 3: Heritage Law, Article 4: The Right to Heritage, Article 5: Diversity and cultural heritages, Article 6: Heritages and human security, Article 7: Education and intercultural dialogue, Article 8: Heritage and conflict prevention, Article 9: Heritage, sustainable development and globalisation, Article 10: Diversity of operators, Article 11: Collective responsibility for cultural heritages and participation, Article 12: From conservation to management, Article 13: Public intervention thresholds, Article 14 Governance instruments.

such as human rights, development, environmental protection, and intellectual property protection; all these underpinned the Convention.

In terms of heritage policy and law-making at the international level, recognition of the variety of manifestations of intangible cultural heritage (ICH) and its values for communities that the international community aimed to address through UNESCO conventions in the late 1990s and the early 2000s has had a trickle-down effect on national and regional approaches towards heritage and its protection around the world. While it is certain that the UNESCO 2003 Convention for the Safeguarding of the Intangible Cultural Heritage moved the heritage field forward, it also continued to use the AHD to frame much of how intangible cultural heritage was to be understood and safeguarded. The idea behind the Faro Convention was therefore to radically challenge the AHD-underpinned policies by offering a framework that would reflect the aspirations and expectations of the citizens regarding their role in public decisions concerning cultural heritage.

The sustainable development agenda was another important framework influencing the conceptualisation of the Faro Convention. The change of development discourse from the understanding that culture is a constraint for development towards the recognition of its constructive role in this process was crucial for the CoE's formulation of its wider policies. The CoE's decision to use a human-based approach to sustainable development as a framework for its policies in different fields, heritage included, was fundamentally a key factor enabling the process of rethinking heritage and heritage discourse as promoted by the Faro Convention.

Lastly, the political context in Europe, triggered by the fall of the Berlin Wall, with the war in ex-Yugoslavia, the accession of Eastern European countries to the CoE, and the new EU 1992 Treaty, all influenced the ideological shift in the CoE's perception of heritage and its role in those political developments. The subjects that emerged from those social and political changes, such as (1) heritage and identity, (2) heritage and society, (3) heritage, information, and training, and (4) methodology for heritage management in a framework of sustainable development all framed the themes of the Faro Convention and allowed for a radical shift in heritage discourse to be defined in the text.

CHAPTER 7

The Convention on the Value of Cultural Heritage for Society

1 Introduction

The Council of Europe Framework Convention on the Value of Cultural Heritage for Society (Faro Convention) was opened for signature in 2005 and entered into force in 2011 after the ten necessary CoE Member States had ratified it. The first step in understanding this rather complex text is to clarify the concept of a 'framework convention' and what it entails in the context of the CoE and international law.[1] The CoE expresses the idea of framework conventions using the following metaphor: 'A framework convention identifies the direction and the destination of an ambitious European journey but is not a detailed route map or timetable'.[2] In their instruction to the Faro drafting committee, the Legal Advice Department and Treaty Office of the CoE elucidate this approach in more detail. In principle, a framework convention contains mostly programme-type provisions that set out objectives the Parties undertake to pursue.[3] In this case, the Parties to the convention are left with a margin of discretion in choosing the means through which they intend to implement the stated objectives. It could be through national legislation and/or through suitable governmental policies.

The use of the framework convention, according to the CoE, may serve several purposes. Firstly, it may consider the different problems and situations the Member States face in the particular field covered by the convention. This approach opens up the possibility for the Parties to the convention to choose the implementing measures best suited to their specific situation. Secondly,

1 Council of Europe, Steering Committee for Cultural Heritage (CDPAT), 'Cultural Heritage, a Vector of Democratic Development – Report of the Cross-Sectoral Seminar, Strasbourg, 20–21 June 2002' [2002] CDPAT (2002) 28;
Council of Europe, Steering Committee for Cultural Heritage (CDPAT), 'Work on Cultural Heritage Conventions – 1st Meeting' [2002] CDPAT (2002) 40.

2 Council of Europe, *Explanatory Report to the Council of Europe Framework Convention on the Value of Cultural Heritage for Society* [2005] CETS No 199, Section C, para 3.

3 Council of Europe, Steering Committee for Cultural Heritage (CDPAT), 'Select Committee of Experts on the Draft Convention on Cultural Heritage – Information Message by the Legal Advice Department and Treaty Office' [2003] CDPAT (2003) 59, 2.

 | DOI:10.1163/9789004756250_008

the framework convention may respond to the will of Member States to establish general rules in particular areas of States' activity. Setting such a framework for adopting more detailed implementing practices also opens the possibility of amending them accordingly in light of future developments in the field covered by the convention. Finally, a framework convention generally does not contain self-executing provisions. This means that this type of convention necessitates the enactment of implementing measures by State Parties, and it is usually not possible to invoke the direct application of the provisions before national courts.[4] Therefore, the Faro Convention does not create enforceable rights for citizens and cannot become the focus of individual legal disputes. Instead, the Faro, as a framework convention, 'links the states which ratified it in joint efforts to find the ways and means of establishing a democratic culture for people's living environment'.[5]

This also means that monitoring the framework convention's implementation differs from regular conventions. While with previous conventions, the focus was on the implementation of their provisions in the national legal systems, with the Faro Convention, at least up to now, the CoE seems less interested in following up on its legal dimension and more focused on promoting the principle of 'shared responsibility' that involves citizens and civil society in mechanisms integrated into public action to identify values and define priorities and managing heritage projects.[6] Even though, as with any other international binding instrument, ratification of the Faro Convention implies the adaptation and modification of domestic legislation, the Convention makes no provision as to timetable or expected level of detail. In this respect, it seems that the CoE took the stance that, although important, the ratification by the state and adaptation of the domestic legal framework is not enough, and the involvement of citizens, elected representatives, and civil society is vital for this Convention to be successful.

Against this background, the Faro Convention emerged as a multifaceted text that many practitioners and heritage administrators find challenging to interpret and understand. To apply a literal, purely linguistic interpretation of the text certainly is not a valuable approach if we want to understand the Convention's meaning and intention appropriately. One must look closely at the different sources to capture this text's value. In this context, the Explana-

---

4 CDPAT (2003) 59 (n 3) 3.

5 Daniel Thérond, 'The Council of Europe Conventions in the Field of Cultural Heritage and Landscape: Trends and Prospects' in Mitja Guštin and Terje Nypan (eds), *Cultural Heritage and Legal Aspects in Europe* (Institute for Mediterranean Heritage 2010) 26.

6 Council of Europe, *The Faro Convention's Role in a Changing Society – Building on a Decade of Advancement 2011–2021* (Council of Europe Publishing, 2021) 10.

tory Report that complements the Convention's text plays a crucial role. It captures the intentions the authors wanted to convey and explains how the Convention text should be understood and translated.

Furthermore, several drafting committee members further explained the purpose and objectives that the Convention is designed to fulfil in the anthology *Heritage and Beyond*.[7] This book is considered critical for understanding Faro and its implications. It addresses the questions of why such a convention was needed and what the benefits for the CoE Member States would be if they ratified it. In this context, the two introductory chapters by Daniel Thérond[8] and Noel Fojut[9] are of specific interest, notably because the two authors 'formed the guiding inspirations and executive force behind the work of the CoE's Committee of Experts that wrote the text'.[10] What new can be added to those efforts to 'decode' the Faro text? Primarily, going back to the evolution of ideas in the drafting process that archival documents expose is a valuable exercise for our understanding of why certain choices have been made. Secondly, the subjective interpretations (that come with hindsight) of the text by a number of interviewees, some of whom participated in the drafting process and some of whom were/are responsible for the Convention's implementation and dissemination, expose the reality between the initial expectations and optimism and the ongoing struggle with implementation and doubt 'if we went too far'.[11] This juxtaposition of the initial ideas, as they emerged from archival research and the current understanding of the text, as presented by interviewees, adds to our understanding of the evolution of the text and its use.

As the Convention is complex in nature, the approach chosen here is to look at it through the several interrelated major themes it covers. The first theme looks at cultural heritage as a resource for social sustainability. Through it, the broader concept of cultural heritage will be addressed, as well as the individual, collective, and European level of cultural heritage as a potential resource for socially sustainable development. The second theme builds on the understanding that the Convention is concerned with heritage rights,

---

7 Council of Europe, *Heritage and Beyond* (Council of Europe Publishing, Strasbourg 2009).

8 Daniel Thérond, 'Benefits and Innovations of the Council of Europe Framework Convention on the Value of Cultural Heritage for Society' in Council of Europe, *Heritage and Beyond* (Council of Europe Publishing, 2009).

9 Noel Fojut, 'The Philosophical, Political and Pragmatic Roots of the Convention' in Council of Europe, *Heritage and Beyond* (Council of Europe Publishing, 2009).

10 Graham Fairclough, 'New Heritage Frontiers' in Council of Europe, *Heritage and Beyond* (Council of Europe Publishing, 2009).

11 Interview with Interviewee 4, former Head of Division of Culture and Cultural Heritage, Council of Europe (10 October 2022).

i.e., 'issues of access to heritage, citizens involvement and participation'.[12] Through it, the relation between heritage and human rights, as well as the concept of 'heritage community', is explored. In this regard, it can be said that the official title of the Convention – the Framework Convention on the Value of Cultural Heritage for Society – sets the tone for its content by asserting the value the cultural heritage can have for society and how it is linked to the concept of sustainable development, especially its sociocultural aspect (sociocultural sustainability). From the title, it is also evident that the Convention plans to question the traditional AHD approach to heritage and offer a fundamentally new approach.

2 Cultural Heritage and Socially Sustainable Development

Central to the understanding of the Faro Convention is the Convention's background in socially sustainable development, where cultural heritage is a resource that can be used constructively in multiple ongoing social processes.[13] Within the theory of the concept of sustainability, the social dimension changed over time, shifting from earlier identified social values such as public health, employment, welfare, equality, and democracy towards more 'soft values' that include social cohesion, social capital, and quality of life.[14] It can be said that today, social sustainability is, above all, about people and their mutual relationships. It is primarily against this background that the Faro Convention's emphasis on a people-centred approach to cultural heritage must be understood.

2.1 *The Faro Convention's Broader Concept of Heritage*

A broader definition of the concept of heritage was a prerequisite for operationalising the use of heritage as a resource for dealing with the different challenges facing Europe. The Convention's preamble clarifies the need for a more comprehensive definition of what heritage is with, 'Recognising the need to put people and human values at the centre of an enlarged and cross-disciplinary concept of cultural heritage' (Preamble, 2nd paragraph). Therefore, the critical Convention's approach is based on the idea that cultural heri-

---

12 CDPAT (2002) 28 (n 1) 2.

13 Graham Fairclough, 'The Cultural Context of Sustainability – Heritage and Living' in Council of Europe, *Heritage and Beyond* (Council of Europe Publishing 2009).

14 Andrea Colantonio, 'Measuring Social Sustainability: Best Practice from Urban Renewal in the EU' (EIBURS Working Paper Series – Traditional and Emerging Prospects in Social Sustainability No 2008/2).

tage must be defined in relation to societal changes and challenges and that consideration needs to be given to human values and functions of cultural heritage in society.[15] To meet the aforementioned Convention's objectives, Article 2a provides a detailed definition of what heritage is considered to be:

> Cultural heritage is a group of resources inherited from the past that people identify, independently of ownership, as a reflection and expression of their constantly evolving values, beliefs, knowledge and traditions. It includes all aspects of the environment resulting from the interaction between people and places through time.

According to the Explanatory Report, this definition is the broadest to appear in any international convention text so far and defies the AHD on multiple levels. The first aspect that needs to be emphasised is that Faro considers that cultural heritage is interactive, which means that heritage is no longer perceived as static or unchangeable (AHD) but rather as something that is constantly being redefined by people and communities.[16] This 'unstable' state of heritage, expressed in the definition by words 'constantly evolving', means that cultural heritage not only considers the past but also implies that heritage is much more about the present and our current use of it, as well as about our consideration of how it should face the future. So again, the AHD understanding of heritage as something static that needs to be protected and preserved unchanged for the future, which in essence excludes present generations, is called into question, and the focus is turned to inclusion and the broader participation of more segments of the population in the discussion of the meaning and value of heritage.

Another welcomed shift in the perception of heritage is embodied in the word 'resources', which implies that the thing so described exists to be utilised and that 'resources' might be eroded or even 'used up' if necessary (2009a, p. 37).[17] Indeed, this was not the case in the AHD way of thinking, wherein heritage has mainly been referred to as an 'asset' to be kept unchanged and untouched. Using the word 'resources' also means that there are users and people (individuals or communities) who will benefit from that use. The

15 Explanatory Report, 2005, Preamble second paragraph: 'The second paragraph sets out the need to consider the human values and functions of cultural heritage, and indeed the need to define cultural heritage itself, in response to major changes in society'.

16 Explanatory Report, 2005, article 2 Definitions, 1 a: 'It pays particular attention to the interactive nature of the cultural heritage, recognising that it is defined and redefined by human actions and that it must not be perceived as either static or immutable'.

17 Fairclough (n 13) 17.

focus of this Convention is to put people at the centre of the debate and decision-making.

The shift away from the paradigm that heritage is 'being served by society' (asset) and towards the new concept where 'heritage must serve society' (resource) needs to be understood as a result of a combination of the philosophical considerations Convention's authors had and organisation's pragmatic politics. As Noel Fojut observes in *Heritage and Beyond*, and as repeated in several interviews,[18] some CoE Member States saw the traditional approach to heritage conservation as a disproportionate drain on national funds, especially in times of prolonged economic challenges. Thus, the clear need for an approach linking conservation costs and heritage value to everyday public life underlines the Faro text. Here again, the reference can be made to Labadi's identification of different relationships between heritage and development, which was already referred to in Chapter 6: (1) heritage conservation in opposition to development, (2) heritage conservation as sustainability, and (3) heritage conservation as community development.[19] As discussed, the CoE has already made some significant shifts from the predominant discourse where heritage was set in opposition to development. The Granada Convention considered architectural heritage to be an important factor in the social life of communities. It introduced this idea in the policy processes with the concept of integrated conservation, which in the 1980s challenged the narrative whereby heritage was portrayed as a burden for society ('served by society'). However, if we follow Labadi's categorisation, the Faro Convention moved much further and needs to be examined through the notion of 'heritage conservation as community development', where heritage must serve the society and where it is considered as a factor (resource) in improving the living environment by strengthening intercultural dialogue and democratic participation. This new approach based on the notion that heritage is a part of everyday life turns the old question of 'what is the price of preserving heritage?' into a question of 'what is the price of not looking after and sensibly using it?'.[20]

Another aspect of the broader definition of cultural heritage offered in Faro is that it draws particular attention to cultural heritage's environmental and

18 Fojut (n 9); Interview with Interviewee 1, former Employee, Council of Europe Directorate of Culture and Cultural and Natural Heritage (1 April 2020); Interview with Interviewee 5, Project Manager, Council of Europe Directorate of Democracy (15 October 2022).

19 Sophia Labadi, 'UNESCO, Heritage and Sustainable Development: International Discourses and Local Impacts' in Peter Gould and Kathryn A Pyburn (eds), *Promise and Peril: Archaeology Engaging with Economic Development* (Springer 2017).

20 Fairclough (n 10) 36.

contextual dimensions. The Convention promotes the idea that living heritage is aligned with a sense of place, (cultural) landscape, and sustainability. Explicitly, its goal is to go beyond the 'historic environment' concept, which tends to be restricted to AHD-underpinned historically defined narratives and predominantly material aspects of the cultural environment.[21] Therefore, Faro's definition tends to be comprehensive, with no inherent time limits nor limits of form or manifestation. According to Faro's definition, how heritage is seen and valued is manifold and based on values, beliefs, traditions, and knowledge. The understanding of heritage that the Faro definition offers underlines the broader democratic aspect that the Convention promotes and provides the basis for a new heritage discourse. Fairclough notes that the Convention points the way forward across many hitherto constraining frontiers built by the AHD and offers the way forward into new territory.[22]

Even though such an innovative way of conceptualising cultural heritage is not unproblematic, it was essential for successfully integrating cultural heritage within the concept of sustainable social development. The Convention promotes cultural heritage's contribution to sustainable social development at three levels – individual, collective, and European.

2.2 *Heritage and Sustainable Development: Individual and Collective Levels*

The whole idea of the Faro Convention is constructed around the transition from an AHD object-focused heritage approach to a people-centred one. This section will reflect on the different roles heritage has as a resource for human (individual) development as well as on the collective level. A few Convention articles reflect a focus on individuals and their opportunities. Article 1c, for example, emphasises that the 'conservation of cultural heritage and its sustainable use have human development and quality of life as their goal'. It reinforces the principle that preserving cultural heritage is not an end in itself, but that it aims to foster the well-being of individuals and the wider community. Ultimately, as expressed in the Explanatory Report, the consequences of this perspective would be a more developed and democratic human society where quality of life is expected to increase for everyone.

Another essential element that plays a critical role in the Convention is the change in participation perspective. As already established in the previous chapters, the AHD was strongly expert-dominated, and the general public was invited, if not positively instructed, to appreciate the experts' choices

21 Explanatory Report (n 16).

22 Fairclough (n 10) 31.

and interpretations. The Faro Convention tends to challenge this deeply rooted discourse and to open space for more meaningful dialogue. The aim of Article 12 is precise when it asks the Parties to 'encourage everyone to participate in the process of identification, study, interpretation, protection, conservation and presentation of the cultural heritage'. Therefore, the Faro Convention invites an open discussion and sees the practice of cultural heritage as a social and cultural activity that is part of an individual's life. This means that democratic participation is the focus, whereby individuals can get involved in the ongoing process of defining and managing cultural heritage. This fundamental change in discourse reflects the broader role the CoE plays in encouraging more active and responsible citizenship by empowering citizens to contribute to and develop a sense of ownership over the activities of decision-making and institutions. The CoE, thus, through its actions and tools, aims to help individuals acquire the attitudes, skills, values, critical understanding, and knowledge required to participate in a democratic society.[23] Conventions such as Faro are vital in this process because they ask the State Parties to create a framework wherein such participation of individuals would be possible, i.e., to create a framework where civil society becomes involved in the design and implementation of national policies. Having in mind the CoE's political nature, the adoption of innovative texts like Faro also sends the political message that the Member States are 'comfortable' with their democratic processes and further involvement of individuals and civil society in the procedures of decision-making.

For the above-examined Convention's call for open dialogue to be successful, the text also requests for more prominent access to cultural heritage (Article 12d), especially for the young and disadvantaged populations in society. Frequently, the notion of greater access to cultural heritage has been understood by heritage professionals as access in a physical sense. This approach, framed by the AHD, continued to perpetuate the privilege of experts in heritage discourse and continued to look at the general public as passive observers. However, the Faro Convention promotes another aspect of accessibility: the intellectual one, which directly opposes the AHD understanding of public passivity. As Meyer-Bisch explains, in the Faro Convention access includes not only material access to the cultural works but also participation, i.e. 'the act of learning to act with this capital, to appropriate it, share it and help transmit

23 It is therefore understandable that the organisation's Culture and Heritage Department is placed in the Directorate of Democracy (which is part of the Directorate General of Democracy and Human Dignity).

it'.[24] This puts the Faro Convention in direct opposition to the AHD in which a 'sense of "action" or critical engagement on the part of non-expert users' is absent, and the 'heritage is [understood to be] about receiving the wisdom and knowledge of historians, archaeologists, and other experts'.[25]

Borrowing from Meyer-Bisch, the following statement perfectly sums up Faro's view on heritage's contribution to sustainable social development on the individual level:

> An individual's dignity can only really be respected if he/she is considered as being able to participate personally, freely, and creatively in recognising and developing cultural references, knowing, maintaining and developing works which are important to him/her and to the milieu in which he/she lives. This involves the freedom to refer to cultural communities or not, as the case may be.[26]

The democratisation of heritage that happens with broader participation and access allows for cultural heritage to demonstrate its potential as a resource for human development and enhancement of the quality of human life. This same standing could be replicated at the broader, collective level. The Faro Convention points out in its different articles how heritage could be used as a resource in diverse social processes. Article 1d emphasises the distinctive perspective of the Convention in general terms. According to this article, the Parties to the Convention are expected to take necessary measures to ensure that cultural heritage can have a role in developing a peaceful and democratic society and in the 'processes of sustainable development and the promotion of cultural diversity' (Article 1d). So, as Fairclough points out in *Heritage and Beyond*, the Faro Convention offers a view of sustainability as a cultural phenomenon, and it touches firmly on how people live, particularly on issues such as quality of life, landscape, society, social cohesion, and social responsibility, as well as rights. Therefore, social sustainability on the individual and collective level, as understood by the Faro Convention, means, in part, creating places where people experience well-being and develop their individual potentials, but also create connections with their surroundings and their past. For Faro,

---

24 Patrice Meyer-Bisch, 'On the "Right to Heritage" – The Innovative Approach of Articles 1 and 2 of the Faro Convention' in Council of Europe, *Heritage and Beyond* (Council of Europe Publishing 2009) 67.

25 Laurajane Smith, *Uses of Heritage* (Routledge 2006) 34.

26 Meyer-Bisch (n 24) 67.

therefore, the value of heritage is based on the presumption of how effectively it can help the lives of all people and the future development of Europe.

2.3 *Heritage and Sustainable Development: European Level*

The European level is the third level, where we can discuss the role of cultural heritage as a source of sustainable social development. Article 3 of the Faro Convention, which defines the 'common heritage of Europe' reads:

> The Parties agree to promote an understanding of the common heritage of Europe, which consists of:
>
> All forms of cultural heritage in Europe which together constitute a shared source of remembrance, understanding, identity, cohesion and creativity, and The ideals, principles and values, derived from the experience gained through progress and past conflicts, which foster the development of a peaceful and stable society, founded on respect for human rights, democracy and the rule of law.

Many commentators consider this attempt to define the 'common heritage of Europe' in the Faro Convention as 'audacious'[27] and the 'most difficult of all' innovative concepts the Convention introduced.[28]

To begin with, it has to be noted that the CoE used the idea of the 'common heritage of Europe' since its creation in 1949 as a part of its goal to build a united Europe based on democracy, freedom, and respect for human rights and the rule of law, as indicated in Article 1 of its Statute. The aim of achieving greater unity among its members by 'safeguarding and realising the ideals and principles which are their common heritage'[29] through the common actions was reiterated in the Preamble of the European Cultural Convention (ECC) in 1954 and represent the starting point for the CoE's policy of cultural cooperation. Article 5 of the ECC, in addition, promotes the idea that Parties to the Convention should regard the objects of 'European cultural value' placed under their control as 'integral parts of the common cultural heritage of Europe' and should take appropriate measures to safeguard them and ensure reasonable access to them.[30] In this early stage, the CoE used the platform of

---

27 Lauso Zagato, 'The Notion of "Heritage Community" in the Council of Europe's Faro Convention: Its Impact on the European Legal Framework' in Nicolas Adell and others (eds), *Between Imagined Communities and Communities of Practice: Participation, Territory and the Making of Heritage* (Universitätsverlag Göttingen 2015).

28 Fojut (n 9) 20.

29 Statute of the Council of Europe (ETS No 1, 1949) art 1.

30 European Cultural Convention (ETS No 18, 1954) art 5.

the common cultural heritage of Europe to encourage European unity by promoting the study of languages, history, and civilisation of other European countries among scholars and students. It was a first step towards 'rendering the common European heritage part of the commonly held baggage of personal culture for an increasing number of Europeans'.[31] This first stage in cultural cooperation and attempts to promote the idea of commonness emerged with the explicit aim of healing the wounds of the World War II.

The same motives of healing the wounds of yet another armed conflict in Europe (the former Yugoslavia) were behind the Faro Convention and its effort to (re)create a common cultural milieu for Europe. At the European level, the CoE, throughout decades, was responsible for preventing armed conflicts among its Member States and building a peaceful and democratic society. This mission became much more demanding with the fall of the Berlin Wall and the socio-political changes in Europe at the time. Notably, the armed conflicts in the early 1990s, where cultural heritage was targeted as a means of erasing the groups' identities, as was the case in Bosnia and Herzegovina, again raised awareness in Western Europe of what had been, over the 1960s, 1970s, and 1980s, the somewhat overlooked value and role of heritage for society. The use/destruction of heritage for the purposes of eliminating an ethnic group showed that the dominant AHD approach to heritage primarily undermined the complexity of the concept of heritage and the problems around it.[32] In 1993, the Vienna Summit recognised common cultural heritage anew as one of the cornerstones of the Council of Europe's actions. Nevertheless, a number of participants at the first meeting of the Drafting Committee of the Faro Convention acknowledged that this aspect of the CoE's work had been obscured for a long time and that the new convention 'would thus highlight the political aspects of the issue of heritage in European integration'.[33] Therefore, the Faro Convention emerged from this recognition of the need for a new doctrine but also from the organisation's decision to use, once again, heritage for its political goals, as was the case with the ECC.[34] The CoE's political direction, which gives prominence to the advancement of human rights, democracy, and the

31 Ugo Mifsud Bonnici, 'The Human Right to Cultural Heritage – The Faro Convention's Contribution to the Recognition and Safeguarding of This Human Right' in Council of Europe, *Heritage and Beyond* (Council of Europe Publishing 2009) 56.

32 Višnja Kisić, *Governing Heritage Dissonance: Promises and Realities of Selected Cultural Policies* (European Cultural Foundation 2016).

33 Council of Europe, Steering Committee for Cultural Heritage (CDPAT), 'Select Committee of Experts on the Preparation of a Framework Convention on Cultural Heritage – Record of the 1st Meeting' [2003] CDPAT (2003) 43, 3.

34 Interview with Former Employee, 1 April 2020 (n 18).

rule of law, as well as to the building of a more cohesive Europe, asked for a transition from the conservation-oriented scientific approach in heritage management to one in which heritage is beneficial and meaningful for societal progress, European unification, and its fundamental values.[35]

With the above-cited definition of the notion of the 'common heritage of Europe' in the Faro Convention, the CoE started seeing cultural heritage in a broader social context. The mutually supporting interaction of defined elements including a common **recourse and source** of identity, memory, and cohesion as well as a common **experience** of both progress and conflict constitutes the unifying theme of the Faro Convention.[36] The thinking behind the construct of the 'common heritage of Europe' in Faro is that all manifestations of cultural heritage in Europe, as a shared source and shared experience, could contribute to the future development of European society built around a consensus on common social values. Here, as Lixinski points out, it is vital to distinguish between the *cultural* heritage of Europe, on the one hand, and the shared *intellectual* heritage, which looks at the CoE's ideal of how a society should operate.[37] Therefore, the idea of the 'common heritage of Europe' represents the notion in which the cultural heritage shared by Europeans interacts with the agreed democratic, political, and social ideals of Europe and generates the sense of a common European responsibility towards cultural heritage.[38] Thus, the innovative aspect of the Faro Convention is that it linked the concept of the 'common heritage of Europe' to human rights and fundamental freedoms for which the CoE remains one of the historic European guardians. In line with Ferracuti's opinion, we should agree that in the Faro Convention, European identity is qualified 'by its heritage of democracy and its capacity to guarantee basic rights to its citizens'.[39] According to this commentator, the 'common heritage of Europe' must be read as the capacity of the

35 Thérond (n 8).

36 Explanatory Report, Article 3: The Convention's aim of addressing the cultural heritage of Europe in its broader social context is expressed by the introduction of the idea of 'common heritage of Europe', composed of two inseparable elements: 'the *cultural* heritage, which represents a resource and a source of collective memory for people in Europe, and the shared *intellectual* heritage of an agreed set of social values, rooted in history, which form the 'European ideal' in terms of how society should operate'.

37 Lucas Lixinski, *Intangible Cultural Heritage in International Law* (Oxford University Press, Oxford 2013).

38 Ondřej Vícha, 'The Concept of the Right to Cultural Heritage within the Faro Convention' (2014) 14(2) *International and Comparative Law Review* 23.

39 Simona Ferracuti, 'L'Etnografo del Patrimonio in Europa: Esercizi di Teoria e Cittadinanza' in Livio Zagato and Marilena Vecco (eds), *Le Culture dell'Europa, l'Europa della Culture* (Franco Angeli, Italy 2011) 217–218.

European institutions (EU and CoE) and their Member States 'to be the guarantors of freedom'.[40]

On the European level, thus, cultural heritage plays the role of a resource for building a peaceful and democratic European society, as well as achieving a greater degree of social and political cohesion among the CoE Member States. Therefore, cultural heritage, on a European level, is considered a decisive element in promoting intercultural dialogue and preventing conflict in the CoE's activities and programmes.[41] The advantage of Faro's proactive promotion of tolerance and the importance of cultural heritage as a means for people to acquire a greater understanding of each other, as well as communicating their *commonness* through the notion of the 'common heritage of Europe', have been particularly evident in the regions of Europe affected by ethnic conflicts in the past decades. This welcomed shift in the understanding of the role of heritage, as promoted by the Faro Convention, was therefore quickly recognised and supported, mainly throughout Eastern European countries, which were largely among the first ones to ratify the Convention.[42]

Regarding this role of heritage in conflict prevention and promotion of intercultural dialogue, Article 7 of the Faro Convention is of specific interest.[43] Regarding conflict prevention, Article 7 reaffirms the role of cultural heritage in creating a peaceful and democratic European society within the framework of sustainable development. The starting point for understanding this particular Article is the awareness that there is cultural diversity in Europe and that culture and cultural heritage have been used in national, ethnic, and

---

40 Ibid, 218.

41 See for example the document prepared by the Secretariat of the Directorate of Cultural and Natural Heritage, *The Role of Cultural Heritage in Conflict Prevention, Transformation, Resolution and Post-Conflict Action: The Council of Europe Approach* (2011).

42 Today the Convention has been ratified by 24 CoE Member States, but if we look at the first 10 countries that enabled Convention to enter into force, they are predominantly Eastern and former communist European countries (8/10): Bosnia and Herzegovina (2009), Croatia (2007), Latvia (2006), Montenegro (2008), Republic of Moldova (2008), Slovenia (2008), Serbia (2010), Georgia (2011), Portugal (2009), and Norway (2008)

43 Article 7 reads The Parties undertake, through the public authorities and other competent bodies, to:

a) encourage reflection on the ethics and methods of presentation of the cultural heritage, as well as respect for diversity of interpretations;

b) establish processes for conciliation to deal equitably with situations where contradictory values are placed on the same cultural heritage by different communities;

c) develop knowledge of cultural heritage as a resource to facilitate peaceful co-existence by promoting trust and mutual understanding with a view to the resolution and prevention of conflicts;

d) integrate these approaches into all aspects of lifelong education and training.

religious-coloured tensions more than was acknowledged in the predominant AHD. Indeed, the background for this Article can be found in the war in the former Yugoslavia, which not only raised the awareness of heritage's complexity and dissonance but also prompted the CoE's work in promoting conflict prevention and peace-building. The roots of Article 7 come from the initial idea that dissonance, conflicts, and the reconciliation of diverse values are critical to our understanding of heritage. The preliminary draft of the Convention signals this transition from the AHD understanding of heritage that camouflages the dissonant nature of heritage by stating that:

> Noting that intolerant movements and distorters of history reduce heritages to a simplistic approach and attempt to place unfair restrictions on access rights;
>
> Considering that human security and conflict prevention are achieved by the preservation of heritage as resources that are necessary for the task of remembrance, dialogue between cultural communities and maintenance of **forums for democratic disagreement.**[44]

Therefore, the specificity of this Article is that it differs from the other forward-looking articles in the Convention, with its roots in the historical experience of ethnic conflicts. Thus, the Faro Convention calls on public authorities to provide space for open discussion and communication on the painful and conflicting aspects of heritage, which could encourage the processes of reconciliation and presumably prevent further conflicts in Europe. This part of the Faro Convention contributes to the broader CoE approach to heritage in conflict processes, in particular as a tool for conflict prevention, as clearly stated in the CoE's document from 2011, which directly refers to the Faro Convention's Article 7:

> – Heritage is both an element of identity common to all Europeans and a factor for differentiation. It is a channel for knowledge and the mutual recognition of diversity, stimulating dialogue between people and communities;
>
> – Heritage is a means for people to understand each other. It contributes, through tolerance, to the prevention of conflicts (*see Article 7 of the Faro Convention*);

44 Council of Europe, Steering Committee for Cultural Heritage (CDPAT), 'Work on Cultural Heritage Conventions – 1st Meeting' [2002] CDPAT (2002) 40, 9, (emphasis added).

> – This approach is particularly important where heritage is likely to become a source of conflict, where it is the expression of contested identities or where conflicts arise from opposing feelings of identity and from 'fear of otherness'. This can result in heritage being seen as exhorting conflict.[45]

By attributing a peace-building role to cultural heritage, which, as noted in Article 7c, asks states to 'develop knowledge of cultural heritage as a resource to facilitate peaceful co-existence by promoting trust and mutual understanding with a view to resolution and prevention of conflicts', it is also expected that cultural heritage will be used to promote intercultural dialogue as another correlated element.[46] The idea behind Article 7 is that cultural heritage should be used as a means for people to acquire a greater understanding of one another. Consequently, this proactive approach to dialogue will result in a more tolerant society, i.e., future conflicts could be avoided this way.

From the discursive point of view, the acknowledgement of the dissonance of heritage is significant. For the most part, while heritage-related conflicts, contestations, and dissonance have always existed, they were obscured by the AHD and its governance models. The same could also be said for the academic approach to the subject; despite the recognition that all heritage is dissonant, a huge body of writing has implicitly created a tendency to separate heritage that is dissonant, 'dark', and problematic from all other consensual, comfortable, and 'normal' heritage.[47] Smith moved the conversation forward by emphasising that all heritage is dissonant and that the AHD continually works to neu-

---

45 Council of Europe, 'The Role of Culture and Cultural Heritage in Conflict Prevention, Transformation, Resolution and Post-Conflict Action: The Council of Europe Approach' [2010] AT (2010) 397 rev 1.

46 The CoE defines the 'intercultural dialogue' in Opatija Declaration (2003) as:
'...this term covers the tools used to promote and protect the concept of cultural democracy and encompasses the tangible and intangible elements likely to foster all forms of cultural diversity, manifesting themselves in multiple identities, whether individual or collective, in changes and in new forms of cultural expression. Intercultural dialogue must extend to every possible element of culture, without exception, whether these be cultural in the strict sense or have a political, economic, social, philosophical or religious dimension. In this context, for instance, interfaith and interreligious dialogue must be viewed in terms of its cultural and social implications vis-à-vis the public sphere' (Opatija Declaration 2003, 9).

47 Among others, see for example: John E Tunbridge and Gregory J Ashworth, 'Dissonant Heritage: The Management of the Past as a Resource in Conflict' (1996) 40(2) Annals of Tourism Research 547;
Brian Graham, Gregory J Ashworth and John E Tunbridge, *A Geography of Heritage: Power, Culture and Economy* (Arnold 2000);

tralise this dissonance through its regulations and management practices.[48] The preliminary draft of the Faro Convention refers to this same understanding by claiming that [cultural heritage] 'should not be limited to a single interpretation or use; its preservation as a source of creativity, reflection and debate belongs to the sphere of public interest'.[49] In this way, the CoE tended to move away from the AHD's understanding of heritage as (only) intrinsically valuable and to link heritage to the concepts of intercultural dialogue, cultural diversity, rights to culture, pluralism, reconciliation, sustainable development, and democratic participation.

However, one specificity that should not be overlooked here is that, as expressed by the Convention's experts drafting group, the text's understanding of the concept of intercultural dialogue should rather proceed from individuals than from cultures.[50] It means that the Faro Convention's principle on intercultural dialogue should not be unilaterally interpreted as exclusively based on an essentialist understanding of culture.[51] Instead, the Convention distances itself from a view of cultures as discrete units (which can lead to increased discrimination) and 'focuses in general on moving away of grouping

---

John J Lennon and Malcolm Foley, 'Interpretation of the Unimaginable: The US Holocaust Memorial Museum, Washington, DC, and "Dark Tourism"' (1999) 38(1) Journal of Travel Research 46;

John J Lennon and Malcolm Foley, *Dark Tourism: The Attraction of Death and Disaster* (2nd edn, Continuum 2000;

Philip R Stone, 'A Dark Tourism Spectrum: Towards a Typology of Death and Macabre Related Tourist Sites, Attractions and Exhibitions' (2006) 54(2) Tourism 145.

48 Laurajane Smith, *Uses of Heritage* (Routledge 2006); but also see Kisić (n 32).

49 CDPAT (2002) 40 (n 44) 10.

50 Council of Europe, Committee of Ministers, 'White Paper on Intercultural Dialogue – Living Together as Equals in Dignity' (2008);

For the purpose of this White Paper, intercultural dialogue is understood as a process that comprises an open and respectful exchange of views between individuals and groups with different ethnic, cultural, religious, and linguistic backgrounds and heritage on the basis of mutual understanding and respect. It requires the freedom and ability to express oneself, as well as the willingness and capacity to listen to the views of others. Intercultural dialogue contributes to political, social, cultural, and economic integration and the cohesion of culturally diverse societies. It fosters equality, human dignity, and a sense of common purpose. It aims to develop a deeper understanding of diverse world views and practices, to increase co-operation and participation (or the freedom to make choices), to allow personal growth and transformation, and to promote tolerance and respect for others.

51 For essentialists, culture is deemed a homogeneous group that is bound, static, and holistic, wherein diversities between people, time, and space are all neglected. Therefore, identity is permanent and fixed, reinforcing national stereotypes (Holliday, 2011, 2013) 32.

people according to the assumption that they would see their own cultural identity as overarching'.[52] As explained by Meyer-Bisch, the starting point is that individuals, with their complex identities, rather than 'cultures', should be included in such a dialogue.[53] This idea derives directly from the 2003 Declaration on the Intercultural Dialogue and Conflict Prevention (known as the Opatija Declaration), which promotes a perspective that challenges the dichotomy of minority/majority communities and attempts to go beyond grouping individuals into specific groups and cultures. It rather positions its understanding of intercultural dialogue within the framework of the principles of freedom of thought, conscience, religion, expression, assembly, and association as defined in Articles 9, 10, 11, and 14 of the European Convention for the Protection of Human Rights and Fundamental Freedoms (ECHR).[54] By reiterating these concepts, the Faro Convention further promotes the flexible, dynamic, and open intercultural dialogue that, it is assumed, will contribute to the CoE's fundamental objective of achieving social cohesion and a peaceful society.

In summary, the Faro Convention emerged from the CoE's vision of cultural heritage's social value and its role in broader social processes, particularly in the CoE's model of social sustainability. The central starting point in this model, and the one we constantly need to return to in interpreting the Faro Convention, is the predominance of the individual's perspective and the individual's role vis-à-vis that of the group. Thus, cultural heritage is seen as an essential resource for human/individual development, and individuals' involvement with cultural heritage is critical for local, national, and European social cohesion.

Building on the ideas developed in the above section, this chapter further explores the fundamental linkage between cultural heritage and the promotion of human rights, as advocated by the Faro Convention. There are two key concepts that are discussed in this context: (1) the Convention's connection to human rights (Article 1) and (2) the innovative concept of 'heritage community' (Article 2b). Both these concepts are essential to the broader democratic aspects that the Faro Convention promotes and thus both contribute to the new heritage discourse that the Convention seeks to frame.

52 Swedish National Heritage Board, *Report – The Faro Convention* (2014) https://historicengland.org.uk/content/docs/research/faro-conventionpdf/ accessed 23 March 2021.

53 Meyer-Bisch (n 24) 62–63.

54 Council of Europe, Committee of Ministers, 'Declaration on Intercultural Dialogue and Conflict Prevention' (adopted at Opatija, 22 October 2003, Appendix, 10).

3 Rights and Responsibilities in the Faro Convention

The present section investigates the Faro Convention's significance in the emergent discussion among heritage and legal scholars and professionals on the fundamental linkage between cultural heritage conservation and management, maintenance of cultural diversity, and human rights. Legal scholars, archaeologists, anthropologists, and heritage scholars increasingly engage with questions on human rights and how a human rights framework can be employed in the context of heritage.[55] Nevertheless, as recognised by Logan, the central concepts of cultural diversity, cultural heritage, and human rights have tended to be studied separately, with different disciplines focusing more on one concept than the others.[56] In addition, the scholarly discussion is predominantly concerned with the UN system, and in the context of heritage, particularly with UNESCO mechanisms and texts; the Faro Convention is one of the CoE instruments sporadically analysed to a certain extent in this context.[57] Nevertheless, the Council of Europe's work, since its foundation in 1949, has been extensively concerned with promoting cultural rights. Having

---

55 See for example, among many others: Janet Blake, 'Taking a Human Rights Approach to Cultural Heritage Protection' (2011) 4(2) Heritage & Society 199;

William S Logan, 'Closing Pandora's Box: Human Rights Conundrums in Cultural Heritage Protection' in Helaine Silverman and D Fairchild Ruggles (eds), *Cultural Heritage and Human Rights* (Springer 2007) 33;

William Logan, 'Cultural Diversity, Cultural Heritage and Human Rights: Towards Heritage Management as Human-Based Cultural Practice' (2012) 18(3) International Journal of Heritage Studies 231;

Melissa F Baird, 'Heritage, Human Rights, and Social Justice' (2014) 7(2) Heritage & Society 139;

Ana Filipa Vrdoljak, *Cultural Heritage in Human Rights and Humanitarian Law* (University of Technology Sydney 2009);

Ana Filipa Vrdoljak, 'Human Rights and Cultural Heritage in International Law' in Federico Lenzerini and Ana Filipa Vrdoljak (eds), *International Law for Common Goods* (Hart Publishing 2014) 139;

Francesco Francioni, 'Culture, Heritage and Human Rights: An Introduction' in Francesco Francioni and Martin Scheinin (eds), *Cultural Human Rights* (Martinus Nijhoff 2008).

56 Logan (2012) (n 55).

57 Eleni Stamatopoulou, *Cultural Rights in International Law: Article 27 of the Universal Declaration of Human Rights and Beyond* (Martinus Nijhoff 2007);

Kimberly Alderman, 'The Human Right to Cultural Property' (2011) 32 Michigan Journal of International Law 1;

Marie Cornu, 'La Convention pour la protection et la promotion de la diversité des expressions culturelles' [2006] Journal du droit international 929;

Ondřej Vícha, 'The Concept of the Right to Cultural Heritage Within the Faro Convention' (2014) 14(2) International and Comparative Law Review 23.

this long understanding of the place of cultural rights in the wider human rights field was crucial for the organisation's reconceptualization of heritage discourse, which suggests that human rights can and should be brought to the centre of heritage management, both as a theme in heritage identification and as a set of policy principles underlying conservation processes.[58] Therefore, it is first necessary to look briefly into the CoE's approach to cultural rights in its policies that would give a context for its heritage discourse.

The end of World War II led to the establishment of the UN organisation and many specialised agencies associated with it, such as UNESCO, among others. The UN sought to encourage cooperation among nation-states in solving global economic, social, cultural, and humanitarian issues as a means of securing and maintaining peace. One of the UN's highest ambitions was to shape a new world order based on the concept of human rights. After WWII and the Holocaust, the need to create new universal human rights standards emerged, building on the so-called 'first generation' human rights (civil and political rights) that surfaced in the seventeenth and eighteenth centuries.[59] The UN Universal Declaration of Human Rights (UDHR), adopted in 1948, expands to include civil, political, economic, social, and cultural rights. The UDHR, it is important to bear in mind, is not legally binding on the states that signed it but represents a moral commitment. Article 27 of the UDHR is of specific importance in the context of this chapter as it makes an explicit reference to cultural rights. Article 27 (1) reads: 'Everyone has the right freely to participate in the cultural life of the community, to enjoy the arts and to share in scientific advancement and its benefits'. In addition, on the international level, it is important to mention two covenants that took the issue of cultural rights further: the International Covenant on Civil and Political Rights (ICCPR) of 1966 and its Article 27[60] and the International Covenant on Economic, Social, and Cultural Rights (ICESCR) of 1966 and its Article 15. Further global recognition of the importance and development of cultural rights came with the creation of the role of Independent Expert on Cultural Rights.[61] Today

58 Logan (2012) (n 55).

59 Ibid.

60 Article 27 of the ICCPR reads: In those States in which ethnic, religious, or linguistic minorities exist, persons belonging to such minorities shall not be denied the right, in community with the other members of their group, to enjoy their own culture, to profess and practice their own religion, or to use their own language.

61 United Nations Human Rights Council, *Resolution 10/23 – Independent Expert in the Field of Cultural Rights* (26 March 2009).

this role is formalised as the UN Special Rapporteur in the field of cultural rights.[62]

At the same time, in the European context, the Council of Europe emerged as an organisation with the priority of building a united Europe based on democracy, freedom, and respect for human rights and the rule of law. Contrary to the UN system, when the CoE was founded in 1949, there was a strong political desire to develop the UNDR further at the European level and to take steps towards a binding convention. The European Convention for the Protection of Human Rights and Fundamental Freedoms (ECHR) emerged in 1950 due to this desire for an advanced monitoring system whereby an independent CoE tribunal can examine the States' commitments: the European Court of Human Rights. While the ECHR, with its additional protocols, primarily accommodates political and civil rights and does not explicitly protect cultural rights as such, the European Court of Human Rights, through its dynamic interpretation of the different Articles of the ECHR, has gradually recognised substantive rights which may fall under the notion of 'cultural rights' in a broad sense, the point I will refer to shortly.[63]

In addition to the ECHR, the CoE recognised the need to address social and economic rights at the international level, which the organisation covered by its specific European Social Charter in 1961 (revised in 1996). And while cultural rights, and especially the right to cultural heritage, have yet to gain deserved recognition in the case law of the Court, the CoE saw the promotion of cultural rights through cultural cooperation and standard-setting instruments as the critical factor in achieving the aims of the organisation as they were specified in the Article 1 of its Statute.[64]

The aims and principles stated in the CoE Statute, such as the principle of common heritage and the need to take joint action to protect it, were again reiterated in the preamble of the ECC of 1954. As discussed in detail in Chapter 2 of this volume, the ECC represents the starting point for the CoE's policy of cultural cooperation and CoE's cultural policy, of which cultural heritage is

---

62 United Nations Human Rights Council, *Resolution 19/6 – Special Rapporteur in the Field of Cultural Rights* (22 March 2012).

63 European Court of Human Rights, *Report – Cultural Rights in the Case-Law of the European Court of Human Rights* (2011).

64 The aim of the Council of Europe is to achieve a greater unity between its members for the purpose of safeguarding and realising the ideals and principles which are their common heritage and facilitating their economic and social progress.

b. This aim shall be pursued through the organs of the Council by discussion of questions of common concern and by agreements and common action in economic, social, cultural, scientific, legal, and administrative matters and in the maintenance and further realisation of human rights and fundamental freedoms.

a part. Since the ECC came into force in 1955, the CoE has been developing the idea of defining and protecting cultural rights. The real impetus in the process of reflecting on cultural rights under the auspice of the CoE came with the 1978 Declaration of Human Rights, where the Committee of Ministers decided:

> ...to give priority to the work undertaken in the Council of Europe of exploring the possibility of extending the list of rights of the individual, notably rights in the social, economic, and **cultural** fields, which should be protected by European conventions or any other appropriate means.[65]

Building on the 1978 Declaration, the CoE launched the process of outlining the cultural rights and principles on which governments could base their policies. In this light, another important event from 1978 contributed largely to putting the issue of cultural rights on the CoE's agenda – the 2nd Conference of European Ministers responsible for Cultural Affairs (Athens, 24–26 October 1978). The Conference adopted Resolution No. 1 on the European Cultural Charter. The objective was to 'lay down guidelines for the conduct of cultural policies in member states'.[66]

In essence, it was recognised that the existing legal instruments do not in any way reflect the progress of ideas on cultural rights at the time and the political importance that became attached to such rights. Therefore, the CoE, in the preliminary studies on the European Cultural Charter posed the question, 'Could the Fundamental Cultural Rights of Europeans be Written Down?' (CDCC (80) 8).[67] In his reply to this question, Mr Lars Gustafsson, one of the ten eminent figures from whom the CoE asked a personal opinion on the content of Charter,[68] mentioned that cultural rights should include, among others: the right to tradition, the right to cultural exchange, the right to access of the citizens to foreign cultural information and productions, access of ordinary citizens to what artists produce, or what thinkers think, the right to cultural variety, and the right to cultural activity.[69] In the same document, Mr Krieps

65 Council of Europe, Committee of Ministers, 'Declaration on Human Rights' (27 April 1978) 8II.

66 Council of Europe, 'Resolution No 1 on the European Cultural Charter' (adopted at the 2nd Conference of European Ministers Responsible for Cultural Affairs, Athens, 24–26 October 1978).

67 Council of Europe, Council for Cultural Co-operation, 'The European Cultural Charter – Preliminary Study' [1980] CDCC (80) 8.

68 The following are the leading figures concerned: Jean-Marie Benoist, Vicenzo Cappelletti, Elena Croce, Lars Gustafsson, Robert Jungk, Lord Kennet, Robert Krieps, Jürgen Moltmann, Jean d'ormesson, Denis de Rougemont, and Olaf schwenke (CDCC (80)8).

69 CDCC (80) 8 (n 67).

argues that 'the right to culture proceeds from the inalienable dignity of man, since everyone has an unquestionable right to the full development of his personality'.[70] The underlying philosophical idea promoted by the cited CoE's preliminary study that would become the basis for subsequent CoE's cultural rights-related texts can be illustrated by Mr Krieps' statement:

> To the extent that culture is the totality of the elements which go to make up the living environment, every man has a right both to respect for the choices he makes and to an improvement of his living environment through the action of community and its solidarity.[71]

The final document from this phase of the CoE's reflection on cultural rights was the European Declaration on Cultural Objectives, adopted by the 4th Conference of European Ministers Responsible for Cultural Affairs in Berlin in 1984. The main idea endorsed in the 1984 Declaration was that the personal fulfilment of everyone in society is deeply linked to culture, which is considered an essential factor in the harmonious development of society. This idea is restated in the Faro Convention.

However, while the discussion on the subject of cultural policies and cultural rights at the CoE during the late 1970s and early 1980s resonated with the ideas promoted internationally (e.g., at the World Conference on Cultural Policies in Mexico City in 1982), the changes brought to the CoE by the collapse of the Soviet system and the emergence of new democracies in Central and Eastern Europe in late 1980s required further and more binding political and normative solutions in its cultural policy. The accession of a large number of newly created European democratic states to the CoE and the conflicts that emerged from the processes of their creation (the wars in the former Yugoslavia) additionally accentuated the need to protect cultural rights, particularly those of persons belonging to national minorities. An important step forward in this process was made through the Final Declaration of the First Summit of Heads of State and Government of the Council of Europe (Vienna, 8–9 October 1993). The political statement was made by the Heads of State asking the CoE:

> ...to begin work on drafting a protocol complementing the European Convention on Human Rights in the cultural field by provisions guaran-

70 Ibid, 46.
71 Ibid, 47.

teeing individual rights, in particular for persons belonging to national minorities.[72]

The follow-up to this request was the CoE's list of cultural rights, principles, and objectives on which governments could base their policies. The Ad Hoc Committee for the Protection of National Minorities (CAHMIN) subsequently used this list in the process of drafting the Framework Convention for the Protection of National Minorities of 1995.[73] This Convention proved to be crucial for turning the general CoE policy on cultural diversity from the earlier texts (underpinned with assimilationism that disregarded the cultural contributions of migrants and minorities) towards an approach that proclaimed the need for protecting diversity and that recognised the social wealth produced by such diversity (Fuentes, 2016). Accordingly, in its Preamble, the Convention states that:

> ...pluralist and genuinely democratic society should not only respect the ethnic, cultural, linguistic and religious identity of each person belonging to a national minority, but also create appropriate conditions enabling them to express, preserve and develop this identity.[74]

The CAHMIN made a further contribution to this debate by drafting proposals for an additional ECHR protocol designed to guarantee individual rights, including respect for cultural identity, access to cultural activities, the right of access to information, and the right to one's cultural heritage. Unfortunately, political and legal difficulties prevented the adoption of the protocol to the ECHR, and the 'fight' for the recognition of cultural rights in binding CoE instruments, such as conventions, had to continue.[75]

Having said that, the failure of cultural rights protocol initiative does not imply that the European Court of Human Rights (ECtHR) has not addressed the culture related issues in its juriprudence. Therefore, it is worth briefly

---

72 Council of Europe, *Vienna Declaration* (adopted at the First Summit of Heads of State and Government, 9 October 1993), Appendix II.

73 Council of Europe, Directorate of Education, Culture and Sport, 'Draft List of Cultural Rights' [1994] CDCC Misc (94) 3 rev 1;
Council of Europe, Ad hoc Committee for the Protection of National Minorities (CAHMIN), 'Preliminary Draft Protocol to the European Convention on Human Rights Concerning the Recognition of Cultural Rights' [1994] CAHMIN (94) 4 rev 2.

74 Council of Europe, *Framework Convention for the Protection of National Minorities* (ETS No 157, 1995).

75 For more details on the reasons of rejecting the protocol to the ECHR (see Vrdoljak, 2005).

acknowledging indications of what some have described as a renewed attention to culture, cultural rights, and cultural identity within the evolving framework of ECHR.[76] While the decision not to extend the competences of the ECtHR explicitly to individual cultural rights was taken in the 1990s, the Court's jurisprudence has continued to develop. Over time, it has gradually expanded its interpretative reach, increasingly engaging with claims that may be understood as pertaining to cultural rights both at the individual and collective levels. This evolving engagement is reflected in a number of reports issued by the ECtHR's Research Division. These note that, through dynamic interpretation of various Convention articles, the Court has progressively recognised substantive rights that fall under a broader understanding of cultural rights.[77] Notably, Articles 8 (respect for private and family life), 9 (freedom of thought, conscience, and religion), and 10 (freedom of expression), along with Article 2 of Protocol No. 1 (right to education), have been central to this interpretative evolution. The Court's case law has, in effect, addressed a range of rights that may be situated within the domain of cultural rights or, at the very least, carry strong cultural dimensions. These include the right to artistic expression, access to culture, the right to cultural identity, linguistic rights, the right to education, the right to seek historical truth, academic freedom, and the right to the protection of cultural and natural heritage. In addition, the Court has made implicit, and at times more explicit, reference to cultural rights when adjudicating cases involving persons or communities belonging to national, cultural, linguistic, or ethnic minorities. Such cases frequently concern claims to maintaining a minority identity and to conducting one's private and family life in accordance with associated cultural traditions. The resolution of these cases, often implicating intercultural dialogue, cultural identity, and freedom of religion, arguably benefits from being framed in terms of cultural rights rather than more politically charged categories such as self-determination or minority rights, which remain highly sensitive for many CoE Member States. Ultimately, this discursive turn towards cultural rights may be seen as a natural, although implicit, extension of the multicultural composition of the Council of Europe's member states, and of the legal and cultural diversity they bring to the ECHR system. It also poses challenges to the Court, which must grapple with tensions that go beyond the original

76 See a critique of such argumentation in Francesco Francioni, 'An Introduction' Francesco Francioni and Martin Scheinin (eds), Cultural Human Rights (Nijhoff, 2008).

77 European Court of Human Rights, *Cultural Rights in the Case-Law of the European Court of Human Rights* (Research Report 2011, updated 2017).

framing of the Convention's preamble, where the notion of a 'common heritage' of political traditions, ideals, and cultures was first articulated.

A more detailed legal analysis of ECtHR jurisprudence on cultural rights has been undertaken by a number of legal scholars, including Jakubowski and Bieczyński (2019), and falls outside the scope of this volume.[78] Nevertheless, this brief acknowledgement of the Court's evolving case law highlights the Council of Europe's longstanding involvement with cultural rights across various domains. In this light, the discursive shift introduced by the Faro Convention appears less as a radical departure and more as a consolidation of a trajectory already embedded within the broader institutional framework.

Thus, building on the extensive work the organisation has done, the Faro Convention emerged as the human-rights-based text that links up all the previous CoE conventions and policies in the cultural field on their common basis, namely, every individual's right to participate in the cultural life of the community. The right to participate in cultural life has been used as the common denominator for all of the CoE's cultural activities, including the right to access to heritage. This principle has been reiterated in the Faro Convention's preamble, with direct reference to two international instruments which concern cultural rights: the United Nations Universal Declaration of Human Rights (1948) and the International Covenant on Economic, Social, and Cultural Rights (1966). This linkage is essential in a few different ways. Firstly, by using the direct reference to international instruments that are designed with an emphasis on the rights **of individuals**, the person's right to take part in cultural heritage, according to the Faro Convention, is designed as an **individual right**, a point to be returned to shortly. Secondly, it served as a reminder of unsuccessful attempts on the European (CoE's) level to amend its core human rights instrument, namely the ECHR and the European Social Charter, with provisions that would regulate cultural rights; thus, reference had to be made to the major international, i.e., non-European, instruments. Finally, as none of the international instruments to which the Faro Convention refers (as non-binding instruments) allow individuals to invoke any right of complaint, it indicates that it is not possible to claim rights under the Faro Convention either.

78 Andrzej Jakubowski (ed), *Cultural Rights as Collective Rights: An International Law Perspective* (Brill 2016);
Mateusz Bieczyński, 'The "Right to Cultural Heritage" in the European Union: A Tale of Two Courts' in Andrzej Jakubowski, Kristin Hausler and Francesca Fiorentini (eds), *Cultural Heritage in the European Union: A Critical Inquiry into Law and Policy* (Brill 2019).

In international human rights law, the basic understanding is that cultural rights, according to their primary definition, mean that it is individuals who have the right to cultural life. Article 27 of the UN Universal Declaration of Human Rights proceeds from this definition, and the Faro Convention, with its direct reference, adheres to the same principle. However, in recent decades, the third generation of human rights (so-called group rights) has stressed that different cultural groups' statuses and cultural identities must be recognised and protected by specific legislation.[79] Therefore, as the Academy of European Law notes:

> Cultural rights are torn between two different but linked meanings: first, as a sub-category of human rights, cultural rights are endowed with universal character, which is a major characteristic and postulate of human rights as a whole; second, cultural rights are clearly related to cultural diversity and cultural diversity is an obvious challenge to the very idea of universal human rights.[80]

Consequently, there is an apparent disjuncture between the universalism of human rights on the one side and cultural diversity and cultural heritage, which are, by definition, culturally and temporally specific, on the other.[81] Without dwelling on the theoretical issues between universalism and cultural relativism, for the purpose of this section, it is essential to be aware that the difference in the design of cultural rights, namely the juxtaposition of the individual versus the collective understanding of them, contributes to the variety and complexity of approaches expressed in international conventions in the field of cultural heritage.

When it comes to UNESCO, for example, the tension between the two approaches is in the essence of UNESCO itself – the contradiction between UNESCO as a modernist organisation with globalising impacts and UNESCO as a supporter of cultural diversity. Logan argued that this contradiction permeates the organisation's various legal instruments.[82] According to Wolferstan and Fairclough, today, UNESCO's view on culture leans more towards

79 Michael Rowlands, 'The Power of Origins: Questions of Cultural Rights' in Victor Buchli (ed), *The Material Culture Reader* (Berg 2002) 105.

80 Cited in: Logan (2007) (n 55) 39.

81 Ibid.

82 William Logan, 'Cultural Diversity, Cultural Heritage and Human Rights: Towards Heritage Management as Human-Based Cultural Practice' (2012) 18(3) International Journal of Heritage Studies, 231.

the homogenisation of cultures in an increasingly globalised world.[83] Therefore, building on the different generations of rights, UNESCO's recent conventions lay closer to the notion that different groups need protection in order to exercise their cultural rights, based on the idea that cultures are seen as limited phenomena. UNESCO's approach has much to do with the definition of culture, which was adopted by the organisation at the World Conference on Cultural Policies in 1982[84] and which served as the basis for several of its conventions. While the 1982 definition has the advantage of proposing a broad sense of culture, according to Meyer-Bisch, it 'remains enumerative, descriptive, and therefore vague, since it does not define either its dynamics or the role of individuals as actors'.[85] With its reference to 'society or a social group', it remains collectivist while disregarding diversity and internal freedoms.

Where does the Faro Convention fit into this context? Article 1a and Article 1b of the Faro Convention read:

> The parties to this Convention agree to
> a. Recognise that rights to cultural heritage are inherent in the right to participate in cultural life, as defined in the Universal Declaration of Human Rights (Article 1a).
> b. Recognise individual and collective responsibility towards cultural heritage.

In addition, Article 4 on Rights and Responsibilities to Cultural Heritage is even more explicit when it asks the Parties to recognise that:

a. Everyone, alone or collectively, has the right to benefit from the cultural heritage and to contribute towards its enrichment;
b. Everyone, alone or collectively, has the responsibility to respect the cultural heritage of others as much as their own heritage and consequently the common heritage of Europe;

---

83 Susan Wolferstan and Graham Fairclough, 'Common European Heritage: Reinventing Identity Through Landscape and Heritage?' in Dirk Callebaut, Jan Marík and Jana Maríková-Kubková (eds), *Heritage Reinvents Europe* (EAC Occasional Paper No 7, Europae Archaeologiae Consilium 2013).

84 Culture must be considered the totality of distinctive spiritual and material, intellectual and affective traits that characterise a society or social group and which in addition to the arts and letters, encompasses lifestyles, ways of living together, value systems, traditions, and beliefs.

85 Patrice Meyer-Bisch, 'Cultural Rights, an Ethical Principle of Cooperation and a Level for Development' (Conference Paper, CROSSROADS Conference, Basel, 8 February 2018) 2.

c. Exercise of the right to cultural heritage may be subject only to those restrictions which are necessary in a democratic society for the protection of the public interest and the rights and freedoms of others.

The above-highlighted links of the Faro Convention to the second generation of rights, with its direct reference to international instruments emanating from an individual perspective, indicate that the Convention aims to convey a new perspective, one differing from the UNESCO approach. The ideological tone of the Convention's human rights discourse signals that the Convention does not put culture/cultural heritage, but rather human beings, at the centre. This notion is clearly expressed in the Explanatory Report of the Convention: '…the Convention deals with heritage as an object of individual rights which give it meaning'.[86] This human rights approach puts the Faro Convention and the heritage discourse it promotes in direct opposition to the AHD. By placing the individual level as the starting point in the Faro Convention's understanding of cultural rights, but, at the same time, being aware that cultural heritage is regarded as a common concern and common resource, it is important to look closer into the specific approach to the individual/collective dilemma of cultural rights adopted by the Faro drafting committee.

The approach embraced in the Faro Convention, it needs to be highlighted, has resulted from the long campaign and influence of the 'Fribourg Group' on the CoE's approach to the subject of cultural rights. Specifically, the work done by Patrice Meyer-Bisch as a coordinator of the Group and as a member of the drafting committee of the Faro Convention was crucial for the ideological shift of 'yet another cultural heritage convention' to the human rights-based instrument.[87] As witnessed by the member of the Secretariat during the drafting process, this human-rights-based approach was not welcomed with enthusiasm by everyone:

> It was exclusively Patrice who was pushing for this human rights agenda. I personally did not agree with it at the beginning, most probably because of my attitude that we were there to protect monuments. My background is in conservation, you know. But as you can see, he was extremely successful in conveying his idea.[88]

---

86 Explanatory Report (n 15) 3.

87 Interview with Interviewee 1, Former Employee of the Council of Europe's Directorate of Culture and Cultural and Natural Heritage (1 April 2020).

88 Ibid.

It has also been highlighted in *Heritage and Beyond* (2009) by many drafting committee members that the Group's work that resulted in the Fribourg Declaration (2007) offers the most suitable way of interpreting the Faro Convention's emphasis on the role of cultural heritage in exercising cultural rights. The Fribourg Group has participated in CoE-organised events and discussions on cultural rights since the early 1990s. For example, what archival documents reveal is that it was the work of the Fribourg Group[89] that influenced and urged the adoption of the protocol on cultural rights to the European Convention on Human Rights in 1993 and 1994, as well as their contribution to the draft to the Framework Convention for the Protection of National Minorities.[90]

A few essential notions defined by the Fribourg Group and expressed in the Fribourg Declaration give the ideological background to the Faro Convention. To start with, and having in mind UNESCO's collectivist idea of culture, in the drafting process of the Faro Convention the CoE leaned more towards the definition of culture proposed by the Fribourg Group, which refocused the definition on people/individuals:

> The term 'culture' refers to values, beliefs, convictions, languages, knowledge and arts, traditions, institutions and ways of life through which a person or group expresses its humanity and the meanings it gives to its existence and its development; 'Culture' itself cannot be a subject; it is a verb, an action – more precisely an interaction – a life which each person must be able to access through knowledge and practices, and to which he or she must also have the freedom to contribute and create.[91]

---

89 For example, the series of colloquies of the Fribourg University Centre for Interdisciplinary Ethical and Human Rights Studies, all devoted to the objectiveness of human rights, and especially the eighth colloquy on *Cultural rights, a neglected category of human rights*. The proceedings have been published with the title 'Les droits culturels, une catégorie sous-développée de droits de 'homme' by P. Meyer-Bisch (ed) in 1993.

90 CAHMIN (94) 4 rev 2 n 73);
The members of the working group were: Denise Bindschedler-Robert (a former judge of the European Court of Human Rights), Sylvie Boiton-Pierre (Lyon University), Marco Borghi (Director of the Fribourg University, Centre for Interdisciplinary Studies), Pascale Boucaud (Director of the Catholic University of Lyon Human Rights Institute), Emmanuel Decaux (Paris University X, Director of the CEDIM), Jean-Bernard Marie (Secretary General of the International Institute for Human Rights, Strasbourg), and Partice Meyer-Bisch (Co-ordinator, Centre for Interdisciplinary Ethical and Human Rights Studies, Fribourg University) (CAHMIN (94) 4).

91 *Fribourg Declaration on Cultural Rights* (University of Fribourg, Interdisciplinary Institute of Ethics and Human Rights 2007).

Building on this understanding of culture, in 1993 the Fribourg Group, as part of their contribution to UNESCO's and the CoE's discussion on the issues of cultural rights, proposed their definition of those rights, which reads:

> Cultural rights are the rights and freedoms that enable an individual, alone or in association with others, and with and for others, to choose and express his or her identity and to accede to cultural references, as well as to such resources as are necessary for his or her process of identification, communication, and creation.[92]

As Meyer-Bisch argues, the hypothesis used in the Group's understanding is that the richer these cultural references are, the more they enable people to develop by exercising real freedoms personally and collectively.[93] 'The wealth of references acquired, recognised, chosen or rejected conditions the freedom of the process of identification that each person develops throughout his or her life'.[94] Therefore, the idea underpinning the Faro Convention is that the protection, respect, and enhancement of cultural heritage are required since, otherwise, the exercise of cultural rights will be hampered and deprived of indispensable resources.[95]

However, if we consider cultural heritage to be a development resource, and here the resource is referred to in terms of knowledge and meaning, access to those resources is critical. Therefore, the Faro Convention promotes the idea that it is the use and knowledge of cultural heritage that constitute the right to participate in cultural life as expressed in the UN Declaration.[96] As described in the Explanatory Report, 'the derivation and consequences of this right largely form the basis for the innovative content of this Convention', i.e., they form the basis for the new heritage discourse.[97]

With the understanding of the background ideas on rights to cultural heritage that underpin the Convention, it can be argued, however, that what 'right to cultural heritage' covered in the Faro Convention is, paradoxically, a relatively narrow and limited area of cultural rights. More specifically, the Convention's purpose is to democratise the process of valuation and participation in heritage issues. As such, its cultural rights approach is primarily about each individual having access to cultural heritage and being given the opportunity

92 Meyer-Bisch (2009) (n 24) 60.
93 Meyer-Bisch (2018) (n 85).
94 Ibid, 2.
95 Meyer-Bisch (2009) (n 24).
96 Stamatopoulou (n 57).
97 Explanatory Report (n 15), Part D – Detailed Commentary on the Text of the Convention.

to be part of and interpret what cultural heritage means.[98] The Faro Convention clearly states that its human rights-based approach should not be understood as providing room to impose legal requirements for a 'right to cultural heritage' (Article 6). The idea promoted in the Convention is not to formulate any legal or cultural requirements for ownership of a specific cultural heritage, but rather the emphasis is on the right of everyone to be part of and to interpret the cultural heritage of their choice.[99] In this respect, as Stamatopoulou argued, the Faro Convention appears to be a weak legal human rights instrument since no rights can be claimed under it, according to Article 6.[100]

In addition to the element of rights, which is primarily about ensuring that people have the right to contribute new interpretations that can enrich and develop cultural heritage, Articles 1b and 4 clearly say that with the rights come responsibilities. In this respect, Article 4b is of specific interest, as it uses the responsibilities element in the Convention to address the existence of multiculturalism in Europe as part of a common European experience, i.e., it underlines the idea behind Europe's common heritage. This idea is rationalised in the Explanatory Report (Article 4) as:

> The responsibility to have as much respect for the heritage of others as for one's own heritage suggests how, through interaction, different cultural heritages may come together to form a common heritage.

In other words, the Faro Convention, with the obligation to respect other people's cultural heritage as much as their own, promotes the interaction and dialogue between different forms of cultural heritage. This dialogue further opens the way for an approach that recognises that there may be multiple interpretations of singular cultural heritage but also that, from a European perspective, there are multiple heritages that together constitute a common European heritage. Therefore, the Faro Convention aims to create an understanding among the public about different cultural heritages in Europe today that have come into being through the interaction between people and cultures over the centuries. This aspect of the Convention, clearly, has been underpinned by the conflicts of the 1990s and the Convention's peace-making and conflict-prevention focus. Cultural heritage is thus attributed an important

98 Wolferstan and Fairclough (n 83).

99 Gabrielle Dolff-Bonekämper, 'The Social and Spatial Frameworks of Heritage – What Is New in the Faro Convention' in Council of Europe, *Heritage and Beyond* (Council of Europe Publishing 2009).

100 Stamatopoulou (n 57).

role in building a peaceful and democratic society, where intercultural dialogue could lead to a greater degree of social and political cohesion among the CoE Member States.

To summarise, in view of the Faro Convention, the subject of the right to heritage is always individual. However, as argued by the members of the drafting committee in *Heritage and Beyond*, the individual exercises this right 'alone or collectively' (Article 4) because the cultural heritage is a common good, a common object, site, or medium.[101] In other words, for an individual to take advantage of this cultural right, one needs to gain access to a context, a community, a group, or an organised collective. As explained by Meyer-Bisch:

> The communities making up the social fabric are essential to the implementation of cultural rights, but from the human rights angle, their exercise of collective rights is only legitimate if it respects the implementation of the rights of all individuals, both inside and outside the community which defines itself by the aim of protecting and developing this heritage.[102]

The next section of the chapter looks into more detail at the concept of 'heritage community' as promoted by the Convention. It is yet another innovative dimension of this text that accentuates the need for broader access to cultural heritage and democratic participation in its interpretation and definition.

4 Heritage Community: A Model for Promoting Democratic Participation

As already recognised, the Faro Convention establishes heritage as an action, a product, and a process *for* society rather than a product in itself and for itself.[103] The main actors undertaking this action are citizens operating under the Faro Convention's notion of 'heritage community'. According to Article 2b of the Convention, a 'heritage community consists of people who value specific aspects of cultural heritage that they wish, within the framework of public action, to sustain and transmit to future generations'. Zagato argues that the word 'people' in this definition is decisive, as it emphasises the collective pro-

---

101 Meyer-Bisch (2009) (n 24).
102 Ibid, 60.
103 Fojut (n 9).

file of the notion of cultural heritage.[104] Whereas the right to cultural access and use of heritage are entitled to individuals, it is 'the people', constituted as a community, who become the subject of action.[105] Consequently, with the Faro Convention, a significant shift happened in our understanding of who has the right to access and the right to interpret cultural heritage. Cultural heritage's significance thus becomes a socially determined process, defined by the group of people with a particular interest in working for and working with an inherited resource. This community is an open and flexible group united by a shared interest rather than a legal entity. Its transversal and flexible nature is best defined by the absence of 'familiar parameters defining the respective value of a heritage as it relates to territory and space', i.e., there is no reference to the local, regional, national, or global importance of heritage in the Faro Convention's definition on 'heritage community'.[106] In addition, there is no reference to predefined societal parameters, whether national, ethnic, religious, professional, or class-based. In the Faro Convention's view, a heritage community can be built across territories and social groups. As noted in the Explanatory Report (Article 2): 'One can be a member of a heritage community simply by valuing a cultural heritage or wishing to pass it on'.

In this respect, the Convention's 'heritage community' differs significantly from the concept of 'natural' communities defined in the UNESCO 2003 Convention. As argued by Bortolotto, while a so-called 'natural' community is based on membership in an ethnic group, a territory, and a shared history, adherence to a heritage community represents a mode of collective aggregation that 'highlights the constructed nature of each community, whose members, dispersed in a space that can be transnational or discontinuous, constantly and voluntarily reaffirm their commitment'.[107]

These circumstances inevitably call for a different approach to cultural heritage, shifting from the AHD's nation-state perspective to one that considers multivocal and intersectional societies. According to Colomer and Catalini (2020), the Convention's concept of 'heritage community' may alleviate identity-related tensions and foster new cultural landscapes. This concept also assists the CoE in promoting a more tolerant and peaceful European society by providing a suitable means to address the complex human geography of contemporary Europe, shaped by both external and internal migrations. The

104 Zagato (n 27).

105 Ibid.

106 Dolff-Bonekämper (n 99) 71.

107 Bortolotto (2012, 88–89) cited in Zagato (n 27) 159.

'heritage community' enables the citizens of Europe to create and negotiate the merging of new identities and cultural narratives (Colomer, 2021).[108]

The Faro Convention's 'heritage community', therefore, is understood as the self-organised, self-managed group of individuals, a 'community of interest' that aims to use cultural heritage both to enhance the well-being of their territories and to enhance democratic participation among citizenries. It became clear that by framing cultural heritage as a mediator of 'intersubjective individual interactions rather than a representation of collective identities',[109] the Faro Convention could be used as a powerful cultural mediator tool in different, and particularly in difficult, scenarios.[110]

On the other hand, the Convention's concept of 'heritage community' challenges the fundamental power-knowledge relations underlying the AHD not only regarding the relationship between public authorities and citizens but also the power/knowledge claims of experts. If, according to the Convention, 'heritage communities' are the subject of action, it is then necessary to define their capacity for action, that is, making the members of the 'heritage community' active creators of knowledge and heritage narratives. According to the Convention, this question of who has access to and the right to interpret cultural heritage, as already established, is central from a democratic perspective. It also turned out to be the most controversial issue of the text, as it challenged the AHD's set boundaries, which were limiting broader debate about established social and cultural values and meanings.

Politically, as evident from the debate on the draft, the particular concern regarding the 'heritage community' concept was that self-defined but vocal minority groups might use the terms of the Convention to promote their extreme views and demands, which could, of course, have numerous consequences.[111] Hence, the inclusion of the need for heritage community to oper-

108 Laia Colomer, 'Exploring Participatory Heritage Governance After the EU Faro Convention' (2021) 13(4) Journal of Cultural Heritage Management and Sustainable Development, 1.

109 Ibid, 5.

110 Faro Convention, Article 7 – Cultural heritage and dialogue.

111 Council of Europe, Steering Committee for Cultural Heritage (CDPAT), '2nd Meeting of the CDPAT – Record' [2003] CDPAT (2003) 61 rev;

Council of Europe, Steering Committee for Cultural Heritage (CDPAT), 'Draft Council of Europe Framework Convention on the Value of Cultural Heritage for Society – Explanatory Report Final Draft' [2004] CDPAT (2004) 24 rev 4;

Council of Europe, Steering Committee for Cultural Heritage (CDPAT), Selected Committee of Experts Responsible for Preparing a Framework Convention on Cultural Heritage, 'Draft Text of Council of Europe Framework Convention on the Value of Cultural Heritage for Society' [2004] CDPAT (2004) 4 rev 10;

ate 'within the framework of public action' (Article 2b). The term 'public action', as pointed out by Jean-Michel Leniaud in his contribution to *Heritage and Beyond*, refers to the public authorities that include not only central government but also the complex and multiple spheres of local, regional, and international authorities.[112]

This understanding of 'public action' opens the debate (in the sphere of political philosophy) on the role that public authorities should play in society. Concerning cultural heritage, the predominant role of public authorities even today presupposes that all heritage powers and responsibilities are concentrated at the central government level (AHD). Heritage has been seen as those things that need public protection either through public spending or state control. As argued by Fojut, 'the weight of current assumptions, political agendas, national and pan-European guidance, and heritage policy within heritage circles strongly favours this old fashioned and increasingly unaffordable approach'.[113] On the opposite side, there is the approach that sees heritage as something that does not necessarily require physical protection or state involvement, i.e., the public sphere should be restricted to the strict minimum. Therefore, Article 2b of the Convention needs to be read with these two extremes in mind. In reality, the relationships that heritage communities may or may not maintain with the public authorities depend on how society itself is structured. Ideally, policy and action should occupy the middle range between two extreme approaches, keeping in mind the goal of making places suitable to live in social, cultural, and economic senses (sustainable communities).

The concept of 'heritage community' derives directly from the actual CoE political agenda on promoting 'democratic participation'. The aim of the CoE's Directorate of Democratic Participation is 'to encourage active and responsible citizenship by empowering citizens to contribute and develop a sense of ownership over the activities of decision-makers and institutions'.[114] It seems that the CoE approach to participation aligned with the ideas of 'coop-

---

Council of Europe, Steering Committee for Cultural Heritage (CDPAT), Selected Committee of Experts Responsible for Preparing a Framework Convention on Cultural Heritage, 'Final Draft Text of Council of Europe Framework Convention on the Value of Cultural Heritage for Society' [2004] CDPAT (2004) 4 rev 11;

Council of Europe, Steering Committee for Cultural Heritage (CDPAT), 'Comments from the German Delegation on the Draft Framework Convention' [2005] CDPAT (2005) 31.

112 Jean-Michel Leniaud, 'Heritage, Public Authorities, Societies' in Council of Europe, *Heritage and Beyond* (Council of Europe Publishing 2009) 137.

113 Fojut (n 9) 35.

114 It is important to notice that in the latest internal reconstruction within the CoE, the Directorate of Democratic Participation that existed at the time of writing this chapter

erativism and assembleary models',[115] aimed both at making up for shortfalls in representative democracy and at reinforcing the governability of the public in a neoliberal context.[116] Therefore, the CoE's work, as expressed in the Faro Convention's Article 12, has been focused on two fronts – civil society and public authorities. Considering that most of the collaborative social initiatives are designed to settle complex social and economic issues in particular territories, the dialogue between the grassroots projects with local authorities is inevitable. While it seems that the concept of 'heritage community' is well understood and welcomed in the civil society sphere, it is also clear that not all (heritage) officials perceive this 'democratic participation' in the same way the emerging 'heritage communities' do. Consequently, as argued by Colomer, the question of democratic participation moves from being a mere topic on heritage management to becoming a full political issue.[117] The 'problem' that the concept of 'heritage community' seems to represent for some countries reluctant to ratify the Faro Convention derives from the simple fact that administrations simply do not agree with sharing spheres of power, knowledge, and heritage decision process with citizens; that is, they want to stay within the AHD realm, with sporadic individual or cosmetic 'participation' initiatives that only accentuate the top-down control of the resulting processes.

And it is not only the role of public authorities that is challenged by the concept of 'heritage community'. According to the Faro Convention, communities are encouraged to define and redefine the value of existing heritage and declare new heritage elements in the light of their interest. This role of active creators of knowledge and heritage narratives is traditionally (AHD) played by heritage experts, and the Faro Convention, with its understanding of the 'heritage community', opens it up to the public as well. The question of how far the heritage sector can (should it wish to) accommodate the heritage communities' alternative views became central, with heritage scholars questioning their role and trying to find ways for more socially engaged heritage practice.[118] The idea of a multitude of approaches and perspectives on a heritage that asks for more inclusive, participatory heritage management is not new, but, as argued

(November 2023) has been renamed to the Directorate for Democracy as of January 2024; therefore the above citation is no longer available at the Directorate's website.

115 Colomer (n 108) 7.

116 Herbert Reiter, 'Participatory Traditions Within the Global Justice Movement' in Donatella della Porta (ed), *Democracy in Social Movements* (Palgrave Macmillan 2009) 44.

117 Colomer (n 108).

118 John Schofield, 'Heritage Expertise and the Everyday: Citizens and Authority in the 21st Century' in John Schofield (ed), *Who Needs Experts?: Counter-Mapping Cultural Heritage* (Ashgate 2014) 1.

by Schofield, 'nowhere is this idea of "everybody's heritage" better or more strongly expressed than in Faro Convention'.[119] The Faro Convention's philosophy in this regard, as put by Robert Palmer, is:

> Heritage involves continual creation and transformation. We can make heritage by adding new ideas to old ideas. Heritage is never merely something to be conserved or protected but rather to be modified or enhanced. Heritage atrophies in the absence of public involvement and public support. This is why heritage processes must move beyond the preoccupations of the experts in government ministries and the managers of public institutions and include the different publics who inhabit our cities, towns, and villages. Such a process is social and creative and is underpinned by the values of individuals, institutions, and societies.[120]

The Convention, therefore, calls for redefining the authoritative position of expert voices, even though, admittedly, the Convention stays quite vague about how this proactive process should be carried out. In line with Smith's argument,[121] Thomas (2014) goes on to argue that the role of experts should be as guides and facilitators.[122] That is:

> Experts should use their knowledge and skills to encourage and enable others to learn about, value and care for the historic environment. They play a crucial role in discerning, communicating and sustaining the established values of places, and in helping people to refine and articulate the values they attach to places.[123]

However, the Faro Convention principles go even further. The Convention acknowledges that people have their own views on heritage and its interpretation and will no longer accept the expert/official narrative. As Olivier points out, 'Certainly we should go further than at present, and this will involve changing our values and behaviours in a way that may make us feel "professionally"

119 John Schofield, 'Forget about "Heritage": Place, Ethics and the Faro Convention' in Tracy Ireland and John Schofield (eds), *The Ethics of Cultural Heritage* (Springer 2015) 198.

120 Robert Palmer, 'Preface' in Council of Europe, *Heritage and Beyond* (Council of Europe Publishing 2009) 8.

121 Smith (2006) (n 25).

122 Suzie Thomas, 'Making Archaeological Heritage Accessible in Great Britain: Enter Community Archaeology' in Suzie Thomas and Jenny Lea (eds), *Public Participation in Archaeology* (Boydell Press 2014).

123 *Conservation Principles, Policies and Guidance* (Historic England 2008) 20.

uncomfortable'.[124] The changing approaches to values coupled with challenges resulting from changing socio-political and economic contexts, according to Faro's approach, require fundamental shifts in professional approaches to heritage, to its protection and regulation, its physical and intellectual access as well as towards public participation, public rights, and responsibilities.[125] How far experts are ready to go to create more meaningful engagement with communities and 'become more respectful of public opinion' will be crucial for implementing the Faro Convention and, as such, to the shift away from the AHD.[126] The opinion supported in this volume goes in line with Olivier's statement that the critical issue is *not* how to implement the specific provisions of the Convention in the regulatory world (even though a new regulatory framework is needed) since the governments and national authorities and agencies will always find this difficult, if not impossible, to achieve. Instead, it focuses on how to give those principles practical meaning that will improve heritage management practice, making it more perceptive and inclusive. This means that the experts should actively create, maintain, and enhance the partnership between all stakeholders in the process. Only in this way 'the role of civil society, with its changing new forms including heritage communities, will grow stronger'.[127] Democratic participation, as promoted by the Faro Convention, requires involving heritage communities in decision-making processes regarding structural matters of heritage management. It means that there is a need to move away from the mere exchange of views among professionals and citizens, which is something that, according to Waterton and Smith, only tends to reinforce expert-based dominance.[128] Therefore, the willingness of heritage experts/officials for a radical shift in their professional practice and approach is a fundamental first step in moving away from the AHD-underpinned practices towards the people-centred, human rights-based perspective framed by the Faro Convention.

---

124 Alex Olivier, 'The Valletta Convention: Twenty Years After – A Convenient Time' in Victoria M Van der Haas and Peter AC Schut (eds), *The Valletta Convention: Twenty Years After – Benefits, Problems, Challenges* (EAC Occasional Paper No 9, Europae Archaeologiae Consilium 2014) 17.

125 Olivier (n 124).

126 Ibid, 17.

127 Ulla Salmela, *Why Finland Signed the Faro Convention and What Is the Added Value* (Finnish Heritage Agency Document, Vilnius, 11 November 2017) https://rm.coe.int/finland-ratification-of-the-faro-convention-in-finland-why-how-what-ne/168077fa9f accessed 4 March 2022, 3.

128 Emma Waterton and Laurajane Smith, 'The Recognition and Misrecognition of Community Heritage' (2010) 16(1–2) International Journal of Heritage Studies 4.

5 Conclusion of the Chapter

From its title, Framework Convention on the Value of Cultural Heritage for Society, it is evident that the Convention plans to question the traditional AHD view of heritage and offer a fundamentally new approach. The ideas presented in this chapter illustrated the Convention's intent to point the way forward across many previously posed constraining frontiers built by the AHD and to offer a path into new territory. The critical Convention's approach is based on the idea that cultural heritage must be defined in relation to societal changes and challenges and that consideration needs to be given to human values and the functions of cultural heritage in society. The convention is therefore constructed around the transition from an AHD object-focused approach to a people-centred one, challenging all the core elements of the AHD.

The definition of cultural heritage, as proposed by the Faro Convention, already indicates the extent to which this Convention aims to be innovative. The first aspect emphasised in this chapter is that the Faro Convention considers that cultural heritage is interactive, which means that heritage is no longer perceived as static or unchangeable (the AHD) but rather as something that is constantly being redefined by people and communities. The AHD understanding of heritage as something static that needs to be protected and preserved unchanged for the future, which in essence excludes present generations, is therefore questioned, and the focus is turned to inclusion and broader participation of more segments of the population in the discussion on the meaning and value of heritage.

Another welcomed shift in the perception of heritage is embodied in the word 'resources', which implies that heritage exists to be utilised in the opposition to the AHD way of thinking, where heritage has mainly been referred to as an 'asset' to be kept unchanged and untouched. Thirdly, the Convention promotes the idea that living heritage is aligned with a sense of place, (cultural) landscape, and sustainability. Explicitly, its goal is to go beyond the 'historic environment' concept, which tends to be restricted to AHD-underpinned, historically defined narratives and predominantly material aspects of the cultural environment. Faro's definition, in this sense, tends to be comprehensive, with no inherent time limits or limits of form or manifestation.

With this innovative conceptualisation of cultural heritage, the Faro Convention invites an open discussion and sees the practice of cultural heritage as a social and cultural activity that is part of an individual's and community's life. This means that the focus is on democratic participation, where individuals can get involved in the ongoing process of defining and managing cultural heritage. This fundamental change in discourse reflects the broader role the CoE plays in encouraging more active and responsible citizenship by empowering citizens to contribute and develop a sense of ownership over the activities of decision-making and institutions. The democratisation of heritage that happens with broader participation and access allows for cultural heritage to demonstrate its potential as a resource for human development, enhancement of the quality of human life, and promotion of cultural rights.

CHAPTER 8

The Faro Convention: Implementation

1 Introduction

It is the opinion of this book that the approach to cultural heritage from a people-centred perspective, as promoted in the Faro Convention, is the CoE's most critical contribution within the realm of European heritage policy-making. As explored in Chapters 6 and 7, it is the recognition of the need to put people and human values at the centre of an expanded, cross-disciplinary concept of cultural heritage, as well as the recognition of the value and potential of cultural heritage used for sustainable development and enhancement of quality of life, that puts the Faro Convention in direct opposition to AHD. The Faro Convention represents the framework for what Fairclough defined as the 'new heritage'.[1] In his words:

> On the one hand, heritage policy might be based on a relatively small, highly managed, and publicly subsidised heritage based on traditional approaches such as national criteria, expert assessment, a concern with authenticity and fabric and selective designation (heritage as constraint, heritage as commodity). On the other hand, it is the new type of heritage that the Faro Convention promotes – a broad, living heritage aligned with a sense of place, landscape, sustainability and comprehensiveness, and context, but which might not allow us to 'keep' everything physically. The first might be said to erect strong walls around a few places, the other to engage with social debates with the risks of loss as well as the potential for much bigger gains in relevance. The first is centred on things, and the second is on people. The first puts heritage into a protected place, and the second places heritage in the economic mainstream.[2]

This idea of the 'new heritage' is further developed by Kisić who described this alternative to AHD as 'inclusive heritage discourse' (IHD).[3] The idea of the 'inclusive heritage' and a need to transition our dialogue about heritage in

1 Graham Fairclough, 'New Heritage Frontiers' in Council of Europe, *Heritage and Beyond* (Council of Europe Publishing 2009) 29.

2 Ibid, 29.

3 Višnja Kisić, *Governing Heritage Dissonance: Promises and Realities of Selected Cultural Policies* (European Cultural Foundation, Amsterdam 2016).

 | DOI:10.1163/9789004756250_009

that direction is getting increasingly integrated into present-day heritage policies and practices and does not meet any visible opposition, at least on the declarative level. The most current national and international policies, texts and declarations follow the concept of 'new/inclusive heritage' to at least some degree. Nevertheless, the crucial question of how to make this new paradigm operational for many local, national, and international heritage players poses a significant challenge, and we need to look at those challenges from a broader political and social perspective. Some decisive questions on the nature and social arrangements of community on the local, national, and international level need to be addressed for the Faro principles to become operational, such as: Is there a presence of an active civil society interested in a specific heritage? Does engaged and supportive political players exist? Is there a willingness among all stakeholders to cooperate? Is there a consensus on an expanded common vision of heritage? And more importantly, is there the aspiration of the state, nation, or local community towards a more democratic socio-economic model? Does the political will for improved democratic participation and social inclusion of all members of society exist? If the answers to those questions do not lean towards the 'yes', the transition to the participatory, human-rights-based model of heritage promoted by the Faro Convention would be extremely challenging to employ. This chapter will explore the challenges the Faro Convention brings and the responses on the institutional CoE and national levels.

2 Implementing the Faro Convention: The Council of Europe's Approach

The level of participation is critical to the idea of 'new/inclusive heritage'. On the other hand, the AHD methods of heritage protection are not sufficiently valuable for achieving any advanced level of social inclusion.[4] It could be said that the AHD model of keeping heritage 'exclusive' and inaccessible with regards to any meaningful public involvement for most of the last century resulted in generations of European citizens who considered heritage to be an exclusively public-sector and expert activity, questioning themselves if the option to participate in the field democratically even exists. The Faro Convention is designed to tackle this issue in particular.

4 As rightly noted by Fairclough (2009, p. 31), 'inclusivity cannot easily be built on a process of finding the most important buildings on a national or expert scale and then looking around to see who might feel "ownership" of them'.

The Faro Convention builds on the inclusive model of participation, encouraging a bottom-up approach that supports citizens and stakeholders, organised in heritage communities, to make decisions regarding the management of cultural heritage. The aim of such a participatory practice may not only be to build long-term sustainable solutions for heritage places, but also to foster democratic governance around heritage practice. Following the broader CoE policy on democratic participation, the Faro Convention aims to 'encourage sustainable development and peaceful and inclusive societies in which heritage is considered a social, political and economic resource'.[5] The 'Faro Way', as the CoE calls it, approaches cultural heritage in terms of sharing responsibilities and promoting the innovative models of participatory governance that will enhance social sustainability through the practice of valuing, interpreting, and managing cultural heritage.[6] In this sense, the Faro Convention makes cultural heritage the means through which the CoE aims to consolidate or enhance citizenship and democracy in Europe.[7] Therefore, the Faro principles represent a powerful political project aiming at the core goals of the CoE regarding its policies on democratic participation. In this respect, the Convention's focus on participation not only contributes to the construction of a more efficient, transparent, and democratic way of governing cultural heritage, but also contributes to the discussion on the redistribution of political capital from representative democracy to participatory democracy. Consequently, as Colomer rightly pointed out, 'the Faro Convention carries participatory democracy over from public European law and political science theory to the realm of heritage management studies'.[8]

To promote its vision of participation and the apparent need to show how the Faro principles could work in practice, the CoE decided to act on multiple fronts. Activities such as the Faro Convention Action Plan (and its Faro Convention Network, Faro Talks, Faro Lab, and Faro Research) and Strategy 21 are direct results of this effort and represent the main field of action of the CoE Heritage Department for the last ten years. According to the official website, the Faro Convention Action Plan that the organisation employed in 2013 aims

5 Noel Fojut, 'The Philosophical, Political and Pragmatic Roots of the Convention' in Council of Europe, *Heritage and Beyond* (Council of Europe Publishing, Strasbourg 2009) 14.

6 Council of Europe, *The Faro Convention at Work in Europe: Selected Examples* (Council of Europe Publishing 2022).

7 Laia Colomer, 'Exploring Participatory Heritage Governance after the EU Faro Convention' (2021) 13(4) *Journal of Cultural Heritage Management and Sustainable Development.*

8 Ibid, 21.

at translating the Faro Convention's principles into practice.[9] What this initiative offers is a look at the field-based projects that represent a variety of interpretations and implementations of the Faro principles. These selected projects inform the CoE on how its texts 'live' in practice and allow for further research and adjustments in line with the political priorities of the Organisation.

The overview of the initiatives, programmes, and actions under the Faro Action Plan suggests a strong focus on civil society actors. However, while this is true to a certain extent, one needs to bear in mind that the Faro Convention is a convention on the *shared responsibility* for cultural heritage on the part of civil society, elected representatives, and public institutions (Section 3 of the Convention). According to Daniel Thérond, this is one of the Convention's strong points, which implies a new state of balance between the respective functions of institutional experts and emerging heritage communities.[10] Therefore, in practice, a wide range of stakeholders may take the initiative of applying the Faro Convention, and the Convention lays down the framework for each of the parties. The selected examples of the Faro-inspired projects presented by the CoE showcase the variety of stakeholders who initiated the projects:

- Heritage curators, as in Marseille (France),
- Mayors, as in Fontecchio (Italy),
- NGOs, as in Viscri (Romania), Cordoba (Spain), and Machkhaani (Georgia),
- Universities, as in Huelva, Castellon (Spain) and Rome (Italy),
- Artists, as in Kaunas (Lithuania),
- Residents in Lisbon (Portugal), Venice (Italy), and Novi Sad (Serbia),
- Local authorities, as in Cervia and Forlì (Italy),
- Central governments, as in the Netherlands, Switzerland, and Norway.[11]

---

9 The Faro Action Plan has the following goals:
- to provide field-based knowledge and expertise for member states to better understand the potential of the convention and fully apply it;
- to help the Council of Europe to highlight and study specific cases in line with the political priorities of the Organization;
- to offer a platform for analysis and recommendations for further action in line with the Faro Convention's principles;

to encourage member states to sign and ratify the convention (Council of Europe, 2022, The Faro Convention at Work in Europe: Selected Examples).

10 Daniel Thérond, 'Benefits and Innovations of the Council of Europe Framework Convention on the Value of Cultural Heritage for Society' in Council of Europe, *Heritage and Beyond* (Council of Europe Publishing, Strasbourg 2009) 9–13.

11 Council of Europe (n 6).

While Articles 11–14 set out the necessity of involving all members of society, within the logic of democratic governance, in all aspects connected with cultural heritage, Article 2 asks all the stakeholders to work 'within the framework of public action'. It means that most of the time, public institutions are still responsible for leading the partnership process. What distinguishes Faro-inspired institutional involvement from the AHD one is the fact that the parties (public institutions, elected representatives) that sign up to the Faro Convention thereby affirm their 'commitment and their desire for democracy'.[12] In other words, they are committed to combating deeply rooted mistrust between civil society, elected representatives, and public institutions (and experts working in those institutions). In no way is this an easy task, and in the words of Interviewee 9, 'it can seem somewhat utopian', but we as an organisation 'have to believe in the commitment of our Member States to a stronger democratic process'.[13]

However, even if the participation of civil society may be more vigorous in some other fields, it is a fact that in the case of heritage, the AHD model resulted in the public authorities, experts, and local elected representatives having little faith in civil society's role in the processes for which they are responsible. Usually, the only benefit the authorities see in participatory processes is in achieving a somewhat better understanding and acceptance by the local community of decisions already made. On the other hand, civil society is more often than not reluctant to take part in the participatory processes insofar as it no longer regards the authorities and elected representatives as reliable partners. Another particularity that needs to be considered is that, as indicated by some of the projects done under the CoE's 'Faro Lab' initiative, some ex-Eastern Bloc countries, in particular, are facing non-negligible obstacles to community engagement in heritage processes. The first reason rests in the fact that it was only recently that civil society, as it is understood by Western European standards, emerged in those countries. Secondly, it needs to be understood that in those states, there is a certain negative perception of collective forms of engagement, such as co-operatives, given their strong resonance with past regimes and the consideration of the potential of the new forms of 'collective democratic engagement' still needs to be understood, developed, and believed in.[14] As rightly pointed out by Aleksandra Chabiera,

---

12 Pascal Wanner, *The Faro Convention Approach and Democratic Socio-Economic Models for Community Engagement – Concluding Memorandum of the Second Faro Action Plan's Faro Lab, Georgia, November 2017* (2017) 7.

13 Interview with Interviewee 9, current employee at the Directorate for Democracy, Council of Europe (October 2022).

14 Wanner (n 12).

'the principles enshrined in the Faro Convention mirror the stage in the development of our societies'.[15] Therefore, the implementation of the Faro Convention principles and ideas is hugely case-/nation-specific and depends mainly on the democratic standards held by the country.

The concept closely connected with participation in the Faro Convention is the 'heritage community' concept. The understanding of the heritage community, as explored in the previous chapter, resonates with Leniaud's statement:

> The heritage only grows to the extent that new 'mediators' succeed in adding further heritage categories to a list that is hedged about by criteria selected in a far from diversified or consensual fashion by routine, prejudice and conflicts of power.[16]

The CoE's work in recent years is heavily oriented towards the growing network of heritage communities under the Faro Convention Network (FCN) project. The network is imagined as a platform comprising heritage communities where good practices are exchanged. The CoE encourages heritage communities to become part of the network through a self-assessed process centred around 12 criteria.[17] Based on the baseline measure of the situation self-assessed by the initiative, it is on the Secretariat of the CoE to review the assessment and provide recommendations and to assist the heritage community with the implementation of their action plan, as well as to decide if the initiative has all the criteria to be included as the active member of the FCN or in some other parts of the Faro Action Plan.[18] The self-assessment exercise is undeniably valuable for every project, and the CoE's role in introducing it widely seems to require more forceful promotion. The current, relatively modest number of 13 active members makes these initiatives merely a 'heritage community of communities'.

On the other hand, not having a significant number of 'officialised' network members does not necessarily mean that the Faro principles are not more

15 Agnieszka Chabiera, *Polish Civil Society and the Aims of the Faro Convention – Report for the Council of Europe*(Council of Europe, 2017) 3 https://rm.coe.int/polish-civil-society-and-the-aims-of-the-faro-convention/1680a1b6dcaccessed 4 April 2022.

16 Jean-Michel Leniaud, 'Heritage, Public Authorities, Societies' in Council of Europe, *Heritage and Beyond* (Council of Europe Publishing, Strasbourg 2009) 139.

17 https://www.coe.int/en/web/culture-and-heritage/fcn-principles-and-criteria

18 Faro Convention Network (appreciation, good practice, etc.);
Faro Convention Promotion (Talks, Meetings, Lab, etc.);
Faro Convention Research (Studies, Camps, etc.);
Faro Convention in Action (Cooperation, Workshops, etc.);
Faro Convention Spotlights (Migration, Marginalised groups, etc.).

widely used. As explained by the current member of the CoE Heritage team, 'those initiatives present a reference point, and the good practice from which to learn. We are certainly not interested in creating yet another list everyone wants to be part of.'[19] Therefore, at least according to the Secretariat, it is inadequate to look at the success of the Convention only through the number of recognised 'heritage communities' on any level. Even more so, as it is not clear if there is a need or not to provide a juridical statute to heritage communities. For the CoE, however, it seems they refer primarily to civil society initiatives that are formalised in some way (NGOs, education establishments, associations, etc.), considering that they need to, according to Article 2b, act 'within the framework of public action'. However, having the heritage community defined in the absence of 'societal parameters, national, ethnic, religious, professional, or based on class', one can argue that heritage communities can exist (and they certainly do) even without a formal associative statute, explicitly taking into account the options of communication and cooperation that modern technology offers (social media, for example).[20] If we take it to the extreme, it is the heritage community's choice to engage in conversation with public authorities or not, depending on their priorities and aims. In this sense, the concept of 'heritage community' offers the response and opportunity for many marginalised communities under the AHD model to develop, protect, and transmit their heritage, even if they decide or do not want to engage with the public authorities.

To exemplify this point of cultural heritage existing and developing within a community and without the recognition of a public authority, the case of the traditional tattoos among Bosnian Croats can be illustrative. The tattoos became widespread among the Roman Catholic population of Bosnia and Herzegovina during the Ottoman rule of their lands (1463–1878). Bosnian Catholics would tattoo their children, hoping it would save them from the Ottoman practice of taking young boys and sending them to Istanbul to become soldiers and convert to Islam. Even if that did subsequently happen, their children would have a permanent reminder of who they were. This practice was even more common among young girls, as parents hoped that tattoos of crosses and other Christian symbols would prevent Turkish men from taking them as their wives. The tradition was well present until the twentieth century, past the

19 Interview with Interviewee 5, current employee at the Directorate of Democracy, Council of Europe (15 October 2022).

20 Gabi Dolff-Bonekämper, 'The Social and Spatial Frameworks of Heritage – What Is New in the Faro Convention' in Council of Europe, *Heritage and Beyond* (Council of Europe Publishing, Strasbourg 2009) 71.

point when the imminent reasons for the practice ceased to exist. More precisely, the tradition was widely used until 1938 and became a sign of identity for Catholic women in Bosnia and Herzegovina. With the creation of communist Yugoslavia, this practice (a sign of religious identity) was undesirable, and it faced a sharp decline.

Nevertheless, today, there is a sign that this heritage survived, adapted, and continues to exist. In present-day society, the practice of tattooing mostly young girls (from the age of 6, in some cases), with an extremely painful technique, would hardly be acceptable. Still, the motifs and their significance (the most essential aspects of this tradition) survived, together with the community which wants to transmit this heritage. There is a growing heritage community that employs this tradition and the motifs used by their ancestors, this time with modern tattoo techniques, to express their identity. However, this heritage community is dispersed worldwide, with a considerable diaspora particularly interested in this tradition. Their way of connecting and forming a 'heritage community' is through social media, where there is an ongoing documentation of patterns used, photos of grandmothers with their traditional tattoos and the modern version of their (great)grandchildren, together with academic work done on the subject and education courses organised for tattoo artists with the aim to familiarising them with this tradition.[21] Therefore, even though the Bosnian public authorities rejected all the attempts to list this tradition on the intangible list of national heritage (as it is no longer a living tradition, in their opinion), the 'unofficial' heritage community of the people who find this expression of their identity important continues to appreciate it and to transmit it in their own 'unofficial' way. This heritage continues to live and develop regardless of whether public authorities recognise it or not.

The diversity of heritage communities and the different levels of engagement with public authorities they are ready to have resulted in moving the CoE's thinking from 'participation' towards 'cooperation'. As established earlier in this part of the book, 'heritage participation' is the critical element of the Faro process. The CoE set it as the essential criteria for assessing the Faro-inspired projects in its first Faro Action Plan. However, as the work moved forward, the term 'cooperation' gradually became preferred over 'participation'.[22] As rightly stated by Wanner, although it is perceived as being inherent to the Faro Convention, the concept of 'participation' has been criticised as

21 https://www.facebook.com/profile.php?id=100063789318338

22 Pascal Wanner, 'Faro Convention and Participation: Shared Responsibility for Cultural Heritage' in Council of Europe, *The Faro Convention's Role in a Changing Society – Building on a Decade of Advancement 2011–2021* (Council of Europe Publishing, Strasbourg 2021) 7–18.

being counterproductive, as it is most of the time initiated by top-down mechanisms.[23] Consequently, terms such as co-operation, co-construction and co-decision turned out to be more meaningful for heritage communities than generic participation, which seems to distribute rights and responsibilities unequally in favour of authorities and experts. The *Faro Convention Action Plan Handbook 2018–2019* reflects this shift from participation towards cooperation. In its glossary, the definition of cooperation is given as follows:

> Cooperation is the action of working together [towards the] same goal, beginning from the first steps and gradually constructing together. A special distinction is made here between participation and cooperation, as participating in something denotes lesser influence in decision-making and may exclude certain groups [from] taking [an] active role in the processes.[24]

Thus, the Faro Convention allows the creation of 'out-of-ordinary dialogue situations' in which cooperation among different stakeholders is based on the desire to share heritage responsibilities.[25] In this new context, all participants, whether heritage experts, elected representatives, local communities, heritage communities, or officials, are '(re)legitimized precisely in relation to a given cultural heritage'.[26] With the Faro process, every stakeholder has respective responsibilities, functions, and knowledge, which are not the same. Yet, they do not conflict with one another if they are suitably designated and recognised: heritage communities relate to a given heritage, experts have a public responsibility, and elected representatives have a political mandate. Therefore, rather than opposing representative democracy and public bodies or institutions, or positioning themselves as the alternative to them, heritage communities, through their adherence to the Faro Convention, confirm their commitment to democracy and the principles and institutions that sustain democracy in the long term. On the other hand, this means that public institutions must create the conditions for action by heritage communities within the framework of public action and commit to cooperation stemming from social demand rather than top-down instructions. The creation of conditions and public framework that stimulate the involvement of citizens, elected representatives, experts,

23 Ibid.

24 Council of Europe, *The Faro Convention Action Plan Handbook 2018–2019* (Council of Europe Publishing, Strasbourg 2018) 23.

25 Wanner 2021 (n 22) 14.

26 Ibid.

institutions, and civil society is vital, since the State's sole ratification of the Faro Convention does not guarantee the emergence of a Faro process by itself. Rather, it must emerge from the common decision to share responsibility for cultural heritage. The shift towards this new Faro-inspired cooperative process in heritage demands, first of all, time for dialogue and building trust. For a long time, the established AHD processes kept this dialogue at a very rudimentary level. With the change in discourse that the Faro Convention promotes, it is essential to develop new ways of entering into dialogue based on the wishes and aspirations of the public regarding what they value the most and consider to be their heritage. As argued by Wanner, future work needs to be focused not only on changes in the partners' attitudes that would allow having the most inclusive conversation but, above all, on the nature of that conversation regarding different partners' values.[27] The implementation of the Faro Convention, therefore, is deeply connected with general democratic practices in the CoE Member States. It undoubtedly represents a critical framework under which heritage communities can strive for greater recognition. Still, for the Faro process to reach its full potential, it is essential that all involved parties, whether elected representatives, (heritage) institutions, or groups of individuals, **choose to cooperate** and to strengthen the sense of shared responsibility for their living environment. For the Faro process, commitment is decisive.

3 Implementing the Faro Convention: National Level

As noticed by many commentators, the Convention is vague in determining how the democratic heritage governance it promotes will be implemented. It does not explicitly explain what it means by 'participation' nor the levels at which heritage communities and the administration have to engage. In addition, the Convention does not explain how the administration is to design participatory processes together with heritage communities so that they share responsibilities in heritage management – the point that most governments find problematic in their need for more precise guidelines that were present under previous Conventions. The CoE's 'Faro Action Plan' that was, therefore, set up 'to translate the Faro Convention principles into practice' and to provide a platform for sharing field-based knowledge and expertise, shows that there is no one-size-fits-all approach to the implementation of the Convention. The disparity between the proposed participatory models and how they are implemented understandably depends on the differences in the legal

27 Ibid.

framework of each CoE Member State and the level of development of their democratic processes. This disparity also signals how heritage and participation is a complex and politically loaded idea that, more often than not, raises conflicts at the heritage management level between regulation and authorities/experts (AHD) on the one hand and engagement and empowerment of heritage communities on the other. As rightly pointed out by the Swedish National Heritage Board, 'because the Convention focuses unilaterally on the positive aspects of this cooperation model, there is a tendency to underestimate the potential practical problems that may arise upon implementation'.[28]

The fact that the Convention aims to establish new approaches and strategies based on cultural heritage from a number of different dimensions, combined with its being a framework convention, inevitably means that for the authorities, it is a very complex document. As was already emphasised, framework conventions are relatively weak instruments because they leave room for the State Parties to adapt the level of implementation. This leaves us with certain doubt about the actual success of the Convention in challenging established AHD-underpinned models of dealing with heritage in practice. The extract from the Swedish National Heritage Board's report exemplifies this attitude when it notes that: 'Sweden could thus ratify [Convention] for "the sake of good cause" and then look for the elements that could enrich, but without the need to reinvent the policies and practices already being used' (2014, p. 5). Therefore, the Convention will be no more alive than is practically and organisationally possible for/desired by the implementing administration. The interviews (interviewees 2 and 4) and reports consulted from Sweden (2014), and Finland (2014) leave the impression that governments and heritage authorities, even from those countries that ratified the Convention, prefer to regard the Convention's text more as a source of ideas rather than as an instrument that requires/obliges the relevant authorities to change their practices. The fact that the Faro Convention contains no instructions on practice or clear guidelines can serve as an alibi for a heritage administration that doesn't wish to implement its principles. Again, the Swedish National Heritage Board is clear in its recommendation to the Swedish government on the text:

> As the Faro Convention contains no instructions on practice but rather has the nature of an ideological, comprehensive concept paper on cul-

---

28 Swedish National Heritage Board, *Report – The Faro Convention* (2014) 12 https://historicengland.org.uk/content/docs/research/faro-conventionpdf/ accessed 23 March 2021.

tural heritage, it should rather, upon ratification, be regarded as support for government administration than a policy document.

Up to now, at least to the author's knowledge, no comprehensive overview of the implementation measures employed by the states or nation-specific or comparative analyses exist. Therefore, it is challenging to establish and talk about how different states approached the Convention and its implementation. Nevertheless, some data extracted from the archival sources could serve as the starting point in our understanding of the nation-specific situations. In this respect, the Review of the Council of Europe Conventions under the Responsibility of the CDCPP: Classification by State (CDCPP (2015) 3 Addendum I Bil.) is of specific interest.[29] Table 8.1 offers insight into the Member States' take on the Faro Convention and its implementation, primarily based on the CDCPP Review (2015), but also on the information available from the CoE HEREIN System, which provides an inventory of European heritage policies in 38 CoE Member States. The information presented in Table 8.1 could be seen as a basis for a desirable, more in-depth analysis of the Convention's implementation in State Parties. For the sake of this chapter, the information from Table 8.1 offers an opportunity to sketch out the initial/current positions of the Member States towards the Convention and its requirements. It also allows us to perceive the level of discomfort the authorities demonstrate with the Convention's principles, in particular, with its request for a more inclusive heritage discourse.

To date (June 2025), the Faro Convention has been ratified by 25 Member States[30] and signed by five countries without ratification (Albania, Bulgaria, Cyprus, Romania, and Netherlands). As the table above shows, the countries differ enormously in their attitude towards the text. On the one side, some countries find the text extremely problematic and ambiguous (France, Germany); others do not consider ratifying the text but recognise its value and implement the 'spirit' of the Convention in their policies and legislation; and some countries have ratified the text and claim not to encounter any problems in its application.

---

29 Council of Europe, Steering Committee for Culture, Heritage and Landscape (CDCPP), 'Review of the Council of Europe Conventions under the Responsibility of the CDCPP – Classification by State' (CDCPP (2015) 3 Addendum I Bil. Rev, 2015).

30 Armenia, Austria, Belgium, Bosnia and Herzegovina, Croatia, Estonia, Finland, Georgia, Hungary, Italy, Latvia, Luxemburg, Montenegro, North Macedonia, Norway, Poland, Portugal, Republic of Moldova, San Marino, Serbia, Slovak Republic, Slovenia, Spain, Switzerland, Ukraine.

TABLE 8.1 National approaches to the Faro Convention

Member state	Status of the Faro Convention ratification	Problems encountered
Austria	Ratification: 23/1/2015	Austria declared that it did not encounter any problems in the Convention's application.
	Entry into Force: 1/5/2015	They suggest that the complementarity of the Convention with other Conventions by the Council of Europe and other international organisations such as UNESCO could be highlighted to explore potential synergies in the implementation.
Belgium	Ratification: 13/5/2022	At the time of the 2015 review, it was only the Flemish part of Belgium that ratified the Convention, so the comments must be understood from that perspective.
	Entry into Force: 01/09/2022	Although Flemish legislation is strongly embedded in this convention, certain themes remain challenging in practice: (1) The (democratic) rights and responsibilities relating to cultural heritage; (2) The concept of 'heritage communities'
Bosnia and Herzegovina	Ratification: 30/04/2009 Entry into Force: 01/06/2011	Bosnia and Herzegovina declared that it did not have any problems with the application of the Convention and that it continues to implement actions in the spirit of Faro. Nevertheless, the government made a comment that the provisions of the Convention relating to public accountability, accessibility, and democratic participation are idealistic. The experience suggests that the implementation of these ideas depends on the overall situation of society, as well as the current needs and interests of individuals and society as a whole. Private and public interests are usually totally opposed when it comes to the use of cultural heritage.

TABLE 8.1 National approaches to the Faro Convention (*cont.*)

Member state	Status of the Faro Convention ratification	Problems encountered
Croatia	Ratification: 06/06/2007	Croatia declared that all its actions and policies are in the spirit and goals of the Convention.
	Entry into Force: 01/06/2011	Convention is implemented through the Strategy of Protection, Preservation and Sustainable Use of Cultural Heritage of Croatia 2011–2015. To the author's knowledge, this document has not been revised.
Czech Republic	No	The Czech Republic commented that its government did not achieve agreement in an internal discussion of the Convention. In addition, it is of the opinion that the convention has a general character and that this is their main reason for not ratifying the text. Nevertheless, it implements documents of a similar character (Strategy of Culture).
Estonia	Ratification: 15/04/2021	Estonia declared in the 2015 CDCPP report that it intends to ratify the Convention, which it did in 2021.
	Entry into Force: 01/08/2021	
Finland	Ratification: 31/05/2018 Entry into Force: 01/09/2018	Finland's first national Cultural Environment Strategy 2014–2020 corresponds to the spirit and goals of the Faro Convention. For example, one of the strategy's goals for 2020 is as follows: 'Cultural environment policies are directed towards citizens and communities. The business sector, public sector, civil society actors and citizens of the area are involved extensively in enhancing the cultural environment. People are aware

TABLE 8.1 National approaches to the Faro Convention (*cont.*)

Member state	Status of the Faro Convention ratification	Problems encountered
		of their own opportunities to participate, and they are able to make use of them.' In addition, Finland is of the opinion that the current Faro Action Plan provides a good basis for the implementation of the Convention. The implementation will benefit from continuous exchange of experience, examples, and good practice between the State Parties and other stakeholders, as well as those who have introduced activities that refer to the Convention but have not signed the Convention.
France	No	France declared that in its case the major obstacle for the ratification of the text is the concept of heritage community: La mission juridique du Conseil d'État auprès du Secrétariat général du ministère de la culture et de la communication a estiméè que la ratification de la convention comportait en l'état un aléa constitutionnel eu égard à la notion de «communauté patrimoniale» qu'elle introduit et à la définition du patrimoine culturel qu'elle donne'.
Germany	No	The German opinion expressed in the CDCPP review was that the important matters regulated by the Convention are already covered by other international conventions (including the UNESCO World Heritage Convention, UNESCO Convention on the Protection and Promotion of the Diversity of Cultural Expressions, European Framework Convention for the Protection of National Minorities, European Charter for Regional or Minority Languages, etc.). Accession to the Convention would potentially

TABLE 8.1 National approaches to the Faro Convention (*cont.*)

Member state	Status of the Faro Convention ratification	Problems encountered
		lead to extensive administrative obligations (e.g., monitoring mechanisms), which would outweigh the concrete benefits in terms of cultural policies. Therefore, Germany does not intend to sign the Convention at present.
Greece	No	Greece did not comment on its decision to not ratify the Convention.
Hungary	Ratification: 27/11/2012 Entry into Force: 01/03/2013	Hungary declared that it does not face any problems in the application of the Convention. The cultural heritage aspects of the Faro Convention are implemented through the 2001 Act LXIV on the protection of cultural heritage and the 393/2012 government decree on the protection of archaeological and built heritage.
Italy	Ratification: 15/12/2020 Entry into Force: 01/04/2021	It is the opinion of Italy that, as a framework convention, Faro cannot be directly implemented in the national legal framework. It rather changes the attitudes and the understanding of the cultural sector towards cultural heritage and heritage communities, even in countries that are not planning to sign implement the framework convention itself. This is slowly producing an evolution that might, over time, prove deeper than the changes introduced by law. Given the spirit of this particular Convention, awareness-raising and other initiatives mobilising a wide range of stakeholders and interested people could contribute to its implementation. The spirit of the Convention is slowly being implemented and producing a change in a

TABLE 8.1 National approaches to the Faro Convention (*cont.*)

Member state	Status of the Faro Convention ratification	Problems encountered
		wide range of public policies. As an example, the EU Council adopted Council conclusions on participatory governance of cultural heritage under the Italian presidency.
Latvia	Ratification: 26/04/2006	Latvia stated that it does not encounter any problems in the application of the Convention.
	Entry into Force: 01/06/2011	According to the statement in the CDCPP review, the Convention is widely used and referenced in order to facilitate necessary amendments and actions according to national legislation and other declarative documents.
Liechtenstein	No	Liechtenstein stated that the ratification is in evaluation, but that 'probably' it does not intend to ratify the Convention in the near future.
Luxembourg	Ratification: 18/05/2011	Luxemburg declared that it does not have any problems with the application of the Convention.
	Entry into Force: 01/09/2011	Its proposal for wider use of the Convention is: 'Il faudrait davantage sensibiliser le public européen'.
Malta	No	Malta stated that its government is examining the possibility of ratifying the Convention (CDCPP 2015); however, Malta, to date, still has not signed or ratified the text. The convention's spirit is implemented through the Cultural Heritage Act, as stated in the Act's preamble, and through (i) regulations inventories, heritage protection,

TABLE 8.1 National approaches to the Faro Convention (*cont.*)

Member state	Status of the Faro Convention ratification	Problems encountered
		excavation regulation, frontier control, etc. (ii) National Strategy Document on Cultural Heritage.
Republic of Moldova	Ratification : 01/12/2008	The Republic of Moldova stated that it does not encounter any problems in application of the Convention.
	Entry into Force: 01/06/2011	Starting from 2009, the first step was to prepare a new law for the protection of specific fields of heritage. All the main goals and principle from the Convention are now logically included in the laws and decision of the Government. Local and civil societies have an active role in promoting the value of the heritage, as well as in preparing legislation and in use of monuments. The Ministry for Culture supports joint projects in local communities, especially between the young generations and older people. Special attention is given to NGOs. The Ministry also supports activities of cultural groups, communities, and the linking of functions and people.
Monaco	No	
The Netherlands	No	The Netherlands declared that there are no concrete plans in the direction of ratification of the Convention. Nevertheless, they support the exchange of (best) practices proposed by the Faro Action Plan. The definition of cultural heritage in the Faro Convention is used as the definition of cultural heritage in a new Heritage Act.

TABLE 8.1 National approaches to the Faro Convention (*cont.*)

Member state	Status of the Faro Convention ratification	Problems encountered
		(2016), and many aspects of the Convention are part and parcel of the Dutch cultural heritage policy.
Norway	Ratification: 27/10/2008	Norway declared that it did not encounter any problems in implementing the Convention.
	Entry into Force: 01/06/2011	According to the statement in the CDCPP review (2015), when Norway ratified the Faro Convention, it was with the understanding that most of the recommendations in the Convention had already been implemented in Norwegian practices. In the last White Paper on cultural heritage, reference is explicitly made to the Faro Convention. The heritage of minorities should possibly be better protected in Norway in order to fully comply with the spirit of Faro.
Poland	Ratification: 29/11/2022 Entry into Force: 01/06/2011	At the time of the CDCPP review, Poland declared that it has already started preparatory works aiming at the ratification of the Convention. The procedure was accomplished in 2022.
Portugal	Ratification: 28/08/2009 Entry into Force: 01/06/2011	Portugal recognised the significance of all the innovative aspects of the Convention. The Portuguese administration has developed a national strategy for bringing cultural heritage closer to communities, which is more visible at the local level. Heritage-related institutions had to go through a major reshuffle so as to be brought up to date.

TABLE 8.1 National approaches to the Faro Convention (*cont.*)

Member state	Status of the Faro Convention ratification	Problems encountered
Slovak Republic	Ratification: 16/08/2013 Entry into Force: 01/12/2013	The Slovak Republic stated that it did not have any problems in the application of the Convention. The performance of the state administration related to the protection of monuments directly pursues the goals of protection stipulated in the Convention. The goals of the Convention are reflected in the Culture Development Strategy of the Slovak Republic for 2014–2020 and have been elaborated in its Action Plan for 2015–2017. There are no latest updates of the Culture Development Strategy, taking into account its end date in 2020.
Slovenia	Ratification: 17/09/2008 Entry into Force: 01/06/2011	Slovenia pointed out some problems in the application of the Convention: the goals of the convention are very extensive. Different concrete actions for implementations are usually more intense at the beginning of each action; it is hard to maintain their advantages over the long term. Huge parts of activities were organised with the support of civil initiatives and different associations. Local initiatives are very important and spread out; small municipalities sometimes do not have enough experts and money for all goals. Nevertheless, Slovenia supports actions in different fields, from legislation and promotion to restoration and the participation of people in protecting and all other activities. The first step was preparing a new law for the protection of heritage. All the main goals from the Convention are logically summarised in general law and decrees. Local and civil societies have an active part in preparing legislation (they are invited to

TABLE 8.1 National approaches to the Faro Convention (*cont.*)

Member state	Status of the Faro Convention ratification	Problems encountered
		give their opinion for each decree, they can propose protections) and in the use of monuments, movable, unmovable, and immaterial heritage. Any protected immovable heritage can be inscribed in special register only with the support and active part of producer/bearer of these activities.
Sweden	No	Sweden produced a report targeting the conditions and consequences of a ratification in 2015. The outcome of the remittance will be the basis for future decision. So far, Sweden has not signed or ratified the Convention.
Switzerland	Ratification: 07/11/2019 Entry into Force: 01/03/2020	Switzerland, if we judge by its decision to ratify the Convention in 2018, radically changed its opinion on the text as it was expressed in the 2015 Review. In the 2015 CDCPP report, the Suisse statement is rather sceptical of the text, stating: 'When it was established, Switzerland expressed certain reservations about the need to establish such a Convention and stressed the need to ensure consistency between this new instrument and existing texts, particularly within UNESCO. As a result, Switzerland considered, on the one hand, that a declaration would have been sufficient and appropriate for achieving the objectives set; and on the other hand, that a prior in-depth discussion on the usefulness of this text and its relationship to existing instruments was essential. This position was then explained by the fact that Article 6c removes any effect directly applicable to this instrument, and that the wording of several provisions remains general and not very binding. As a result, the framework

TABLE 8.1 National approaches to the Faro Convention (*cont.*)

Member state	Status of the Faro Convention ratification	Problems encountered
		convention risked not having the expected effects and undermining legal certainty. A declaration would also have had the advantage of not establishing new monitoring mechanisms to be financed by the Member States (and which can prove very costly for a federalist country like Switzerland). The strengthening and improvement of the implementation of the Conventions in force which have already been ratified therefore remains a priority over the adoption of additional instruments from Switzerland's point of view.'[a]
Turkey	No	

a Original text in French reads: 'Lors de son établissement, la Suisse a émis certaines réserves quant à la nécessité d'établir une telle Convention et a souligné le besoin de veiller à la cohérence entre ce nouvel instrument et les textes existants, notamment au sein de l'UNESCO. De ce fait, la Suisse estimait d'une part qu'une déclaration aurait été suffisante et adaptée à l'atteinte des objectifs fixés ; et d'autre part qu'une discussion de fonds préalable sur l'utilité de ce texte et sa relation aux instruments existants était indispensable. Cette position avait alors été expliquée par le fait que l'article 6c, enlève tout effet directement applicable à cet instrument, et que la formulation de plusieurs dispositions demeure générale et peu contraignante. De ce fait, la convention-cadre risquait de ne pas déployer les effets escomptés et de porter atteinte à la sécurité juridique. Une déclaration aurait par ailleurs eu l'avantage de ne pas établir de nouveaux mécanismes de suivi devant être financés par les États membres (et qui peuvent s'avérer très coûteux pour un pays fédéraliste comme la Suisse). Le renforcement et l'amélioration de la mise en œuvre des Conventions en vigueur déjà ratifiées demeurent à ce titre prioritaire sur l'adoption d'instruments additionnels du point de vue de la Suisse.'

TABLE 8.1 National approaches to the Faro Convention (*cont.*)

Member state	Status of the Faro Convention ratification	Problems encountered
United Kingdom	No	The UK Government declared that currently it has no plans to ratify the Convention. It is the opinion of the UK, expressed in the CDCPP Review, that it implements the actions in line with the Faro principle through its State Party status to the World Heritage Convention.

Note: Table composed by author using the data from multiple sources.

For the countries reluctant to ratify the text, along with the critique that the Convention does not offer a clear guideline for its implementation and that it is too 'theoretical' and 'inspirational', the Convention is also portrayed as overly ambitious.[31] It is perceived by many governments that the Convention wants to cover 'just about everything' and that it is 'trying to do too much'.[32] In addition, there is a widespread view that the Convention's understanding of cultural heritage as the solution for a number of social problems is somewhat 'naïve'.[33] This critique, mainly from the governments, as argued by a former CoE Secretariate member, reflects their uneasiness with the text. The Swedish report once again articulates this discomfort:

> If this 'list' of prospective areas of society were actually to be implemented on all points, based on the same high level of ambition, a number of consequences would become visible. These consequences would probably include a series of constitutional amendments being actualised within a number of policies. This would, in turn, require a change to the instructions and a change to the way Swedish cultural environments are managed: a change of target that can be both costly and resource-intensive. Moreover, a consequence could also be that the Swedish public cultural environment administration would need to increase its cross-sectoral cooperation.[34]

The uneasiness with the Convention's principles expressed in the quotes above illustrates not only the tenacity of the AHD but also shows on how many levels the governments feel that the Faro Convention challenges the established heritage discourse. In line with this understanding is Portugal's comment in the CDCPP Review, stating that the heritage-related institutions had to go through a 'major reshuffle so as to be adjusted to the signs of the times' and principles advocated by the Convention.[35] This obviously presents a major challenge for most countries. Germany, in addition, considers that 'an accession to the Convention would potentially lead to extensive administrative obligations which would outweigh the concrete benefits in terms of cultural policies', suggesting that the advantages of the more democratic participation are not worth the

31 Swedish National Heritage Board (n 28).

32 Interview with Interviewee 4, former head of the Division of Culture and Cultural Heritage, Council of Europe (10 October 2022).

33 Ibid.

34 Swedish National Heritage Board (n 28) 65.

35 CDCPP (2015) 3 Addendum 1 Bil. Rev (n 29) 173.

'expensive' changes in established heritage management arrangement.[36] In line with the UK's understanding, Germany considers that the heritage field is already sufficiently regulated by other international conventions, particularly the UNESCO Conventions.[37]

The case of Switzerland is interesting to look at, as it shows that even governments with strong opposition to the text, such as Germany and the UK, might change their position at some point. Switzerland's first opinion of the Convention was rather disapproving, asking for a simple declaration on the subject instead of the Convention, as seen from the CDCPP Review. However, the situation and opinion of the Swiss government changed during 2017–2018, when the Département fédéral de l'intérieur (DFI) opened the consultation process concerning the ratification of the Convention. According to the Report on the results of the consultation process (2018), 124 organisations, collectives, and institutions were invited to participate in this process (cantons, political parties, local communities, the private sector, and NGOs in the heritage field). Fifty-one of them expressed their opinion and, with a majority of 46 votes, voted in favour of ratification.[38] Switzerland's consultation report offers a fascinating view of the Convention – one not simply from the national/governmental perspective but that discloses the stance of different stakeholders on the text. For example, all the NGOs and associations in the heritage domain were in favour of the text. At the same time, there was a considerable disparity of opinions coming from the political parties, with the Green Party (PVL) and Social Democratic Party (PSS) calling for immediate ratification of the text, the Liberals (PLR) supporting the heritage policies already in place with rather

36 German opposition to the text can be summarised: A framework convention, due to its lack of clear definition of purpose and objectives, the lack of limitation of scope, and the lack of clarity concerning the relationship to other international legal instruments, is not acceptable. As demonstrated, the project in its present form would create a number of undesirable and potentially damaging political and legal effects for the CoE and its Member States. As a consequence, the only feasible way to advance on the path towards an improved protection of cultural heritage would be the instrument of a declaration (CDPAT(2005)31, p. 7).

37 Council of Europe, Steering Committee for Cultural Heritage (CDPAT), 'Comments from the German Delegation on the Draft Framework Convention' [2005] CDPAT (2005) 31.

38 A l'exception de SZ, tous les cantons se rallient aux objectifs, principes et contenus de la Convention et se prononcent en faveur de la ratification. Les Verts et le PSSsoutiennent nettement la proposition, alors que le PLR émet d'importantes réserves sur l'utilité de la Convention et que l'UDC rejette explicitement la ratification;

L'Union des villes suisses et la Conférence des villes en matière culturelle soutiennent la Convention et saluent les efforts faits par le Conseil fédéral pour la ratifier. Les associations faîtières de l'économie sont partagées : le Centre patronal et l'Union suisse des arts et métiers rejettent la ratification, alors que l'Union syndicale suisse la soutient.

significant opposition to the Faro Convention, and the Swiss People's Party (UDC) rejecting the Convention 'because its usefulness does not seem to have been demonstrated'.[39] This political understanding of the Convention as an 'extremely liberal text', according to Interviewee 5, results in a rather open rejection of the text from the conservative side of the political spectrum and consequently poses an obvious problem with the ratification process.[40]

In addition to the uneasiness with the Faro principles expressed by some governments on the national level, the same attitude is noticeable in the intergovernmental (CoE) discussions on the subject. During the Convention's drafting process, Germany expressed its opposition to the text in rather strong language:

> Going ahead with the project of a framework convention – in spite of fundamental opposition against this specific instrument by an important number of Member States – would raise serious concerns of compatibility with the general goals of the Council of Europe: Instead of eliminating dividing lines in Europe, this would create a conceptual division in the perception of European history and cultural heritage. As far as Germany is concerned, we will not be able to sign a framework convention, not even at a later stage.[41]

The case commented on by Interviewee 2 exemplified this aspect of strong disagreement with the Convention's principles even a decade after its adoption.[42] According to him, during the discussion on the Recommendation CM/Rec (2020)7 on Promoting the Continuous Prevention of Risks in the day-to-day Management of Cultural Heritage: Co-operation with States, Specialists and Citizens, in 2020, there was some intense opposition to even including the reference to the Faro Convention in the text. Some governments went as far as to question the adoption of the Recommendation if the Faro principles were to be included. He stated, 'they want to use any opportunity to undermine the Faro and to keep the heritage management practice confined in the

39 Département fédéral de l'intérieur (DFI), Office fédéral de la culture (OFC), *Message du 30 novembre 2018 concernant la ratification de la convention-cadre du Conseil de l'Europe sur la valeur du patrimoine culturel pour la société (convention de Faro)* (2018); Original text reads : 'Car son utilité ne lui semble pas démontrée'.

40 Interview with Interviewee 5 (n 19).

41 CDPAT (2005) 31 (n 39) 3.

42 Interview with Interviewee 2, current employee at the Council of Europe's Directorate for Democracy (4 December 2020).

established Grenada and Valletta principles'.[43] In other words, almost 20 years after the adoption of the Faro Convention, governments still show reluctance towards transformations in their heritage discourse. At the same time, it could be argued that the Faro Convention, through this hesitancy towards it, further heightens its position as the 'manifesto' of a new European heritage discourse, specifically among ever-growing heritage communities. Even though its implementation comes with a number of challenges, the fact that this kind of document was drafted and adopted by the governments sends the signals that there is prospective space for dialogue in and democratisation of the heritage field. As stated by the Italian government, the spirit of the Convention is slowly being implemented and producing a change in a wide range of public policies.[44]

In line with Italy's statement above, there are currently 25 State Parties that, at least based on their ratification of the text, feel comfortable with the ideas and principles promoted by the Faro Convention. One of the important ideas that makes the transition towards 'new heritage' for many governments more appealing needs to be borne in mind; as understood from the Explanatory Report's quote below, the Faro Convention aims not to replace but rather to complement the dominant aesthetic and scholarly understanding of heritage:

> The foundation of this Convention is that a functional view of the cultural heritage can and should **supplement** the aesthetic and scholarly view, provided always that proposed uses accord with the principles of sustainability.[45]

The understanding is that aesthetic, historical, and expert-driven views on heritage are only some of the possible approaches to heritage, and according to the Convention, a great synergy of skills and competencies as well as uses of heritage among public, institutions, and private players can occur if they are allowed to participate in heritage processes on an equal footing. Therefore, with sustainable development in mind, the Faro Convention looks at how the diversity of heritage and its interpretations and values can contribute and be used continuously to enrich society's economic, political, social, and cultural development.

---

43 Ibid.

44 CDCPP (2015) 3 Addendum 1 Bil.Rev (n 29).

45 Explanatory Report to the Council of Europe Framework Convention on the Value of Cultural Heritage for Society (CETS No. 199. Article 1d) (emphasis added).

As visible from Table 8.1, many State Parties declared that they did not have any problems with the application of the Convention, and this attitude could easily be understood taking into account the stated diversity of options offered by the Faro framework. Therefore, governments feel free to choose which aspects of the Convention (and to what degree) to concentrate on and accordingly declare that they do not encounter any problems in the Convention's application. Some examples and statements from certain State Parties could be illustrative of this multiplicity of approaches, but also of some governments' rather 'unambitious' and, one could say, disappointing interpretations of the Convention.

Croatia, for example, adopted the Strategy of Protection, Preservation and Sustainable Use of Cultural Heritage of Croatia 2011–2015 in order to implement the Convention. Nevertheless, the document appeared still largely underpinned by the AHD. To start with, the definition of cultural heritage given at the beginning of the document is in line with the definition promoted by the Faro Convention. Nevertheless, in the following chapters of the document, it became clear that heritage is primarily understood as the 'non-renewable and limited resource which demands protection, safeguarding, valuing and use according to the principles of sustainability'.[46] Furthermore, on the crucial issue of participation, the document shows a surprising misunderstanding of the Faro concept of participation and bases its approach on the need to 're-activate' an 'inactive' public that, according to the experts working on the document, is 'insufficiently aware of cultural heritage'.[47] Therefore, there is an urgent need to 'raise the awareness of the local population of the need to protect cultural heritage and to use it as an economic resource'.[48] Having the Strategy as a document through which the Faro Convention is supposed to be implemented in Croatia also signals how big a challenge the point of participation in the text is facing nationally. The following quote summarises the Croatian standing on the heritage issues, which extensively reson-

46 'Kulturna je baština neobnovljiv i ograničen resurs koji zahtijeva očuvanje, skrb, vrednovanje i korištenje prema načelu održivosti' (Ministarstvo Kulture Republike Hrvatske, 2011, 4).

47 Ministarstvo kulture Republike Hrvatske, 'Strategija zaštite, očuvanja i održivog gospodarskog korištenja kulturne baštine Republike Hrvatske za razdoblje 2011–2015' (2011) 4 (translated by author) https://bit.ly/48xPJlQ accessed 5 April 2022.

48 Ibid 10–1 (translated by author);

'Nedovoljna senzibiliziranost za kulturnu baštinu u lokalnim zajednicama utječe na neadekvatno korištenje kulturne baštine kao gospodarskog resursa' (p. 10);

'Poticati odgojno-obrazovne, ekološke i turističke aktivnosti mjesnog stanovništva radi jačanja svijesti o potrebi očuvanja kulturne baštine i njezina gospodarskog korištenja' (p. 11).

ates with the AHD model, and which leaves the reader doubting the government's intention and capability to follow the Faro principles:

> The policy of protection and preservation of cultural heritage is mainly focused on recognizing, registering, restoring (restoring and conserving) and preserving cultural **assets** and **presenting them to the public.** The objectives, measures and organization are focused primarily on the functions of protection and conservation. At the same time, cultural heritage, as well as cultural goods, are hardly perceived as an important development potential, as a resource for the economic and all-round development not only of local communities and regions, but also of the country. On the other hand, the economic, social, and spiritual use of cultural heritage is currently dominated by the interests of different users without sufficient awareness and responsibility for its preservation and protection.[49]

Furthermore, on the point of sustainability and the use of heritage, Croatia is exclusively promoting the role of heritage in tourism and for economic purposes. From the document it seems that the government promotes the cultural tourism as almost the only option possible. What is missing in this strategy is an in-depth consideration of whether 'betting on tourism' will pay off for local communities, and what impact on their quality of life or living environment this approach will have. The overall understanding of the Strategy is that the local communities will be interested in cultural heritage only if they can see the potential economic gain from its use.

In Bosnia and Herzegovina's case, the authorities maintain that there is insufficient compatibility between cultural heritage protection interest and the interests of economic development, echoing the long-prevailing understanding of cultural heritage as an obstacle to development:

> Difficult economic conditions have led to the society hardly recognising cultural heritage, as well as other segments of culture, as an important factor in sustainable development goals. This is directly reflected in the sustainable use of cultural heritage. In most cases, when implementing projects in which cultural heritage is used in accordance with the current legislation and the provisions of the relevant heritage protection service,

---

49 Ministarstvo Kulture Republike Hrvatske (n 49) 51, translated by author (emphasis added).

> potential private investors generally believe that the initial investment is too high and the period when it becomes profitable too long.[50]

Some other countries, for example Turkey and Slovenia, seem to understand the 'participation' aspect of the Convention in terms of greater physical accessibility to the museums and sites. Turkey declared that it implemented actions that correspond to the spirit and goals of the Convention; these consist of the 'opportunities of cheaper entrance fees or free entrances to museums for the public'.[51] In the same spirit, Slovenia stated that its new law for the protection of heritage is based on the Faro Convention, and the new regulation demands from 'all newly declared monuments to be open for general public without entrance fee at least several times a year'.[52] Whether this also applies to the 'old' monuments and sites is not clear. However, Slovenia also declared that its Ministry of Culture supports joint activities in local communities, especially between children, the younger generation, and older people: 'Ministry also supports activities of cultural groups, communities and linking of [heritage] functions and people.'[53] At the same time, Bosnia and Herzegovina, while declaring that its administration supports projects that present heritage as a resource for human development and the enhancement of cultural diversity and intercultural dialogue, also considers the Convention's provisions relating to public accountability, accessibility, and democratic participation 'idealistic'.[54]

4 Conclusion of the Chapter

The conclusion that can be drawn from the above examples is that the Faro Convention undeniably disturbed the prevailing heritage discourse in Europe to a certain degree. It is a feeling that, as much as the Convention's provisions sound 'idealistic', they are at the centre of slow but steady changes in heritage policies around the continent. The amount and vigour of the opposition displayed by some governments testifies to the long and challenging road faced by the Convention. The way in which the Faro Convention challenges the power/knowledge claims of experts institutionalised in state cultural agencies

50 CDCPP (2015) 3 Addendum 1 Bil.Rev (n 29) 53.
51 Ibid, 332.
52 Ibid, 297.
53 Ibid, 297.
54 Ibid, 53.

certainly provokes a rather 'defensive mood' on the part of public authorities. However, the fact that the Convention has been ratified by 25 countries leaves us with the hope that a paradigm shift is possible and that the need for it was recognised. For now, as some of the above examples illustrate, the well-intentioned official responses from the governments that support the Convention seem to still be constrained in their attempts for change because of the conceptual and administrative frameworks established by the AHD. Nevertheless, the ever-growing network of heritage communities could potentially trigger a more noticeable transformation, hopefully at the cultural, economic, and institutional levels, and move the discussion from promoting access to heritage (most of the time in the physical sense) towards a more articulated expression of the right to take part in cultural life in the policy process. Having the framework for this transition in the form of the Convention is a non-negligible success and should not be dismissed easily. As concluded by Interviewee 10:

> Maybe Faro's overambitious and idealistic goals will never be achieved, but in the situation as we have it now where heritage is considered exclusive and inaccessible, we need to consider even the smallest progress towards more democratic participation in heritage as a great success.[55]

55 Interview with Interviewee 10, current Project Manager at the Directorate of Democracy, Council of Europe (October 2022).

CHAPTER 9

Concluding Thoughts

The aim of this book was to map out and critically analyse the evolution of distinctive heritage discourses within the policy framework developed by the CoE. In particular, the core characteristics of the AHD, as described by Smith,[1] were used as the reference point against which to measure the deviations the CoE developed in its policies and texts and the evolution of the specific ensuing CoE heritage discourse. In addition, an exploration of the 'family' of the CoE's heritage-related conventions not only allowed for a more nuanced understanding of the CoE's discourse and its relation to the AHD but also provided an opportunity to take stock of more than 70 years of CoE heritage activities and examine the context, history, personalities, and politics behind those texts and, consequently, their discourses. In this respect, the CoE's contribution to the development of international heritage doctrine and law appeared to be largely overlooked by academia, and this volume aimed to fill this gap.

As such, what this book has demonstrated is that the CoE played a significant role in international heritage discussions. Along with UNESCO, ICOMOS, and ICCROM, the CoE is an organisation that legitimised the AHD during the 1950s and 1960s but that also constructed a genuinely counteractive approach for understanding and managing heritage in a new millennium that challenges the AHD on multiple levels. A significant body of research demonstrates that while demands for more inclusion, dialogue, diversity, and participation on the international level (with UNESCO texts) as well as on the national policy level have resulted in a subtly altered conceptualisation of heritage, those texts and policies still very much stay within the parameters of the AHD.[2] This volume, nevertheless, has determined that the 'new/inclusive heritage discourse' (Chapter 8) framed by the CoE's Faro Convention offers an innovative way of 'doing heritage' and making it a noteworthy resource for broader social issues.

1 Laurajane Smith, *Uses of Heritage* (Routledge, Taylor & Francis Group 2006).

2 For example: Emma Waterton, *Rhetoric & 'Reality' – Politics, Policy and the Discourse of Heritage in England* (PhD thesis, University of York 2007);
John Pendlebury, 'Conservation Values, the Authorized Heritage Discourse and the Conservation-Planning Assemblage' (2013) 19(7) International Journal of Heritage Studies 709;
Lucas Lixinski, 'Selecting Heritage: The Interplay of Art, Politics and Identity' (2011) 22(1) European Journal of International Law 8;
Natsuko Akagawa, 'Rethinking the Global Heritage Discourse – Overcoming "East" and "West"?' (2016) 22(1) International Journal of Heritage Studies 14.

 | DOI:10.1163/9789004756250_010

The research presented in this book primarily drew from the theoretical and methodological contributions of Smith,[3] Waterton,[4] and Fairclough,[5] but also from the many authors whose work is based on the critique of dominant discourse (AHD) from multiple perspectives (Part 1). Laurajane Smith proposed the existence of an authorised heritage discourse (AHD) and clarified its characteristics;[6] Waterton,[7] but also Pendlebury,[8] Labadi,[9] Kisić,[10] and many others offered examples of how public policies can be explored in relation to the AHD; and Fairclough's understanding of CDA argued for the dialectics of discourse. These contributions facilitated an exploration of the construction of a distinctive articulation of what heritage is and what it does in the CoE's heritage policy and standard-setting documents. Although, as indicated by other authors,[11] the AHD has varied over time and context, its fundamental characteristics appeared to continue to be at the core of international heritage policies. Nevertheless, of interest to this research was how the AHD's features within the CoE's policies were affected by the organisation's broader aims of promoting human rights and democracy. What became particularly striking about the CoE's agenda of human rights is that it had underpinned the organisation's heritage discourse from its earliest phase and led to the conceptualisation of the 'new heritage discourse' (Chapters 7 and 8), which does not only constitute a slight variation on the AHD but rather objects to its core postulates.

---

3 Smith (n 1).

4 Waterton (n 2).

5 Norman Fairclough, 'Critical Discourse Analysis as a Method in Social Scientific Research' in Ruth Wodak and Michael Meyer (eds), *Methods of Critical Discourse Analysis* (SAGE Publications 2001).
   – *Analysing Discourse: Textual Analysis for Social Research* (Routledge 2003).
   – *Critical Discourse Analysis* (2nd edn, Longman 2010).

6 Smith (n 1).

7 Waterton (n 2).

8 Pendlebury 2013 (n 2); John Pendlebury, *Conservation in the Age of Consensus* (Routledge 2009).

9 Sophia Labadi, *UNESCO, Cultural Heritage, and Outstanding Universal Value: Value-Based Analyses of the World Heritage and Intangible Cultural Heritage Conventions* (Alta-Mira Press 2013);
   'Historical, Theoretical and International Considerations on Culture, Heritage and (Sustainable) Development' in Peter Larsen and William Logan (eds), *World Heritage and Sustainable Development: New Directions in World Heritage Management* (Routledge 2018).

10 Višnja Kisić, *Governing Heritage Dissonance: Promises and Realities of Selected Cultural Policies* (European Cultural Foundation 2016).

11 For example: Waterton (n 2) and Pendlebury 2013 (n 2).

The overall aim of this concluding chapter is to highlight the particularities of the CoE's discourse and the impact it has had on how heritage is managed in Europe today. To do this, the arguments that emerged from the CoE conventions and activities analysed will be framed by the three sets of research questions that framed this research, as they allow for capturing and illustrating the stages through which the CoE's heritage sector has progressed as well as describing the evolution of the organisation's heritage discourse. While the structure of the book may offer the appearance of a linear progression, the analysis showed that the relationships between each 'stage' are complex and dynamic, and each legitimises and incorporates the others in different combinations. It means that heritage processes have continually undergone a process of creation and recreation in reaction to the organisation's changing political and social interests. Therefore, the structure ultimately employed here allowed for a more detailed illustration of the political, ideological, and social underpinnings guiding the CoE's understanding of heritage from 'monuments and sites' towards a human rights-based approach wherein the focus is on the role of heritage in social processes.

Which Historical, Political, and Social Circumstances Fostered the Emergence and Development of the CoE's Heritage Discourse?

Taking stock of the 70 years of the CoE's heritage-related activities, as presented in this volume, offers a unique look at the timing, context, politics, individual influences, and institutional dynamics that shaped how heritage is perceived and managed in Europe today. This section addresses some of the main findings with respect to the research question: **Which Historical, Political, and Social Circumstances Fostered the Emergence and Development of the CoE's Heritage Discourse?**

The political nature of the organisation inevitably means that the CoE used heritage in the service of its wider political goals – European unity based on the promotion of human rights, the rule of law, and democracy. As shown throughout this volume, the first political goal that underpinned the entirety of the CoE's heritage work was building European unity and promoting the common European heritage. In line with the AHD's notion of 'nation', where monuments and archaeological sites demonstrative of significant time-depth were considered meaningful aspects of heritage capable of constructing the narrative of the nation's history and past, the CoE in its role of promoting European unity employed the same model by evoking the 'common European heritage'. Attempts to consciously design and articulate European unity and common history were intended to counterbalance the extensive use of heritage in national contexts. By recognising the contributions of every Member State to the common European heritage, the blending of 'us', 'Europeanness', and 'heritage' offered an opportunity for building a more peaceful and democratic European society. Acknowledging our 'commonness', the CoE argues, helps to build a cohesive European community.

While this use of heritage for political goals comes as no surprise, the analysis of the chain of texts throughout this research disclosed how the emphasis on the notion of common European heritage changed depending on the political context at a specific time – it emerged as a central concept around which to build European unity in the formative years of the organisation; it was highly neglected during the 1960s, 1970s, and 1980s, when the organisation was of the opinion that the core values it propagates are firmly established in its Member States, and therefore there was no need to use heritage for ideological purposes (which resulted in 'technical' conventions on architecture and archaeology); and it again came into focus with the political and social changes and challenges provoked by the collapse of the Berlin Wall. Therefore, as shown in Chapter 7, today the idea of the 'common heritage of Europe' mainly represents the notion in which the cultural heritage shared by Europeans (irrespective of their origin) interacts with the agreed democratic, political, and social ideals of Europe and generates a sense of shared European responsibility towards cultural heritage.

Another critical outcome of the analysis undertaken is the CoE's early recognition of the social aspects of heritage. The identification of the social facets of heritage as early as in the 1970s (Chapters 3 and 4) intensified the pressure on experts to consider the public, its values, and its participation in their approach to heritage and its management. By covering seven decades of development of the CoE's heritage policy, it was possible to reach a comprehensive understanding of how the notion of public inclusion and values of heritage for society evolved from extreme passiveness and exclusion in the earlier texts to policies based on democratic participation and that include rather radical concepts, such as 'heritage community', in its latest convention.

The debates regarding the public's value in the CoE's heritage policies, as discussed in Chapters 3–5 in particular, reflected the AHD approach where the notions/aspects relating to the 'public' and 'people' were almost completely removed from the realm of heritage management. Social aspects of heritage were acknowledged in its earlier conventions. Nevertheless, as the findings from Part 2 suggest, the social component served as a reminder for the 'experts' to take into account during the management processes rather than as a genuine call to include the public in heritage processes. Public inclusion, at this point, was used by experts as the 'opportune' element they referred to in political debates when arguing for higher public spending on cultural heritage. However, in reality, their intention was never to start a genuine dialogue with the 'public'; the 'inclusion' and 'participation' they were referring to meant that the public was expected to support their work and passively accept the knowledge they produced. Consequently, it could be argued the setting framed by the AHD model in the last century created the situation of a complete detachment of heritage and experts 'taking care' of it from not only the 'public' but also from the 'public representatives' who consequently find it difficult today to understand the value of heritage for society and to include it more actively in a broader political agenda (local, national, and international). The enormous advocacy work of the heritage professional community that needs to be done in promoting and 'making' others (public and politicians) aware of the role that heritage could play in tackling global challenges comes as the direct result of the AHD-underpinned approach that the same experts' community was propagating throughout the years. The only option at heritage professionals' disposal today is to recognise the limitations that the AHD represents for them and to engage in genuine dialogue with other stakeholders.

With the shift of its heritage discourse during the 1990s and 2000s, the CoE seems to offer a framework in which a democratisation of heritage could be possible. For the CoE, it was the social and political changes in the 1990s that accentuated the limitations of the AHD model, and the organisation started to think about and promote heritage as a part of its wider policies of democratic participation, human rights, and European active citizenship. The CoE today differentiates four dimensions of citizenship: the political/legal, social, cultural, and economic dimensions.[12] Here, the cultural dimension is of particular interest as it refers to the consciousness of a common heritage, which should be developed through the knowledge of cultural heritage, history, and language. Citizenship is also understood as a practice of playing an active role (participating) in society, which implies working towards improving life for all members of society. In addition, participation is not only a condition for effective democratic citizenship but also a core principle of human rights. Therefore, the CoE argues that without participation, many human rights are difficult to access. It is participation through which we can build a society based on human rights, develop social cohesion, and influence decision makers. Consequently, these broader aims begged a change in the CoE's twentieth-century

12 Council of Europe, Council for Cultural Cooperation, 'Education for Democratic Citizenship: Dimensions of Citizenship, Core Competences, Variables and International Activities – prepared by Ruud Veldhuis' [1997] DECS/CIT (97) 23.

AHD-based heritage policies and its view on the participation of the 'public' in heritage processes.

The Faro Convention's concept of 'heritage community' (Charter 7) as a 'community of interest', the self-organised, self-managed group of individuals that aims to use cultural heritage both to enhance the well-being of their territories and to enhance democratic participation among citizenries, presents a response to previous AHD-imposed limitations regarding participation. It is hoped that the Convention's 'heritage community' concept might help relieve identity-related tensions and facilitate new cultural landscapes. It also allows the CoE to achieve a more tolerant and peaceful European society, since it offers a suitable approach to address the complex human geography of Europe today caused by outside and inner migrations. The 'heritage community' concept allows European citizens to generate and negotiate the merging of new identities and cultural narratives.[13] Indeed, the Faro discourse emerging from the human rights-based understanding of heritage has the clear aim of tackling the problem of participation of the 'public' and its passivity when it comes to managing heritage. While the privilege of experts and public authorities is clearly challenged, the Faro discourse does not make experts 'redundant' or public administration unnecessary. Instead, it calls for genuine cooperation of all interested stakeholders, putting experts, authorities, and the public in equal positions of power.

Hence, the findings presented in this volume, derived from a broad exploration of the background of the particular heritage conventions and actions, add a further layer to our understanding of *why* the CoE made certain choices, not only when it comes to the subjects of the conventions but also in their substance and political aim. In addition, the coverage of the chain of CoE texts allowed for a better understanding of their correlations as well as their links with other international texts (particularly those of UNESCO and ICOMOS) and global developments in the field, which additionally enhances our understanding of the particular texts (in comparison to, for example, their analysis in isolation). The importance of these findings for the field of heritage rests in the fact that they accentuate the importance of acknowledging regional approaches to heritage, as it is (most often) through the influence of more progressive ideas developed regionally that global standards are set and discourse enhanced. It is therefore important to have a close look at and a thor-

13 Laia Colomer, 'Exploring Participatory Heritage Governance after the EU Faro Convention' (2021) 13(4) Journal of Cultural Heritage Management and Sustainable Development.

ough understanding of regional developments, for they frame and shape global heritage policies and legislation.

What Are the Characteristics of the Distinctive CoE Discourse, and How Have They Evolved over Time? How Do They Compare to the Generalised Characteristics of the AHD?

Mapping the evolution of the CoE's heritage discourse is a central aspect of this volume, which aims to contribute to the ongoing discussion in heritage studies, where the need to identify multiple discourses among different international and regional institutions, rather than gloss over them by only recognising the generalised character of the AHD (as characterised by Smith), is recognised. Nevertheless, the generalised characteristics of the AHD were used as the reference point against which to measure the specificities and deviations authorised in the CoE's heritage texts. This section, therefore, addresses the findings coming from the consideration of 'how' the CoE framed core notions, such as 'heritage' and the role of 'experts' in its texts. The importance of these findings rests in their ability to demonstrate the existence of multiple heritage discourses and the fascinating ability of the field to adjust and progress depending on the wider institutional, national, regional, or international political and social contexts. An exploration of the CoE heritage texts and activities through discursive lenses allowed for a far more comprehensive understanding of how heritage is perceived and managed across Europe, especially keeping in mind that it is largely through the CoE standard-setting instruments and the discourse they frame that the Member States' heritage policies and legislation are structured. Therefore, by acknowledging the existence of the distinctive CoE heritage discourse, the conversation (and critique) in the heritage field on the 'Eurocentric' nature of global heritage practice turns out to be much more nuanced than it is usually the case, as it shows additional, mostly omitted, layers of the European approach to the subject.

Charting the existence of Smith's AHD within the heritage policy of the CoE proved to be relatively straightforward, with a number of core features extracted at the early stages of the CoE's heritage policy texts (Part 1). Those features emerged as a concrete product, not only of the Critical Discourse Analysis but also as a clear resonance within the responses in some of the in-depth interviews. As characterised by Smith, these core AHD features revolved around the protection of material, monumental, aesthetically pleasing monuments and sites and a belief in the privileged position of (predominantly male) experts as the only ones capable of 'speaking' to and 'educating' the otherwise passive general public.[14] The belief propagated about the intrinsic value of the fabric and great age of monuments brought to the surface a focus on their fragility and their finite and non-renewable nature, and with it an inevitable sense of threat in a rapidly changing world.

Nevertheless, while this understanding of heritage underpinned the CoE's early heritage policies as something old, beautiful, tangible, and monumental, selected by experts, the organisation realised that if it wanted its heritage policies to be aligned with its broader aims, certain restrictions of AHD needed to be addressed. The first (technical) phase of the CoE's heritage activities developed in the 1970s and across the 1980s and 1990s (Part 1) mainly emerged as the reaction to the limitations of the discourse encapsulated, primarily in the 1964 Venice Charter and further in the UNESCO World Heritage Convention. As the analysis in Chapters 3 and 4 identified, the CoE's crucial innovative approach from this period – integrated conservation – moved away from the protection of singular monuments and argued for protecting the monument's surroundings (historical centres), including vernacular architecture and less aesthetically pleasing buildings. This also meant enlarging the definition of heritage to cover industrial, rural, underwater and technical architecture and, with it, undermining the importance of the 'old age' characteristic of the AHD.

Furthermore, with this approach the CoE significantly moved away from UNESCO's quite limiting focus on the monuments with outstanding universal value, which in reality covered/and still does just a small fraction of heritage. This departure allowed for a more holistic, community-based approach which takes into account the way of life of those communities living in historic centres. In addition, the integrated conservation approach brought heritage conservation into the context of spatial planning, legitimising conservators' and archaeologists' roles in broader city planning processes. Admittedly, the decision-making firmly stayed within the realm of experts. Still, the CoE argued for collaboration among different services, notably city planners, conservators, and archaeologists, in order to protect the historic centres and the way of life in them. By framing its approach via integrated conservation, the CoE also moved away from a concept of the 'fragility' and non-renewable nature of heritage that must remain unchanged towards an understanding of heritage as a resource that needs to be used and adapted to present needs. It is an opinion of this book that the concept of 'integrated conservation', introduced in the 1970s, was crucial in introducing heritage in the broader political and economic concerns, shifting the perception of heritage from being a burden for the public budget

14 Smith (n 1).

towards it being a resource for society. It offered a workable framework for all future social, political, and economic challenges. It was the critical step that brought heritage issues and experts into the broader political debate on the development of society.

Essential to the concept of integrated conservation was the acknowledgement (as early as 1973) of the role that heritage (at this point, still only its material manifestation) has on the way of life and full development of the individual. While the analysis of a range of documents emerging from the CoE heritage sector from the 1970s was underpinned mainly by the core postulates of the AHD (such as the materiality of monuments, aesthetics, beauty, and experts' privilege), the recognition of the *social aspects* of the monuments and historic centres is one of the most critical points of the CoE heritage discourse at the time. If the concept of integrated conservation was to be successful, the social aspects of the historical cities could not be ignored. In this respect, the pioneering role of the CoE heritage policy must be recognised, as it allowed for a further reconceptualisation of heritage to emerge at the end of the twentieth century.

An increased reconceptualisation of heritage that happened at the end of the 1990s, in the case of the CoE, underpinned by the broader political and social changes that came with the fall of the Berlin Wall, led to fundamental changes in how heritage and its role were perceived within the CoE's heritage texts and actions. The analysis of the range of documents emerging from the preparatory work for the 2005 Faro Convention and the Convention itself offers a view of the CoE's radical recreation of the heritage discourse. To start with, the Faro Convention proposed what appears to be the broadest definition of heritage in any of the international conventions' texts. Building on its new people-centred approach to heritage, the focus moved from the question of 'What is heritage?' to reflection on 'What heritage does'. This 'new/inclusive heritage' (Chapter 8) puts individuals, and the values heritage has for them individually and collectively, in the centre rather than focusing on the historical and artistic values that experts attach to monuments and sites.[15] Heritage moved from being fragile, limited, and something that needs to be protected for nebulous future generations to being considered a vital resource to be used actively by current generations in various social and political processes. It has been argued in Part 2 that the CoE, with its Faro Convention, emerged as the rare organisation willing to diverge radically from the AHD and put a new way of 'doing' and understanding heritage in motion. The framework pro-

15 Graham Fairclough, 'New Heritage Frontiers' in Council of Europe, *Heritage and Beyond* (Council of Europe Publishing 2009) and Kisić (n 10).

posed by the Faro Convention can indeed be considered the foundation for the inclusive heritage discourse. Its human rights-based approach to heritage, offers, among others, the solutions and the way forward from the AHD-underpinned lack of acknowledgement of heritage as a resource for wider social issues in global and national policies and puts heritage at the heart of the broader political discussion on the future of humanity.

Another recurrent AHD element is the dominance of experts, who were called upon to increase proper and immaculate care for a fragile and non-renewable heritage. In this regard, the analysis in this volume offers a look at the evolution of the place of experts in the CoE's heritage discourse from expert exclusivity (Part 1) to democratic participation (Part 2). The findings emerging from examining the CoE's documents from the formative years (the 1960s and early 1970s) of its heritage policies revealed the intriguing network of heritage scholars and experts working their way to authorising their positions in the international heritage policy arena. They used a motif of 'crisis' and 'threats' coming with rapid development intertwined with the notion of their – that is, the experts – moral obligation to *save* heritage for future generations. In the case of the CoE's policies, this positioning afforded those legitimised as 'experts' not only intellectual and physical access to a range of heritage debates but also secured them a significant position in wider spatial planning processes. The integrated conservation approach basically moved conservation and, especially, archaeology (Part 2) from being predominantly academic disciplines into the role of important players in planning policies on the local, national, and international levels. Disciplinary groups, including architects and archaeologists, used the CoE's heritage initiatives to firmly secure their positions as the only groups capable of identifying and safeguarding Europe's heritage. Their influence was such that the CoE's early conventions completely lost the political dimension expected from the texts adopted by political organisations such as the CoE. That is why the organisation's Secretariat refers to those conventions as 'technical'. The 'technicality' of those 'first generation conventions' also meant that individuals and the public were rarely acknowledged as engaging in any active type of preservation, protection, or conservation. The authorisation of experts that happened during the 1960s and 1970s established the clear difference between 'us' (experts) and 'them' (everyone else). It allowed the architects, conservators, and archaeologists to establish themselves, through the standard-setting documents of the CoE, as the only legitimate 'spokespersons' for heritage on behalf of the Europeans.

The change introduced with the inclusion of heritage in the CoE's wider democratic participation debate at the beginning of the 2000s, which culminated in the Faro Convention, deeply challenged the experts' privileges enshrined in the AHD and the CoE's 'technical' conventions. As analyses of documents and in-depth interviews suggest, there is still unnecessary reluctance from the expert groups towards the new approach proposed by the CoE. In this regard, this volume suggests, it is essential that heritage experts understand that the current model underpinned by the AHD, even though it gives them a feeling of dominance in the field, essentially keeps them out of the more considerable political debate and strategic planes when it comes to the future of our societies. In other words, perpetuating the AHD understanding of heritage as something that needs experts' protection, that is detached from social processes, and that is a subject that only a small group of experts can understand keeps heritage matter away from more significant political discussions, and thus heritage rarely takes an important position in strategic political documents (such as the Sustainable Development Goals, for example). As long as heritage, in political discussions, is considered to be a significant financial burden on public funds that is taken care of by a small group of experts rather than a resource that needs to be used by and for the benefit of all, experts will have a hard time advocating for heritage's place in strategic political decisions. Therefore, this volume argues, heritage professionals and their respective institutions should have a particular interest in changing their AHD-based practices if they want to have a more significant role in the broader conversation on sustainable development and peacebuilding or a general discussion on improving the living conditions of communities. The currently promoted CoE approach offers a possible framework for the new discourse, which would address the limitations the AHD model imposes.

What Was/Is the CoE's Impact on the Global Heritage Discourse? What Was/Is Its Impact on the Member States' Heritage Legislation, Taking into Account the Legally Binding Nature of Its Conventions?

One of the findings from the overview of the CoE's heritage activities in this book relates to the impact the ideas and notions developed at the CoE have had on global and European heritage policies and practices. When it comes to the international level, the formative years of international heritage practice and policies can be characterised as a period of intense cooperation among major international heritage bodies. This cooperation allowed for the circulation of ideas and, as such, for defining and authorising the dominant heritage discourse legitimised through the chain of adopted heritage texts. In this context of intense collaboration and interaction, the role and influence of the CoE have mostly been overlooked. Therefore, the importance of the findings presented in this section for the field of heritage rest in the fact that they elucidate the background of some of the important developments in international heritage legislation and standard-setting instruments that had their origin under the auspices of the CoE. They also highlight the idea that underpins this research, namely that it is important to acknowledge the existence of multiple heritage (institutional) discourses (among them the CoE's heritage discourse) instead of glossing over them with a generalised AHD characterisation, which has the tendency to undermine important nuance, that, as demonstrated with the example of the CoE, were decisive in the evolution of the field in general.

As the analysis of the archival documents (Part 1) illustrated, the CoE played a significant role in this process and was at the origin of some pioneering ideas that were further enshrined in the documents on a global and national level. Among those ideas were, for example, the CoE's early recognition of the problem of illicit trafficking of cultural goods, which was a main incentive for drafting its 1969 Convention on Protection of the Archaeological Heritage. Furthermore, the initiative for the Convention on Underwater Heritage (1987), which conceptualised the central notions that would later be enshrined in the UNESCO Convention on the Protection of the Underwater Cultural Heritage (2001), serves as an example of the reciprocal influence organisations have had on each other's work. The CoE's recognition of vernacular heritage and its value to society also moved the discussion forward on the international level and inspired an enlargement of the concept of heritage and the values attached to it. While some of these achievements, from today's perspective, sound relatively minor, at the time when they were articulated and negotiated, they presented a ground-breaking development that allowed the field to progress. Therefore, the global impact of the CoE's heritage approach is not negligible; however, being a key European standard-setting organisation in the field meant that the organisation has primarily had a central role in harmonising European heritage legislation. Its concepts, such as integrated conservation, have been enshrined in the legislation of all the CoE Member States. It became the cornerstone of how conservation has been perceived and practised across the continent. When it comes to archaeology, as stated by Schut, the CoE Valletta Convention (1992) has become such an integrated part of the European archaeological practice that the younger generation of archaeologists can hardly imagine the pre-Valletta era.[16] The conventions on the protection of architectural and archaeological heritage introduced heritage into special planning and ensured that the voice of heritage had to be taken into

---

16 Peter Schut, 'Foreword' in Victoria M. van der Haas and Peter A.C. Schut (eds), *The Valletta Convention: Twenty Years After – Benefits, Problems, Challenges – EAC Occasional Paper No. 9* (Europae Archaeologiae Consilium 2014) 9.

account in any development plans. Praised by conservators and archaeologists, these conventions are still the core of European heritage management today.

The new developments arising from the decision to formulate its heritage discourse based on the human rights approach (Part 2) once again highlighted the CoE as an organisation that is capable and willing to question existing practices and challenge them. This book argues that the new framework outlined in the Faro Convention has significant potential to be a major influence on the development of global international law in the field. The fact that the Convention aims to leave the closed realm of the AHD-framed heritage field and to enter into dialogue and participate in a broader social and political context means that its implementation depends on the range of social arrangements on local, national, and international levels rather than on standard-setting declarations.

For the Faro Convention to be operational, certain conditions need to be met, such as the presence of an active civil society interested in specific heritage; a presence of consensus on an expanded common vision of heritage; a presence of supportive political players and other stakeholders and their willingness to cooperate; and, more importantly, a presence of a local, national, or international ambition for a more democratic socio-economic model. It is clear that the Faro Convention represents a rather powerful political project that challenges many well-established policies and practices and, as such, encounters significant resistance and opposition.

The importance of the CoE is that it succeeded in articulating and legalising the framework that presents a genuine philosophical and methodological shift in our understanding of what heritage is and what it does. It, therefore, has the potential to become the canonical text of the new/inclusive heritage discourse, making the heritage process more inclusive and democratic in the new millennia. The proposed framework offers a clear path for dialogue and the dismantling of the AHD-framed notions of heritage, passive audience, and expert privileges. It is time for the heritage sector, followed by the heritage standard-setting instruments, to fully come to terms with the role and consequences of the AHD and to promote and implement genuine and successful policies of cooperation and dialogue which will secure a place for heritage in broader political and social policies and processes. It seems that the CoE is attentive to play a significant role in this process, which once again is framing the international heritage discourse, this time by challenging the same AHD postulates that it helped to legitimise in its twentieth-century heritage treaties. In this context (and paradoxically) the CoE as the 'Eurocentric' organisation proved to be leading heritage player in the 'fight' against 'Eurocentric' dominant international discourse (AHD), by offering a framework for a new, inclusive way forward.

Primary Sources: Council of Europe Archival Documents

Council of Europe Documents

Council of Europe (1948). *Congress of Europe (The Hague, 7–11 May 1948)*

Council of Europe (1949). *Statute of the Council of Europe*, European Treaty Series – No.1

Council of Europe, Committee of Ministers (1949). *Minutes of the Meetings* (CM (49) PV2E)

Council of Europe, Committee of Ministers (1949). *Resolution* (49) 29 – *Cultural Recommendations*

Council of Europe (1950), *Convention for the Protection of Human Rights and Fundamental Freedoms*, ETS No. 005

Council of Europe, Committee of Ministers (1950). *Resolution* (50) 27 – *Cultural Questions*

Council of Europe, Committee of Ministers (1950). *Minutes of the Meetings* (CM (50) PV3E) Council of Europe, Committee of Cultural Experts (1950). Report of the Committee of Cultural Experts to the Committee of Ministers (CM(50)34)

Council of Europe, Committee of Cultural Experts (1951). *Cultural Relations and the Council of Europe – Note by Mr Seymour* (CM/WP III (51) 45)

Council of Europe, Committee of Cultural Experts (1952). *Proposal Concerning the Organisation of a Series of European Exhibitions – Submitted by the Belgian Delegation* (EXP/Cult (52) 27 Appendix D)

Council of Europe, Committee of Cultural Experts (1952). *Report* (CM/12 (52) 49)

Council of Europe (1952). *Agreement between the Council of Europe and the United Nations Educational, Scientific and Cultural Organisation*

Council of Europe, Committee of Cultural Experts (1952). *Tentative draft European Cultural Convention* (EXP/Cult (52) 24)

Council of Europe, Committee of Cultural Experts (1952). *Tentative draft European Cultural – Amendments proposed by the Secretary-General* (EXP/Cult (52) 24 Amendment No.1)

Council of Europe, Committee of Cultural Experts (1952). *Tentative draft European Cultural – Amendments proposed by the Belgian Delegation* (EXP/Cult (52) 24 Amendment No.2)

Council of Europe (1953). The European Round Table Discussion (Rome, 13th-16th October, 1953)

Council of Europe, Committee of Cultural Experts (1953). *Draft European Cultural Convention – Submitted by the United Kingdom Delegation* (EXP/Cult B (53) 2)

Council of Europe, Committee of Cultural Experts (1953). *Draft European Cultural Convention – Amended version of the draft submitted by the UK delegation* (EXP/Cult B (53) 1)

Council of Europe, Committee of Cultural Experts (1953). *Draft European Cultural Convention – Amendments proposed by the Secretariat-General* (Amendment to EXP/Cult (53) 1)

Council of Europe, Committee of Cultural Experts (1953). *Draft European Cultural Convention – Amended version of the draft submitted by the UK delegation* (EXP/Cult/ B (53) 2Revised)

Council of Europe, Committee of Cultural Experts (1953). *Memorandum of the Irish Delegation on the Draft European Cultural Convention* (Amendment 2 to EXP/Cult (53) 1)

Council of Europe, Committee of Cultural Experts (1953). *Draft European Cultural Convention – Drafting amendments proposed by the United Kingdom Delegation* (Amendment 3 to EXP/Cult (53) 1)

Council of Europe, Committee of Cultural Experts (1953). *Draft European Cultural Convention* (EXP/Cult (53) 15)

Council of Europe, Committee of Cultural Experts (1953). *Draft European Cultural Convention – Text proposed by the Drafting Sub-Committee (composed of Haigh (UK), Bizos (France), Hayes (Ireland) and Reinink (Netherlands)* (EXP/Cult (53) 17)

Council of Europe, Committee of Cultural Experts (1953). *Draft European Cultural Convention – Revised text submitted by the Secretariat-General*) (EXP/Cult (53) 20)

Council of Europe, Committee of Cultural Experts (1953). *Meeting of the Art Specialists – Report to the Committee of Cultural Experts* (EXP/Cult (53) 21)

Council of Europe, Committee of Cultural Experts (1953). *Draft European Cultural Convention – Explanatory Memorandum by the Secretariat-General* (EXP/Cult (53) 22)

Council of Europe, Committee of Cultural Experts (1953). *Draft European Cultural Convention – Observations of the United Kingdom Delegation of the present text of the Convention* (EXP/Cult (53) 31)

Council of Europe, Committee of Cultural Experts (1953). *Draft European Cultural Convention – Observations of the Norwegian Delegation* (EXP/Cult (53) 46)

Council of Europe, Committee of Cultural Experts (1953). *Draft European Cultural Convention – Revised text submitted by the Secretariat-General* (EXP/Cult (53) 20 Revised)

Council of Europe, Committee of Cultural Experts (1953). *Draft Report of the Seventh Session (1s – 3rd December 1953)* (EXP/Cult (53) 48)

Council of Europe, Committee of Cultural Experts (1953). *Memorandum presented by the Belgian delegation in the Meeting of Art Specialists* (EXP/Cult/Art (53) 1)

Council of Europe, Committee of Cultural Experts (1954). *Draft European Cultural Convention – Memorandum by the Secretariat-General* (EXP/Cult (54) 3)

Council of Europe, Committee of Ministers (1954). *Report of the Eight Session of the Committee of Cultural Experts* (CM (54) 61)

Council of Europe, Committee of Ministers (1954). *UNESCO Proposals for the Programme of Work of the Council of Europe – Letter from the Director General of UNESCO* (CM (54) 19)

Council of Europe, Committee of Ministers (1954). *The Conference of Sao Paulo on the Cultural Relations between the Old World and the New* (CM (54) 25)

Council of Europe, Committee of Ministers (1954). *Twenty-second Meeting of the Ministers' Deputies – European Cultural Convention (Memorandum circulated by the United Kingdom Deputy during the Twenty-Second Meeting)* (CM (54) 125)

Council of Europe, Committee of Ministers (1954). *Twenty-second Meeting of the Ministers' Deputies – European Cultural Convention (Explanatory Memorandum by the Secretariat-General)* (CM (54) 110)

Council of Europe, Committee of Cultural Experts (1954). *Summary of the Conclusions* (EXP/Cult (54) 28)

Council of Europe (1954). *European Cultural Convention (ETS No. 018)*

Council of Europe, Committee of Cultural Experts (1955). *Report of the Council of Europe/UNESCO inter-Secretariat meeting to Cultural and Scientific Questions of Mutual Interest* (EXP/Cult/CE-UNESCO (55) 1)

Council of Europe, Committee of Cultural Experts (1955). *Examination of Questions of European Interest in the UNESCO Programme and of any other Questions of Interest to the Two Organisations* (EXP/Cult (55) 35)

Council of Europe, Committee of Cultural Experts (1956). *Report of the Special Meeting for the Examination of Questions Included in the UNESCO Programme of Interest to the Council of Europe* (EXP/Cult (56) 27)

Council of Europe, Committee of Cultural Experts (1957). *Report of Mr Reinink, Observer of the Council of Europe at the Ninth Session of the General Conference of UNESCO* (EXP/Cult (57) 64)

Council of Europe, Committee of Cultural Experts (1958). *Report of the Sub-committee on the participation of the Council of Europe in the Major Project of UNESCO* (EXP/Cult (58) 33)

Council of Europe (1969). *European Convention on the Protection of the Archaeological Heritage (ETS No. 066)*

Council of Europe, Committee of Ministers (1954). *Memorandum by the Secretariat of UNESCO on the Conference of Sao Paolo on the cultural relations between the Old World and the New* (CM (54) 25)

Council of Europe, Committee of Ministers (1958). *Resolution (58) 13 – Cultural Fund of the Council of Europe*

Council of Europe, Committee of Ministers (1960). *Resolution (60) 32 – Cultural and scientific cooperation in Europe*

Council of Europe, Committee of Ministers (1961). *Resolution (61) 39 – Cultural and scientific co-operation: Setting up of the Council for Cultural Co-operation*

Council of Europe, Committee of Ministers (1961). *Resolution (61) 40 – Cultural and scientific co-operation: Transfer to the Council for Cultural Co-operation of the cultural activities listed in the Appendix to Resolution (59) 23*

Council of Europe, Committee of Ministers (1961). *Resolution (61) 41 – Cultural and scientific co-operation: Activities of member Governments with a view to European Co-operation in the fields of education and of cultural and scientific affairs*

Council of Europe, Committee of Ministers (1961). *Resolution (61) 42 – Cultural and scientific co-operation: Payment of the travel and subsistence expenses of members of the Council of Cultural Co-operation and its permanent Committees*

Council of Europe (1961, revised in 1996). *European Social Charter* (*ETS No. 163*)

Council of Europe, Committee of Experts for the Conservation of Nature and Landscape (1962). *Text of Recommendation concerning the Safeguarding of the beauty and character of landscapes and sites adopted by the UNESCO General Conference* (EXP/Nat (63) 15)

Council of Europe, Council for Cultural Cooperation (1963). *Fifth Session – Draft Agenda* (*CCC (63) OJ 2*)

Council of Europe, European Conference of Local Authorities (1963). *Arrangements for the European Conference on the Preservation and Development of Ancient Buildings and Historic or Artistic Sites* (CPL/P (4) 44)

Council of Europe, Council for Cultural Cooperation (1964). *7th Session – Project for European action to protect the archaeological heritage: Draft European Convention Presented by the Italian Delegation* (DECS/Cult (64) 12)

Council of Europe, Council for Cultural Cooperation (1965). *Report by Massimo Pallottino – Proposal for European Action for the Protection of the Archaeological Heritage* (CCC/AC (65) 13)

Council of Europe, Committee of Ministers (1965). *Memorandum presented by Mr. Pietro Gazzola on Preservation and Development of Groups and Areas of Buildings of Historical or Artistic Interest* (CCC/CDS/CT (65) 8)

Council of Europe, Committee of Ministers – Committee of Technical Advisers (1965). *Report – Preservation and Development of Groups and Areas of Buildings of Historical or Artistic Interest* (CCC/CDS/CT (65) 5)

Council of Europe, Committee of Ministers (1965). *Confrontation B – Problèmes posés par la réanimation des monuments dans leur cadre esthétique ou naturel, offrant un intérêt culturel, qui ne remplissent plus les fonctions pour lesquelles ils ont été conçus* (CCC/CDS/B (65) 27')

Council of Europe, Council for Cultural Cooperation (1966). *Ninth Session – Cultural activities: Supplementary report presented by the Cultural Affairs Division* (CCC/AC (65) 14)

Council of Europe, Council for Cultural Cooperation (1966). *10th Session – Annotated draft European Convention on the prohibition of the illicit export and import of articles of cultural and archaeological interested presented by the Italian Delegation* (CCC/AC (65) 19 Revised 2)

Council of Europe, Council for Cultural Cooperation (1966). *9th Session – Cultural Activities Draft Report* (CCC (66) Misc 3)

Council of Europe, Council for Cultural Cooperation (1966). *10th Session – Report by the Cultural Affairs Division* (CCC/AC (66) 40)

Council of Europe, Committee of Technical Advisers (1966). *Protection and Enhancement of Historical or Artistic Buildings and Sites – Text of a letter addressed to the Secretariat by Professor Raymond M. Lemaire* (CCC/AC (66) 82)

Council of Europe, Committee of Ministers (1966). *Resolution (66) 19 – Criterial and Methods of Cataloguing Ancient Buildings and Historical or Artistic Sites*

Council of Europe, Committee of Ministers (1966). *Resolution (66) 20 – The Reviving of Monuments*

Council of Europe, Council for Cultural Cooperation (1966). *11th Session – Working Party on the problem of protecting the European Archaeological Heritage* (CCC/AC (66) 164)

Council of Europe, Committee of Ministers (1966). *Preservation and development of groups and areas of buildings of historical or artistic interest – Symposium B, Vienna 1965* (CCC/AC (66) 52 Provisional)

Council of Europe, Committee of Ministers (1967). *Symposium C – Principles and practice of active preservation and rehabilitation of groups and areas of buildings of historical or artistic interest, Bath 1966* (COE.H.2.4/67 PR)

Council of Europe, Committee of Ministers (1967). *Symposium D – Active maintenance of monuments, groups and areas of buildings of historical or artistic interest within the context of regional planning, The Hague 1967* (COE.H.2.4/AC)

Council of Europe, Council for Cultural Cooperation (1967). *Eleventh Session – Working Party on the problem of protecting the European archaeological heritage* (CCC/AC (66) 164)

Council of Europe, Council for Cultural Cooperation (1967). *Draft European Convention on the Protection of the Archaeological Heritage* (CCC/AC (67) 40 Provisional)

Council of Europe, Council for Cultural Cooperation (1967). *Working Party for the preparation of a European Convention on the protection of the archaeological heritage – Second Meeting* (CCC/AC (67) 41)

Council of Europe, Council for Cultural Cooperation (1967). *Twelfth Session – Fourth Draft of a European Convention on the protection of the archaeological heritage* (CCC/AC (67) 51)

Council of Europe, Council for Cultural Cooperation (1967). *Thirteenth Session – Fifth Draft of a European Convention on the protection of the archaeological heritage* (CCC/AC (67) 100)

Council of Europe, Committee of Ministers (1968). *Symposium E – Policy for the preservation and rehabilitation, Avignon 1968* (COE.H.2.3/68 PO)

Council of Europe, Committee of Ministers (1968). *Note on the action taken by the Council of Europe in the field of the preservation and rehabilitation of groups and areas of building of historical or artistical interest* (CCC/ACV (68) 62)

Council of Europe, Council for Cultural Cooperation (1968). *Draft European Convention on the protection of the archaeological heritage adopted by the Council for Cultural Cooperation at its Thirteenth Session* (CCC/ACV (68) 15)

Council of Europe, Committee of Ministers (1968). *Resolution (68) 11 – on the Principles and Practice of the Active Preservation and Rehabilitation of Groups and Areas of Buildings of Historical or Artistic Interest*

Council of Europe, Committee of Ministers (1968). *Resolution (68) 12 – on the active Maintenance of Monuments, Groups and Areas of Buildings of Historical or Artistic Interest within the Context of Regional Planning*

Council of Europe, Committee of Ministers (1968). *Resolution (68) 16 – organisation of a Conference of Ministers most Directly Responsible for the Preservation and Rehabilitation of Groups and areas of Buildings of Historical or Artistic Interest*

Council of Europe, Committee of Ministers (1969). *Conclusions of the 177th Meeting of the Ministers' Deputies* (CM/Del/Dec (69) 177)

Council of Europe, Committee of Ministers (1969). *Forty-Fourth Session of the Committee of Ministers (5–6 May 1969, London)*

Council of Europe (1969). *20 Years of Educational and Cultural Activity in the Service of Europe (1949 – 1969)* (COE.H.I.9/69 ED)

Council of Europe, Conference of Ministers Chiefly Responsible for the Preservation and Rehabilitation of Groups and Areas of Buildings of Historic or Artistic Interest (1969). *Report – Bases for common European action to protect the architectural heritage of the past* (B (69) 71)

Council of Europe (1969). *First Conference of European Ministers Responsible for the Preservation and Rehabilitation of the Cultural Heritage of Monuments and Sites – Resolutions of the Conference (Brussels, 25–27 November 1969)*

Council of Europe (1969). *European Convention on the Protection of the Archaeological Heritage*, ETS No. 66

Council of Europe (1969). *Explanatory Report to the European Convention on the Protection of the Archaeological Heritage*, ETS No. 66

Council of Europe (1970). *Preservation and Rehabilitation of the European Cultural Heritage of Monuments and Sites – Speech of his Highness the Prince de Liege to the PACE* (CCC/ACV (70) 3)

Council of Europe, Committee of Ministers (1970). *Conférence des Ministres Européens Responsables de la Sauvegarde et de la Réanimation du Patrimoine Culturel Immobilier – Bruxelles 1969 – Note du Secrétariat General* (CM (70) 44)

Council of Europe, Committee of Ministers (1970). *Conclusions of the 187th Meeting of the Ministers' Deputies* (CM/Del/Dec (70) 187)

Council of Europe, Committee of Ministers (1970). *Conclusions of the 188th Meeting of the Ministers' Deputies* (CM/Del/Dec (70) 188)

Council of Europe, Committee of Ministers (1970). *Conclusions of the 191st Meeting of the Ministers' Deputies* (CM/Del/Dec (70) 191)

Council of Europe, Committee of Ministers (1970). *Conclusions of the 192nd Meeting of the Ministers' Deputies* (CM/Del/Dec (70) 192)

Council of Europe, Committee of Ministers (1970). *Conclusions of the 194th Meeting of the Ministers' Deputies* (CM/Del/Dec (70) 194)

Council of Europe, Committee of Ministers (1971). *Conclusions of the 196th Meeting of the Ministers' Deputies* (CM/Del/Dec (71) 196)

Council of Europe, Committee of Ministers (1971). *Conclusions of the 198th Meeting of the Ministers' Deputies* (CM/Del/Dec (71) 198)

Council of Europe, Committee of Ministers (1971). *Conclusions of the 204th Meeting of the Ministers' Deputies* (CM/Del/Dec (71) 204)

Council of Europe, Committee on Monuments and Sites (1971). *Council of Europe Action for the Preservation and Rehabilitation of the Cultural Heritage of Monuments and Sites* (DELA/MS (71) 1)

Council of Europe, Committee on Monuments and Sites (1971). *1st Meeting – Annotated Agenda* (DELA/MS (71) 2)

Council of Europe, Committee on Monuments and Sites (1971). *1st Meeting – Background Material relating to the Preservation and Rehabilitation of the Cultural Heritage of Monuments and Sites* (DELA/MS (71) 3)

Council of Europe, Committee on Monuments and Sites (1971). *Towards a new European polity for the Preservation and Rehabilitation of Groups of Buildings and Sites of Historical Value – Extracts from the consolidated report on the possibilities resulting from the CCC's work 1964–69* (DELA/MS (71) 5)

Council of Europe, Committee on Monuments and Sites (1971). *The Present-Day Value of Europe's Heritage of Historic Monuments and Sites – Document prepared by Mr. Raymond Lemaire* (DELA/MS (71) 6 Revised)

Council of Europe, Committee on Monuments and Sites (1971). *Split Declaration – European Symposium of Towns of Historic Interest* (DELA/MS (71) 7)

Council of Europe, Committee on Monuments and Sites (1971). *Protection of Europe's Architectural Heritage – Memorandum submitted by Europa Nostra* (DELA/MS (71) 8)

Council of Europe, Committee on Monuments and Sites (1971). *Year Devoted to the Preservation and Rehabilitation of the Cultural Heritage of Monuments and Sites – Secretariat Memorandum* (DELA/MS (71) 10)

Council of Europe, Committee on Monuments and Sites (1971). *Structural and Operational Organisation of the Committee's Work* (DELA/MS (71) 11)

Council of Europe, Committee on Monuments and Sites (1971). *"A Future for the Past" – A Civic Trust Film – Information Paper* (DELA/MS (71) 13)

Council of Europe, Committee on Monuments and Sites (1971). *European Year 1975 – Memorandum by Mr Duncan Sandys* (DELA/MS (71) 16)

Council of Europe, Committee on Monuments and Sites (1971). *1st Session – Report of the General Discussion* (DELA/MS (71) 17)

Council of Europe, Committee on Monuments and Sites (1971). *1st Session – Report* (DELA/MS (71) 18)

Council of Europe, Committee on Monuments and Sites (1972). *Economic and Social Problems Arising from the Revival of the Cultural and Artistic Heritage of Buildings – Study by Mr Jean-Paul Pigeat* (DELA/MS (72) 1)

Council of Europe, Committee on Monuments and Sites (1972). *Publications relating to the Preservation and Rehabilitation of the Cultural Heritage of Monuments and Sites* (DELA/MS (72) 2)

Council of Europe, Committee on Monuments and Sites (1972). *Technical Assistance – Secretariat Memorandum* (DELA/MS/CD (72) 2)

Council of Europe, Committee on Monuments and Sites (1972). *Proposal for a Programme for the 1975 Year – Organising Committee of the Year (1st Meeting)* (DELA/MS/CO (72) 3)

Council of Europe, Committee on Monuments and Sites (1972). *Co-operation with UNESCO* (DELA/MS/CD (72) 4)

Council of Europe, Committee on Monuments and Sites (1972). *Man in a European Society – The Improvement of Man's Physical Environment in the Town and in the Country: Extract for the Intergovernmental Work Programme of the Council of Europe 1973–1974* (DELA/MS (72) 4)

Council of Europe, Committee on Monuments and Sites (1972). *Report of the Meeting* (DELA/MS (72) 5)

Council of Europe, Committee on Monuments and Sites (1972). *Report of the 1st meeting of the Organising Committee* (DELA/MS/CO (72) 6)

Council of Europe, Committee on Monuments and Sites (1972). *General Principles – Secretariat Memorandum* (DELA/MS/CD (72) 6)

Council of Europe, Committee on Monuments and Sites (1972). *European Programme of Pilot Projects – Criteria for the Selection and Implementation of the Programme* (DELA/MS (72) 8)

Council of Europe, Committee on Monuments and Sites (1972). *European Architectural Heritage Year 1975 – Report of the 2nd meeting of the Organising Committee* (DELA/MS (72) 9

Council of Europe, Committee on Monuments and Sites (1972). *Technical Assistance – Secretariat Memorandum* (DELA/MS/CD (72) 11

Council of Europe, Committee on Monuments and Sites (1972). *Historic Buildings: Their Care and Repair – The Availability of Manpower Specialised in Traditional Techniques* (DELA/MS (72) 13)

Council of Europe, Committee on Monuments and Sites (1972). *Report of the 2nd Meeting* (DELA/MS (72) 17)

Council of Europe, Committee on Monuments and Sites (1972). *European Architectural Heritage Year 1975 – Aims, Organisation and Activities* (DELA/MS/CO (72) 19)

Council of Europe, Committee of Ministers (1972). *Resolution (72) 20 – Interim Measures for the Protection of the Cultural Heritage of Monuments and Sites*

Council of Europe, Committee of Ministers (1972). *Resolution (72) 21 – On the Compilation of National Inventories of Monuments, Groups of Buildings and Sites of Historical or Artistic Interest*

Council of Europe, Committee on Monuments and Sites (1973). *Towards a Comprehensive Policy of Conservation of the Architectural Heritage: General Principles – Professor R. Lemaire* (DELA/MS/CD (73) 1)

Council of Europe, Committee on Monuments and Sites (1973). *European Architectural Heritage Campaign – Organising Committee Report* (DELA/MS/CO (73) 2)

Council of Europe, Committee on Monuments and Sites (1973). *Report of the 3rd Meeting* (DELA/MS (73) 2)

Council of Europe, Committee on Monuments and Sites (1973). *Technical Assistance* (DELA/MS (73) 4)

Council of Europe, Committee on Monuments and Sites (1973). *EAHY Congress 1975 – International Organising Committee Note* (DELA/MS/CO (73) 7)

Council of Europe, Committee on Monuments and Sites (1973). *European Architectural Heritage Year 1975 – Report of the International Organising Committee* (DELA/MS/CO (73) 9)

Council of Europe, Committee on Monuments and Sites (1973). *Economic and Social Problems Arising from the Revival of the Cultural and Artistic Heritage of Buildings – Study by Jean-Paul Pigeat* (DELA/MS (73) 12)

Council of Europe, Committee on Monuments and Sites (1973). *General Principles – Comments on Mr. Lemaire's report made by the Sub-Committee appointed by the Committee on Monuments and Sites* (DELA/MS (73) 13)

Council of Europe, Committee on Monuments and Sites (1973). *Report – 2nd Session of the Committee on Monuments and Sites (Strasbourg, 22–26 May 1973)* (DELA/MS (73) 15)

Council of Europe, Committee on Monuments and Sites (1973). *Sauvons le Visage de l'Europe –Série d'Étude: François Sorlin, Piero Gazzola et Raymond Lemaire* (DELA/MS (73) 16)

Council of Europe, Committee on Monuments and Sites (1973). *The Social and Economic Implications of Conservation – European Programme of Pilot Projects: Symposium No. 1*) (DELA/MS (73) 19 revised)

Council of Europe, Committee on Monuments and Sites (1973). *European Programme of Pilot Projects – Purpose, Structure and Scope* (DELA/MS (73) 25)

Council of Europe, Committee on Monuments and Sites (1974). *European Charter for the Preservation and Rehabilitation of the Architectural Heritage – Preliminary Draft (DELA/MS (73) 27)*

Council of Europe, Committee on Monuments and Sites (1974). *Adaptation of Laws and Regulations to meet the Requirements of the Active Preservation of the Cultural Heritage of Monuments and Sites and its Integration into Contemporary Society – Draft Recommendation to Governments* (DELA/MS/CD (74) 1)

Council of Europe, Committee on Monuments and Sites (1974). *Report of the 4th Meeting* (DELA/MS (74) 4)

Council of Europe, Committee on Monuments and Sites (1974). *Report of the 5th Meeting* (DELA/MS (74) 9)

Council of Europe, Committee on Monuments and Sites (1974). *EAHY 1975 International Organising Committee – Report of the 5th Meeting* (DELA/MS/CO (74) 10)

Council of Europe, Committee on Monuments and Sites (1974). *Council of Europe Action after 1975* (DELA/MS (74) 12)

Council of Europe, Committee on Monuments and Sites (1974). *Report of the 3rd Session* (DELA/MS (74) 23)

Council of Europe, Committee on Monuments and Sites (1974). *Amsterdam Congress – Themes* (DELA/MS (74) 24)

Council of Europe, Committee on Monuments and Sites (1974). *Report of the 6th Meeting* (DELA/MS (74) 27)

Council of Europe, Committee on Monuments and Sites (1974). *Report of the 7th Meeting* (DELA/MS (74) 29)

Council of Europe, Committee on Monuments and Sites (1975). *Draft European Charter of the Architectural Heritage – Adopted at the 4th Session of the Committee on Monuments and Sites* (DELA/MS (75) 32 / CM (75) 171)

Council of Europe, Committee on Monuments and Sites (1975). EAHY 1975 – *Table of Activities undertaken by the National Committees* (DELA/MS/Inf (75) 4)

Council of Europe, Committee on Monuments and Sites (1975). *Report of the 9th Meeting* (DELA/MS (75) 25)

Council of Europe, Committee on Monuments and Sites (1975). *Draft European Charter of the Architectural Heritage* (DELA/MS (75) 26)

Council of Europe, Committee on Monuments and Sites (1975). *Draft Programme 1976* (DELA/MS (75) 27)

Council of Europe, Committee on Monuments and Sites (1975). *Summary of the Comments made by National Committees on the Draft on the Draft Recommendation to Governments* (DELA/MS/CD (74) *12 revised*) *prepared by the Secretariat* (DELA/MS (75) 28)

Council of Europe, Committee on Monuments and Sites (1975). *Draft European Charter of the Architectural Heritage – Adopted at the 4th Session* (DELA/MS (75) 32)

Council of Europe, Committee on Monuments and Sites (1975). *Report of the 4th Session* (DELA/MS (75) 33)

Council of Europe, Committee on Monuments and Sites (1975). *Social Cost of the Integrated Conservation of Historic Centres – Symposium II* (DELA/MS (75) 34)

Council of Europe, Committee on Monuments and Sites (1975). *Recommendations to Governments – Amended Draft by Mr Pirlot* (DELA/MS (75) 35)

Council of Europe, Committee on Monuments and Sites (1975). *European Programme of Pilot Projects* (DELA (75) 37)

Council of Europe – Congress on the European Architectural Heritage, Amsterdam (1975). *Amsterdam Declaration*

Council of Europe (1975). *European Charter of the Architectural Heritage*

Council of Europe, Committee of Ministers (1976). *Intergovernmental Work Programme – Draft Medium-Term Plan 1976–1980* (CM (76) 113)

Council of Europe, Committee on Monuments and Sites (1976). Projet de recommandation concernant l'adaptation des system législatifs et réglementaires en vue de faire face aux exigences de la conservation active et de l'intégration du patrimoine culturel immobilier dans la société contemporaine (CM (76) 22 / DELA/MS (76) 1)

Council of Europe, Committee on Monuments and Sites (1976). *Rapport de la reunion ad hoc* (CM (76) 22 / DELA/MS (76) 2)

Council of Europe, Committee on Monuments and Sites (1976). *Rapport de la 6e Session* (CM (76) 199)

Council of Europe, Committee of Ministers (1976). *Resolution (76) 28 – Concerning the Adaptation of Laws and Regulations to the Requirements of Integrated Conservation of the Architectural Heritage*

Council of Europe, Steering Committee for Regional Planning and the Architectural Heritage (CDAT) (1977). *Report of the 1st Meeting* (CM (77) 112 / CDAT (77) 13)

Council of Europe, Steering Committee for Regional Planning and the Architectural Heritage (CDAT) (1978). *Report of the 2nd Meeting* (CM (78) 197 / CDAT (78) 15)

Council of Europe, Conference of Local and Regional Authorities of Europe (1978). *Environment and Town Planning Committee – Urban Renewal Campaign* (CPL/Env (12) 17)

Council of Europe, Committee of Ministers (1978). *Declaration on Human Rights*

Council of Europe, 2nd Conference of European Ministers responsible for Cultural Affairs 1978). *Resolution No.1 on the European Cultural Charter* (Athens, 24–26 October 1978)

Council of Europe, Directorate of Environment and Local Authorities (1979). *Conservation of the European Architectural Heritage: List of Available Council of Europe Documents* (DELA/Centre/MS (79) 2)

Council of Europe, Steering Committee for Regional Planning and the Architectural Heritage (CDAT) (1979). *Rapport final sur la situation du patrimoine architectural en Europe* (CM (79) 64 / CDAT (78) 4 révisé 2)

Council of Europe, Steering Committee for Regional Planning and the Architectural Heritage (CDAT) (1979). *Report of the 3rd Meeting* (CM (79) 148 / CDAT (79) 10)

Council of Europe, Steering Committee for Regional Planning and the Architectural Heritage (CDAT) (1980). *Report of the 4th Meeting* (CM (80) 220 / CDAT (80) 20)

Council of Europe, Committee of Ministers (1980). *Recommendation No. R (80) 16) – of the Committee of Ministers to Member States on the Specialised Training of Architects, Town Planners, civil Engineers and Landscape Designers.*

Council of Europe, Council for Cultural Co-operation (1980). *The European Cultural Charter – Preliminary Study* (CDCC (80) 8)

Council of Europe, Committee of Ministers (1981). *Recommendation No. R (81) 13 on the action in aid of certain declining craft trades in the context of craft activity*

Council of Europe, Conference of Local and Regional Authorities of Europe (1981). *4th European Symposium of Historic Towns (Fribourg, Switzerland) – Final Declaration* (CONF/Hist (81) 9-E)

Council of Europe, Steering Committee for Urban Policies and the Architectural Heritage (CDUP) (1981). *Report of the Meeting of the Plenary Committee* (CM (81) 95/ CDUP (81) 12)

Council of Europe, Steering Committee for Urban Policies and the Architectural Heritage (CDUP) (1981). *Report on the Situation of the Architectural Heritage in Europe* (CDUP (81) 16)

Council of Europe, European Committee on Crime Problems (CDPC) (1981). *Meeting Report XXXth Plenary Session* (CM (81) 125/ CDPC (81) 13 revised)

Council of Europe, European Committee on Crime Problems (CDPC) (1981). *Draft European Convention on Offences against Cultural Property – Text adopted by the Selected Committee of Experts on International Cooperation in the Field of Offences relating to Works of Art* (PC-R-OA) (CDPC (81) 16)

Council of Europe (1981). *Third Conference of European Ministers Responsible for Cultural Affairs (Luxembourg) – European Cultural Co-operation: Achievements and Prospects* (CM (81) 192)

Council of Europe, Committee of Senior Officials (1981). *Report on the Third Conference of European Ministers Responsible for Cultural Affairs (Luxembourg)* (MAC-3-HF 19)

Council of Europe, Committee of Ministers (1981). *Written Question No. 238 by Lord Duncan Sandys on the UNESCO Convention of 1972 concerning the Protection of the World Cultural and Natural Heritage* (CM (81) 104)

Council of Europe, Steering Committee for Urban Policies and the Architectural Heritage (CDUP) (1982). *Report of the Second Meeting* (CM (82) 97/ CDUP (82) 18)

Council of Europe, Steering Committee for Urban Policies and the Architectural Heritage (CDUP) (1982). *The Possibility and Desirability of Preparing a European Convention for the Protection of the Architectural Heritage* (CDUP (82) 4)

Council of Europe, Steering Committee for Urban Policies and the Architectural Heritage (CDUP) (1982). *Ad Hoc Terms of Reference Addressed to the CDUP* (CDUP (82) 15)

Council of Europe, Steering Committee for Urban Policies and the Architectural Heritage (CDUP) (1982). *Rapport sur la Situation du Patrimoine Architectural en Europe, par Mr. H.L. Warburton* (CDUP (82) 59)

Council of Europe, Conference of Local and Regional Authorities of Europe (1982). *Resolution 127 (1982) on the 4th European Symposium of Historic Towns* (Resolution 127)

Council of Europe, European Committee on Legal Co-operation (CDCJ) (1982). *Meeting Report (37th meeting)* (CM (82) 146/ CDCJ (82) 33)

Council of Europe, European Committee on Legal Co-operation (CDCJ) (1982). *Request by the CDPC for the CDCJ's opinion on certain provisions of the draft Convention on Offences against Cultural Property* (CDCJ (82) 7)

Council of Europe, Committee of Ministers (1982). *Progress of European Co-operation – Report by the Secretary General of the Council of Europe* (CM (82) 65)

Council of Europe, European Committee on Legal Co-operation (CDCJ) (1982). *Report by the Select Committee of Experts on International Co-operation in the Field of Offences Relating to Works of Art* (CDPC (82) 1)

Council of Europe (1983). *13th Colloquy on European Law – International Legal Protection of Cultural Property: The Harmonisation of Criminal Law and International Criminal Co-operation as Instruments of Protection* (CJ-DE/13 (83) 6)

Council of Europe, Steering Committee for Urban Policies and the Architectural Heritage (CDUP) (1983). *Report of the 3rd Meeting of the Plenary Committee* (CM (83) 59/ CDUP (83) 15)

Council of Europe, Steering Committee for Urban Policies and the Architectural Heritage (CDUP) (1983). *Study on the Legal Feasibility and Desirability of a European Convention on the Protection of the Architectural Heritage – by the European University Centre Nancy* (CDUP (83) 4)

Council of Europe, Steering Committee for Urban Policies and the Architectural Heritage (CDUP) (1983). *Comparative Analysis of Legislation in the Field of Conservation of Monuments and Sites* (CDUP (83) 62)

Council of Europe, Steering Committee for Urban Policies and the Architectural Heritage (CDUP) (1983). *Comparative Analysis of Legislation in the Field of Conservation of Monuments and Sites – Report of the Meeting* (CDUP (83) 89)

Council of Europe, Steering Committee for Urban Policies and the Architectural Heritage (CDUP) (1983). *Letter and Memorandum from the Spanish Delegation* (CM (83) 86)

Council of Europe, Conference of Local and Regional Authorities of Europe (1983). *The Renaissance of Towns in Regions of Old Industry in Europe – Proposal for the Conference* (CPL/P (17) 18)

Council of Europe, Committee of Ministers (1983). *Conclusions of the 358th Meeting of the Ministers' Deputies* (CM/Del/Concl (83) 358)

Council of Europe, Committee of Ministers (1983). *European Conference of Ministers Responsible for the Conservation of the Architectural Heritage – Secretariat Memorandum* (CM (83) 163)

Council of Europe, Committee of Ministers (1983). *Conclusions of the 359th and 360th Meetings of the Ministers' Deputies* (CM/Del/Concl (83) 359 and 360)

Council of Europe, Committee of Ministers (1984). *Draft Convention on Offences Relating to Cultural Property – Comments by the Delegation of the United Kingdom and Observations by the Secretariat* (Addendum I to CM (84) 191)

Council of Europe, European Committee on Crime Problems (CDPC) (1984). *Offences Relating to Works of Art – Final Activity Report prepared by the Selected Committee of Experts on International Co-operation in the Field of Offences relating to Works of Art* (Addendum II to CM (84) 107/ CDPC (84) 8)

Council of Europe, Committee of Ministers (1984). *Draft Convention on Offences Relating to Cultural Property – Views expressed at the 374th meeting of the Ministers' Deputies* (CM (84) 191)

Council of Europe, Steering Committee for Urban Policies and the Architectural Heritage (CDUP) (1984). *Report of the 4th Meeting of the Plenary Committee* (CM (84) 72/ CDUP (84) 27)

Council of Europe, Steering Committee for Urban Policies and the Architectural Heritage (CDUP) (1984). *European Convention for the Conservation of the Architectural Heritage – Preliminary draft revised by the Secretariat following the meeting of the group of experts* (CDUP (84) 1)

Council of Europe, Steering Committee for Urban Policies and the Architectural Heritage (CDUP) (1984). *Information on the Architectural Heritage* (CDUP (84) 6)

Council of Europe, Steering Committee for Urban Policies and the Architectural Heritage (CDUP) (1984). *Commentaires des Membres du Comite Restreint d'Experts sur le Projet revise No 1 du Secretariat* (CDUP (84) 46)

Council of Europe, Steering Committee for Urban Policies and the Architectural Heritage (CDUP), Selected Committee of Experts Responsible for Drafting a European

Convention for the Protection of the Architectural Heritage (1984). *2nd Revised Draft of the Convention* (CDUP (84) 73)

Council of Europe, Steering Committee for Urban Policies and the Architectural Heritage (CDUP), Selected Committee of Experts Responsible for Drafting a European Convention for the Protection of the Architectural Heritage (1984). *Working Paper for the meeting 27–29 November 1984* (CDUP (84) 92)

Council of Europe, 4th Conference of European Ministers Responsible for Cultural Affairs (1984). *European Declaration on Cultural Objectives (Berlin 1984)*

Council of Europe, Steering Committee for Urban Policies and the Architectural Heritage (CDUP) (1985). *Report of the 5th Meeting of the Plenary Committee* (CM (85) 61/ CDUP (85) 20)

Council of Europe (1985). *Convention for the Protection of the Architectural Heritage of Europe* (*ETS No. 121*)

Council of Europe (1985). *Explanatory Report to the Convention for the Protection of the Architectural Heritage of Europe* (European Treaty Serious – No. 121)

Council of Europe (1985). *European Convention on Offences relating to Cultural Property* (European Treaty Serious – No. 119)

Council of Europe (1985). *Explanatory Report to the European Convention on Offences relating to Cultural Property* (European Treaty Serious – No. 119)

Council of Europe, Steering Committee for Urban Policies and the Architectural Heritage (CDUP), Selected Committee of Experts Responsible for Drafting a European Convention for the Protection of the Architectural Heritage (1985). *Final Activity Report* (Addendum to CM (85) 61 / CDUP (85) 20)

Council of Europe, Committee of Ministers, Ministers' Deputies (1985). *Convention for the Protection of the Architectural Heritage of Europe – Date of opening for signature* (CM (85) 135)

Council of Europe, Committee of Ministers, Ad Hoc Committee of Experts on the Underwater Cultural Heritage (CAHAQ) (1985). *Final Activity Report* (CAHAQ (85) 5)

Council of Europe, Steering Committee for Urban Policies and the Architectural Heritage (CDUP) (1986). *Report of the 6th Meeting of the Plenary Committee* (CM (86) 71/ CDUP (86) 35)

Council of Europe, Steering Committee for Urban Policies and the Architectural Heritage (CDUP) (1986). *Promotion of European Cultural Routes* (CDUP (86) 60)

Council of Europe, Committee of Ministers (1986). *Draft Third Medium-Term Plan 1987–91 – Democratic Europe: Humanism, Diversity, Universality* (CM (86) 2)

Council of Europe, Committee of Ministers (1987). *Conclusions of the 404th Meeting of the Ministers' Deputies* (CM/Del/Concl (87) 404)

Council of Europe (1984). *Archaeology and Planning – Report of the Florence Colloquy* (PUBDGIV008)

Council of Europe, Steering Committee for Integrated Conservation of the Historic Heritage (CDPH) (1987). *Meeting Report – 1st Meeting* (CM (87) 120 / CDPH (87) 12)

Council of Europe, Steering Committee for Integrated Conservation of the Historic Heritage (CDPH) (1987). *Archaeology and Major Public Works – The Law and its Application: Comparative Study of the situation in several European countries* (CDPH/Nice (87) 1)

Council of Europe, Committee of Ministers (1987). *Draft Intergovernmental Programme of Activities for 1988* (CM (87) 136)

Council of Europe, Committee of Ministers (1987). *Recommendation No. R (87)24 on the Committee of Ministers to Member States on European Industrial Towns*

Council of Europe, Steering Committee for Integrated Conservation of the Historic Heritage (CDPH) (1988). *Meeting Report – 2+ Meeting* (CM (88) 20 / CDPH (87) 32

Council of Europe, Steering Committee for Integrated Conservation of the Historic Heritage (CDPH) (1988). *Meeting Report – 3rd Meeting* (CM (88) 81 / CDPH (88) 13)

Council of Europe, Steering Committee for Integrated Conservation of the Historic Heritage (CDPH) (1988). *Select Committee of Experts on Archaeology and Planning (PH-R-MA) – Meeting Report* (CDPH (88) 66)

Council of Europe, Steering Committee for Integrated Conservation of the Historic Heritage (CDPH) (1988). *Select Committee of Expert on the Effects of Atmospheric Pollution on the Architectural Heritage* (CM (88) 20 / CDPH (87) 32)

Council of Europe, Steering Committee for Integrated Conservation of the Historic Heritage (CDPH), Select Committee of Experts on Archaeology and Planning (1989). *Document de Travail soumis par la Délégation Française pour la Réunion des 12–13 juin 1989* (CDPH (89) 28)

Council of Europe, Committee of Ministers (1989). *Recommendation No. R (89) 5 of the Committee of Ministers to Member States Concerning the Protection and Enhancement of the Archaeological Heritage in the Context of Town and Country Planning Operations*

Council of Europe, Committee of Ministers (1989). *Recommendation No. R (89) 6 on the protection and enhancement of the rural architectural heritage*

Council of Europe, Steering Committee for Integrated Conservation of the Historic Heritage (CDPH) (1989). *Select Committee of Experts on Archaeology and Planning (PH-R-MA) – Revision of the European Convention on the Protection of the Archaeological Heritage (1st meeting)* (CDPH (89) 35)

Council of Europe, Steering Committee for Integrated Conservation of the Historic Heritage (CDPH) (1989). *4th Plenary Meeting – Report* (CDPH (89) 12 / CM (89) 65)

Council of Europe, Steering Committee for Integrated Conservation of the Historic Heritage (CDPH) (1989). *Select Committee of Experts on Archaeology and Planning (PH-R-MA) – Final Activity Report* (Addendum 1 to CDPH (89) 12 / Addendum 1 to CM (89) 65)

Council of Europe, Steering Committee for Integrated Conservation of the Historic Heritage (CDPH) (1989). *Select Committee of Experts on the Rural Architectural Heritage – Interim Activity Report* (Addendum 2 to CM (89) 65 / Addendum 2 to CDPH (89) 12)

Council of Europe (1989). *Archaeology and Major Public Works – Report of the Nice Colloquy* (PUBDGIV018)

Council of Europe, European Committee on Crime Problems (CDPC) (1989). *Interdisciplinary Meeting of Experts on the Legal Protection of Cultural Property – Information Document* (CDPC (89) 11)

Council of Europe, Steering Committee for Integrated Conservation of the Historic Heritage (CDPH) (1990). *Report of the 5th meeting* (CM (90) 104)

Council of Europe, Committee of Ministers (1990). *Recommendation* (90) 20 *on the protection and conservation of the industrial, technical and civil engineering heritage in Europe*

Council of Europe, Steering Committee for Integrated Conservation of the Historic Heritage (CDPH) (1990). *Select Committee of Experts on Archaeology and Planning (PH-R-MA) – Revision of the European Convention on the Protection of the Archaeological Heritage (2nd meeting)* (CDPH (90) 14)

Council of Europe, Steering Committee for Integrated Conservation of the Historic Heritage (CDPH) (1990). *Select Committee of Experts on Archaeology and Planning (PH-R-MA) – Revision of the European Convention on the Protection of the Archaeological Heritage (2nd meeting – Report)* (CDPH (90) 22)

Council of Europe, Steering Committee for Integrated Conservation of the Historic Heritage (CDPH) (1990). *Select Committee of Experts on Archaeology and Planning (PH-R-MA) – Revision of the European Convention on the Protection of the Archaeological Heritage (3rd meeting – Report)* (CC-PAT (90) 17)

Council of Europe, Committee of Ministers (1990). *Preliminary Draft Intergovernmental Programme of Activities for 1991* (CM (90) 67)

Council of Europe, Steering Committee for Integrated Conservation of the Historic Heritage (CDPH) (1990). *Select Committee of Experts on Archaeology and Planning (PH-R-MA) – Revision of the European Convention on the Protection of the Archaeological Heritage (4th meeting – Working Paper Prepared by the Secretariat)* (CC-PAT (90) 18 rev.2)

Council of Europe, Steering Committee for Integrated Conservation of the Historic Heritage (CDPH) (1991). *Select Committee of Experts on Archaeology and Planning (PH-R-MA) – Revision of the European Convention on the Protection of the Archaeological Heritage (5th meeting – Revised Preliminary Draft)* (CC-PAT (91) 21 rev.)

Council of Europe, Cultural Heritage Committee (1991). *Draft Revised European Convention on the Protection of the Archaeological Heritage – Final Activity Report and Draft Revised Convention* (CM (91) 122 / CC-PAT (91) 41)

Council of Europe, Cultural Heritage Committee (1991). *Draft Recommendation No. R (91) ... on the Protection of the Twentieth Century Architectural Heritage – Final Activity Report* (CM (91) 116 / CC-PAT (91) 42)

Council of Europe, Cultural Heritage Committee (1991). *Select Committee of Experts on Archaeology and Planning – Final Activity Report* (CC-PAT (91) 31)

Council of Europe, Cultural Heritage Committee (1991). *Third European Conference of Ministers Responsible for Cultural Heritage – Preparations for the Conference* (MPC (91) 4)

Council of Europe, Council for Cultural Co-operation (1991). *Meeting Report (59th Session)* (CDCC (91) 5)

Council of Europe (1992). *European Convention on the Protection of the Archaeological Heritage (Revised)*, ETS No. 143

Council of Europe (1992). *Explanatory Report to the European Convention on the Protection of the Archaeological Heritage (Revised)*, ETS No. 143

Council of Europe (1992). *Third European Conference of Ministers responsible for the Cultural Heritage – Resolutions 1–4*

Council of Europe, Cultural Heritage Committee (1992). *European Plan for Archaeology, Meeting of the Group of Specialists on the Archaeological Heritage* (CC-PAT (92) 55)

Council of Europe, Conference of Local and Regional Authorities of Europe (1992). *Committee on the Natural and Built Environment – Report on the Rio Earth Summit and its implications (presented by Mr. H. Lässing)* (CPL/ENV (27) 12)

Council of Europe, Committee of Ministers (1993). *Draft Recommendation No. R (93) ... on the Protection of the Architectural Heritage against Natural Disasters* (CM (93) 141)

Council of Europe, Cultural Heritage Committee (1993). *Report of the discussion on European Plan for Archaeology – Committee of Experts on the Archaeological Heritage* (CC-PAT (93) 50)

Council of Europe, Cultural Heritage Committee (1993). *Report of the Organising Committee for the Bronze Age Campaign* (CC-PAT (93) 110)

Council of Europe, Cultural Heritage Committee (1993). *Comparative Study of the Situation in Urban Archaeology in Europe* (CC-PAT (93) 84)

Council of Europe (1993). *Declaration of the Council of Europe's First Summit of Heads of State and Governments of the Council of Europe (Vienna Declaration)*

Council of Europe, Committee of Ministers (1994). *Intergovernmental Programme of Activities for 1994* (MEP (94) 2)

Council of Europe, Cultural Heritage Committee (1994). *Council of Europe Archaeological Heritage – Information Document* (CC-PAT (94) 35 rev.2)

Council of Europe, Cultural Heritage Committee (1994). *Organising Committee for the Bronze Age Campaign – Meeting Report* (CC-PAT (94) 43)

Council of Europe, Cultural Heritage Committee (1994). *Report of joint meeting of the Scientific and Organising Committee for the Bronze Age Campaign* (CC-PAT (94) 127)

Council of Europe, Cultural Heritage Committee (1994). *European Network of Ancient Places of Performance – Abridged Report of the Seminar* (CC-PAT (94) 124)

Council of Europe, Directorate of Education, Culture and Sport (1994). *Draft List of Cultural Rights* (CDCC Misc (94) 3 rev 1)

Council of Europe, Ad hoc Committee for the Protection of National Minorities (CAHMIN) (1994). *Preliminary draft protocol to the European Convention for the Protection of Human Rights and Fundamental Freedoms on the recognition of cultural rights, prepared by the working party following up the 8th Fribourg Colloquy* (CAHMIN (94) 4 rev 2)

Council of Europe, Ad Hoc Committee for the Protection of National Minorities (CAHMIN) (1995). *Draft articles and alternative versions for possible inclusion in a protocol complementing the ECHR in the cultural field* (CAHMIN (95) 1 rev.3)

Council of Europe, Ad Hoc Committee for the Protection of National Minorities (CAHMIN) (1995). *Preparation of an additional draft to the European Convention on Human Rights (ECHR) in the cultural field – Proposals from the Swiss delegation* (CAHMIN (95) 13)

Council of Europe, Ad Hoc Committee for the Protection of National Minorities (CAHMIN) (1995). *Activity Report* (CAHMIN (95) 22 Addendum)

Council of Europe, Ad Hoc Committee for the Protection of National Minorities (CAHMIN) (1995). *Report of the 11th meeting* (CM (95) 80)

Council of Europe, Ad Hoc Committee for the Protection of National Minorities (CAHMIN) (1995). *Report of the 12th meeting* (CM (95) 119)

Council of Europe, Ad Hoc Committee for the Protection of National Minorities (CAHMIN) (1995). *Report of the 13th meeting* (CM (95) 153)

Council of Europe (1995). *Framework Convention for the Protection of National Minorities* (ETS No. 157)

Council of Europe, Committee of Ministers (1996). *4th European Conference of Ministers Responsible for the Cultural Heritage (Helsinki) – Report by the Secretary General* (CMD037494/ CM (96) 97)

Council of Europe, Committee of Ministers (1996). *IVth European Conference of Ministers Responsible for the Cultural Heritage (Helsinki) – Helsinki Declaration on the political dimension of cultural heritage conservation in Europe*

Council of Europe, Committee of Ministers (1996). *IVth European Conference of Ministers Responsible for the Cultural Heritage (Helsinki) – Resolution No. 1 on the cultural hertiage as a factor in building Europe*

Council of Europe, Committee of Ministers (1996). *IVth European Conference of Ministers Responsible for the Cultural Heritage (Helsinki) – Resolution No. 2. – The Cultural Heritage as a Factor of Sustainable Development*

Council of Europe, Cultural Heritage Committee (1996). *Protection of the Cultural Heritage Against Unlawful Acts – Interim activity report and draft Recommendation* CM (96) 70

Council of Europe, Committee of Ministers, Ministers' Deputies (1996). *Draft Recommendation No. R (96) … on the Protection of the Cultural Heritage against Unlawful Acts* (CM (96) 33 / CM (96) 70)

Council of Europe, Committee of Ministers (1997). *Cultural Heritage Committee* (CC-PAT) *– Extension of Terms of Reference* (No. 97/338

Council of Europe, Council for Cultural Cooperation (1997). *Education for Democratic Citizenship: dimensions of citizenship, core competences, variables and international activities – prepared by Ruud Veldhuis* (DECS/CIT (97) 23)

Council of Europe, Committee of Ministers (1998). *Campaign "Europe, A Common Heritage" – State of Preparation* (GT-SUIVI (98) 27)

Council of Europe, Technical Co-operation and Consultancy Programme related to the Integrated Conservation of Cultural Heritage (1999). *Housing Rehabilitation in Old City Centres as a Factor of Social Cohesion and Economic Development* (CC-PAT (99) 24)

Council of Europe, Ministers' Deputies Rapporteur Groups (2000). *Situation and future of the Activity "Heritage, identity and diversity"* (GR-C (2000) 27

Council of Europe (2000). *Council of Europe Landscape Convention* (ETS No. 176).

Council of Europe (2001). *Fifth European Conference of Ministers Responsible for the Cultural Heritage – Resolutions and Declarations*

Council of Europe, Ministers' Deputies Rapporteur Groups (2001). *Parliamentary Assembly Recommendation 1486 (2000) on "Maritime and Fluvial Cultural Heritage" – Draft reply* (GR-C (2001) 18)

Council of Europe (2001). *Res (2001)6 on access to Council of Europe documents*

Council of Europe, Steering Committee for Cultural Heritage (CDPAT) (2002). *1st meeting of the CDPAT Bureau* (CDPAT (2002) 11)

Council of Europe, Steering Committee for Cultural Heritage (CDPAT) (2002). *Cultural Heritage, a Vector of Democratic Development* – Report of the Cross-sectoral seminar, Strasbourg, 20–21 June 2002 (CDPAT (2002) 28)

Council of Europe, Steering Committee for Cultural Heritage (CDPAT) (2002). *Implementation of the Activities of the Committee 2002–2004* (CDPAT (2002) 33)

Council of Europe, Steering Committee for Cultural Heritage (CDPAT) (2002). *Work on Cultural Heritage Conventions – 1st meeting* (CDPAT (2002) 40)

Council of Europe, Steering Committee for Cultural Heritage (CDPAT) (2002). *Reference Framework for the Technical Co-operation Programme: Sustainable Development Strategy 2003–2005* (CDAPT (2002) 45)

Council of Europe, Steering Committee for Cultural Heritage (CDPAT) (2003). *Heritage's Place in Globalisation and Local Development – Contribution to a basic text* (CDPAT (2003) 17)

Council of Europe, Steering Committee for Cultural Heritage (CDPAT) (2003). *Heritage interpretation – players, methods and ethics: Pointers to the situation in Europe* (CDPAT (2003) 35)

Council of Europe, Steering Committee for Cultural Heritage (CDPAT) (2003). *Exchange of Views on the Future Aims of Council of Europe Co-operation in the Field of Cultural Heritage in the Light of European Union Enlargement* (CDPAT (2003) 37)

Council of Europe, Steering Committee for Cultural Heritage (CDPAT) (2003). *Select Committee of Experts on the preparation of a Framework Convention on Cultural Heritage – Record of the 1st Meeting* (CDPAT (2003) 43)

Council of Europe, Steering Committee for Cultural Heritage (CDPAT) (2003). *Select Committee of Experts on the draft Convention on cultural heritage – Information message by the legal Advice Department and Treaty Office* (CDPAT (2003) 59)

Council of Europe, Steering Committee for Cultural Heritage (CDPAT) (2003). *2nd meeting of the CDPAT – Record* (CDPAT (2003) 61 rev)

Council of Europe, Committee of Ministers (2003). *Declaration on intercultural dialogue and conflict prevention* – Adopted by the European ministers responsible for cultural affairs, Opatija (Croatia), 22 October 2003

Council of Europe, Steering Committee for Cultural Heritage (CDPAT) (2004). *3rd Bureau Meeting – Report* (CDPAT (2004) 29)

Council of Europe, Directorate General for Education, Culture, Heritage, Youth and Sport (2004). *50 Years of Council of Europe Art Exhibitions*

Council of Europe (2004). *50 Years of the European Cultural Convention – Report by the Secretary General to the Wrocław Conference*

Council of Europe, Steering Committee for Cultural Heritage (CDPAT) (2004). *Preparation of a Framework Convention on Cultural Heritage in a Changing Europe – Draft final activity Report* (CDPAT (2004) 51)

Council of Europe, Steering Committee for Cultural Heritage (CDPAT) (2004). *Draft Council of Europe Framework Convention on the Value of Cultural Heritage for Society – Explanatory Report Final Draft* (CDPAT (2004) 24 rev 4)

Council of Europe, Steering Committee for Cultural Heritage (CDPAT), Selected Committee of Experts Responsible for Preparing a Framework Convention on Cultural Heritage (2004). *Draft text of Council of Europe Framework Convention on the Value of Cultural Heritage for Society* (CDPAT (2004) 4 rev 10)

Council of Europe, Steering Committee for Cultural Heritage (CDPAT), Selected Committee of Experts Responsible for Preparing a Framework Convention on Cultural Heritage (2004). *Final Draft Text of Council of Europe Framework Convention on the Value of Cultural Heritage for Society* (CDPAT (2004) 4 rev 11)

Council of Europe, Steering Committee for Cultural Heritage (CDPAT) (2004). *A Council of Europe Initiative: Heritage from Elsewhere, Heritage of Others* (CDPAT (2004) 30 final)

Council of Europe, Steering Committee for Cultural Heritage (CDPAT) (2004). *Technical Co-operation and Consultancy Programme Related to the Integrated Conservation of the Cultural Heritage – Intermediate State of Progress Report* (CDPAT (2004) 65)

Council of Europe, Steering Committee for Cultural Heritage (CDPAT) (2005). *Final Activity Report – Preparation of a framework convention on cultural heritage in a changing Europe* (CM (2005) 17. Addendum)

Council of Europe, Steering Committee for Cultural Heritage (CDPAT) (2005). *Proposed Revised CDPAT Terms of References – 4th Plenary Session* (CDPAT (2005) 25)

Council of Europe, Steering Committee for Cultural Heritage (CDPAT) (2005). *Comments from the German Delegation on the Draft Framework Convention* (CDPAT (2005) 31)

Council of Europe, Steering Committee for Cultural Heritage (CDPAT) (2005). *European Heritage Days – Draft Proposal for the Future Organisation of the European Heritage Days* (CDPAT (2005) 36)

Council of Europe (2005). *Council of Europe Framework Convention on the Value of Cultural Heritage for Society*, CETS No. 199

Council of Europe, Directorate General IV – Education, Culture and Heritage, Youth and Sport (2005). *Sustainable Development at the Council of Europe: proposal for its strategic development* (GR-C (2005) 13)

Council of Europe, Rapporteur Group on Administrative and Budgetary Questions (2006). *Vedovato library and archives* (GR-AB (2006) 17)

Council of Europe, Committee of Ministers (2008). *White Paper on Intercultural Dialogue – Living Together as Equals in Dignity*

Council of Europe, Steering Committee for Cultural Heritage and Landscape (CDPATEP) (2008). *Draft List of Decisions* (CDPATEP (2008) 25)

Council of Europe, Steering Committee for Cultural Heritage and Landscape (CDPATEP) (2009). *Meeting Report – 2nd Plenary Session* (CDPATEP (2009) 20)

Council of Europe, Steering Committee for Cultural Heritage and Landscape (CDPATEP) (2009). *Guidelines on the Medium-Term Assignments of the CDPATEP* (CM (2009) 112)

Council of Europe, Steering Committee for Cultural Heritage and Landscape (CDPATEP) (2010). *Meeting Report – 3rd Plenary Session* (CDPATEP (2010) 25)

Council of Europe (2010). *The Role of Culture and Cultural Heritage in Conflict Prevention, Transformation, Resolution and Post-conflict Action: The Council of Europe Approach* (AT (2010) 397 rev.1)

Council of Europe, European Court of Human Rights (2011). Report- *Cultural rights in the case-law of the European Court of Human Rights*

Council of Europe, Steering Committee for Cultural Heritage and Landscape (CDPATEP) (2011). *Report of the 4th Plenary Session* (CDPATEP (2011) 18)

Council of Europe, Steering Committee for Cultural Heritage and Landscape (CDPATEP) (2011). *Bureau Meeting Report – 4th meeting* (CDPATEP (2011) 24)

Council of Europe, Steering Committee for Culture, Heritage and Landscape (CDCPP) (2012). *Cultural Heritage and Technical Consultancy – 1st meeting of the Bureau* (CDCPP (2012) 41)

Council of Europe, Steering Committee for Culture, Heritage and Landscape (CDCPP) (2012). *Initial Reflections towards a Future Vision for the CDCPP: Works and Working Methods 2013 Onwards* (CDCPP (2012) 42)

Council of Europe, Steering Committee for Culture, Heritage and Landscape (CDCPP) (2012). *List of Decisions – 1st Plenary Session* (CDCPP (2012) 35 rev.)

Council of Europe, Steering Committee for Culture, Heritage and Landscape (CDCPP) (2012). *Meeting Report – 1st meeting of the Bureau* (CDCPP (2012) 57)

Council of Europe, Steering Committee for Culture, Heritage and Landscape (CDCPP) (2012). *Meeting Report – 2nd meeting of the Bureau* (CDCPP (2012) 64)

Council of Europe, Steering Committee for Culture, Heritage and Landscape (CDCPP) (2012). *Medium-term orientations and perspectives for cultural heritage activities in the Council of Europe* (CDCPP (2012) 5

Council of Europe, Steering Committee for Culture, Heritage and Landscape (CDCPP) (2013). *Meeting Report – 3rd meeting of the Bureau* (CDCPP (2013) 9)

Council of Europe, Steering Committee for Culture, Heritage and Landscape (CDCPP) (2012). *List of Decisions – 4th meeting of the Bureau* (CDCPP (2013) 17)

Council of Europe, Steering Committee for Culture, Heritage and Landscape (CDCPP) (2013). *Contributions of the CDCPP to the objectives and priorities of the Council of Europe* (CDCPP (2013) 19)

Council of Europe, Steering Committee for Culture, Heritage and Landscape (CDCPP) (2013). *Draft Programme of Work 2014–2015* (CDCPP (2013) 20)

Council of Europe, Steering Committee for Culture, Heritage and Landscape (CDCPP) (2013). *Meeting Report – 2nd meeting* (CDCPP (2013) 29)

Council of Europe, Steering Committee for Culture, Heritage and Landscape (CDCPP) (2014). *Meeting Report – 3rd meeting* (CDCPP (2014) 20)

Council of Europe, Steering Committee for Culture, Heritage and Landscape (CDCPP) (2014). *List of Decisions Concerning the Committee of Ministers and Meeting Report – 5th meeting of the Bureau* (CDCPP (2014) 10)

Council of Europe, Steering Committee for Culture, Heritage and Landscape (CDCPP) (2014). *Addendum to the Report of the Bureau – 6th meeting of the Bureau* (CDCPP-Bu (2014) 19 Add)

Council of Europe, Steering Committee for Culture, Heritage and Landscape (CDCPP) (2015). *Review of the Council of Europe Conventions under the Responsibility of the CDCPP* (CDCPP (2015) 3)

Council of Europe, Steering Committee for Culture, Heritage and Landscape (CDCPP) (2015). *Meeting Report – 7th meeting of the Bureau* (CDCPP (2015) 13)

Council of Europe, Steering Committee for Culture, Heritage and Landscape (CDCPP) (2015). *Meeting Report – 8th meeting of the Bureau* (CDCPP-Bu (2015) 19)

Council of Europe, Steering Committee for Culture, Heritage and Landscape (CDCPP) (2015). *Meeting Report – 9th meeting of the Bureau* (CDCPP-Bu (2015) 33)

Council of Europe, Steering Committee for Culture, Heritage and Landscape (CDCPP) (2015). *Meeting Report – 4th meeting* (CDCPP (2015) 19)

Council of Europe, Steering Committee for Culture, Heritage and Landscape (CDCPP) (2015). *Review of the Council of Europe Conventions under the Responsibility of the CDCPP – Classification by State* (CDCPP (2015) 3 Addendum I Bil.Rev)

Council of Europe (2015). The Namur Declaration adopted at the 6th session of the Council of Europe Conference of Ministers responsible for Cultural Heritage (Namur, Belgium, 23–24 April 2015)

Council of Europe, Steering Committee for Culture, Heritage and Landscape (CDCPP) (2016). *Meeting Report – 5th meeting* (CDCPP (2016) 19)

Council of Europe, Steering Committee for Culture, Heritage and Landscape (CDCPP) (2016). *Meeting Report – 10th meeting of the Bureau* (CDCPP-Bu (2016) 14)

Council of Europe, Steering Committee for Culture, Heritage and Landscape (CDCPP) (2016). *Meeting Report – 11th meeting of the Bureau* (CDCPP-Bu (2016) 27)

Council of Europe, Steering Committee for Culture, Heritage and Landscape (CDCPP) (2017). *List of Decisions and Texts Adopted – 6th Plenary Session* (CDCPP (2017) 18)

Council of Europe, Steering Committee for Culture, Heritage and Landscape (CDCPP) (2017). *Meeting Report – 12th meeting of the Bureau* (CDCPP-Bu (2017) 9)

Council of Europe, Steering Committee for Culture, Heritage and Landscape (CDCPP) (2017). *List of Decisions – 13th meeting of the Bureau* (CDCPP-Bu (2017) 16 rev)

Council of Europe (2017). *Council of Europe Convention on Offences relating to Cultural Property* (CETS No. 221)

Council of Europe, Steering Committee for Culture, Heritage and Landscape (CDCPP) (2018). *List of Decisions and Texts Adopted – 7th Plenary Session* (CDCPP (2018) 10)

Council of Europe, Steering Committee for Culture, Heritage and Landscape (CDCPP) (2018). *List of Decisions – 14th meeting of the Bureau* (CDCPP-Bu (2018) 7)

Council of Europe, Steering Committee for Culture, Heritage and Landscape (CDCPP) (2018). *List of Decisions – 15th meeting of the Bureau* (CDCPP-Bu (2018) 11)

Council of Europe, Committee of Ministers (2018). *Recommendation (CM/Rec (2018)3) of the Committee of Ministers to member States on Cultural Heritage Facing Climate Change: Increasing Resilience and Promoting Adaptation*

Council of Europe, EUR-OPA Major Hazards Agreement (2018). *Report on the International Conference on Culture Against Disasters – Protecting Cultural Landscapes as Prevention of Natural Disasters* (APCAT (2018) 08)

Council of Europe, Steering Committee for Culture, Heritage and Landscape (CDCPP) (2019). *Cultural Heritage: Strategy 21; the Faro Convention Action Plan; "The Faro Way: Enhanced Participation in Cultural Heritage"; Herein; Council of Europe Convention on Offences relating to Cultural Property; European Heritage Days* (CDCPP (2019) 6)

Council of Europe, Steering Committee for Culture, Heritage and Landscape (CDCPP) (2019). *List of Decisions and Texts Adopted at the 8th Plenary Session* (CDCPP (2019) 11)

Council of Europe, Steering Committee for Culture, Heritage and Landscape (CDCPP) (2019). *List of Decisions – 16th meeting of the Bureau* (CDCPP-Bu (2019) 6)

Council of Europe, Steering Committee for Culture, Heritage and Landscape (CDCPP) (2019). *List of Decisions – 17th meeting of the Bureau* (CDCPP-Bu (2019) 11)

Council of Europe (2020). *Strategic Framework of the Council of Europe* (SG/Inf (2020) 34)

Council of Europe, Steering Committee for Culture, Heritage and Landscape (CDCPP) (2020). *Meeting Report (Online Meeting)* (CDCPP (2020) 6)

Council of Europe, Steering Committee for Culture, Heritage and Landscape (CDCPP) (2020). *Meeting Report – 9th Session* (CDCPP (2020) 14)

Council of Europe, Steering Committee for Culture, Heritage and Landscape (CDCPP) (2020). *Meeting Report – 18th meeting of the Bureau* (CDCPP-Bu (2020) 6)

Council of Europe, Committee of Ministers (2020). *Recommendation CM/Rec (2020)7 on Promoting the Continuous Prevention of Risks in the day-to-day Management of Cultural Heritage: Co-operation with States, Specialists and Citizens*

Council of Europe, Steering Committee for Culture, Heritage and Landscape (CDCPP) (2021). *Meeting Report (Extraordinary Session)* (CDCPP (2021) 2)

Council of Europe, Steering Committee for Culture, Heritage and Landscape (CDCPP) (2021). *Meeting Report – 10th Session (Part I)* (CDCPP (2021) 11)

Council of Europe, Steering Committee for Culture, Heritage and Landscape (CDCPP) (2021). *Meeting Report – 10th Session (Part II)* (CDCPP (2021) 23)

Council of Europe (2021). *State of Democracy, Human Rights and the Rule of Law: A Democratic Renewal for Europe – Report by the Secretary General of the Council of Europe*

Council of Europe, Steering Committee for Culture, Heritage and Landscape (CDCPP) (2022). *LINKED – Guiding Principles for an Integrated Culture, Nature and Landscape Management* (CDCPP (2022) 5)

Council of Europe, Steering Committee for Culture, Heritage and Landscape (CDCPP) (2022). *Meeting Report – 11th Session* (CDCPP (2022) 13)

Council of Europe (2022). *Moving Forward – Annual Report of the Secretary General of the Council of Europe*

Council of Europe, Steering Committee for Culture, Heritage and Landscape (CDCPP) (2022). *Terms of Reference 2022–2025*

Parliamentary Assembly (PACE)

Parliamentary Assembly – Committee on Culture, Science and Education (1949). *Report – Methods by which the Council of Europe can develop cultural cooperation between its members* (Doc. 59)

Parliamentary Assembly (1949). *Recommendation 24 – Cultural Conventions*

Parliamentary Assembly (1949). *Recommendation 25 – Free circulation of books*

Parliamentary Assembly (1949). *Recommendation 26 – Collaboration in Scientific Research*

Parliamentary Assembly (1949). *Recommendation 27 – Private Association which are working to promote European Culture*

Parliamentary Assembly (1949). *Recommendation 28 – Meeting of the Ministers of Education and University Authorities*

Parliamentary Assembly (1949). *Recommendation 29 – European University*

Parliamentary Assembly (1949). *Recommendation 30 – Employment of teachers displaced by war*

Parliamentary Assembly (1949). *Recommendation 31 – European Cultural Centre*

Parliamentary Assembly (1949). *Recommendation 32 – Liaison with UNESCO*

Parliamentary Assembly, Committee on Cultural and Scientific Questions (1950). *List of Cultural Resolutions Adopted by the Consultative Assembly at its First Session in 1949 and the Measures Taken to Implement Them* (AS/CS (2) 1)

Parliamentary Assembly, Committee on Culture, Science and Education (1950). *Report – Cooperation in Cultural Matters* (Doc. 3)

Parliamentary Assembly, Committee on Culture, Science and Education (1950). *Report – Cultural and Scientific Matters* (Doc. 83)

Parliamentary Assembly, Committee on Culture, Science and Education (1950). *Conclusions – Cultural and Scientific Matters* (Doc. 101)

Parliamentary Assembly (1950). *Recommendation 32 – Cultural Agreements*

Parliamentary Assembly, Committee on Cultural and Scientific Questions (1950). *UNESCO Draft Agreement on the Importation of Educational, Scientific and Cultural Materials* (AS/CS (50) 3)

Parliamentary Assembly, Committee on Cultural and Scientific Questions (1950). *UNESCO Draft Agreement on the Importation of Educational, Scientific and Cultural Materials – Observations of the Secretariat-General* (AS/CS (50) 4)

Parliamentary Assembly (1950). *Note of the Secretariate General of the Council of Europe on the Fifth Annual Conference of UNESCO* (AS/CS (50)5)

Parliamentary Assembly, Committee on Cultural and Scientific Questions (1951). *Table showing the Cultural recommendations Adopted by the Consultative Assembly in 1949 and 1950 and the progress made in implementing them* (AS/CS (3) 2)

Parliamentary Assembly (1951). *Report of the Committee of Ministers to the Consultative Assembly (Chapter 5 – Cultural Questions)* (Doc. 5)

Parliamentary Assembly (1951). *Recommendation 19 – Protection, in the event of war, of works of artistic or historic value*

Parliamentary Assembly, Committee on Cultural and Scientific Questions (1954). *Working Party – First Report tabled by UNESCO in the Consultative Assembly* (AS/CS/WP I (6) 7)

Parliamentary Assembly (1954). *Chapter IV of the Special Message from the Committee of Ministers – Cultural Field* (Doc. 281)

Parliamentary Assembly (1954). *Report transmitted to the Council of Europe by the United Nations Educational, Scientific and Cultural Organisation* (Doc.282)

Parliamentary Assembly (1954). *Draft European Cultural Convention – Request for an opinion* (Doc. 269)

Parliamentary Assembly (1955). *Five Years' Work by the Committee of Cultural Experts – Report presented on behalf of the Committee of Cultural Experts by M. Reinink* (AS/CS (6) 41)

Parliamentary Assembly (1955). *Draft Recommendation on the establishment of a Cultural Fund of the Council of Europe* (Doc. 354)

Parliamentary Assembly, Committee on Cultural and Scientific Questions (1955). *Recommendation 74* (AS/CS (7) 35)

Parliamentary Assembly, Committee on Cultural and Scientific Questions (1955). *Cultural Agreements – Analytical Study Prepared by the Secretariat of UNESCO* (AS/CS (6) 52)

Parliamentary Assembly, Committee on Cultural and Scientific Questions (1955). *Draft Reply to the Second Progress Report of UNESCO* (AS/CS (7) 15)

Parliamentary Assembly (1955). *Second Report to the Consultative Assembly of the Council of Europe by the UNESCO* (Doc. 366)

Parliamentary Assembly (1957). *Draft Agenda – Joint Cultural Committee* (AS/EXP/Cult (57) OJ1)

Parliamentary Assembly, Committee on Cultural and Scientific Questions (1957). *Co-operation Between the Council of Europe and UNESCO – Draft Recommendations and Resolutions arising out of UNESCO's Third Report to the PACE* (AS/CS (8) 51)

Parliamentary Assembly, Cultural Committee (1958). *Cultural Activities within NATO – Report of the Conference of Members of PACE from the NATO Countries* (AS/Cult (9) 30)

Parliamentary Assembly, Cultural Committee (1958). *Co-operation with UNESCO – Preliminary Draft Reply to the 4th Report of UNESCO to the PACE* (AS/Cult (9) 50)

Parliamentary Assembly (1959). *Report on NATO cultural Activities* (Doc. 1020)

Parliamentary Assembly, Cultural and Scientific Committee (1960). *Protection of Centres Containing Historical and Artistic Monuments – Final Declaration adopted by the first National Conference on the Preservation and Restoration of Historic Sites (Gubbio, September 1960)* (AS/Cult (14) 44)

Parliamentary Assembly (1960). *Resolution 186 (1960) – Reply to the First Report of the Administrative Board of the Cultural Fund*

Parliamentary Assembly, Cultural Committee (1960). *NATO Cultural Co-operation – Information note publisher by the NATO Secretariat* (AS/Cult (12) 29)

Parliamentary Assembly (1961). *Recommendation 300 – Development of cultural cooperation in Europe*

Parliamentary Assembly (1961). *Resolution 214 – Development of cultural cooperation in Europe*

Parliamentary Assembly, Cultural and Scientific Committee (1961). *Outline Reply by the Consultative Assembly to the 1961 UNESCO Memorandum* (AS/Cult (13) 52)

Parliamentary Assembly, Cultural and Scientific Committee (1962). *Action taken on Recommendations and Resolutions presented by the Cultural Committee during the XIIIth Session* (AS/Cult (14) 1)

Parliamentary Assembly, Cultural and Scientific Committee (1962). *Draft Resolution in Reply to the 1961 Memorandum by UNESCO to the Consultative Assembly of the Council of Europe* (AS/Cult (13) 59)

Parliamentary Assembly, Cultural and Scientific Committee (1962). *Protection of Centres Containing Monuments – Plan for an International Campaign for Historical Monuments sponsored by UNESCO* (AS/Cult (14) 24)

Parliamentary Assembly, Cultural and Scientific Committee (1962). *Activities and Programme of Work for the 14th Session* (AS/Cult (14) 2)

Parliamentary Assembly (1963). *Report on the preservation and development of ancient buildings and historical and artistic sites (presented by Mr. Weiss)* (Doc. 1570)

Parliamentary Assembly (1963). *Recommendation 365*

Parliamentary Assembly, Cultural and Scientific Committee (1963). *Preparation of the European Conference advocated in Recommendation 365* (CMH (63) 2)

Parliamentary Assembly, Cultural and Scientific Committee (1963). *Co-operation with UNESCO – Memorandum (1961–1963)* (AS/Cult (15) 14)

Parliamentary Assembly, Cultural and Scientific Committee (1964). *Cooperation in the Cultural and Scientific Fields* (AS/Cult (16) 23)

Parliamentary Assembly (1965). *Report – Action Programme of the Council of Europe in the Field of the Preservation and Development of Ancient Buildings and Historical or Artistic Sites* (Doc. 1957)

Parliamentary Assembly, Cultural and Scientific Committee (1966). *Summary of the debate in the Consultative Assembly on the speech made by Mr Maheu, Director General of UNESCO on 30th September 1966* (AS/Cult (18) 51)

Parliamentary Assembly, Cultural and Scientific Committee (1966). *Co-operation between Council of Europe and UNESCO – Cultural co-operation and Peace, UNESCO and Europe* (AS/Cult (18) 47)

Parliamentary Assembly (1967). *List of texts adopted by the Consultative Assembly on UNESCO's activities* (AS/Cult/UNESCO (19) 1)

Parliamentary Assembly, Cultural Committee (1967). *Memorandum on European Cultural Policy and UNESCO* (AS/Cult (19) 15)

Parliamentary Assembly, Cultural and Scientific Committee, Sub-committee on UNESCO (1967). *Declaration of Principles of International Cultural Co-operation adopted at the General Conference of UNESCO at its 14th session* (AS/Cult/UNESCO (18) 2)

Parliamentary Assembly, Committee on Culture and Education (1969). *Sub-Committee on Historical and Artistic Monuments and Sites – Draft Minutes of the meeting* (AS/Cult/Monuments (21) PV 1)

Parliamentary Assembly, Committee on Culture and Education (1969). *Information Document on 6th General Assembly of Europa Nostra* (AS/Cult (21) 13)

Parliamentary Assembly (1969). *Recommendation 567 – Twenty years of European cultural cooperation*

Parliamentary Assembly (1969). *Resolution 408 (1969) – Responsibility of Local Authorities in the Preservation and Rehabilitation of Ancient Buildings and Historical or Artistic Sites*

Parliamentary Assembly (1969). *Recommendation 567 (1969) – Twenty years of European cultural co-operation*

Parliamentary Assembly, Committee on Culture and Education (1970). *Draft Report on the European Conference of Ministers responsible for the preservation and rehabilitation of the cultural heritage of monument and sites, Rapporteur Mr. A. Premoli* (AS/Cult (21) 29)

Parliamentary Assembly (1970). *Report on a draft outline law for the active protection of immovable cultural property in Europe* (Doc. 2819)

Parliamentary Assembly (1970). *Recommendation 612 (1970) – Draft outline law for the Active Protection of Immovable Property in Europe*

Parliamentary Assembly, Committee on Culture and Education (1970). *Draft Minutes of the Meeting* (AS/Cult (21) PV 6)

Parliamentary Assembly (1971). *Memorandum 1971 by UNESCO* (Doc. 3016)

Parliamentary Assembly, Committee on Culture and Education (1971). *Draft reply to the UNESCO Memorandum 1971* (AS/Cult (23) 22)

Parliamentary Assembly, Committee on Culture and Education (1972). *Draft Report on European co-operation with regard to Monuments and Sites – Presented by Mr Duncan Sandys* (AS/Cult (24) 13)

Parliamentary Assembly, Committee on Culture and Education (1972). *Draft Report on the Protection of Europe's Architectural Heritage – Presented by Mr Duncan Sandys* (AS/Cult (24) 16)

Parliamentary Assembly (1972). *Recommendation 681 (1972) – Protection of Europe's Architectural Heritage*

Parliamentary Assembly, Committee on Culture and Education (1974). *Sub-Committee on Monuments and Sites – Proposal for a further report in 1975 on specific aspects (particularly social) of the conservation of the architectural heritage* (AS/Cult/MS (26) 7)

Parliamentary Assembly (1974). *Recommendation 742 (1974) – Future Action of the Council of Europe for the Conservation of the Architectural Heritage after 1975*

Parliamentary Assembly (1975). *Recommendation 750 – Conservation of Europe's Architectural Heritage*

Parliamentary Assembly, Committee on Culture and Education (1975). *Sub-Committee on Monuments and Sites – Draft Minutes of the Meeting* (AS/Cult/MS (26) PV 6)

Parliamentary Assembly, Committee on Culture and Education (1975). *Sub-Committee on Monuments and Sites – The Social Aspects of Conservation of the Architectural Heritage (Report)* (AS/Cult/MS (27) 3)

Parliamentary Assembly, Committee on Culture and Education (1975). *Activities of the European Communities in the field of Culture and Education* (AS/Cult (26) 36)

Parliamentary Assembly, Committee on Culture and Education, Sub-committee on UNESCO and other International Organisations (1975). *Fields of Activity of the Various Organisations Concerned with Culture and Education* (AS/Cult/Int. (27) 1 provisional)

Parliamentary Assembly, Committee on Culture and Education (1976). *Sub-Committee on Monuments and Sites – Future Assembly Activity in the field of monuments and sites* (AS/Cult/MS (27) 18)

Parliamentary Assembly, Committee on Culture and Education, Sub-committee on UNESCO and other International Organisations (1975). *Activities of the European Communities in the field of Culture and Education – Second Interim Report on the European Parliament* (AS/Cult/Int (27) 2)

Parliamentary Assembly, Committee on Culture and Education (1976). *Sub-committee on the Architectural and Artistic Heritage of Europe – Future work of the Sub-committee* (AS/Cult/AA (28) 14)

Parliamentary Assembly, Committee on Culture and Education (1976). *Sub-Committee on Monuments and Sites – Draft Minutes of the Meeting* (AS/Cult/MS (27) PV 6)

Parliamentary Assembly (1976). *Recommendation 788 (1976) – Arrangements for Reviewing the Progress of Architectural Conservation*

Parliamentary Assembly (1976). *Resolution 617 (1976) – Follow-up to the Amsterdam Congress on the European Architectural Heritage*

Parliamentary Assembly, Committee on Culture and Education, Sub-committee on UNESCO and other International Organisations (1976). *Draft Minutes of the Meeting* (AS/Cult/Int (27) PV 2)

Parliamentary Assembly, Committee on Culture and Education, Sub-committee on UNESCO and other International Organisations (1976). *Draft Minutes of the Meeting* (AS/Cult/Int (27) PV 3)

Parliamentary Assembly, Committee on Culture and Education, Sub-committee on UNESCO and other International Organisations (1976). *Draft Report on Co-operation with UNESCO (presented by Mrs Wolf)* (AS/Cult/Int (28) 1 / Doc.3846)

Parliamentary Assembly, Committee on Culture and Education, Sub-committee on UNESCO and other International Organisations (1976). Verbatim *Account of the Assembly Debate of Mrs Wolf's Report on Co-operation with UNESCO* (AS/Cult/Int (28) 4)

Parliamentary Assembly (1977). *Resolution 667 (1977) – Establishment of Parliamentary Heritage Groups*

Parliamentary Assembly (1977). *Written Question No. 194 by Lord Duncan-Sandys on the UNESCO Convention of 1970 for the Protection of Art Treasures against Theft* (Doc. 3972)

Parliamentary Assembly (1977). *Reply from the Committee of Ministers to Written Question No.194 by Lord Duncan-Sandys on the UNESCO Convention of 1970 for the Protection of Art Treasures against Theft* (Doc. 4071)

Parliamentary Assembly, Committee on Culture and Education, Sub-committee on UNESCO and other International Organisations (1977). *Mandate and Work Programme* (AS/Cult/Int (29) 1)

Parliamentary Assembly, Committee on Culture and Education, Sub-committee on UNESCO and other International Organisations (1977). *UNESCO General Conference (Nairobi 1976) – Intervention made by Mr de Pange representing the Secretary General of the Council of Europe in the course of the General Policy Debate* (AS/Cult/Int (28) 5)

Parliamentary Assembly, Committee on Culture and Education, Sub-committee on UNESCO and other International Organisations (1977). *Draft Minutes of the Meeting* (AS/Cult/Int (29) PV 1)

Parliamentary Assembly, Committee on Culture and Education, Sub-committee on UNESCO and other International Organisations (1977). *Draft Minutes of the Meeting* (AS/Cult/Int (28) PV 2)

Parliamentary Assembly, Committee on Culture and Education, Sub-Committee on the Architectural and Artistic Heritage of Europe (1978). *Draft Minutes of the Meeting (14 September 1978)* (AS/Cult/AA (30) PV 2)

Parliamentary Assembly (1978). *Report on the Underwater Cultural Heritage (Rapporteur: Mr. Roper)* (Doc. 4200)

Parliamentary Assembly (1978). *Recommendation 848 (1978) – Underwater Cultural Heritage*

Parliamentary Assembly, Committee on Culture and Education, Sub-committee on UNESCO and other International Organisations (1978). *Draft Minutes of the Meeting* (AS/Cult/Int (30) PV 1)

Parliamentary Assembly, Committee on Culture and Education, Sub-committee on UNESCO and other International Organisations (1978). *Draft Minutes of the Meeting* (AS/Cult/Int (29) PV 3)

Parliamentary Assembly (1978). *Report on the European Foundation Pro Venetia Viva and the European Centre for the training of craftsmen in the conservation of the architectural heritage* (Doc. 4190)

Parliamentary Assembly (1978). *Report on co-operation with UNESCO* (Doc. 4228)

Parliamentary Assembly (1979). *Communication from the Committee of Ministers transmitting to the Assembly the report of the Steering Committee for Regional Planning and the Architectural Heritage on the situation of the architectural heritage in Europe* (Doc. 4300)

Parliamentary Assembly (1979). *Report on European cultural cooperation* (Doc. 4214)

Parliamentary Assembly (1979). *Report on the conservation of the European architectural heritage – Rapporteur Lord Duncan Sandys* (Doc. 4396)

Parliamentary Assembly (1979). *Recommendation 880 – Conservation of the European architectural heritage*

Parliamentary Assembly (1979). *Recommendation 881 – Rural Architectural Heritage*

Parliamentary Assembly, Committee on Culture and Education, Sub-committee on the Architectural and Artistic Heritage (1979). *Draft Minutes of the Meeting* (AS/Cult/AA (30) PV 4)

Parliamentary Assembly, Committee on Culture and Education, Sub-committee on UNESCO and other International Organisations (1979). *Draft Minutes of the Meeting* (AS/Cult/Int (30) PV 2)

Parliamentary Assembly, Committee on Culture and Education (1979). *Discussion Paper on the Future of the Committee* (AS/Cult (31) 13)

Parliamentary Assembly, Committee on Culture and Education (1980). *Co-operation with UNESCO – Preparation of the Exchange of Views with the Director General of UNESCO* (AS/Cult (32) 4)

Parliamentary Assembly, Committee on Culture and Education, Sub-committee on UNESCO and other International Organisations (1980). *Draft Minutes of the Meeting* (AS/Cult/Int (31) PV 5)

Parliamentary Assembly, Committee on Culture and Education, Sub-committee on UNESCO and other International Organisations (1980). *Draft Minutes of the Meeting* (AS/Cult/Int (32) PV 1)

Parliamentary Assembly (1980). *Report on co-operation with UNESCO* (Doc. 4528)

Parliamentary Assembly (1980). *Recommendation 892 (1980) – Co-operation with UNESCO*

Parliamentary Assembly (1981). *Report on Metal Detectors and Archaeology* (Doc. 4741)

Parliamentary Assembly (1981). *Recommendation 921 (1981) – Metal detectors and archaeology*

Parliamentary Assembly, Committee on Culture and Education, Sub-Committee on the Architectural and Artistic Heritage (1982). *European Cooperation on the Cultural Heritage – Review of Council of Europe work on Archaeology* (AS/Cult/AA (34) 13)

Parliamentary Assembly, Committee on Culture and Education (1982). *UNESCO World Conference on Cultural Policies (Mexico 1982) – Declaration on Cultural Policies* (As/Cult (34) 34)

Parliamentary Assembly, Committee on Culture and Education (1982). *UNESCO Conference on Cultural Policies (Mexico 1982) – Report* (AS/Cult (34) 38)

Parliamentary Assembly, Committee on Culture and Education, Sub-Committee on the Architectural and Artistic Heritage (1984). *European Convention on the Architectural Heritage* (AS/Cult/AA (36) 3)

Parliamentary Assembly, Committee on Culture and Education, Sub-Committee on the Architectural and Artistic Heritage (1984). *Hearing on the Movement of Works of Art* (AS/Cult/AA (35) 21)

Parliamentary Assembly, Committee on Culture and Education (1984). *Report on the Activities of UNESCO and Co-operation with the Council of Europe* (AS/Cult (36) 6 / Doc. 5274)

Parliamentary Assembly, Committee on Culture and Education (1984). *Draft Report on European Cultural Cooperation 1982–1984* (AS/Cult (36) 7)

Parliamentary Assembly, Committee on Culture and Education (1986). *Assembly Texts and Other Reports relating to the Committee's field of Activity (since 1970)* (AS/Cult (38) 13 rev.)

Parliamentary Assembly, Committee on Culture and Education, Sub-Committee on the Architectural and Artistic Heritage (1989). *Draft Minutes of the Meeting* (AS/Cult/AA (41) PV 1)

Parliamentary Assembly, Committee on Culture and Education (1990). *Draft Comments on the Preliminary draft Intergovernmental Programme of Activities for 1991* (AS/Cult (42) 5)

Parliamentary Assembly, Committee on Culture and Education, Sub-Committee on the Architectural and Artistic Heritage (1991). *European Symposium of Firms Specialising in the Restoration of Buildings of Major Importance* (AS/Cult/AA (43) 7 rev.)

Parliamentary Assembly, Committee on Culture and Education (1991). *Assembly Texts and Other Reports relating to the Committee's Field of Activity (since 1970)* (AS/Cult (43) 28)

Parliamentary Assembly, Committee on Culture and Education, Sub-Committee on the Architectural and Artistic Heritage (1993). *Current Action by the Assembly Relating to the Cultural Heritage* (AS/Cult/AA (44) 34)

Parliamentary Assembly, Committee on Culture and Education, Sub-Committee on the Architectural and Artistic Heritage (1993). *Destruction by war of the cultural heritage in Croatia and Bosnia-Herzegovina – Information Report (rapporteur Mr. Jacques Baumel)* (AS/Cult/AA (44) 16)

Parliamentary Assembly, Committee on Culture and Education (1993). *Information Report on the destruction by war of the cultural heritage in Croatia and Bosnia-Herzegovina* (Doc. 6756)

Parliamentary Assembly, Committee on Culture and Education, Sub-Committee on the Architectural and Artistic Heritage (1994). *Draft Minutes of the Meeting* (AS/Cult/AA (94) PV 1)

Parliamentary Assembly, Committee on Culture and Education, Sub-Committee on the Architectural and Artistic Heritage (1996). *The European Plan for Archaeology – Memorandum by the Secretariat General* (AS/Cult/AA (1996) 3)

Parliamentary Assembly, Committee on Culture and Education, Sub-Committee on the Architectural and Artistic Heritage (1996). *Draft Minutes of the Meeting* (AS/Cult/AA (1996) PV 1)

Parliamentary Assembly (2000). *Recommendation 1485 (2000) – Disused hospitals and military buildings*

Parliamentary Assembly (2000). *Recommendation 1486 (2000) – Maritime and Fluvial Cultural Heritage*

Parliamentary Assembly, Committee on Culture and Education, Sub-committee on the Cultural Heritage (2001). *Access to the European Heritage in Museums – Conclusions of the European Museum Forum Workshop* (AS/Cult/AA (2001) 15)

Parliamentary Assembly (2002). *Recommendation 1566 (2002) – European Cultural Co-operation and the Future Role of the Assembly*

Parliamentary Assembly (2003). *Recommendation 1634 (2003) – Tax incentives for cultural heritage conservation*

Parliamentary Assembly (2004). *Recommendation 1651 (2004) – Ending the Plundering of African Cultural Objects*

Parliamentary Assembly (2005). *Recommendation 1730 (2005) – The Private management of Cultural Property*

Parliamentary Assembly, Committee on Culture, Science and Education (2005). *50th Anniversary of the European Cultural Convention (Closing Ministerial Conference) – "Intercultural dialogue – the way ahead"* (As/Cult (2005)43)

Parliamentary Assembly (2006). *Recommendation 1758 (2006) – Follow-up to the Third Summit: Priority for Cultural Co-operation*

Parliamentary Assembly (2008). *Recommendation 1851 (2008) – Crafts and Cultural Heritage Conservation Skills*

Parliamentary Assembly (2010). *Recommendation 1942 (2010) – A balanced Approach to the Rescuing of Archaeological Finds from Development Projects*

Parliamentary Assembly (2014). *Recommendation 2038 (2014) – Europe's Endangered Heritage*

Parliamentary Assembly (2015). *Recommendation 2071 (2015) – Cultural Heritage in Crisis and Post-crisis Situations*

Parliamentary Assembly, Committee on Culture, Science, Education and Media (2019). *Report: Safeguarding and Enhancing Intangible Cultural Heritage in Europe* (Doc. 14832)

Parliamentary Assembly, Committee on Culture, Science, Education and Media (2019). *Report: The Value of Cultural Heritage in a Democratic Society (Provisional Version)*

Other International Organisations

UNESCO

UNESCO (1954). *Convention for the Protection of Cultural Property in the Event of Armed Conflict*

UNESCO (1956). *Recommendation on International Principle Applicable to Archaeological Excavations*

UNESCO (1958). Records of the General Conference, tenth session, Paris – Resolution 4.62

UNESCO (1964). Records of the *General Conference – Resolutions*

UNESCO (1964). *Recommendation on the Means of Prohibiting and Preventing the Illicit Export, Import and Transfer of Ownership of Cultural Property*

UNESCO (1968). *Appraisal of the Major Project on Mutual Appreciation of Eastern and Western Cultural Values (1957–1966)*

UNESCO (1968). *Recommendation concerning the Preservation of Cultural Property Endangered by Public or Private works*

UNESCO (1970). *Convention on the Means of Prohibiting and Preventing the Illicit Import, Export and Transfer of Ownership of Cultural Property*

UNESCO (1970). List of the State Parties to the *Convention on the Means of Prohibiting and Preventing the Illicit Import, Export and Transfer of Ownership of Cultural Property*

UNESCO (1970). *Protection of mankind's cultural heritage: Sites and Monuments*. Paris: UNESCO

UNESCO (1972). *Intergovernmental Conference on Cultural Policies in Europe (Helsinki 1972) – Final Report*

UNESCO (1972). *Address by Mr René Maheu, Director-General of the UNESCO at the opening meeting of the Intergovernmental Conference on Cultural Policies in Europe* (DG/72/12)

UNESCO (1972). *Report of the Director-General on the Intergovernmental Conference on Cultural Policies in Europe* (17 C/70)

UNESCO (1972). *Convention Concerning the Protection of the World Cultural and Natural Heritage* (The World Heritage Convention)

UNESCO (1973). *Cultural co-operation in Europe – Situation and Prospects*

UNESCO (1983). General Conference – *Measures Taken with a view to Implementing 21 C/Resolution 7.06, Paragraph 3(k) on European Co-operation: Report of the Director-General* (22 C/101)

UNESCO (2001). *Convention on the Protection of the Underwater Cultural Heritage*

UNESCO (2001). *UNESCO Universal Declaration on Cultural Diversity*

UNESCO (2002). *The Budapest Declaration on World Heritage* (WHC-02/CONF.202/5)
UNESCO (2003). *Convention for the Safeguarding of the Intangible Cultural Heritage*
UNESCO (2005). *Convention on the Protection and Promotion of the Diversity of Cultural Expressions*
UNESCO (2011). *Operational Guidelines for the Implementation of the World Heritage Convention* (WHC. 11/01)

United Nations (UN)

United Nations (1948). *Universal Declaration of Human Right*
United Nations (1966). *International Covenant on Civil and Political Rights*
United Nations (1966). *International Covenant on Economic, Social and Cultural Rights*
United Nations (1982). *Convention on the Law of the Sea*
Report of the World Commission on Environment and Development: Our Common Future. United Nations General Assembly; *document*; A/42/42
United Nations, General Assembly (1992). *Rio Declaration on Environment and Development*, document A/CONF.151/26 (Vol.I)
United Nations, Human Rights Council (2009). *Resolution 10/23 – Independent expert in the field of cultural rights*
United Nations, Human Rights Council (2012). *Resolution 19/6 – Special Rapporteur in the field of cultural rights*
United Nations (2015). *Transforming our world: the 2030 Agenda for Sustainable Development*

ICOMOS

Second International Congress of Architects and Technicians of Historic Monuments (1964). *International Charter for the Conservation and Restoration of Monuments and Sites* (*The Venice Charter*)
The Second General Assembly of ICOMOS (1969). *The value for tourism of the conservation and presentation of monuments and sites with special reference to experience and practice in Great Britain, Oxford, United Kingdom*
ICOMOS Australia (1979/1999/2013). *The Burra Charter – The Australia ICOMOS Charter for Places of Cultural Significance*
ICOMOS (1990). *Charter for the Protection and Management of the Archaeological Heritage (1990)*
ICOMOS (1998). *The Stockholm Declaration: Declaration of ICOMOS marking the 50th anniversary of the Universal Declaration of Human Rights (1998)*

ICOM

ICOM (1986, 2001, 2004). *Code of Ethics for Museums*

European Union

European Parliament (1973). *Motion for a Resolution submitted by Mr. Hougardy on behalf of the Liberal and Allies Group on measures to protect the European Cultural Heritage* (Document 73/73)

European Commission (1974). *Recommendation to Member States concerning the protection of the architectural and natural heritage* (75/65/EEC)

European Parliament (1974). *Report drawn up on behalf of the Committee on Cultural Affairs and Youth on the motion for a resolution submitted by Mr. Premoli on behalf of the Liberal and Allies Group on measures to protect the European cultural heritage; Rapporteur – Lady Elles* (Document 54/74)

European Union (1992). *Treaty of Maastricht on European Union*

Council of the European Union (2014). *Conclusions on cultural heritage as a strategic resource for a sustainable Europe*

European Commission (2014). *Towards an integrated approach to cultural heritage for Europe* (COM (2014) 477 final)

European Commission (2014). *Mapping of cultural heritage actions in European Union policies, programmes and activities*

Western European Union

Assembly of Western European Union (1957). *Proceedings – Third Session*

NATO

NATO (1953). *Social and Cultural Co-operation – Interim Report by the Working Group* (C-M (53) 25)

NATO, Working Group on Social and Cultural Co-operation (1953). *Draft Recommendations Relating to Cultural Exchange Between the NATO Countries* (AC/31-D/7)

NATO, Committee on Information and Cultural Relations (1954). *Report to the Secretary General from the Temporary Cultural Consultant on Strengthening Cultural Co-operation Among NATO Countries* (AC/52-D/53)

NATO, The Committee of Three (1956). *Summary Record of the Meeting of the Council* (C-R (56) 23)

NATO, The Committee of Three (1956). *Report of the Committee of Three on Non-military Cooperation in NATO* (C-M (56) 126)

African Union

African Union (1981). *African charter on human and people's right*

African Union (2006). *Charter for African cultural renaissance*

African Union (2013). *Agenda 2063: The Africa we want*

Organisation of American States (OAS)

Organisation of Americas, Fourth Summit of the Americas (2005). *Declaration of Mar del Plata*

Organisation of Americas, Fifth Summit of the Americas (2009). *Declaration of Commitment of Port of Spain*

Organisation of Americas (2011), *Final Report* of the Fifth Inter-American Meeting of Ministers of Culture and Highest Appropriate Authorities (on 9–10 November 2011 at OAS Headquarters, Washington, DC) [OAS Doc OEA/Ser.K/XXVII.3 CIDI/REMIC-III/doc.6/11 rev]

Other Inernational Documents

United States of America (1974). *Archaeological and Historical Preservation Act*

Association of Southeast Asian Nations – ASEAN (2007). *The Charter of the Association of Southeast Asian Nations, Singapore 2007*

Swedish National Heritage Board (2014). *Report – The Faro Convention*

University of Fribourg, Interdisciplinary Institute of Ethnics and Human Rights (2007). *Fribourg Declaration on Cultural Rights*

Bibliography

Assemblee Europeenne 1949–1969 (Hansard Society for Parliamentary Government 1969)

Abousnnouga G and Machin D, *The Language of War Monuments* (Bloomsbury Publishing 2013)

Ahmad Y, 'The Scope and Definitions of Heritage: From Tangible to Intangible' (2006) 12 *International Journal of Heritage Studies* 292

Akagawa N, 'Rethinking the Global Heritage Discourse – Overcoming "East" and "West"?' (2016) 22 *International Journal of Heritage Studies* 14

Akagawa N and Smith L, *Safeguarding Intangible Heritage: Practice and Politics* (Routledge 2018)

Albert M-T (ed), *Perceptions of Sustainability in Heritage Studies* (De Gruyter 2015)

Albert M-T, Bandarin F and Pereira Roders A (eds), *Going Beyond: Perceptions of Sustainability in Heritage Studies No 2* (Springer 2017)

Alderman K, 'The Human Right to Cultural Property' (2011) 32 *Michigan Journal of International Law* 2

Anderson B, *Imagined Communities: Reflections on the Origins and Spread of Nationalism* (Verso 1983)

Archer M, *Realist Social Theory: The Morphogenic Approach* (CUP 1995)

Arnstein S, 'A Ladder of Citizen Participation' (1969) 35 *Journal of the American Institute of Planners* 216

Ashurst J, *Conservation of Ruins* (Routledge 2007)

Ashworth GJ and Graham B (eds), *Senses of Place: Senses of Time* (Routledge 2005)

Ashworth GJ and Larkham PJ (eds), *Building a New Heritage: Tourism, Culture and Identity in the New Europe* (Routledge 1994)

Ashworth GJ, Graham B and Tunbridge JE, *Pluralising Pasts: Heritage, Identity and Place in Multicultural Societies* (Pluto Press 2007)

Askew M, 'The Magic List of Global Status: UNESCO, World Heritage and the Agendas of State' in Labadi S and Logan C (eds), *Heritage and Globalisation* (Routledge 2010) 19

Avrami E, Mason R and de la Torre M, *Values and Heritage Conservation* (Getty Conservation Institute 2000)

Babić, S., Karl, R., Milosavljević, M., Mizoguchi, K., Paludan-Müller, C., Murray, T., Robb, J., Schlanger, N. and Vanzetti, A. (2017) 'What Is 'European Archaeology'? What Should it be?' *European Journal of Archaeology*, 20(1), pp. 4–35.

Baillie, B. and Sørensen, M.L.S. (2021) 'Heritage Challenges in Africa: Contestations and Expectations', in: Baillie, B. and Sørensen, M.L.S. (eds) *African Heritage Chal-*

lenges. Communities and Sustainable Development. Singapore: Palgrave Macmillan, pp. 1–43.

Baird, M.F. (2014) 'Heritage, human rights, and social justice', *Heritage & Society*, 7(2), pp. 139–155.

Barnett, C. (2001) 'Culture, policy and subsidiarity in the European Union: from symbolic identity to the governmentalisation of culture', *Political Geography*, 20, pp. 405–426.

Barthel, D. (1996) *Historic Preservation: Collective Memory and Historical Identity.* New Brunswick: Rutgers University Press.

Basu, P. and Modest, W. (eds) (2015) *Museums, Heritage and International Development.* New York: Routledge.

Bauer, A. A. (2007) 'New Ways of Thinking About Cultural Property: A Critical Appraisal of the Antiquities Trade Debates', *Fordham International Law Journal*, 31(3), pp. 690–724.

Bauer, A. A. (2015) 'Cultural Property – Building Communities of Stewardship beyond Nationalism and Internationalism', in: Samuels, K. L. and T. Rico (eds) *Heritage Keywords: Rhetoric and Redescription in Cultural Heritage.* Colorado: University Press of Colorado, pp. 81–94.

Bauman, Z. (2004) *Europe: An Unfinished Adventure.* Cambridge: Polity

Bellucci, P., Sanders, D. and Serricchio, F. (2012) 'Explaining European Identity', in: Sanders, D., Bellucci, P., Tóka, G. and Torcal, M. (eds) *The Europeanization of National Polities? Citizenship and Support in a Post-enlargement Union.* Oxford: Oxford University Press, pp. 61–91.

Beloff, M. (1957) *Europe and the Europeans – an international discussion.* London: Chatto & Windus.

Beloff, M. (1961) *New Dimensions in Foreign Policy: A Study in British Administrative Experience 1947–59.* New York: Routledge.

Benwell, B. and Stokoe, E. (2006) *Discourse and Identity.* Edinburgh: Edinburgh University Press.

Berger, S., Dicks, B. and Fontaine, M. (2020) 'Community: a useful concept in heritage studies?', *International Journal of Heritage Studies*, 26(4), pp. 325–351.

Bertacchini, E., Liuzza, C., Meskell, L. and Saccone, D. (2016) 'The politicization of UNESCO World Heritage decision making', *Public Choice*, 167, pp. 95–129.

Bhaskar, R. (1978) *A Realist Theory of Science.* London: Routledge.

Bhaskar, R. (1986) *Scientific Realism and Human Emancipation.* London: Verso.

Bhaskar, R. (1989) *Reclaiming Reality. A Critical Introduction to Contemporary Philosophy.* London: Verso.

Bhaskar, R. and Danermark, B. (2006) 'Metatheory, interdisciplinarity and disability research: A critical realist perspective', *Scandinavian Journal of Disability Research*, 8(4), pp. 278–297.

Biehl, P. F., Gramsch, A. and Marciniak, A. (eds) (2002) *Archaeologies of Europe: History, Methods, and Theories*. Berlin: Waxmann.

Billing, M. (2008) 'The language of critical discourse analysis: The case of nominalisation', *Discourse & Society*, 19(6), pp. 783–800.

Bitsch, M.-T. (1986) 'Le rôle de la France dans la naissance du Conseil de l'Europe' in: R. Poidevin (ed.) *Histoire des débuts de la construction européenne*. Bruxelles: Bruylant, pp. 165–198.

Bitsch, M.-T. (2004) *Histoire de la construction européene de 1945 à nos jours*. Edition Complexe.

Blake, J. (1996) 'The protection of the underwater cultural heritage', *International & Comparative Law Quarterly*, 45(4), pp.819–843.

Blake, J. (2000) 'On Defining the Cultural Heritage', *The International and Comparative Law Quarterly*, 49(1), pp. 61–85.

Blake, J. (2009) 'UNESCO's 2003 Convention on Intangible Cultural Heritage: The Implications of Community Involvement in 'Safeguarding'', in: Smith, L. and N. Akagawa (eds) *Intangible Heritage*. London and New York: Routledge, pp. 45–73.

Blake J. (2011) 'Taking a human rights approach to cultural heritage protection', *Heritage & Society*, 4(2), pp. 199–238.

Blake, J. (2015) *International Cultural Heritage Law*. Oxford: Oxford University Press.

Blake, J. (2016) 'Development of UNESCO's 2003 Convention – Creating a new heritage protection paradigm?', in: Stefano, M.L. and P. Davis (eds) *The Routledge Companion to Intangible Cultural Heritage*. London: Routledge, pp. 11–21.

Blake, J. (2018) 'Gender and intangible heritage: illustrating the inter-disciplinary character of international law', in: Grahn, W. and R.J. Wilson (eds) *Gender and Heritage: Performance, Place and Politics*. New York: Routledge, pp. 207–220.

Blommaetr, J. (2005) *Discourse: A Critical Introduction*. Cambridge: Cambridge University Press.

Bold, J. (2016) 'The technical co-operation programme: context and evolution', in: Bold, J. and M. Cherry (eds) *The politics of heritage regeneration in South-East Europe*. Strasbourg: Council of Europe Publishing, pp. 17–26.

Bold, J. and Pickard, R. (eds) (2018) *An Integrated Approach to Cultural Heritage – The Council of Europe's Technical Co-operation and Consultancy Programme*. Strasbourg: Council of Europe Publishing.

Bond, M. (2012) *The Council of Europe – Structure, history and issues in European politics*. London and New York: Routledge.

Bonnici, U.M. (2009) 'The human right to cultural heritage – the Faro Convention's contribution to the recognition and safeguarding of this human right', in: Council of Europe *Heritage and beyond*. Strasbourg: Council of Europe Publishing, pp. 53–58.

Borneman, J. and Fowler, N. (1997) 'Europeanization', *Annual Review of Anthropology*, 26(1), pp. 487–514.

Boswell, D. and Evans, J. (eds) (1999) *Representing the Nation: A Reader Histories, Heritage and Museums*. London and New York: Routledge.

Bourdeau, L., Gravari-Barbas, M. and Robinson, M. (eds) (2016) *World Heritage, Tourism and Identity: Inscription and Co-production*. London: Routledge.

Boylan, P. J. (1993) *Review of the Convention for the Protection of Cultural Property in the Event of Armed Conflict (The Hague Convention of 1954)*. Paris: UNESCO

Boylan, P. J. (2002) 'The Concept of Cultural Protection in Times of Armed Conflict: From the Crusades to the New Millennium', in: Brodie, N. and W. K. Tubb (eds) *Illicit Antiquities: The Theft of Culture and the Extinction of Archaeology*. New York: Routledge, pp. 43–108.

Brumann, C. (2014) 'Shifting tides of world-making in the UNESCO World Heritage Convention: cosmopolitanism colliding', *Ethnic and Racial Studies*, 37(12), pp. 2176–2192.

Brumann, C. (2015) 'Community as Myth and Reality in the UNESCO World Heritage Convention', in: Adell, N., Bendix, R. F., Bartolotto, C. and M. Tauschek (eds) *Between Imagined Communities and Communities of Practice*. Göttingen: Universitätsverlag Göttingen, pp. 273–289.

Burman, P. and Rodwell, D. (2015) 'The Contribution of the United Kingdom to European Architectural Heritage Year 1975', in: Falser, M. and W. Lipp (ICOMOS Austria) (eds) *A Future for Our Past: The 40th Anniversary of European Architectural Heritage Year (1975–2015)*. Berlin: Hendrik Bäßler Verlag.

Byrne, D. (1991) 'Western hegemony in archaeological heritage management', *History and Anthropology*, 5(2), pp. 269–276.

Calligaro O, *Negotiating Europe: EU Promotion of Europeanness since the 1950s* (Palgrave Macmillan 2013)

Calligaro O, 'From "European Cultural Heritage" to "Cultural Diversity"? The Changing Core Values of European Cultural Policy' (2014) 45 *Politique Européenne* 60

Calligaro O, 'Which Culture(s) for Europe?: The Contrasting Conceptions of the Council of Europe and the European Union from 1949 to the Present Day' (2017) 13 *Cambio: rivista sulle trasformazioni sociali* 67

Carman J, *Archaeology and Heritage: An Introduction* (Continuum 2002)

Cave C and Negussie E, *World Heritage Conservation: The World Heritage Convention, Linking Culture and Nature for Sustainable Development* (Routledge 2017)

Chabiera A, *Polish Civil Society and the Aims of the Faro Convention – Report for the Council of Europe*(2017) https://rm.coe.int/polish-civil-society-and-the-aims-of-the-faro-convention/1680a1b6dcaccessed 4 April 2022

Chalturin AG, 'The Fifth General Assembly of ICOMOS – 1978' (1995) 5 *Scientific Journal: Thirty Years of ICOMOS* 38

Chirikure S and others, 'Unfulfilled Promises? Heritage Management and Community Participation as Some of Africa's Cultural Heritage Sites' (2010) 16 *International Journal of Heritage Studies* 30

Churchill W, *Speech delivered at the University of Zurich* (19 September 1946) https://rm.coe.int/16806981f3 accessed 3 March 2018

Choay F, *The Invention of the Historic Monument* (CUP 2001)

Chouliaraki L and Fairclough N, *Discourse in Late Modernity: Rethinking Critical Discourse Analysis*(Edinburgh UP 1999)

Clarke D, 'Archaeology: The Loss of Innocence' (1973) 47 *Antiquity* 6

Clarke R, 'Heritage in Trust: Sustainable Stewardship in Transition?' (1996) 2 *International Journal of Heritage Studies* 145

Clarke A, 'Heritage Diplomacy' in Watanabe Y (ed), *Handbook of Cultural Security* (Edward Elgar 2018) 417

Cleere H (ed), *Archaeological Heritage Management in the Modern World* (Routledge 2000)

Cleere H (ed), 'The Charter for the Protection and Management of the Archaeological Heritage' (1993) 67 *Antiquity* 402

Cleere H (ed), 'The Uneasy Bedfellows: Universality and Cultural Heritage' in Layton R, Stone PG and Thomas J (eds), *Destruction and Conservation of Cultural Property* (Routledge 2001) 22

Clive B, 'Culture, Policy, and Subsidiarity in the European Union: From Symbolic Identity to the Governmentalisation of Culture' (2001) 20 *Political Geography* 405

Colantonio A, 'Measuring Social Sustainability: Best Practice from Urban Renewal in the EU' (2008) EIBURS Working Paper Series 2008/2

Colella S, 'Not a Mere Tangential Outbreak: Gender, Feminism and Cultural Heritage' (2018) 18 *Il Capitale culturale* 251

Coleman J (ed), *The Council of Europe* (Council of Europe Publishing 1999)

Colomer L and Catalani A (eds), *Heritage Discourses in Europe: Responding to Migration, Mobility and Cultural Identity in the 21st Century* (Arc Humanities Press 2020)

Colomer L, 'Exploring Participatory Heritage Governance After the EU Faro Convention' (2021) 13 *Journal of Cultural Heritage Management and Sustainable Development*

Confédération Suisse, *Consultation concernant la ratification de la Convention-cadre du Conseil de l'Europe sur la valeur du patrimoine culturel pour la société* (2018) http://bit.ly/3ShO7a3 accessed 5 April 2022

Congress Internationaux d'Architecture moderne, *La Charte d'Athènes* (1933, trans Tyrwhitt J 1946)

Cornu M, 'La Convention pour la protection et la promotion de la diversité des expressions culturelles' (2006) 3 *Journal du droit international* 929 Council of Europe, *The First Five Years – 5.V.1949 – 5.V.1954* (1954)

Cornu M, *European Yearbook/Annuaire Européen vol 1* (Brill/Nijhoff 1955)

Cornu M, *European Yearbook/Annuaire Européen vol 3* (Brill/Nijhoff 1957)

Cornu M, *20 Years of Education and Cultural Activity in the Service of Europe – 1949–1969* (1969)

Cornu M, *Manual of the Council of Europe* (Stevens & Sons 1970)

Cornu M, *An Experiment in Multilateral Cultural Cooperation in Europe: The Council for Cultural Cooperation*(1972)

Cornu M, *Congress of Europe* (1999)

Cornu M, *The Council of Europe and Cultural Heritage – 1954–2000* (2001)

Cornu M, *50 Years of the European Cultural Convention* (2004a) https://www.coe.int/t/dg4/CulturalConvention/Source/Bilan50_EN.pdf accessed 3 March 2018

Cornu M, *50 Years of Council of Europe Art Exhibitions* (2004b)

Cornu M, *Analysis and Reform of Cultural Heritage Policies in South-East Europe* (2008) Cornu M, *Heritage and Beyond* (2009)

Cornu M, *The Faro Convention Action Plan Handbook 2018–2019* (2018)

Cornu M, *The Faro Convention's Role in a Changing Society – Building on a Decade of Advancement 2011–2021* (2021)

Cornu M, *The Faro Convention at Work in Europe: Selected Examples* (2022)

Crang M, 'Living History: Magic Kingdoms or a Quixotic Quest for Authenticity?' (1996) 23 *Annals of Tourism Research* 415

Crooke E, 'The Politics of Community Heritage: Motivations, Authority and Control' (2010) 16 *International Journal of Heritage Studies* 16

Crouch D, 'Places Around Us: Embodied Lay Geographies in Leisure and Tourism' (2000) 19 *Leisure Studies* 63

Crouch D, 'Spatialities and the Feeling of Doing' (2001) 2 *Social and Cultural Geography* 61

Crouch D, 'Spacing, Performing, and Becoming: Tangles in the Mundane' (2003) 35 *Environment and Planning* 1945

Dalibard J, 'The Next 20 Years' (1989) 21 *APT Bulletin* 4

Deacon H and Smeets R, 'Authenticity, Value and Community Involvement in Heritage Management under the World Heritage and Intangible Heritage Conventions' (2013) 6 *Heritage & Society* 1

De Cesari C, *Cultural Heritage Beyond the "State": Palestinian Heritage between Nationalism and Transnationalism* (PhD Thesis, Stanford University 2009)

De Cesari C, 'Memory Voids and the New European Heritage: A Proposal for Studying Transnational Memory' (2012) 25 *Journal of Museum Ethnography* 152

De La Torre M, 'Values and Heritage Conservation' (2013) 6 *Heritage & Society* 155

De La Torre M and Mason R, 'Introduction' in De La Torre M (ed), *Assessing the Values of Cultural Heritage* (Getty Conservation Institute 2002) 3

De Marco L, 'The Issue of the Historic Centres and the Italian Contribution to the European Architectural Heritage Year 1975: Precedents and Current Perspectives' (2015) 3 *Monumenta* 301

Deering MJ, *Denis de Rougemont l'Européen* (Fondation Jean Monnet pour l'Europe 1991)

Delafons J, *Politics and Preservation – A Policy History of the Build Heritage, 1882–1996* (E&FN Spon 1997)

Delanty G, *Inventing Europe: Idea, Identity, Reality* (St Martin's Press 1995)

Delanty G, 'The European Heritage: History, Memory, and Time' in Rumford C (ed), *The Sage Handbook of European Studies* (SAGE 2009) 36

Delanty G, *The Cosmopolitan Imagination: The Renewal of Critical Social Theory* (CUP 2009)

Delanty G, *The European Heritage: A Critical Re-interpretation* (Routledge 2018)

Delanty G and Rumford C, *Rethinking Europe: Social Theory and the Implications of Europeanization*(Routledge 2005)

Demoule J-P, 'Rescue Archaeology: The French Way' (2002a) 2 *Public Archaeology* 170

Demoule J-P, 'Answer to Roger Thomas' (2002b) 2 *Public Archaeology* 239

Depaepe P, 'Preventive Archaeology, Scientific Research and Public Outreach: Some Non-politically Correct Thoughts' in Novaković P and others (eds), *Recent Developments in Preventive Archaeology in Europe* (Ljubljana University Press 2016)

Díaz-Andreu M and Champion T, 'Nationalism and Archaeology in Europe: An Introduction' in Díaz-Andreu M and Champion T (eds), *Nationalism and Archaeology in Europe* (Routledge 1996) 1

Díaz-Andreu M, *A World History of Nineteenth-Century Archaeology – Nationalism, Colonialism, and the Past* (OUP 2007)Díaz-Andreu M, 'Heritage Values and the Public' (2017) 4 *Journal of Community Archaeology & Heritage* 2

Diner D, 'Restitution and Memory: The Holocaust in European Political Cultures' (2003) 90 *New German Critique* 36

Dolff-Bonekämper G, 'The Social and Spatial Frameworks of Heritage – What Is New in the Faro Convention' in Council of Europe, *Heritage and Beyond* (Council of Europe Publishing 2009) 69

Douglas M, 'Traditional Culture: Let's Hear No More About It' in Rao V and Walton M (eds), *Culture and Public Action* (Stanford UP 2004) 85

Dromgoole S, '2001 UNESCO Convention on the Protection of the Underwater Cultural Heritage' (2003) 18 *International Journal of Marine and Coastal Law* 59

Dromgoole S, *Underwater Cultural Heritage and International Law* (CUP 2013)

During R, 'European Heritage Discourses, a Matter of Identity Construction' in During R (ed), *Cultural Heritage and Identity Politics* (Wageningen Academic Publishers 2011) 17

Eder K and Spohn W (eds), *Collective Memory and European Identity: The Effects of Integration and Enlargement* (Ashgate 2005)

Edensor T, *Industrial Ruins: Space, Aesthetics and Materiality* (Berg 2005)

Edensor T and Kothari U, 'The Masculinisation of Stirling's Heritage' in Kinnaird V and Hall DR (eds), *Tourism: A Gender Analysis* (Wiley 1994) 164

Egloff B and Comer D, 'Conserving the Archaeological Soul of Places: Drafting Guidelines for the ICAHM Charter' (ICOMOS General Assembly 2008)

Ekern S and others, 'Human Rights and World Heritage: Preserving Our Common Dignity Through Rights-Based Approaches to Site Management' (2012) 18 *International Journal of Heritage Studies* 213

Emerick K, *Conserving and Managing Ancient Monuments: Heritage, Democracy, and Inclusion* (Boydell Press 2014)

Erder C, *The Venice Charter under review* (1977) https://www.icomos.org/venicecharter2004/erder.pdfaccessed 7 June 2020

Erder C, *Facing Europeanism* (2000) 7 *Archaeological Dialogues* 2

Fairclough N, *Language and Power* (Longman 1989)

Fairclough N, *Discourse and Social Change* (Polity Press 1992)

Fairclough N, 'Critical Discourse Analysis and the Marketization of Public Discourse: The Universities' (1993) 4 *Discourse & Society* 133

Fairclough N, *Critical Discourse Analysis: The Critical Study of Language* (Pearson 1995)

Fairclough N, 'Linguistic and Intertextual Analysis in Discourse Analysis' in Jaworski A and Coupland N (eds), *The Discourse Reader* (Routledge 1999) 183

Fairclough N, 'Critical Discourse Analysis as a Method in Social Scientific Research' in Wodak R and Meyer M (eds), *Methods of Critical Discourse Analysis* (SAGE 2001) 121

Fairclough N, *Analysing Discourse – Textual Analysis for Social Research* (Routledge 2003)

Fairclough N, *Critical Discourse Analysis* (2nd edn, Longman 2010)

Fairclough N and Wodak R, 'Critical Discourse Analysis' in Van Dijk TA (ed), *Discourse as Social Interaction* (SAGE 1997) 258

Fairclough N and others, 'Introduction' (2004) 1 *Critical Discourse Studies* 1

Fairclough N, Jessop B and Sayer A, 'Critical Realism and Semiosis' in Joseph J and Roberts JM (eds), *Realism Discourse and Deconstruction* (Routledge 2004) 23

Fairclough G, 'New Heritage Frontiers' in Council of Europe, *Heritage and Beyond* (Council of Europe Publishing 2009a) 29

Fairclough N, 'The Cultural Context of Sustainability – Heritage and Living' in Council of Europe, *Heritage and Beyond* (Council of Europe Publishing 2009b) 125

Falser M and Lipp W (eds), *A Future for Our Past: The 40th Anniversary of European Architectural Heritage Year (1975–2015)* (Hendrik Bäßler Verlag 2015)

Ferracuti S, 'L'Etnografo del patrimonio in Europa: esercizi di teoria e cittadinanza' in Zagato L and Vecco M (eds), *Le culture dell'Europa, l'Europa della culture* (Franco Angeli 2011) 206

Farrell M, Fella S and Newman M (eds), *European Integration in the 21st Century: Unity in Diversity* (SAGE 2002)

Faulkner N, 'Archaeology from Below' (2000) 1 *Public Archaeology* 21

Fischer A and Kristiansen K (eds), *The Neolithization of Denmark: 150 Years of Debate* (JR Collis Publications 2002)

Fitch KL and Sanders RE (eds), *Handbook of Language and Social Interaction* (1st edn, Psychology Press 2004)

Fligstein N, Polyakova A and Sandholtz W, 'European Integration, Nationalism and European Identity' (2012) 50 *Journal of Common Market Studies* 106

Fojut N, 'The Philosophical, Political and Pragmatic Roots of the Convention' in Council of Europe, *Heritage and Beyond* (Council of Europe Publishing 2009) 13

Forrest C, *International Law and the Protection of Cultural Heritage* (Routledge 2010)

Foucault M, *The Order of Discourse* (Gallimard 1971)

Foucault M, *The Order of Things* (Tavistock 1974)

Foucault M, *The Archaeology of Knowledge* (Tavistock 1977)

Foucault M, *The History of Sexuality, Volume One: An Introduction* (Penguin 1981)

Francioni F, 'Culture, Heritage and Human Rights: An Introduction' in Francioni F and Scheinin M (eds), *Cultural Human Rights* (Martinus Nijhoff 2008) 1

Fuentes JL, 'Cultural Diversity in the Council of Europe Documents: The Role of Education and the Intercultural Dialogue' (2016) 14 *Policy Futures in Education* 377

Gauthier M, 'The Origins and Aims of the Valletta Convention: Its Implementation in France' in Van der Haas VM and Schut PAC (eds), *The Valletta Convention: Twenty Years After* (EAC Occasional Paper No 9, 2014) 31

Gazzola P, *The Past in the Future* (DAPCO 1969)

Gee JP, *Social Linguistics and Literacies: Ideology in Discourse* (5th edn, Taylor & Francis 2011)

Gee JP, *An Introduction to Discourse Analysis: Theory and Method* (2nd edn, Routledge 2005)

Gibson L and Pendlebury J (eds), *Valuing Historic Environments* (Ashgate 2009)

Gilroy P, *After Empire: Melancholia or Convivial Culture* (Routledge 2004)

Giuditta G, 'The Principle of International Restitution of Cultural Property in the 1954 Hague Convention: The UNIDROIT Contribution' (2018) 23 *Uniform Law Review* 42

Gladwyn L, *The European Idea* (New English Library 1967)

Glendinning M, 'The Conservation Movement: A Cult of the Modern Age' (2003) 13 *Transactions of the Royal Historical Society* 359

Glendinning M, *Modern Architect: The Life and Times of Robert Matthew* (RIBA Publishing 2008)

Glendinning M, *The Conservation Movement: A History of Architectural Preservation – Antiquity to Modernity* (Routledge 2013)

Glendinning M, 'The European Architectural Heritage Year and UNESCO World Heritage: The Hare and the Tortoise?' in Falser M and Lipp W (eds), *A Future for Our Past* (Hendrik Bäßler Verlag 2015)

Gould PG and Pyburn A (eds), *Collision or Collaboration: Archaeology Encounters Economic Development* (Springer 2017)

Graham B, Ashworth GJ and Tunbridge JE, *A Geography of Heritage: Power, Culture and Economy*(Arnold 2000)

Graham B, 'The Uses and Abuses of Heritage' in Corsane G (ed), *Heritage, Museums and Galleries: An Introductory Reader* (Routledge 2005) 26

Graham B and Howard P (eds), *The Routledge Research Companion to Heritage and Identity* (Routledge 2008)

Graham SE, 'The (Real) Politics of Culture: U.S. Cultural Diplomacy in UNESCO, 1946–1954' (2006) 30 *Diplomatic History* 231

Gramsch A, '"Reflexiveness" in Archaeology, Nationalism and Europeanism' (2000) 7 *Archaeological Dialogues* 4

Gramsch A, 'Theory in Central European Archaeology: Dead or Alive?' in Bintliff J and Pearce M (eds), *The Death of Archaeological Theory?* (Oxbow Books 2011) 48

Gramsch A and Sommer U (eds), *A History of Central European Archaeology – Theory, Methods, and Politics* (Archaeolingua 2011)

Grosjean E, *Forty Years of Cultural Co-operation at the Council of Europe, 1954–94* (Council of Europe Publishing 1997)

Guerrieri S, 'From the Hague Congress to the Council of Europe: Hopes, Achievements and Disappointments in the Parliamentary Way to European Integration (1948–51)' (2014) 34 *Parliaments, Estates and Representation* 216

Haas E, 'International Integration: The European and the Universal Process' (1961) 15 *International Organization* 366

Haigh A, 'The Council for Cultural Co-operation' (1970) 16 *European Yearbook* 129

Haigh A, *Cultural Mission of the Council of Europe* (Council of Europe 1970)

Haigh A, *Cultural Diplomacy in Europe* (Council of Europe 1974)

Hakenbeck SE, 'Migration in Archaeology: Are We Nearly There Yet?' (2008) 23 *Archaeological Review from Cambridge* 9

Haigh A, 'Genetics, Archaeology and the Far Right: An Unholy Trinity' (2019) 51 *World Archaeology* 517

Halbwachs M, *On Collective Memory* (University of Chicago Press 1992)

Hall S, 'Representation, Meaning and Language' in Hall S (ed), *Representation: Cultural Representations and Signifying Practices* (SAGE 1997) 15

Hall S, 'Introduction and the Work of Representation' in Hall S (ed), *Representation: Cultural Representations and Signifying Practices* (SAGE 1997) 1

Hall S, 'Whose Heritage? Un-settling "The Heritage", Re-imagining the Post-nation' (1999) 13 *Third Text* 3

Hall S, 'Foucault: Power, Knowledge and Discourse' in Wetherell M, Taylor S and Yates SJ (eds), *Discourse Theory and Practice: A Reader* (SAGE 2001) 72

Haller B, *An Assembly for Europe – The Council of Europe's Parliamentary Assembly 1949–1989* (Council of Europe Publishing 2006)

Hamilakis Y and Duke P, *Archaeology and Capitalism: From Ethics to Politics* (Left Coast Press 2008)

Hardy M (ed), *The Venice Charter Revisited: Modernism, Conservation and Tradition in the 21st Century*(Cambridge Scholars Publishing 2009)

Harrison R, *Heritage: Critical Approaches* (Routledge 2013)Harrison R, 'Beyond "Natural" and "Cultural" Heritage: Toward an Ontological Politics of Heritage in the Age of Anthropocene' (2015) 8 *Heritage & Society* 24

Hermann R, Brewer T and Risse T (eds), *Transnational Identities: Becoming European in the EU* (Rowman & Littlefield 2004)

Harré R and Bhaskar R, 'How to Challenge Reality: Story v. Structure' in López J and Potter G (eds), *After Postmodernism: An Introduction to Critical Realism* (Athlone Press 2001) 22

Harvey D, 'Heritage Pasts and Heritage Presents: Temporality, Meaning and the Scope of Heritage Studies' (2001) 11 *International Journal of Heritage Studies* 269

Historic England, *Conservation Principles, Policies and Guidance* (2008) https://bit.ly/3tRRPhk accessed 4 March 2022

Hoggart R, *An Idea and Its Servants: UNESCO from Within* (Chatto & Windus 1978)

Hodder I, 'Interpretive Archaeology and Its Role' (1991) 56 *American Antiquity* 7

Hodder I, 'Cultural Heritage Rights: From Ownership and Descent to Justice and Well-being' (2010) 83 *Anthropological Quarterly* 861

Hodder I, *Archaeological Theory in Europe – The Last Three Decades* (Routledge 2015)

Hølleland H, 'Spells of History: Childe's Contribution to the European Identity Discourse' (2010) 20 *Bulletin of the History of Archaeology* 30

Hølleland H and Skrede J, 'What's Wrong with Heritage Experts? An Interdisciplinary Discussion of Experts and Expertise in Heritage Studies' (2019) 25 *International Journal of Heritage Studies* 825

Houbart C, 'Deconsecrating a Doctrinal Monument: Raymond M. Lemaire (1921–1997) and the Revisions of the Venice Charter' (2014) 4 *Change Over Time* 218

Houbart C, 'Towards an "Integrated Conservation": The Contribution of R.M. Lemaire and Piero Gazzola during the First Decade of ICOMOS (1965–1975)' (2016) 1 *Heritage for Future* 117

Huxley J, *UNESCO: Its Purpose and Philosophy* (UNESCO 1948)

Ifversen J, 'The Meaning of European Civilization: A Historical-Conceptual Approach' (1998) 1 *European Studies Newsletter* 20

Ifversen J, 'Europe and European Culture – A Conceptual Analysis' (2002) 4 *European Societies* 1

Ignatieff M, *Human Rights as Politics and Idolatry* (Princeton UP 2001)

Ismay HL, *NATO, the First Five Years 1949–1954* (NATO 1955)

James L, 'The Symbolic Value of Expertise in International Heritage Diplomacy' (2016) 13 *Future Anterior* 83

Jakobson R, 'Linguistics and Poetics' in Jaworski A and Coupland N (eds), *The Discourse Reader*(Routledge 1999) 54

Janks H, 'Critical Discourse Analysis as a Research Tool' (1997) 18 *Discourse: Studies in the Cultural Politics of Education* 329

Johansen B and Mogren M, 'Valetta and Beyond – Ideas and Practice in Sweden' in Van der Haas VM and Schut PAC (eds), *The Valletta Convention: Twenty Years After* (EAC Occasional Paper No 9, 2014) 143

Jokilehto J, *Comments on the Venice Charter with Illustrations* (1995) https://www.icomos.org/venicecharter2004/jokilehto.pdf accessed 16 June 2018

Jokilehto J, 'The Context of the Venice Charter (1964)' (1998a) 2 *Conservation and Management of Archaeological Sites* 229

Jokilehto J, 'International Trends in Historic Preservation: From Ancient Monuments to Living Cultures' (1998b) 29 *APT Bulletin: The Journal of Preservation Technology* 17

Jokilehto J, *History of Architectural Conservation* (Routledge 1999a)

Jokilehto J, 'A Century of Heritage Conservation' (1999b) 5 *Journal of Architectural Conservation* 14

Jokilehto J, 'Considerations on Authenticity and Integrity in World Heritage Context' (2006a) 2 *City & Time* 1

Jokilehto J, 'World Heritage: Defining the Outstanding Universal Value' (2006b) 2 *City & Time* 1

Jokilehto J, 'International Charters on Urban Conservation: Some Thoughts on the Principles Expressed in Current International Doctrine' (2007) 3 *City & Time* 23

Jokilehto J, 'ICCROM's First Fifty Years' (2009) 61 *Museum International* 26

Jokilehto J, 'Heritage, Values and Valuation' in Quagliuolo M (ed), *Quality in Cultural Heritage Management*(DRI-Fondazione Enotria 2010)

Jokilehto J, 'Human Rights and Cultural Heritage: Observations on the Recognition of Human Rights in the International Doctrine' (2012) 18 *International Journal of Heritage Studies* 226

Jokilehto J and Soheil M-A, 'Development of ICCROM's Architectural Conservation Training in Reference to Council of Europe Initiatives' in Falser M and Lipp W (eds), *A Future for Our Past* (Hendrik Bäßler Verlag 2015) 104

Jones S and Graves-Brown P, 'Introduction: Archaeology and Cultural Identity in Europe' in Graves-Brown P, Jones S and Gamble C (eds), *Cultural Identity and Archaeology* (Routledge 1996) 1

Jones S, 'Wrestling with the Social Value of Heritage: Problems, Dilemmas and Opportunities' (2017) 4 *Journal of Community Archaeology & Heritage* 21

Jones S and Leech S, *Cultural Value: Valuing the Historic Environment* (AHRC 2015)

Karlström A, 'Spiritual Materiality: Heritage Preservation in a Buddhist World?' (2005) 5 *Journal of Social Archaeology* 338

Kisić V, *Governing Heritage Dissonance: Promises and Realities of Selected Cultural Policies* (European Cultural Foundation 2016)

Kisić V, 'Shaking the Solid – Heritage in the Era of Plurality' in Halme A-M and others (eds), *Heritage Is Ours*(Europa Nostra Finland 2018a) 134

Kisić V, 'Beyond Celebrations and Divisions: Re-politicizing Heritage Dissonance in Europe' (2018b) 4 *Economia della Cultura* 465

Kisić V, 'Heritage Research in the 21st Century' in Stegmeijer E and Veldpaus L (eds), *A Research Agenda for Heritage Planning* (Elgar 2021) 21

Kleinsorge TEJ (ed), *Council of Europe* (Kluwer Law International 2015)

Kobylinski Z (ed), *Quo Vadis Archaeologia? Whither European Archaeology in the 21st Century?* (Polish Academy of Sciences 2001)

Kohl PL and Fawcett C (eds), *Nationalism, Politics and the Practice of Archaeology* (CUP 1995)

Kohl PL, 'Nationalism and Archaeology: On the Constructions of Nations and the Reconstructions of the Remote Past' (1998) 27 *Annual Review of Anthropology* 223

Kohli M, 'The Battlegrounds of European Identity' (2000) 2 *European Societies* 113

Koziol C, 'From International to Cosmopolitan: Taking the Venice Charter Beyond the "State-Party" Politics of Experts' (2014) 4 *Change Over Time* 204

Kreck V, 'European Identity Concept and the European Idea' (2015) 45 *Journal of Intercultural Studies*117

Kristiansen K, 'Do We Need the "Archaeology of Europe"?' (2008) 15 *Archaeological Dialogues* 5

Kristiansen K, 'Archaeological Communities and Languages' in Skeates R and others (eds), *The Oxford Handbook of Public Archaeology* (OUP 2012) 461

Kuipers M, 'Dutch Conversions in Conservation' in Falser M and Lipp W (eds), *A Future for Our Past* (Hendrik Bäßler Verlag 2015) 238

Kurin R, 'Safeguarding Intangible Cultural Heritage in the 2003 UNESCO Convention: A Critical Appraisal' (2004) 56 *Museum International* 66

Labadi S, 'A Review of the Global Strategy for a Balanced, Representative and Credible World Heritage List 1994–2004' (2005) 7 *Conservation and Management of Archaeological Sites* 89

Labadi S, 'Representations of the Nation and Cultural Diversity in Discourses on World Heritage' (2007) 7 *Journal of Social Archaeology* 147

Labadi S, 'Intangible Heritage and Sustainable Development: Realistic Outcome or Wishful Thinking?' (2011) 4 *Heritage and Society* 115

Labadi S, 'The National Museum of Immigration History (Paris, France), Neo-colonialist Representations, Silencing, and Re-appropriation' (2013) 13 *Journal of Social Archaeology* 310

Labadi S, *UNESCO, Cultural Heritage, and Outstanding Universal Value* (AltaMira Press 2013)

Labadi S, 'Sustainable Development: Heritage, Community, Economics' in Meskell L (ed), *Global Heritage* (Wiley-Blackwell 2015) 196

Labadi S and Logan W (eds), *Urban Heritage, Development, and Sustainability* (Routledge 2015)

Labadi S, 'UNESCO, Heritage and Sustainable Development' in Gould P and Pyburn K (eds), *Promise and Peril* (Springer 2017) 45

Labadi S, 'UNESCO World Heritage Convention (1972)' in Smith C (ed), *Encyclopedia of Global Archaeology* (Springer 2018a) 1

Labadi S, 'Historical, Theoretical and International Considerations on Culture, Heritage and (Sustainable) Development' in Larsen P and Logan W (eds), *World Heritage and Sustainable Development* (Routledge 2018b) 37

Labadi S, 'Re-examining World Heritage and Sustainable Development' in Bharne V and Sandmeier T (eds), *Routledge Companion to Global Heritage Conservation* (Routledge 2019) 15

Labadi S and others, *Heritage and the Sustainable Development Goals* (ICOMOS 2021)

Labadi S, 'The World Convention at 50' (2022a) *Journal of Cultural Heritage Management and Sustainable Development*

Labadi S, *Rethinking Heritage for Sustainable Development* (UCL Press 2022b)

Lähdesmäki T, 'Politics of Tangibility, Intangibility, and Place in the Making of a European Cultural Heritage in EU Heritage Policy' (2016) 22 *International Journal of Heritage Studies* 766

Lähdesmäki T, 'Founding Myths of EU Europe and the Workings of Power in the EU Heritage and History Initiatives' (2019) 22 *European Journal of Cultural Studies* 781

Lähdesmäki T and others (eds), *Dissonant Heritages and Memories in Contemporary Europe* (Palgrave Macmillan 2019)

Langfield M, Logan W and Craith MN (eds), *Cultural Diversity, Heritage and Human Rights* (Routledge 2009)

Larsen PB and Logan W (eds), *World Heritage and Sustainable Development* (Routledge 2018)

Lascoumes P and Le Galès P, 'Understanding Public Policy through Its Instruments' (2007) 20 *Governance* 1

Last K, 'Heritage and Identity' in Sassatelli M (ed), *Landscape as Heritage* (European University Institute 2006)

Ledig C, 'The Faro Convention and the Information Society' in Council of Europe, *Heritage and Beyond*(Council of Europe Publishing 2009) 159

Lemaire R, *Prémices de la Charte de Venise* (1964) https://www.icomos.org/venicecharter2004/lemaire1.pdf accessed 15 June 2018

Lemaire R, *Report of the President of ICOMOS, 1965–1975* (1981) https://www.icomos.org/public/publications/JS5_11.pdf accessed 20 June 2018

Lemaire R, *A Propos de la Charte de Venise* (1995) https://www.icomos.org/venicecharter2004/lemaire1995.pdf accessed 16 June 2018

Lemaire R, *Faut-il Revoir la Charte de Venise?* (1995) https://www.icomos.org/venicecharter2004/lemaire2.pdfaccessed 16 June 2018

Lemelin RH and others, 'Conflicts, Battlefields, Indigenous Peoples and Tourism' (2013) 7 *International Journal of Culture, Tourism and Hospitality Research* 257

Leniaud J-M, 'Heritage, Public Authorities, Societies' in Council of Europe, *Heritage and Beyond*(Council of Europe Publishing 2009) 137

Lennon JJ and Foley M, 'Interpretation of the Unimaginable' (1999) 38 *Journal of Travel Research* 46

Lennon JJ and Foley M, *Dark Tourism* (2nd edn, Continuum 2000)

Levy D and Sznaider N, 'Memory Unbound' (2002) 5 *European Journal of Social Theory* 87

Levy J, 'Gender, Feminism, and Heritage' in Bihel P and Prescott C (eds), *Heritage in the Context of Globalization* (Springer 2013) 85

Lipp W and Falser M, 'Thresholds of Monument Awareness' in Falser M and Lipp W (eds), *A Future for Our Past* (Hendrik Bäßler Verlag 2015) 21

Lipe W, 'Value and Meaning in Cultural Resources' in Cleere H (ed), *Approaches to the Archaeological Heritage* (CUP 1984) 1

Lixinski L, 'Selecting Heritage' (2011) 22 *European Journal of International Law* 81

Lixinski L, *Intangible Cultural Heritage in International Law* (OUP 2013a)

Lixinski L, 'International Cultural Heritage Regimes, International Law, and the Politics of Expertise' (2013b) 20 *International Journal of Cultural Property* 407

Lixinski L, 'Regional and International Treaties on Intangible Cultural Heritage' in Waelde C and others (eds), *Research Handbook on Contemporary Intangible Cultural Heritage* (Edward Elgar 2018) 15

Logan W, 'Voices from the Periphery' (2004) 18 *Historic Environment* 2

Logan W, 'Closing Pandora's Box' in Silverman H and Ruggles DF (eds), *Cultural Heritage and Human Rights*(Springer 2007) 33

Logan W, 'Cultural Diversity, Cultural Heritage and Human Rights' (2012) 18 *International Journal of Heritage Studies* 231

Logan W and Wijesuriya G, 'The New Heritage Studies and Education, Training, and Capacity-Building' in Logan W and others (eds), *A Companion to Heritage Studies* (Wiley 2015) 557

Logan W, Craith MN and Kockel U (eds), *A Companion to Heritage Studies* (Wiley 2015)

Loulanski T, 'Revising the Concept for Cultural Heritage' (2006) 13 *International Journal of Cultural Property* 207

Lowenthal D, *The Past Is a Foreign Country* (CUP 1985)

Lowenthal D, 'Conserving Nature and Antiquity' in Baark E and Svedin U (eds), *Man, Nature and Technology*(Macmillan 1988) 122

Lowenthal D, 'Heritages for Europe' (1995) 4 *International Journal of Cultural Property* 377

Lowenthal D, *The Heritage Crusade and the Spoils of History* (Viking 1997)

Lowenthal D, 'Fabricating Heritage' (1998) 10 *History and Memory* 5

Lowenthal D, 'Natural and Cultural Heritage' (2005) 11 *International Journal of Heritage Studies* 81

Ludwig C, 'From Bricks and Mortar to Social Heritage' (2016) 22 *International Journal of Heritage Studies* 811

Luke A, 'Beyond Science and Ideology Critique' (2002) 22 *Annual Review of Applied Linguistics* 96

Luxen J-L, 'Les fondateurs de l'ICOMOS et la Campagne européenne de 1975' in Falser M and Lipp W (eds), *A Future for Our Past* (Hendrik Bäßler Verlag 2015) 86

Maarleveld TJ, 'The Maritime Paradox: Does International Heritage Exist?' (2012) 18 *International Journal of Heritage Studies* 418

Macdonald S, 'Museums, National, Postnational and Transnational Identities' (2003) 1 *Museum and Society* 1

Macdonald S, *Memorylands: Heritage and Identity in Europe Today* (Routledge 2013)

Machin D and Mayr A, *How to Do Critical Discourse Analysis: A Multimodal Introduction* (SAGE 2012)

Makuvaza S (ed), *Aspects of Management Planning for Cultural World Heritage Sites* (Springer 2018)

Manacorda S, 'Criminal Law Protection of Cultural Heritage: An International Perspective' in Manacorda S and Chappell D (eds), *Crime in the Art and Antiquities World* (Springer 2011) 17

Martinelli A, 'The European Identity' (2017) 2 *Glocalism: Journal of Culture, Politics and Innovation* 1

Marsh D, 'Marxism' in Marsh D and Stoker G (eds), *Theory and Methods in Political Science* (Palgrave Macmillan 1995) 153

Marsh D and Furlong P, 'A Skin, Not a Sweater: Ontology and Epistemology in Political Science' in Marsh D and Stoker G (eds), *Theory and Methods in Political Science* (Palgrave Macmillan 1995) 17

Martin J and Wodak R, 'Introduction' in Martin J and Wodak R (eds), *Re/reading the Past* (John Benjamins 2003) 19

Mastalir RW, 'A Proposal for Protecting the "Cultural" and "Property" Aspects of Cultural Property Under International Law' (1992) 16 *Fordham International Law Journal* 1033

Matsuda A, 'The Concept of "the Public" and the Aims of Public Archaeology' (2004) 15 *Papers from the Institute of Archaeology* 90

Mauter WR, 'Churchill and the Unification of Europe' (1998) 61 *The Historian* 67

McManamon FP, 'Archaeological Messages and Messengers' (2000) 1 *Public Archaeology* 5

Mehan H, 'The Construction of an LD Student' in Wetherell M, Taylor S and Yates SJ (eds), *Discourse Theory and Practice* (SAGE 2001) 345

Merriman N, *Beyond the Glass Case* (Leicester UP 1991)

Merriman N, 'The Public Interest in Archaeology' in Wise P (ed), *Significant Others* (Society of Museum Archaeologists 2000) 20

Merriman N, 'Archaeology, Heritage and Interpretation' in Cunliffe B and others (eds), *Archaeology: The Widening Debate* (British Academy 2002) 541

Merriman N, (ed), *Public Archaeology* (Routledge 2004)

Merryman JH, 'Two Ways of Thinking About Cultural Property' (1986) 80 *American Journal of International Law* 831

Merryman JH, 'The Retention of Cultural Property' (1988) 21 *UC Davis Law Review* 477

Merryman JH, 'The Nation and the Object' (1994) 3 *International Journal of Cultural Property* 61

Merryman JH, 'Cultural Property Internationalism' (2005) 12 *International Journal of Cultural Property* 11

Meskell L, 'Negative Heritage and Past Mastering in Archaeology' (2002) 75 *Anthropological Quarterly* 557

Meskell L, 'The Intersections of Identity and Politics in Archaeology' (2002) 31 *Annual Review of Anthropology* 279

Meskell L, 'Human Rights and Heritage Ethics' (2010) 83 *Anthropology Quarterly* 839

Meskell L, 'The Social Life of Heritage' in Hodder I (ed), *Archaeological Theory Today* (2nd edn, Polity Press 2012) 229

Meskell L, 'UNESCO's World Heritage Convention at 40' (2013) 54 *Current Anthropology* 483

Meskell L, 'States of Conservation' (2014) 87 *Anthropological Quarterly* 217

Meskell L, *A Future in Ruins* (OUP 2018)

Meskell L and others, 'Multilateralism and UNESCO World Heritage' (2014) 21 *International Journal of Heritage Studies* 423

Meskell L and others, 'World Heritage Regionalism' (2015) 22 *International Journal of Cultural Property* 437

Meyer-Bisch P, 'On the "Right to Heritage"' in Council of Europe, *Heritage and Beyond* (Council of Europe Publishing 2009) 59

Meyer-Bisch P,*Cultural Rights, an Ethical Principle of Cooperation and a Level for Development* (Conference Paper, CROSSROADS 2018)

Meyer-Bisch P and Bidault M, *Déclarer les Droits Culturels* (Bruylant 2010)

Milisauskas S, 'Archaeology in the Soviet Bloc' (1997) 99 *American Anthropologist* 390

Ministarstvo Kulture Republike Hrvatske, *Strategija zaštite, očuvanja i održivog gospodarskog korištenja kulturne baštine Republike Hrvatske* (2011) https://bit.ly/48xPJlQ accessed 5 April 2022

Mitchell JM, *International Cultural Relations* (Allen & Unwin 1986)

Moghadam M and Senftova L, 'Measuring Women's Empowerment' (2015) 57 *International Social Science Journal* 389

Morris W, *Manifesto of the Society for the Protection of Ancient Buildings* (SPAB 1877)

Morris W, *Address at the Twelfth Annual Meeting* (1889) https://www.marxists.org/archive/morris/works/1889/spab16.htm accessed 7 November 2020

Nassar N, 'Planning for Urban Heritage Places: Reconciling Conservation, Tourism, and Sustainable Development' (2003) 17 *Journal of Planning Literature* 467

Ndoro W and Wijesuriya G, 'Heritage Management and Conservation: From Colonisation to Globalisation' in Meskell L (ed), *Global Heritage* (Wiley 2015) 131

Nic Craith M, Kockel U and Lloyd K, 'The Convention for the Safeguarding of the Intangible Cultural Heritage' in Akagawa N and Smith L (eds), *Safeguarding Intangible Heritage* (Routledge 2018) 118

Nicholas GP, 'Touching the Intangible' in Geismar H and Anderson J (eds), *The Routledge Companion to Cultural Property* (Routledge 2017) 212

Niklasson E, 'The Janus-face of European Heritage' (2017) 17 *Journal of Social Archaeology* 138

O'Keefe PJ, 'The European Convention on the Protection of the Archaeological Heritage' (1993) 67 *Antiquity* 406

O'Keefe PJ, 'Fourth Meeting of Governmental Experts to Consider the Draft Convention on the Protection of Underwater Cultural Heritage' (2002) 11 *International Journal of Cultural Property* 168

O'Keefe PJ and Nafziger JA, 'The Draft Convention on the Protection of the Underwater Cultural Heritage' (1994) 25 *Ocean Development and International Law* 391

O'Keefe PJ and Prott LV, *Law and the Cultural Heritage vol 3* (Butterworths 1989)

O'Keefe PJ and Prott LV, *Cultural Heritage Conventions and Other Instruments* (Institute of Art and Law 2011)

O'Keefe R, *The Protection of Cultural Property in Armed Conflict* (CUP 2006)

Olivier A, 'The Valletta Convention: Twenty Years After' in Van der Haas VM and Schut PAC (eds), *The Valletta Convention* (EAC Occasional Paper No 9, 2014) 11

Olivier A, 'Communities of Interest' (2017) 4 *Journal of Community Archaeology & Heritage* 7

Olivier A and Van Lindt P, 'Valletta Convention Perspectives' in Van der Haas VM and Schut PAC (eds), *The Valletta Convention* (EAC Occasional Paper No 9, 2014) 165

Paganoni MC, 'Cultural Heritage in the Discourse of European Institutions' (2015) 2 *Lingue Culture Mediazioni* 117

Pagden A (ed), *The Idea of Europe from Antiquity to the European Union* (CUP 2002)
Palmer R, 'Preface' in Council of Europe, *Heritage and Beyond* (Council of Europe Publishing 2009) 7
Palmer M and Lambert J, *A Handbook of European Organizations vol 10* (Allen & Unwin 1968)
Palmer M and others, *European Unity* (Allen & Unwin 1968)
Papa-Sokal M, 'Beyond the Nationalist-Internationalist Polarization' (2009) 14 *Art Antiquity and Law* 237
Papa-Sokal M, 'Who "Owns" the Euphronios Krater?' (2011) 3 *Present Pasts* 2
Parkinson A, Scott M and Redmond D, 'Competing Discourses of Built Heritage' (2016a) 22 *International Journal of Heritage Studies* 261
Parkinson A, 'Defining "Official" Built Heritage Discourses' (2016b) 24 *European Planning Studies* 277
Parry J, *Companies of Clouds* (PhD Thesis, University of Warwick 2000)
Passerini L, 'Gender, Subjectivity, Europe' in Passerini L and others (eds), *Women Migrants from East to West* (Berghahn Books 2007) 251
Patel KK (ed), *The Cultural Politics of Europe* (Routledge 2013)
Patel KK and Calligaro O, 'The True "EURESCO"?' (2017) 24 *European Review of History* 399
Pearce S, 'The Construction and Analysis of the Cultural Heritage' (1998) 4 *International Journal of Heritage Studies* 1
Pearson M and Sullivan S, *Looking After Heritage Places* (Melbourne UP 1995)
Pendlebury J, *Conservation in the Age of Consensus* (Routledge 2009)
Pendlebury J, 'Conservation Values' (2013) 19 *International Journal of Heritage Studies* 709
Petaux J, *Democracy and Human Rights for Europe* (Council of Europe Publishing 2009)
Petzet M, *Principles of Preservation* (2004) https://www.icomos.org/venicecharter2004/petzet.pdfaccessed 16 June 2018
Pickard R (ed), *Management of Historic Centres* (Spon Press 2001)
Pickard R (ed), 'Area-Based Protection Mechanisms for Heritage Conservation' (2002a) 8 *Journal of Architectural Conservation* 69
Pickard R(ed), 'A Comparative Review of Policy for the Protection of the Architectural Heritage of Europe' (2002b) 8 *International Journal of Heritage Studies* 349
Pickard R (ed), European Cultural Heritage vol 2 (Council of Europe Publishing 2002c)
Pickard R (ed), 'Management Strategies for Historic Towns in Europe' in Labadi S and Logan W (eds), *Urban Heritage, Development and Sustainability* (Routledge 2015) 151
Plenderleith HJ, 'A History of Conservation' (1998) 43 *Studies in Conservation* 129
Prott LV and O'Keefe PJ, *Law and the Cultural Heritage vol 3* (Butterworths 1989)

Prott LV and O'Keefe PJ, '"Cultural Heritage" or "Cultural Property"?' (1992) 1 *International Journal of Cultural Property* 307

Prott LV, 'International Standards for Cultural Heritage' in UNESCO *World Culture Report* (UNESCO 1998) 222

Prott LV, 'The International Movement of Cultural Objects' (2005) 12 *International Journal of Cultural Property* 225

Potter J, *Representing Reality* (SAGE 1996)

Potter J and Wetherell M, *Discourse and Social Psychology* (SAGE 1987)

Potter J and Wetherell M, 'Unfolding Discourse Analysis' in Wetherell M and others (eds), *Discourse Theory and Practice* (SAGE 2001) 198

Povolo C, 'An Historical Dimension of European Cultural Heritage' (2013) 21 *Acta Historiae* 1

Reiter H, 'Participatory Traditions within the Global Justice Movement' in Della Porta D (ed), *Democracy in Social Movements* (Palgrave Macmillan 2009) 44

Riedlmayer A, *Destruction of Cultural Heritage in Bosnia-Herzegovina, 1992–1996* (ICTY 2002)

Riegl A, 'The Modern Cult of Monuments' in Stanley-Price N and others (eds), *Historical and Philosophical Issues in the Conservation of Cultural Heritage* (Getty Conservation Institute 1996) 69

Rizzo I and Thorsby D, 'Cultural Heritage' in Ginsburg V and Throsby D (eds), *Handbook of the Economics of Art and Culture vol 1* (North-Holland 2006) 983

Roberts A, *Churchill: Walking with Destiny* (Penguin 2018)

Robertson AH, *The Council of Europe* (Praeger 1961)

Rodwell D, *Conservation and Sustainability in Historic Cities* (Blackwell 2007)

Rodwell D, 'Urban Conservation in the 1960s and 1970s' (2010) 21 *Architectural Heritage* 1

Rojas E, 'Historic Cities and the Venice Charter' (2014) 4 *Change Over Time* 196

Rose G, 'The Cultural Politics of Place' (1994) 19 *Transactions of the Institute of British Geographers* 46

Ross M, *Planning and the Heritage* (Routledge 2003)

Rougemont D, *The Meaning of Europe* (Sidgwick & Jackson 1965)

Rouse J, *Knowledge and Power* (Cornell UP 1987)

Rouse J, 'Power/Knowledge' in Gutting G (ed), *The Cambridge Companion to Foucault* (2nd edn, CUP 1994) 95

Rowlands M, 'The Power of Origins' in Buchli V (ed), *The Material Culture Reader* (Berg 2002) 105

Rudolff B and Buckley K, 'World Heritage' in Logan W and others (eds), *A Companion to Heritage Studies* (Wiley 2015) 522

Ruskin J, *The Seven Lamps of Architecture* (Longmans 1903 [1849])

Salmela U, *Why Finland Signed the Faro Convention* (2017) https://rm.coe.int/finland-ratification-of-the-faro-convention-in-finland-why-how-what-ne/168077fa9f accessed 4 March 2022

Sandys D, 'European Architectural Heritage Year' (1975) 23 *Annuaire Européen* 124

Sassatelli M, 'Imagined Europe' (2002) 5 *European Journal of Social Theory* 435

Sassatelli M, *Becoming Europeans* (Routledge 2009)

Sassatelli M, 'European Identity between Flows and Places' (2010) 44 *Sociology* 67

Sayer A, *Realism and Social Science* (SAGE 2000)

Schadla-Hall T, 'Editorial' (1999) 2 *European Journal of Archaeology* 147

Schmahl S and Breuer M (eds), *The Council of Europe* (OUP 2017)

Schofield J, 'Heritage Expertise and the Everyday' in Schofield J (ed), *Who Needs Experts?* (Ashgate 2014) 1

Schofield J, 'Forget about "Heritage"' in Ireland T and Schofield J (eds), *The Ethics of Cultural Heritage*(Springer 2015) 197

Schut P, 'Foreword' in Van der Haas VM and Schut PAC (eds), *The Valletta Convention* (EAC Occasional Paper No 9, 2014) 9

Scollon R, *Analysing Public Discourse* (Routledge 2008)

Shahin J and Wintle M (eds), *The Idea of a United Europe* (St Martins Press 2000)

Shortliffe S, 'Gender and (World) Heritage' in Bourdeau L and others (eds), *World Heritage, Tourism, and Identity* (Routledge 2015) 107

Silberman N, 'Heritage Interpretation and Human Rights' (2010) 18 *International Journal of Heritage Studies* 245

Silberman N, 'Changing Vision of Heritage Value' (2014) 36 *Ethnologies* 433

Silva R, *The Significance of the Venice International Charter* (1983) https://www.icomos.org/venicecharter2004/silva.pdf accessed 15 June 2018

Silva KD, 'Paradigm Shift in Global Heritage Discourse' (2015) 1 *Space and Communication* 1

Silverman H and Ruggles DF (eds), *Cultural Heritage and Human Rights* (Springer 2007)

Skrede J and Hølleland H, 'Uses of Heritage and Beyond' (2018) 18 *Journal of Social Archaeology* 77

Skrede J, 'Discourse Analysis and Non-representation Theories in Heritage Studies' (2020) 37 *Journal of Cultural Geography* 88

Smith AD, 'Towards a Global Culture?' (1990) 7 *Theory, Culture and Society* 71

Smith AD, 'National Identity and the Idea of European Unity' (1992) 68 *International Affairs* 55

Smith L, *Archaeological Theory and the Politics of Cultural Heritage* (Routledge 2004)

Smith L, *Uses of Heritage* (Routledge 2006)

Smith L, 'Indigenous Archaeologies' (2008) 82 *Antiquity* 236

Smith L, *Missing Out on Heritage* (Conference Paper, English Heritage 2009)

Smith L, 'Intangible Heritage' (2015) 40 *Revista D'Etnologia de Catalunya* 133

Smith L and Akagawa N, 'Introduction' in Smith L and Akagawa N (eds), *Intangible Heritage* (Routledge 2009) 1

Smith L and Campbell G, 'The Elephant in the Room' in Logan W and others (eds), *A Companion to Heritage Studies* (Wiley-Blackwell 2016) 443

Smith L and Campbell G, 'The Tautology of "Intangible Values"' (2017) 10 *Heritage & Society* 26

Smith L and Waterton E, *Heritage, Communities and Archaeology* (Bloomsbury 2016)

Spohn W, 'National Identities and Collective Europe' in Eder K and Spohn W (eds), *Collective Memory and European Identity* (Ashgate 2005) 1

Stamatopoulou E, *Cultural Rights in International Law* (Martinus Nijhoff 2007)

Stamatoudi IA, *Cultural Property Law and Restitution* (Edward Elgar 2011)

Starn R, 'Authenticity and Historic Preservation' (2002) 15 *History of the Human Science* 1

Stavenhagen R, 'Cultural Rights' in Niec H (ed), *Cultural Rights and Wrongs* (UNESCO 1998) 1

Stoianovich T, *Balkan Worlds* (Routledge 2015)

Stone PR, 'A Dark Tourism Spectrum' (2006) 54 *Tourism* 145

Stråth B (ed), *Europe and the Other and Europe as the Other* (Peter Lang 2000)

Stråth B (ed), 'A European Identity' (2002) 5 *European Journal of Social Theory* 387

Strati A, 'The Notion of the Underwater Cultural Heritage' in Strati A, *The Protection of the Underwater Cultural Heritage* (Brill Nijhoff 1995) 7

Stubbs JH, *Time Honored* (Wiley 2009)

Swenson A, 'The First Heritage International(s)' (2016) 13 *Future Anterior* 1

Thérond D, 'Benefits and Innovations of the Council of Europe Framework Convention' in Council of Europe, *Heritage and Beyond* (Council of Europe Publishing 2009) 9

Thérond D, 'The Council of Europe Conventions in the Field of Cultural Heritage and Landscape' in Guštin M and Nypan T (eds), *Cultural Heritage and Legal Aspects in Europe* (Institute for Mediterranean Heritage 2010) 20

Thomas R, 'Comment' (2002) 2 *Public Archaeology* 236

Thomas S, 'Making Archaeological Heritage Accessible in Great Britain' in Thomas S and Lea J (eds), *Public Participation in Archaeology* (Boydell Press 2014) 23

Thompson MV, *Ruins: Their Preservation and Display* (British Museum Publications 1981)

Thompson MV, *Ruins Reused* (Heritage Marketing and Publications 2006)

Toman J, *The Protection of Cultural Property in the Event of Armed Conflict* (Routledge 1996)

Toye R, 'Churchill and the "United States of Europe"' in Packwood A (ed), *The Cambridge Companion to Winston Churchill* (CUP 2023) 362

Trigger BG, 'Anglo-American Archaeology' (1981) 13 *World Archaeology* 138

Trigger BG, 'Archaeology at the Crossroads' (1984) 13 *Annual Review of Anthropology* 275

Trigger BG, *A History of Archaeological Thought* (CUP 1989)

Trigger BG, 'Romanticism, Nationalism, and Archaeology' in Kohl PL and Fawcett C (eds), *Nationalism, Politics, and the Practice of Archaeology* (CUP 1995) 263

Trotzig G, 'The New European Convention on the Protection of the Archaeological Heritage' (1993) 67 *Antiquity* 414

Tunbridge JE and Ashworth GJ, 'Dissonant Heritage' (1996) 40 *The Management of the Past as a Resource in Conflict* 547

Ulph J and Vigneron S, 'The Significance of the Convention on Offences Relating to Cultural Property 2017' in Fabiani DM and others (eds), *Cultural Property Crime and the Law* (Routledge forthcoming 2024)

Van Balen K and Vandesande A (eds), *Community Involvement in Heritage* (Garant 2015)

Van den Dries M, 'The Good, the Bad and the Ugly?' (2011) 43 *World Archaeology* 594

Van den Dries M, 'From Malta to Faro' in Schut P and others (eds), *EAC Occasional Paper No 10* (Europae Archaeologia Consilium 2015) 45

Van den Dries M, Van der Linde S and Strecker A (eds), *Crossing Borders and Connecting People in Archaeological Heritage Management* (Sidestone Press 2015)

Van der Linde S and Van den Dries M, 'Creative Archaeology' in Van den Dries M and others (eds), *Crossing Borders and Connecting People* (Sidestone Press 2015) 51

Van Dijk TA, 'Discourse, Power and Access' in Caldas CR (ed), *Studies in Critical Discourse Analysis*(Routledge 1993)

Van Dijk TA, (ed), *Discourse as Structure and Process vol 1* (SAGE 1997)

Van Dijk TA, 'Multidisciplinary CDA' in Wodak R and Meyer M (eds), *Methods of Critical Discourse Analysis* (SAGE 2001) 95

Van Leeuwen T, *Discourse and Practice* (OUP 2008)

Vícha O, 'The Concept of the Right to Cultural Heritage within the Faro Convention' (2014) 14 *International and Comparative Law Review* 23

Von Truetzschler W, *The Evolution of "Cultural Heritage" in International Law* (ICOMOS General Assembly 2005)

Vrdoljak AF, *Minorities, Cultural Rights and the Protection of Intangible Cultural Heritage* (European Society for International Law 2005)

Vrdoljak AF, *Cultural Heritage in Human Rights and Humanitarian Law* (University of Technology Sydney 2009)

Vrdoljak AF, 'Human Rights and Cultural Heritage in International Law' in Lenzerini F and Vrdoljak AF (eds), *International Law for Common Goods* (Hart Publishing 2014) 139

Vrdoljak AF, 'Challenges for International Cultural Heritage Law' in Logan W and others (eds), *A Companion to Heritage Studies* (Wiley 2015) 541

Wagner P, 'From Monuments to Human Rights' in Council of Europe, *Forward Planning* (Council of Europe 2000) 9

Walsh K, *The Representation of the Past* (Routledge 1992)

Wanner P, *The Faro Convention Approach* (2017) https://rm.coe.int/-the-faro-convention-approach-and-democratic-socio-economic-models-for/1680780489 accessed 4 April 2022

Wanner P, 'Faro Convention and Participation' in Council of Europe, *The Faro Convention's Role in a Changing Society* (Council of Europe Publishing 2021) 7

Wassenberg B, *History of the Council of Europe* (Council of Europe Publishing 2013)

Waterton E, Smith L and Campbell G, 'The Utility of Discourse Analysis to Heritage Studies' (2006) 12 *International Journal of Heritage Studies* 339

Waterton E, *Rhetoric & 'Reality'* (PhD Thesis, University of York 2007)

Waterton E, *Politics, Policy and the Discourse of Heritage in Britain* (Palgrave Macmillan 2010)

Waterton E and Watson S (eds), *Culture, Heritage and Representation* (Ashgate 2010)

Waterton E and Watson S (eds), *Heritage and Community Engagement* (Routledge 2011)

Waterton E and Watson S (eds), 'Framing Theory' (2013) 19 *International Journal of Heritage Studies* 546

Waterton E and Smith L, 'The Recognition and Misrecognition of Community Heritage' (2010) 16 *International Journal of Heritage Studies* 4

Wetherell M, 'Themes in Discourse Research' in Wetherell M and others (eds), *Discourse Theory and Practice* (SAGE 2001a) 14

Wetherell M, 'Debates in Discourse Research' in Wetherell M and others (eds), *Discourse Theory and Practice* (SAGE 2001b) 380

Wight AC, 'Philosophical and Methodological Praxes in Dark Tourism' (2006) 12 *Journal of Vacation Marketing* 119

Willems WJH, 'Archaeology and Heritage Management in Europe' (1998) 1 *European Journal of Archaeology* 293

Willems WJH, *The Future of European Archaeology* (Oxbow Books 1999)

Willems WJH, 'The Work of Making Malta' (2007) 10 *European Journal of Archaeology* 57

Willems WJH, 'Archaeology in the Netherlands' (2008) 165 *Archaeological Journal* 8

Willems WJH, 'Archaeological Resources Management and Academic Archaeology in Europe' in D'Agata AL and Alaura S (eds), *Quale future per l'archeologia* (Gangemi Editore 2009) 89

Willems WJH, 'Malta and Its Consequences' in Van der Haas VM and Schut PAC (eds), *The Valletta Convention* (EAC Occasional Paper No 9, 2014) 151

Willems WJHo and Van den Dries MH (eds), *Quality Management in Archaeology* (Oxbow Books 2007)

Winter T, 'Clarifying the Critical in Critical Heritage Studies' (2013) 19 *International Journal of Heritage Studies* 532

Winter T, 'Heritage Conservation Futures' (2014) 14 *Journal of Social Archaeology* 319

Winter T, 'Beyond Eurocentrism?' (2014) 20 *International Journal of Heritage Studies* 123

Winter T, 'Heritage Diplomacy' (2015) 21 *International Journal of Heritage Studies* 997

Winter T, 'Heritage Diplomacy' (2016) 13 *Future Anterior* 17

Winter T, 'Heritage and the Politics of Cooperation' in Labrador AM and Silberman NA (eds), *The Oxford Handbook of Public Heritage Theory and Practice* (OUP 2018) 1

Wodak R, *Disorders of Discourse* (Longman 1996)

Wodak R and Meyer M (eds), *Methods of Critical Discourse Studies* (SAGE 2001)

Wodak R and Meyer M (eds), 'Critical Discourse Analysis' (2009) 2 *Methods of Critical Discourse Analysis* 1

Wolferstan S and Fairclough G, 'Common European Heritage' in Callebaut D and others (eds), *Heritage Reinvents Europe* (EAC Occasional Paper No 7, 2013) 43

Wu Z and Hou S, 'Heritage and Discourse' in Waterton E and Watson S (eds), *The Palgrave Handbook of Contemporary Heritage Research* (Palgrave Macmillan 2015) 37

York Archaeological Trust, *Discovering the Archaeologists of Europe 2012–14* (2014)

Zagato L, 'Intangible Cultural Heritage and Human Rights' (2012) 1 *Il patrimonio culturale intangibile nelle sue diverse dimensioni* 29

Zagato L, 'The Notion of "Heritage Community"' in Adell N and others (eds), *Between Imagined Communities and Communities of Practice* (Universitätsverlag Göttingen 2015) 141

Zancheti SM and Jokilehto J, 'Values and Urban Conservation Planning' (1997) 3 *Journal of Architectural Conservation* 37

Zito AR and others, 'The Instruments of European Heritage' in Whitehead C and others (eds), *Dimensions of Heritage and Memory* (Routledge 2019) 50

Zucconi G, 'Gustavo Giovannoni' (2014) 4 *Change Over Time* 76

Index

www.ingramcontent.com/pod-product-compliance
Lightning Source LLC
Chambersburg PA
CBHW051401240926
51852CB00002B/78
9789004726260